WITHDRAWN

11-31

VIEWS
ON
CAPITALISM

LIBRARY
BRYAN COLLEGE
DAYTON, TN. 37321

VIEWS
ON
CAPITALISM

RICHARD ROMANO
ASSISTANT PROFESSOR
DEPARTMENT OF ECONOMICS
BROOME TECHNICAL COMMUNITY COLLEGE

MELVIN LEIMAN
ASSOCIATE PROFESSOR
DEPARTMENT OF ECONOMICS
STATE UNIVERSITY OF NEW YORK
AT BINGHAMTON

GLENCOE PRESS
A DIVISION OF THE MACMILLAN COMPANY
BEVERLY HILLS, CALIFORNIA

38065

Copyright © 1970 by Glencoe Press
A Division of The Macmillan Company.

Printed in the United States of America.

All rights reserved. No part of this book may be reproduced or transmitted in any form or by any means, electronic or mechanical, including photocopying, recording, or by any information storage and retrieval system, without permission in writing from the Publisher.

Glencoe Press
A Division of The Macmillan Company.
8701 Wilshire Boulevard
Beverly Hills, California 90211
Collier-Macmillan Canada, Ltd., Toronto, Canada.

Library of Congress catalogue card number: 71-109445.

Second Printing, 1971

to two Ellens

CONTENTS

PART 3   The Radical View

PREFACE

This book is intended primarily for use as supplementary reading for the introductory economics course and aims at stimulating student interest and discussion. It is during this course that the student begins to develop a method of reasoning which helps him to evaluate the operation of the economy and its socio-economic institutions. Among these institutions are private property, the market system, the business corporation, the union, the family household, and the government. They comprise the basic "organs" through which and upon which the economy operates. While the introductory student studies the dynamics of economic growth, he is seldom given an opportunity to see how the "organic composition" of the economy is changing. These essays attempt to focus attention on the nature and direction of this change. The editors wish to impress upon the student that he cannot fully appreciate his economic environment by concentrating merely on static economic theory; however, they do not wish to suggest that this volume is a substitute for that theory. It is our hope that these essays will help the student realize that the economic system and its institutions are in a constant state of evolution, and that economic problems must be viewed against this changing background. The readings presented here were chosen with this in mind. They attempt to shed light on the forces which are molding, or are likely to mold, the future of the economy. How our economic institutions are being restructured and what their future might be are fertile areas for student involvement. If the student is motivated to develop his own concept of the evolution of capitalism, all the better, for in doing so he will gain valuable insights into the nature and functioning of the economy.

The material presented here provides the student with a diversity of opinion on the forces and directions of change within capitalism; no attempt has been made, however, to include all schools of thought. Whenever possible references are restricted to views of the American economy, although many of the arguments go beyond our own system. The readings are a sampling of opinion from the eighteenth century to the present time. Although emphasis is placed on twentieth-century capitalism, earlier selections, from works that have become classics, are included to enable the student to evaluate their influence on, or similarity to, contemporary views. Although the predictions expressed in many of the selections may seem to have fallen wide of the mark, a critical analysis of them will help the student to sharpen his own ability to evaluate and influence current trends.

The readings are divided into three broad categories of opinion —Conservative, Liberal, and Radical. Admittedly these terms have suffered from overuse and have undergone significant semantic change during the period encompassed by this volume. The fact that some of the views presented here seem to resist any single classification should serve to warn the student against attempting a categorization that is too strict. Indeed, many people reject the conservative–liberal dichotomy altogether. For our purpose, however, the categories are still useful when they are properly defined in their modern context. The general introduction to each part of this volume will explain the rationale behind a category and will show how the representative selections follow that rationale.

Additional introductions preceding the individual selections trace the main line of the author's thinking and show how it compares with that of others in the volume. Included in these discussions is material that is pertinent to understanding of the author's position but is not necessarily implied in the selections. These additional introductions also contain a certain amount of editorial analysis. Since this criticism reflects the editors' own biases, perhaps it is only fair to state at the outset what these biases are. Professor Romano may be viewed as a liberal reformer who, although not hoping to speak for the majority of economists, sees himself as being close to the mainstream of modern economic thinking. Professor Leiman's views are clearly in the radical tradition. Although each introduction represents the combined effort of both editors, the initials at the end of each indicate who is chiefly responsible for that piece. The selected bibliography at the end of each of the three parts should serve as a guide to further representative readings.

These essays have been used as part of the principles of economics course at Broome Technical Community College and in the introductory social science course at the State University of New York at Binghamton. The editors hope that this volume will also find acceptance outside of these areas. In addition to their wives, whose editorial comments were invaluable, the editors wish to thank their students whose reactions have helped to narrow the selections to a a practicable number.

RICHARD ROMANO
MELVIN LEIMAN

OCTOBER, 1969
BINGHAMTON, N.Y.

VIEWS
ON
CAPITALISM

PART 1

THE CONSERVATIVE VIEW

INTRODUCTION

An economic conservative places primary responsibility for the organization and distribution of production on the market system. He views governmental intervention in the market system as undesirable and generally relegates the role of the government to one of protecting individual property rights, promoting competition, maintaining law and order, and defending the country against foreign military aggression. Although conservatives differ over the specific functions that they believe government should perform within the economy, it is fair to say that they all feel that its role should be a limited one. For this reason they are considered advocates of laissez-faire. The selections presented here under the conservative label have this element in common.

Contemporary conservative philosophy, and for that matter liberal philosophy as well, is concerned with maximizing individual freedom. The conservative feels that this goal is obtainable only under a system of laissez-faire capitalism. Modern liberals, on the other hand, stress the positive role that government can play in expanding and guaranteeing individual freedoms. With this view in mind, both are concerned with eliminating the abuses of excessive economic power. To the conservative, the best method of limiting this power is through the competitive market system. To him the interference of government tends to lead to monopoly power and thus subverts the very thing which competitive capitalism guarantees, a highly stable, efficient, and egalitarian means of production and distribution. In addition, the conservative views the growing power of government as leading to authoritarianism. Thus the powerful state poses a serious threat to human rights and political freedom. Following this philosophy, the economic conservative (believer in laissez-faire) might also become a conservative on noneconomic questions such as civil rights or foreign policy. But if the solution of an essentially noneconomic problem—Civil Rights—necessitated an increased role for the government, which might infringe on the right of private property, then the conservative is likely to revert to the philosophy that "the best government is one which governs least." Although the lines between economic and political ideology are often difficult to distinguish, this volume is concerned mainly with economic questions.

The economic conservatives represented here are proponents of the laissez-faire philosophy and are concerned about the future of capitalism. As they look at the system they are obviously disturbed by what they see. For Adam Smith this meant a condemnation of the mercantilist system which artificially diverted capital toward the trade sector and under which government-protected monopolies were allowed to grow. For Hayek, Friedman and Rothbard, it means concern for the growing size and power of the federal government and the movement toward the welfare state. Each presents his case against the growing power of the state, but all feel that the future of capitalism lies in a reversal of the direction in which it seems to be going; all warn of the dangers inherent in a system that deviates too far from the laissez-faire philosophy.

An excerpt from Adam Smith's *Wealth of Nations*, published in 1776, is included here because it is the classic statement on the virtues of competitive capitalism. This book is still widely read by students of economics and its influence on contemporary thinking is evidenced by the numerous references to it by the other authors in this volume. At the time *The Wealth of Nations* appeared, Britain was in the early stages of the Industrial Revolution. The philosophy of Smith and his followers, the Classical Economists, provided the theoretical underpinning for the rising industrial sector of the economy and helped move Britain close to a laissez-faire economy by the middle of the nineteenth century. The Classical Economists of this time were not considered conservatives. Indeed, they were "liberals" in the Lockean tradition who fought the existing power structure in an effort to establish free trade, a competitive market, and parliamentary reform. For this reason proponents of the laissez-faire philosophy are often called "liberals." Thus Smith is a liberal in the nineteenth century tradition but a conservative when viewed against a modern background. Hayek, Friedman, and Rothbard also can be considered either nineteenth-century liberals or modern conservatives. The approach here is to view them as the latter.

An important twentieth-century extension of Smith's laissez-faire philosophy is provided by Friedrich Hayek's *The Road to Serfdom*. Written against the background of the totalitarianism of the second World War period, Hayek's words have served as an inspiration for those who were to follow him. Hayek warns of the dangers to political freedom inherent in a planned economy. His overriding question is whether economic planning and political freedom are compatible, and his emphatic answer is that they are not. In the selection presented here Hayek attempts to refute the arguments of some modern liberals that the complexity and structure of modern capitalism require planning.

The fact that the selection by Milton Friedman follows that by Hayek is apropos of Friedman's intellectual debt to him. Friedman is modern America's most well-known conservative. His economic philosophies have been linked with the political campaign of Barry Goldwater. In his book *Capitalism and Freedom* Friedman shows his distaste for the liberals whom he sees as moving the country toward the welfare state. As with Hayek, this means a growing limitation on individual freedom. To Friedman, competitive capitalism is synonymous with economic freedom, which in turn is a necessary condition for political freedom. The main part of the selection presented here examines the connection between economic and political freedom and reflects in all its essential points the basic philosophy of Hayek presented almost twenty years earlier.

The selection by Rothbard is perhaps the most difficult to classify. While professing a distaste for the growing size of the public sector, many of his attitudes on noneconomic issues indicate an alliance with more radical views such as those of the New Left. Although Rothbard's article is more limited in scope than the others in this part, it serves as a useful contrast and shows the range of opinion that one can expect to find among the conservative group.

—R. R.

1

◀ ADAM SMITH* ▶

from

An Inquiry into the Nature and Causes of the Wealth of Nations (1776)

Adam Smith did not set out to predict the future of capitalism. As this selection indicates, however, he was concerned that those forces which would ensure a bright future be allowed to operate. Writing in a period of commercial capitalism, he preached the partially heretical notion that the abandonment of the comprehensive mercantile regulations and the adoption of the laissez-faire rules of the game would unleash a country's vast economic potential. The "invisible hand" (the competitive market system) would efficiently allocate society's human and material resources among the various sectors so as to foster economic development and class harmony.

Reacting against the mercantilist tendency to concentrate its capital in the tariff-protected foreign trade sector, Smith advocated a gradual, balanced growth pattern in which investment in agriculture received top priority at an early stage followed in due time by manufacturing and trade. Facilitating this growth would be, according to Smith, the increased employment of productive labor (those engaged in turning out tangible products) and the utilization of the division of labor principle (illustrated by his famous "pin factory"). A component of the latter factor is represented in modern times as technological

---

*(1723–1790)

change, and Smith placed great emphasis on its role within the laissez-faire system. He undoubtedly felt that the two were consistent with one another, a view which may be contrasted with those of Schumpeter* and Galbraith.† Growth, then, was Smith's chief concern, and the crucial initiator of this economic activity was the savings of the propertied class. These savings set in motion a dynamic growth process in which the "wages fund" (money available for wage payments) advanced by the capitalists in the current period, out of earnings in the previous period, was replenished by the productive workers by an amount greater than the advance. This in turn aided economic growth in the following period. The possibilities of uninvested savings or inadequate effective demand (which would cause unemployment) were not explored by Smith. His perspective was the grand theme of economic development, within the framework of a competitive capitalist order, rather than short-run cyclical phenomena. Operating under a competitive system, with the profit motive as the main incentive for production, the concentration of economic power would be limited and an efficient allocation of resources as well as a growing economy would result. The possibility of a stationary state at some advanced stage of capitalism is mentioned by Smith, but this possibility is not fully explored until the middle of the nineteenth century by John Stuart Mill.‡

An adequate appraisal of Smith's economic thinking requires historical perspective. Smith represents a fusion of the economic theorist and the political statesman. His *Wealth of Nations* is both an economic treatise and a practical political program. It represents the thinking of an intellectual keenly aware of the main streams of theoretical political economy, and a cautious reformer attempting to influence public policy. The England of Smith's day was one where the mercantile restrictions and subsidies were becoming more and more arbitrary and oppressive, and where commercial and military rivalries imposed a drain on the economy. With England, the world's leading commercial center, on the threshold of the Industrial Revolution, it was not unreasonable for Smith to believe that the free market was a more effective instrument for furthering the wealth of nations and maintaining political freedom than the "planned economy" administered by the mercantilist statesmen.

Monopoly privileges, public corruption, and economic inefficiency were all too obvious, and evasion of personal political rights was becoming increasingly manifest. In championing free trade and a decentralized economy, which separated the business sector from governmental control, Smith was providing a rationale for a widely prevalent practice—mass evasion of the burdensome mercantile regulations by a growing entrepreneurial class actively and skillfully pur-

---

*See chapter 7.
† See chapter 8.
‡See chapter 5.

suing its self-interest. It was the pursuit of this self-interest which Smith characterized as economic man's basic psychological drive. Because of his belief in the existence of a natural order in the universe, Smith felt that this drive would automatically work for the betterment of society as a whole. To ensure that this natural order would be preserved, a noninterventionist government was necessary. The role of the government, according to Smith, ought to be restricted to military protection, administration of laws, and erection of a limited amount of public works which the private sector had insufficient economic incentive to engage in. Smith's arguments and those of his followers, combined with the success of the system which seemingly operated under their principles, became so dominant that they helped to foster the idea of a relationship between economic and political freedom and competitive capitalism. This feeling has carried down to the present time and is expressed here, with various personal twists and modern connotations, by Hayek, Friedman, and Rothbard.

Even though Smith underestimated the thrust that the mercantilist system had imparted to early capitalist economic development, he did recognize that the interests of society could not be best served by operating under that institutional arrangement. Despite the ready adaptability of his doctrines to the propertied interests, Smith's sympathies were with the laboring class and the actual tiller of the soil. Although Smith is sometimes regarded by businessmen and modern conservatives as being favorable to big business, a close examination of the selection presented here will show this view to be a false one. He believed, and probably with validity under the existing institutional arrangements, that impersonal competitive markets could more effectively restrain the ability of the capitalists to exploit the public than a government he regarded as an "engine of oppression." The irresponsibility of the business class and the State toward the condition of the masses in the period of industrial mobilization does not destroy the historical validity of Smith's theory. It was not unreasonable for him to assume that capital accumulation would necessarily raise the standard of living of the working class, since it was not yet typical for capital accumulation to take the form of fixed capital (such as machinery and factories) which could result in economic growth without an accompanying rise in economic welfare.

Two of Adam Smith's notions deserve attention because they are of concern to many of today's undeveloped countries. They are the alleged benefits of stressing agriculture at an early stage of development as opposed to industry or commerce, and the idea that free trade is beneficial from the standpoint of growth and welfare. There are serious shortcomings to both of these positions. A strong case can be made for the view that free trade, based on the principle of comparative advantage, could freeze a country's productive pattern and prevent the diversified development of industry. The all-too-frequent result is a reinforcement of the circle of poverty and a widening gap between the advanced and backward countries. The stress on agriculture also has certain weaknesses except in cases, like early America, where the land:labor ratio is exceptionally favorable. Agriculture is likely to be carried on in an unproductive manner in a society with a weak industrial sector. Although agricultural development may, under certain favorable circumstances, ease the transition to an industrial society, in a world characterized by rapidly rising expectations, the peoples of undeveloped countries will almost certainly view the price of gradual balanced growth as too severe.

Smith's *Wealth of Nations,* nevertheless, remains one of the great classics of economic thought. It gave a precision and rigor to economic analysis that was indispensable for the development of the discipline. But more than that, it presented a model of an economic system that is rigorously defended by a number of modern theorists, some of whom have expanded its implications far beyond the scope of economic theory. The mystique of Smith's market system remains the ideal to which American capitalism often pays lip service but which it refuses to practice.

———M. L.

from

An Inquiry into the Nature and Causes of the Wealth of Nations

ECONOMIC GROWTH AND THE MARKET SYSTEM

The annual labor of every nation is the fund which originally supplies it with all the necessaries and conveniences of life which it annually consumes, and which consist always either in the immediate produce of that labor or in what is purchased with that produce from other nations.

According, therefore, as this produce, or what is purchased with it, bears a greater or smaller proportion to the number of those who are to consume it, the nation will be better or worse supplied with all the necessaries and conveniences for which it has occasion.

But this proportion must in every nation be regulated by two different circumstances: first, by the skill, dexterity, and judgment with which its labor is generally applied; and, secondly, by the proportion between the number of those who are employed in useful labor and that of those who are not so employed. Whatever be the soil, climate, or extent of territory of any particular nation, the abundance or scantiness of its annual supply must, in that particular situation, depend upon those two circumstances.

The abundance or scantiness of this supply too seems to depend more upon the former of those two circumstances than upon the latter. Among the savage nations of hunters and fishers, every individual who is able to work is more or less employed in useful labor and endeavors to provide, as well as he can, the necessaries and conveniences of life for himself, or such of his family or tribe as are either too old, or too young, or too infirm to go hunting and fishing. Such nations, however, are so miserably poor that, from mere want, they are frequently reduced, or, at least, think themselves reduced, to the necessity sometimes of directly destroying, and sometimes of abandoning, their infants, their old people, and those afflicted with lingering diseases to perish with hunger or to be devoured by wild beasts. Among civilized and thriving nations, on the contrary, though a great number of people do not labor at all, many of whom consume the produce of ten times, frequently of a hundred times more labor than the greater part of those who work; yet the produce of the whole labor of the society is so great that all are often abundantly supplied, and a workman, even of the lowest and poorest order, if he is frugal and industrious, may enjoy a greater share of the necessaries and conveniences of life than it is possible for any savage to acquire. . . .

Whatever be the actual state of the skill, dexterity, and judgment with which labor is applied in any nation, the abundance or scantiness of its annual supply must depend, during the continuance of that state, upon the proportion between the number of those who are annually employed in useful labor and that of those who are not so employed. The number of useful and productive laborers, it will hereafter appear, is everywhere in proportion to the quantity of capital stock which is employed in setting them to work and to the particular way in which it is so employed. . . .

Nations tolerably well advanced as to skill, dexterity, and judgment in the application of labor have followed very different plans in the general conduct or direction of it; and those plans have not all been equally favorable to the greatness of its produce. The policy of some nations has given extraordinary encouragement to the industry of the country; that of others to the industry of towns. Scarce any nation has dealt equally and impartially with every sort of industry. Since the downfall of the Roman Empire, the policy of Europe has been more favorable to arts, manufacturers, and commerce, the industry of towns, than to agriculture, the industry of the country. . . .

Though those different plans were, perhaps, first introduced by the private interests and prejudices of particular orders of men, without any regard to, or foresight of, their consequences upon the general welfare of the society, yet they have given occasion to very different theories of political economy, of which some magnify the importance of that industry which is carried on in towns, others of that which is carried on in the country. Those theories have had a considerable influence, not only upon the opinions of men of learning, but upon the public conduct of princes and sovereign states. . . .

Of the Causes of Improvement in the Productive Powers of Labor

The greatest improvement in the productive powers of labor and the greater part of the skill, dexterity, and judgment with which it is anywhere directed, or applied, seem to have been the effects of the division of labor. . . .

To take an example . . . from a very trifling manufacture, but one in which the division of labor has been very often taken notice of, the trade of the pin-maker; a workman not educated to this business (which the division of labor has rendered a distinct trade), nor acquainted with the use of the machinery employed in it (to the invention of which the same division of labor has probably given occasion), could scarce, perhaps, with his utmost industry, make one pin in a day, and certainly could not make twenty. But in the way in which this business is now carried on, not only the whole work is a peculiar trade, but it is divided into a number of branches, of which the greater part are likewise peculiar trades. One man draws out the wire, another straightens it, a third cuts it, a fourth points it, a fifth grinds it at the top for receiving the head; to make the head requires two or three distinct operations; to put it on is a peculiar business, to whiten the pins is another; it is even a trade by itself to put them into the paper; and the important business of making a pin is, in this manner, divided into about eighteen distinct operations, which, in some manufactories, are all performed by distinct hands, though in others the same man will sometimes perform two or three of them. I have seen a small manufactory of this kind where ten men only were employed, and where some of them consequently performed two or three distinct operations.

But though they were very poor, and therefore but indifferently accommodated with the necessary machinery, they could, when they exerted themselves, make among them about twelve pounds of pins in a day. There are in a pound upward of four thousand pins of a middling size. Those ten persons, therefore, could make among them upward of forty-eight thousand pins in a day. Each person, therefore, making a tenth part of forty-eight thousand pins, might be considered as making four thousand eight hundred pins in a day. But if they had all wrought separately and independently, and without any of them having been educated to this peculiar business, they certainly could not each of them have made twenty, perhaps not one pin in a day; that is, certainly, not the two hundred and fortieth, perhaps not the four thousand eight hundredth part of what they are at present capable of performing in consequence of a proper division and combination of their different operations.

In every other art and manufacture the effects of the division of labor are similar to what they are in this very trifling one; though, in many of them, the labor can neither be so much subdivided nor reduced to so great a simplicity of operation. The division of labor, however, so far as it can be introduced, occasions, in every art, a proportionable increase of the productive powers of labor. The separation of different trades and employments from one another seems to have taken place in consequence of this advantage. This separation too is generally carried furthest in those countries which enjoy the highest degree of industry and improvement, what is the work of one man in a rude state of society being generally that of several in an improved one. . . .

This great increase of the quantity of work which, in consequence of the division of labor, the same number of people are capable of performing is owing to three different circumstances; first, to the increase of dexterity in every particular workman; secondly, to the saving of the time which is commonly lost in passing from one species of work to another; and, lastly, to the invention of a great number of machines which facilitate and abridge labor and enable one man to do the work of many. . . .

It is the great multiplication of the productions of all the different arts, in consequence of the division of labor, which occasions, in a well-governed society, that universal opulence which extends itself to the lowest ranks of the people. Every workman has a great quantity of his own work to dispose of beyond what he himself has occasion for;

and every other workman being exactly in the same situation, he is enabled to exchange a great quantity of his own goods for a great quantity or, what comes to the same thing, for the price of a great quantity of theirs. He supplies them abundantly with what they have occasion for, and they accommodate him as amply with what he has occasion for, and a general plenty diffuses itself through all the different ranks of the society. . . .

Of the Principle Which Gives Occasion to the Division of Labor

This division of labor, from which so many advantages are derived, is not originally the effect of any human wisdom, which foresees and intends that general opulence to which it gives occasion. It is the necessary, though very slow and gradual, consequence of a certain propensity in human nature which has in view no such extensive utility; the propensity to truck, barter, and exchange one thing for another.

Whether this propensity be one of those original principles in human nature, of which no further account can be given; or whether, as seems more probable, it be the necessary consequence of the faculties of reason and speech, it belongs not to our present subject to inquire. It is common to all men, and to be found in no other race of animals, which seem to know neither this nor any other species of contracts. . . .

As it is by treaty, by barter, and by purchase, that we obtain from one another the greater part of those mutual good offices which we stand in need of, so it is this same trucking disposition which originally gives occasion to the division of labor. In a tribe of hunters or shepherds a particular person makes bows and arrows, for example, with more readiness and dexterity than any other. He frequently exchanges them for cattle or for venison with his companions; and he finds at last that he can in this manner get more cattle and venison, than if he himself went to the field to catch them. From a regard to his own interest, therefore, the making of bows and arrows grows to be his chief business, and he becomes a sort of armorer. Another excels in making the frames and covers of their little huts or movable houses. He is accustomed to be of use in this way to his neighbors, who reward him in the same manner with cattle and with venison, till at last he finds it his interest to dedicate himself entirely to this employment, and to become a sort of house-carpenter. In the same manner a third becomes a smith, or a brazier; a fourth a tanner or dresser of hides or skins, the principal part of the clothing of savages. And thus the certainty of being able to exchange all that surplus part of the produce of his own labor, which is over and above his own consumption, for such parts of the produce of other men's labor as he may have occasion for, encourages every man to apply himself to a particular occupation, and to cultivate and bring to perfection whatever talent or genius he may possess for that particular species of business. . . .

Among men, . . . the most dissimilar geniuses are of use to one another; the different produces of their respective talents, by the general disposition to truck, barter, and exchange, being brought, as it were, into a common stock, where every man may purchase whatever part of the produce of other men's talents he has occasion for. . . .

That the Division of Labor Is Limited by the Extent of the Market

As it is the power of exchanging that gives occasion to the division of labor, so the extent of this division must always be limited by the extent of that power, or, in other words, by the extent of the market. When the market is very small, no person can have any encouragement to dedicate himself entirely to one employment, for want of the power to exchange all that surplus part of the produce of his own labor, which is over and above his own consumption, for such part of the produce of other men's labor as he has occasion for.

There are some sorts of industry, even of the lowest kind, which can be carried on nowhere but in a great town. A porter, for example, can find employment and subsistence in no other place. . . .

As, by means of water-carriage, a more extensive market is open to every sort of industry than what land-carriage alone can afford it, so it is upon the sea-coast, and along the banks of navigable rivers, that industry of every kind naturally begins to subdivide and improve itself; and it is frequently not till a long time after that those improvements extend themselves to the inland parts of the country. . . .

Since such therefore are the advantages of water-carriage, it is natural that the first improvements of art and industry should be made where this conveniency opens the whole world for a market to the produce of every sort of labor, and that they should always be much later in extending themselves into the inland parts of the country. The inland parts of the country can for a long time have no other market for the greater part of their goods, but the country which lies round about them, and separates them from the sea-coast, and the great navigable rivers. The extent of their market, therefore, must for a long time be in proportion to the riches and populousness of that country, and consequently their improvement must always be posterior to the improvement of that country. . . .

The nations that, according to the best authenticated history, appear to have been first civilized, were those that dwelt round the coast of the Mediterranean Sea. That sea, by far the greatest inlet that is known in the world, having no tides, nor consequently any waves except such as are caused by the wind only, was, by the smoothness of its surface, as well as by the multitude of its islands, and the proximity of its neighboring shores, extremely favorable to the infant navigation of the world; when, from their ignorance of the compass, men were afraid to quit the view of the coast, and from the imperfection of the art of ship-building, to abandon themselves to the boisterous waves of the ocean. . . .

OF THE NATURE, ACCUMULATION, AND EMPLOYMENT OF STOCK

In that rude state of society in which there is no division of labor, in which exchanges are seldom made, and in which every man provides everything for himself, it is not necessary that any stock should be accumulated or stored up beforehand, in order to carry on the business of the society. Every man endeavors to supply by his own industry his own occasional wants as they occur. When he is hungry, he goes to the forest to hunt; when his coat is worn out, he clothes himself with the skin of the first large animal he kills; and when his hut begins to go to ruin, he repairs it, as well as he can, with the trees and the turf that are nearest it.

But when the division of labor has once been thoroughly introduced, the produce of a man's own labor can supply but a small part of his occasional wants. The far greater part of them are supplied by the produce of other men's labor, which he purchases with the produce, or what is the same thing, with the price of the produce of his own. But this purchase cannot be made till such time as the produce of his own labor has not only been completed but sold. A stock of goods of different kinds, therefore, must be stored up somewhere sufficient to maintain him, and to supply him with the materials and tools of his work, till such time, at least, as both these events can be brought about. A weaver cannot apply himself entirely to his peculiar business unless there is beforehand stored up somewhere, either in his own possession or in that of some other person, a stock sufficient to maintain him, and to supply him with the materials and tools of his work, till he has not only completed but sold his web. This accumulation must, evidently, be previous to his applying his industry for so long a time to such a peculiar business.

As the accumulation of stock must, in the nature of things, be previous to the division of labor, so labor can be more and more subdivided in proportion only as stock is previously more and more accumulated. The quantity of materials which the same number of people can work up increases in a great proportion as labor comes to be more and more subdivided; and, as the operations of each workman are gradually reduced to a greater degree of simplicity, a variety of new machines come to be invented for facilitating and abridging those operations. As the division of labor advances, therefore, in order to give constant employment to an equal number of workmen, an equal stock of provisions, and a greater stock of materials and tools than what would have been necessary in a ruder state of things must be accumulated beforehand. But the number of workmen in every branch of business generally increases with the division of labor in that branch, or rather it is the increase of their number which enables them to class and subdivide themselves in this manner.

As the accumulation of stock is previously necessary for carrying on this great improvement in the productive powers of labor, so that accumulation naturally leads to this improvement. The person who employs his stock in maintaining labor necessarily wishes to employ it in such a manner as to produce as great a quantity of work as possible. He endeavors, therefore, both to make among his workmen the most proper distribution of employment and to furnish them with the best machines which he can either invent or afford to purchase. His abilities in both these respects are generally in proportion to the extent of his stock or to the number of people whom it can employ. The quantity of industry, therefore, not only increases in every country with the increase of the stock which employs it, but, in consequence of that increase, the same quantity of industry produces a much greater quantity of work. . . .

Capitals are increased by parsimony and diminished by prodigality and misconduct.

Whatever a person saves from his revenue he adds to his capital and either employs it himself in maintaining an additional number of productive hands or enables some other person to do so, by lending it to him for an interest, that is, for a share of the profits. As the capital of an individual can be increased only by what he saves from his annual revenue or his annual gains, so the capital of a society, which is the same with that of all the individuals who compose it, can be increased only in the same manner.

Parsimony, and not industry, is the immediate cause of the increase of capital. Industry, indeed, provides the subject which parsimony accumulates. But whatever industry might acquire, if parsimony did not save and store up, the capital would never be the greater.

Parsimony, by increasing the fund which is destined for the maintenance of productive hands, tends to increase the number of those hands whose labor adds to the value of the subject upon which it is bestowed. It tends therefore to increase the exchangeable value of the annual produce of the land and labor of the country. It puts into motion an additional quantity of industry, which gives an additional value to the annual produce.

What is annually saved is as regularly consumed as what is annually spent, and nearly in the same time too; but it is consumed by a different set of people. That portion of his revenue which a rich man annually spends is in most cases consumed by idle guests, and menial servants, who leave nothing behind them in return for their consumption. That portion which he annually saves, as for the sake of the profit it is immediately employed as a capital, is consumed in the same manner, and nearly in the same time too, but by a different set of people, by laborers, manufacturers, and artificers, who reproduce with a profit the value of their annual consumption. His revenue, we shall suppose, is paid him in money. Had he spent the whole, the food, clothing, and lodging which the whole could have purchased would have been distributed among the former set of people. By saving a part of it, as that part is for the sake of the profit immediately employed as a capital either by himself or by some other person, the food, clothing, and lodging which may be purchased with it are necessarily reserved for the latter. The consumption is the same, but the consumers are different.

By what a frugal man annually saves, he not only affords maintenance to an additional number of productive hands, for that or the ensuing year, but, like the founder of a public workhouse, he establishes, as it were, a perpetual fund for the maintenance of an equal number in all times to come. The perpetual allotment and destination of this fund, indeed, is not always guarded by any positive law, by any trust-right or deed of mortmain. It is always guarded, however, by a very powerful principle, the plain and evident interest of every individual to whom any share of it shall ever belong. No part of it can ever afterward be employed to maintain any but productive hands, without an evident loss to the person who thus perverts it from its proper destination.

The prodigal perverts it in this manner. By not confining his expense within his income, he encroaches upon his capital. Like him who perverts the revenues of some pious foundation to profane purposes, he pays the wages of idleness with those funds which the frugality of his forefathers had, as it were, consecrated to the maintenance of industry. By diminishing the funds destined for the employment of productive labor, he necessarily diminishes, so far as it depends upon him, the quantity of that labor which adds a value to the subject upon which it is bestowed, and, consequently, the value of the annual produce of the land and labor of the whole country, the real wealth and revenue of its inhabitants. If the prodigality of some was not compensated by the frugality of others, the conduct of every prodigal, by feeding the idle with the bread of the industrious, tends not only to beggar himself but to impoverish his country. . . .

Great nations are never impoverished by private, though they sometimes are by public prodigality and misconduct. The whole, or almost the whole, public revenue is in most countries employed in maintaining unproductive hands. Such are the people who compose a numerous and splendid court, a great ecclesiastical establishment, great fleets and armies, who in time of peace produce nothing, and in time of war acquire nothing which can compensate the expense of maintaining them, even while the war lasts. Such people, as they themselves produce nothing, are all maintained by the produce of other men's labor. When multiplied, therefore, to an unnecessary number, they may in a particular year consume so great a share of this produce as not to leave a sufficiency for maintaining the productive laborers, who should reproduce it next year. The next year's produce, therefore, will be less than that of the foregoing, and if the same disorder should continue, that of the third year will be still less than that of the second. Those unproductive hands, who should be maintained by a part only of the spare revenue of the people, may consume so great a share of their whole revenue, and therefore oblige so great a number to encroach upon their capitals, upon the funds destined for the maintenance of productive labor, that all the frugality and good conduct of individuals may not be able to compensate the waste and degradation of produce occasioned by this violent and forced encroachment.

This frugality and good conduct, however, is upon most occasions, it appears from experience, sufficient to compensate, not only the private prodigality and misconduct of individuals but the public extravagance of government. The uniform, constant, and uninterrupted effort of every man to better his condition, the principle from which public and national, as well as private opulence is originally derived, is frequently powerful enough to maintain the natural progress of things toward improvement, in spite both of the extravagance of government and of the greatest errors of administration. Like the unknown principle of animal life, it frequently restores health and vigor to the constitution, in spite, not only of the disease, but of the absurd prescriptions of the doctor.

The annual produce of the land and labor of any nation can be increased in its value by no other means but by increasing either the number of its productive laborers or the productive powers of those laborers who had before been employed. The number of its productive laborers, it is evident, can never be much increased, but in consequence of an increase of capital, or of the funds destined for maintaining them. The productive powers of the same number of laborers cannot be increased, but in consequence either of some addition and improvement to those machines and instruments which facilitate and abridge labor; or of a more proper division and distribution of employment. In either case an additional capital is almost always required. It is by means of an additional capital only that the undertaker of any work can either provide his workmen with better machinery or make a more proper distribution of employment among them. When the work to be done consists of a number of parts, to keep every man constantly employed in one way requires a much greater capital than where every man is occasionally employed in every different part of the work. When we compare, therefore, the state of a nation at two different periods and find that the annual produce of its land and labor is evidently greater at the latter than at the former, that its lands are better cultivated, its manufactures more numerous and more flourishing, and its trade more extensive, we may be assured that its capital must have increased during the interval between those two periods and that more must have been added to it by the good conduct of some than had been taken from it either by the private misconduct of others or by the public extravagance of government....

Of the Accumulation of Capital, or of Productive and Unproductive Labor

There is one sort of labor which adds to the value of the subject upon which it is bestowed: there is another which has no such effect. The former, as it produces a value, may be called productive; the latter, unproductive labor. Thus the labor of a manufacturer adds, generally, to the value of the materials which he works upon, that of his own maintenance, and of his master's profit. The labor of a menial servant, on the contrary, adds to the value of nothing. Though the manufacturer has his wages advanced to him by his master, he, in reality, costs him no expense, the value of those wages being generally restored, together with a profit, in the improved value of the subject upon which his labor is bestowed. But the maintenance of a menial servant never is restored. A man grows rich by employing a multitude of manufacturers: he grows poor by maintaining a multitude of menial servants. The labor of the latter, however, has its value, and deserves its reward as well as that of the former. But the labor of the manufacturer fixes and realizes itself in some particular subject or vendible commodity, which lasts for some time at least after that labor is past. It is, as it were, a certain quantity of labor stocked and stored up to be employed, if necessary, upon some other occasion. That subject, or what is the same thing, the price of that subject, can afterwards, if necessary, put into motion a quantity of labor equal to that which had originally produced it. The labor of the menial servant, on the contrary, does not fix or realize itself in any particular subject or vendible commodity. The services of the menial generally perish in the very instant of their performance, and seldom leave any trace or value behind them, for which an equal quantity of service could afterwards be procured.

The labor of some of the most respectable orders in the society is, like that of menial servants, unproductive of any value, and does not fix or realize itself in any permanent subject, or vendible commodity, which endures after that labor is past, and for which an equal quantity of labor could afterwards be procured. The sovereign, for example, with all the officers both of justice and war who serve under him, the whole army and navy, are unproductive laborers. They are the servants of the public, and are maintained by a part of the annual produce of the industry of other people. Their service, how honorable, how useful, or how necessary soever, produces nothing for which an equal quantity of service can afterwards be procured. The protection, security, and defence of the commonwealth, the effect of their labor this year, will not purchase its protection, security, and defence for the year to come. In the same class must be ranked, some both of the gravest and most important, and some of the most frivolous professions: churchmen, lawyers, physicians, men of letters of all kinds; players, buffoons, musicians, opera-singers, opera-dancers, etc. The labor of the meanest of these has a certain value, regulated by the very same principles which regulate that of every other sort of labor; and that of the noblest and most useful produces nothing which could afterwards purchase or procure an equal quantity of labor. Like the declamation of the actor, the harangue of the orator, or the tune of the musician, the work of all of them perishes in the very instant of its production.

Both productive and unproductive laborers, and those who do not labor at all, are all equally maintained by the annual produce of the land and labor of the country. This produce, how great soever, can never be infinite, but must have certain limits. According, therefore, as a smaller or greater proportion of it is in any one year employed in maintaining unproductive hands, the more in the one case and the less in the other will remain for the productive, and the next year's produce will be greater or smaller accordingly; the whole annual produce, if we except the spontaneous productions of the earth, being the effect of productive labor.

Though the whole annual produce of the land and labor of every country is, no doubt, ultimately destined for supplying the consumption of its inhabitants, and for procuring a revenue to them, yet when it first comes either from the ground, or from the hands of the productive laborers, it naturally divides itself into two parts. One of them, and frequently the largest, is, in the first place, destined for replacing capital, or for renewing the provisions, materials, and finished work, which had been withdrawn from capital; the other for constituting a revenue either to the owner of this capital, as the profit of his stock; or to some other person, as the rent of his land. Thus, of the produce of land, one part replaces the capital of the farmer; the other pays his profit and the rent of the landlord; and thus constitutes a revenue both to the owner of this capital as the profits of his stock, and to some other person as the rent of his land. Of the produce of a great manufacture, in the same manner, one part, and that always the largest, replaces the capital of the undertaker of the work; the other pays his profit, and thus constitutes a revenue to the owner of this capital. . . .

The proportion, therefore, between the productive annd unproductive hands, depends very much in every country upon the proportion between that part of the annual produce, which, as soon as it comes either from the ground or from the hands of the productive laborers, is destined for replacing a capital, and that which is destined for constituting a revenue, either as rent, or as profit. This proportion is very different in rich from what it is in poor countries. . . .

OF THE DIFFERENT EMPLOYMENTS OF CAPITAL

Though all capitals are destined for the maintenance of productive labor only, yet the quantity of that labor, which equal capitals are capable of putting into motion, varies extremely according to the diversity of their employment; as does likewise the value which that employment adds to the annual produce of the land and labor of the country.

A capital may be employed in four different ways: either, first, in procuring the rude produce annually required for the use and consumption of the society; or, secondly, in manufacturing and preparing that rude produce for immediate use and consumption; or, thirdly, in transporting either the rude or manufactured produce from the places where they abound to those where they are wanted; or, lastly, in dividing particular portions of either into such small parcels as suit the occasional demands of those who want them. In the first way are employed the capitals of all those who undertake the improvement of cultivation of lands, mines, or fisheries; in the second, those of all master manufacturers; in the third, those of all wholesale merchants; and in the fourth, those of all retailers. It is difficult to conceive that a capital should be employed in any way which may not be classed under some one or other of those four.

Each of those four methods of employing a capital is essentially necessary either to the existence or extension of the other three, or to the general conveniency of the society. . . .

The persons whose capitals are employed in any of those four ways are themselves productive laborers. Their labor, when properly directed, fixes and realizes itself in the subject or vendible commodity upon which it is bestowed, and generally adds to its price the value at least of their own maintenance and consumption. The profits of the farmer, of the manufacturer, of the merchant, and retailer, are all drawn from the price of the goods which the two first produce, and the two last buy and sell. Equal capitals, however, employed in each of those four different ways, will immediately put into motion very different quantities of productive labor, and augment too in very different proportions the value of the annual produce of the land and labor of the society to which they belong. . . .

No equal capital puts into motion a greater quantity of productive labor than that of the farmer. Not only his laboring servants, but his laboring cattle, are productive laborers. In agriculture too nature labors along with man; and though her labor costs no expence, its produce has its value, as well as that of the most expensive workmen. The most important operations of agriculture seem intended, not so much to increase, though they do that too, as to direct the fertility of nature towards the production of the plants most profitable to man. A field overgrown with briars and brambles may frequently produce as great a quantity of vegetables as the best cultivated vineyard or corn field. Planting and tillage frequently regulate more than they animate the active fertility of nature; and after all their labor, a great part of the work always remains to be done by her. The laborers and laboring cattle, therefore, employed in agriculture, not only occasion, like the workmen in manufactures, the reproduction of a value equal to their own consumption, or to the capital which employs them, together with its owners profits; but of a much greater value. Over and above the capital of the farmer and all its profits, they regularly occasion the reproduction of the rent of the landlord. This rent may be considered as the produce of those powers of nature, the use of which the landlord lends to the farmer. It is greater or smaller according to the supposed extent of those powers, or in other words, according to the supposed natural or improved fertility of the land. It is the work of nature which remains after deducting or compensating every thing which can be regarded as the work of man. It is seldom less than a fourth, and frequently more than a third of the whole produce. No equal quantity of productive labor employed in manufactures can ever occasion so great a reproduction. In them nature does nothing; man does all; and the reproduction must always be in proportion to the strength of the agents that occasion it. The capital employed in agriculture, therefore, not only puts into motion a greater quantity of productive labor than any equal capital employed in manufactures, but in proportion too to the quantity of productive labor which it employs, it adds a much greater value to the annual produce of the land and labor of the country, to the real wealth and revenue of its inhabitants. Of all the ways in which a capital can be employed, it is by far the most advantageous to the society. . . .

After agriculture, the capital employed in manufactures puts into motion the greatest quantity of productive labor, and adds the greatest value to the annual produce. That which is employed in the trade of exportation, has the least effect of any of the three.

The country, indeed, which has not capital sufficient for all those three purposes, has not arrived at that degree of opulence for which it seems naturally destined. To attempt, however, prematurely and with an insufficient capital, to do all the three, is certainly not the shortest way for a society, no more than it would be for an individual, to acquire a sufficient one. The capital of all the individuals of a nation, has its limits in the same manner as that of a single individual, and is capable of executing only certain purposes. The capital of all the individuals of a nation is increased in the same manner as that of a single individual, by their continually accumulating and adding to it whatever they save out of their income. It is likely to increase the fastest, therefore, when it is employed in the way that affords the greatest revenue to all the inhabitants of the country, as they will thus be enabled to make the greatest savings. But the revenue of all the inhabitants of the country is necessarily in proportion to the value of the annual produce of their land and labor. . . .

The capital employed in the home-trade of any country will generally give encouragement and support to a greater quantity of productive labor in that country, and increase the value of its annual produce more than an equal capital employed in the foreign trade of consumption: and the capital employed in this latter trade has in both these respects a still greater advantage over an equal capital employed in the carrying trade. The riches, and so far as power depends upon riches, the power of every country, must always be in proportion to the value of its annual produce, the fund from which all taxes must ultimately be paid. But the great object of the political economy of every country, is to increase the riches and power of that country. It ought, therefore, to give no preference nor superior encouragement to the foreign trade of consumption above the home-trade, nor to the carrying trade above either of the other two. It ought neither to force nor to allure into either of those two channels, a greater share of the capital of the country than what would naturally flow into them of its own accord.

Each of those different branches of trade, however, is not only advantageous, but necessary and unavoidable, when the course of things, without any constraint or violence, naturally introduces it. When the produce of any particular branch of industry exceeds what the demand of the country requires, the surplus must be sent abroad, and exchanged for something for which there is a demand at home. Without such exportation, a part of the productive labor of the country must cease, and the value of its annual produce diminish. The land and labor of Great Britain produce generally more corn, woollens, and hard ware, than the demand of the home-market requires. The surplus part of them, therefore, must be sent abroad, and exchanged for something for which there is a demand at home. It is only by means of such exportation, that this surplus can acquire a value sufficient to compensate the labor and expence of producing it. The neighborhood of the sea coast, and the banks of all navigable rivers are advantageous situations for industry, only because they facilitate the exportation and exchange of such surplus produce for something else which is more in demand there. . . .

In a country which had acquired that full complement of riches which the nature of its soil and climate, and its situation with respect to other countries, allowed it to acquire; which could, therefore, advance no further, and which was not going backwards, both the wages of labor and the profits of stock would probably be very low. In a country fully peopled in proportion to what either its territory could maintain or its stock employ, the competition for employment would necessarily be so great as to reduce the wages of labor to what was barely sufficient to keep up the number of laborers, and, the country being already fully peopled, that number could never be augmented. In a country fully stocked in proportion to all the business it had to transact, as great a quantity of stock would be employed in every particular branch as the nature and extent of the trade would admit. The competition, therefore, would everywhere be as great, and consequently the ordinary profit as low as possible. . . .

OF THE NATURAL AND MARKET PRICE OF COMMODITIES

. . . When the price of any commodity is neither more nor less than what is sufficient to pay the rent of the land, the wages of the labor, and the profits of the stock employed in raising, preparing, and bringing it to market, according to their natural rates, the commodity is then sold for what may be called its natural price.

The commodity is then sold precisely for what it is worth, or for what it really costs the person who brings it to market; for though in common language what is called the prime cost of any commodity does not comprehend the profit of the person who is to sell it again, yet if he sells it at a price which does not allow him the ordinary rate of profit in his neighborhood, he is evidently a loser by the trade, since by employing his stock in some other way he might have made that profit. His profit, besides, is his revenue, the proper fund of his subsistence. As, while he is preparing and bringing the goods to market, he advances to his workmen their wages, or their subsistence, so he advances to himself, in the same manner, his own subsistence, which is generally suitable to the profit which he may reasonably expect from the sale of his goods. Unless they yield him this profit, therefore, they do not repay him what they may very properly be said to have really cost him.

Though the price, therefore, which leaves him this profit is not always the lowest at which a dealer may sometimes sell his goods, it is the lowest at which he is likely to sell them for any considerable time; at least where there is perfect liberty, or where he may change his trade as often as he pleases.

The actual price at which any commodity is commonly sold is called its market price. It may either be above, or below, or exactly the same with its natural price.

The market price of every particular commodity is regulated by the proportion between the quantity which is actually brought to the market and the demand of those who are willing to pay the natural price of the commodity, or the whole value of the rent, labor, and profit which must be paid in order to bring it thither. Such people may be called the effectual demanders, and their demand the effectual demand, since it may be sufficient to effectuate the bringing of the commodity to market. It is different from the absolute demand. A very poor man may be said in some sense to have a demand for a coach and six; he might like to have it; but his demand is not an effectual demand, as the commodity can never be brought to market in order to satisfy it.

When the quantity of any commodity which is brought to market falls short of the effectual demand, all those who are willing to pay the whole value of the rent, wages, and profit which must be paid in order to bring it thither cannot be supplied with the quantity which they want. Rather than want it altogether, some of them will be willing to give more. A competition will immediately begin among them, and the market price will rise more or less above the natural price, according as either the greatness of the deficiency or the wealth and wanton luxury of the competitors happen to animate more or less the eagerness of the competition. Among competitors of equal wealth and luxury the same deficiency will generally occasion a more or less eager competition, according as the acquisition of the commodity happens to be of more or less importance to them. Hence the exorbitant price of the necessaries of life during the blockade of a town or in a famine.

When the quantity brought to market exceeds the effectual demand, it cannot be all sold to those who are willing to pay the whole value of the rent, wages, and profit which must be paid in order to bring it thither. Some part must be sold to those who are willing to pay less, and the low price which they give for it must reduce the price of the whole. The market price will sink more or less below the natural price, according as the greatness of the excess increases more or less the competition of the sellers, or according as it happens to be more or less important to them to get immediately rid of the commodity. The same excess in the importation of perishables will occasion a much greater competition than in that of durable commodities; in the importation of oranges, for example, than in that of old iron.

When the quantity brought to market is just sufficient to supply the effectual demand and no more, the market price naturally comes to be either exactly, or as nearly as can be judged of, the same with the natural price. The whole quantity upon hand can be disposed of for this price and cannot be disposed of for more. The competition of the different dealers obliges them all to accept of this price but does not oblige them to accept of less.

The quantity of every commodity brought to market naturally suits itself to the effectual demand. It is the interest of all those who employ their land, labor, or stock, in bringing any commodity to market, that the quantity never should exceed the effectual demand; and it is the interest of all other people that it never should fall short of that demand.

If at any time it exceeds the effectual demand, some of the component parts of its price must be paid below their natural rate. If it is rent, the interest of the landlords will immediately prompt them to withdraw a part of their land; and if it is wages or profit, the interest of the laborers in the one case, and of their employers in the other, will prompt them to withdraw a part of their labor or stock from this employment. The quantity brought to market will soon be no more than sufficient to supply the effectual demand. All the different parts of its price will rise to their natural rate, and the whole price to its natural price.

If, on the contrary, the quantity brought to market should at any time fall short of the effectual demand, some of the component parts of its price must rise above their natural rate. If it is rent, the interest of all other landlords will naturally prompt them to prepare more land for the raising of this commodity; if it is wages or profit, the interest of all other laborers and dealers will soon prompt them to employ more labor and stock in preparing and bringing it to market. The quantity brought thither will soon be sufficient to supply the effectual demand. All the different parts of its price will soon sink to their natural rate, and the whole price to its natural price.

The natural price, therefore, is, as it were, the central price, to which the prices of all commodities are continually gravitating. Different accidents may sometimes keep them suspended a good deal above it, and sometimes force them down even somewhat below it. But whatever may be the obstacles which hinder them from settling in this center of repose and continuance, they are constantly tending toward it.

The whole quantity of industry annually employed in order to bring any commodity to market naturally suits itself in this manner to the effectual demand. It naturally aims at bringing always that precise quantity thither which may be sufficient to supply, and no more than supply, that demand.

But in some employments the same quantity of industry will in different years produce very different quantities of commodities; while in others it will produce always the same, or very nearly the same. The same number of laborers in husbandry will, in different years, produce very different quantities of corn, wine, oil, hops, etc. But the same number of spinners and weavers will every year produce the same or very nearly the same quantity of linen and woolen cloth. It is only the average produce of the one species of industry which can be suited in any respect to the effectual demand; and, as its actual produce is frequently much greater and frequently much less than its average produce, the quantity of the commodities brought to market will sometimes exceed a good deal, and sometimes fall short a good deal, of the effectual demand. Even though that demand therefore should continue always the same, their market price will be liable to great fluctuations, will sometimes fall a good deal below, and sometimes rise a good deal above, their natural price. In the other species of industry, the produce of equal quantities of labor being always the same, or very nearly the same, it can be more exactly suited to the effectual demand. While that demand continues the same, therefore, the market price of the commodities is likely to do so too, and to be either altogether, or as nearly as can be judged of, the same with the natural price. That the price of linen and woolen cloth is liable neither to such frequent nor to such great variations as the price of corn, every man's experience will inform him. The price of the one species of commodities varies only with the variations in the demand. That of the other varies not only with the variations in the demand but with the much greater and more frequent variations in the quantity of what is brought to market in order to supply that demand.

The occasional and temporary fluctuations in the market price of any commodity fall chiefly upon those parts of its price which resolve themselves into wages and profit. That part which resolves itself into rent is less affected by them. A rent certain in money is not in the least affected by them either in its rate or in its value. A rent which consists either in a certain proportion or in a certain quantity of the rude produce is no doubt affected in its yearly value by all the occasional and temporary fluctuations in the market price of that rude produce; but it is seldom affected by them in its yearly rate. In settling the terms of the lease, the landlord and the farmer endeavor, according to their best judgment, to adjust that rate, not to the temporary and occasional, but to the average and ordinary price of the produce.

Such fluctuations affect both the value and the rate either of wages or of profit, according as the market happens to be either overstocked or understocked with commodities or with labor; with work done, or with work to be done. A public mourning raises the price of black cloth (with which the market is almost always understocked upon such occasions) and augments the profits of the merchants who possess any considerable quantity of it. It has no effect upon the wages of the weavers. The market is understocked with commodities, not with labor; with work done, not with work to be done. It raises the wages of journeymen tailors. The market is here understocked with labor. There is an effectual demand for more labor, for more work to be done than can be had. It sinks the price of colored silks and cloths and thereby reduces the profits of the merchants who have any considerable quantity of them upon hand. It sinks too the wages of the workmen employed in preparing such commodities, for which all demand is stopped for six months, perhaps for a twelvemonth. The market is here overstocked both with commodities and with labor.

But though the market price of every particular commodity is in this manner continually gravitating, if one may say so, toward the natural price, yet sometimes particular accidents, sometimes natural causes, and sometimes particular regulations of police, may, in many commodities, keep up the market price, for a long time together, a good deal above the natural price.

When by an increase in the effectual demand, the market price of some particular commodity happens to rise a good deal above the natural price, those who employ their stocks in supplying that market are generally careful to conceal this change. If it was commonly known, their great profit would tempt so many new rivals to employ their stocks in the same way that, the effectual demand being fully supplied, the market price would soon be reduced to the natural price and perhaps for some time even below it. If the market is at a great distance from the residence of those who supply it, they may sometimes be able to keep the secret for several years together and may so long enjoy their extraordinary profits without any new rivals. Secrets of this kind, however, it must be acknowledged, can seldom be long kept; and the extraordinary profits can last very little longer than they are kept.

Secrets in manufactures are capable of being longer kept than secrets in trade. A dyer who has found the means of producing a particular color with materials which cost only half the price of those commonly made use of, may, with good management, enjoy the advantage of his discovery as long as he lives, and even leave it as a legacy to his posterity. His extraordinary gains arise from the high price which is paid for his private labor. They properly consist in the high wages of that labor. But as they are repeated upon every part of his stock, and as their whole amount bears, upon that account, a regular proportion to it, they are commonly considered as extraordinary profits of stock.

Such enhancements of the market price are evidently the effects of particular accidents, of which, however, the operation may sometimes last for many years together.

Some natural productions require such a singularity of soil and situation that all the land in a great country which is fit for producing them may not be sufficient to supply the effectual demand. The whole quantity brought to market, therefore, may be disposed of to those who are willing to give more than what is sufficient to pay the rent of the land which produced them, together with the wages of the labor, and the profits of the stock which were employed in preparing and bringing them to market, according to their natural rates. Such commodities may continue for whole centuries together to be sold at this high price; and that part of it which resolves itself into the rent of land is in this case the part which is generally paid above its natural rate. The rent of the land which affords such singular and esteemed productions, like the rent of some vineyards in France of a peculiarly happy soil and situation, bears no regular proportion to the rent of other equally fertile and equally well-cultivated land in its neighborhood. The wages of the labor and the profits of the stock employed in bringing such commodities to market, on the contrary, are seldom out of their natural proportion to those of the other employments of labor and stock in their neighborhood.

Such enhancements of the market price are evidently the effect of natural causes which may hinder the effectual demand from ever being fully supplied, and which may continue, therefore, to operate forever.

A monopoly granted either to an individual or to a trading company has the same effect as a secret in trade or manufactures. The monopolists, by keeping the market constantly understocked, by never fully supplying the effectual demand, sell their commodities much above the natural price and raise their emoluments, whether they consist in wages or profit, greatly above their natural rate.

The price of monopoly is upon every occasion the highest which can be got. The natural price, or the price of free competition, on the contrary, is the lowest which can be taken, not upon every occasion indeed, but for any considerable time together. The one is upon every occasion the highest which can be squeezed out of the buyers, or which, it is supposed, they will consent to give; the other is the lowest which the sellers can commonly afford to take and at the same time continue their business.

The exclusive privileges of corporations, statutes of apprenticeship, and all those laws which restrain, in particular employments, the competition to a smaller number than might otherwise go into them have the same tendency, though in a less degree. They are a sort of enlarged monopolies and may frequently, for ages together and in whole classes of employments, keep up the market price of particular commodities above the natural price and maintain both the wages of the labor and the profits of the stock employed about them somewhat above their natural rate.

Such enhancements of the market price may last as long as the regulations of police which give occasion to them.

The market price of any particular commodity, though it may continue long above, can seldom continue long below, its natural price. Whatever part of it was paid below the natural rate, the persons whose interest it affected would immediately feel the loss and would immediately withdraw either so much land, or so much labor, or so much stock, from being employed about it that the quantity brought to market would soon be no more than sufficient to supply the effectual demand. Its market price, therefore, would soon rise to the natural price. This at least would be the case where there was perfect liberty.

OF SYSTEMS OF POLITICAL ECONOMY

OF THE PRINCIPLE OF THE COMMERCIAL OR MERCANTILE SYSTEM

That wealth consists in money, or in gold and silver, is a popular notion which naturally arises from the double function of money as the instrument of commerce and as the measure of value. . . .

In consequence of these popular notions, all the different nations of Europe have studied, though to little purpose, every possible means of accumulating gold and silver in their respective countries. Spain and Portugal, the proprietors of the principal mines which supply Europe with those metals, have either prohibited their exportation under the severest penalties or subjected it to a considerable duty. The like prohibition seems anciently to have made a part of the policy of most other European nations. It is even to be found, where we should least of all expect to find it, in some old Scotch acts of Parliament, which forbid under heavy penalties the carrying gold or silver *forth of the kingdom.* The like policy anciently took place both in France and England.

When those countries became commercial, the merchants found this prohibition, upon many occasions, extremely inconvenient. They could frequently buy more advantageously with gold and silver than with any other commodity the foreign goods which they wanted, either to import into their own or to carry to some other foreign country. They remonstrated, therefore, against this prohibition as hurtful to trade....

The importation of gold and silver is not the principal, much less the sole, benefit which a nation derives from its foreign trade. Between whatever places foreign trade is carried on, they all of them derive two distinct benefits from it. It carries out that surplus part of the produce of their land and labor for which there is no demand among them and brings back in return for it something else for which there is a demand. It gives a value to their superfluities by exchanging them for something else which may satisfy a part of their wants and increase their enjoyments. By means of it, the narrowness of the home market does not hinder the division of labor in any particular branch of art or manufacture from being carried to the highest perfection. By opening a more extensive market for whatever part of the produce of their labor may exceed the home consumption, it encourages them to improve its productive powers, and to augment its annual produce to the utmost, and thereby to increase the real revenue and wealth of the society. These great and important services foreign trade is continually occupied in performing to all the different countries between which it is carried on. They all derive great benefit from it, though that in which the merchant resides generally derives the greatest, as he is generally more employed in supplying the wants, and carrying out the superfluities of his own, than of any other particular country. To import the gold and silver which may be wanted, into the countries which have no mines, is, no doubt, a part of the business of foreign commerce. It is, however, a most insignificant part of it. A country which carried on foreign trade merely upon this account could scarce have occasion to freight a ship in a century....

I thought it necessary, though at the hazard of being tedious, to examine at full length this popular notion that wealth consists in money or in gold and silver. Money in common language, as I have already observed, frequently signifies wealth; and this ambiguity of expression has rendered this popular notion so familiar to us that even they, who are convinced of its absurdity, are very apt to forget their own principles and in the course of their reasonings to take it for granted as a certain and undeniable truth. Some of the best English writers upon commerce set out with observing that the wealth of a country consists, not in its gold and silver only, but in its lands, houses, and consumable goods of all different kinds. In the course of their reasonings, however, the lands, houses, and consumable goods seem to slip out of their memory, and the strain of their argument frequently supposes that all wealth consists in gold and silver and that to multiply those metals is the great object of national industry and commerce.

The two principles being established, however, that wealth consisted in gold and silver and that those metals could be brought into a country which had no mines only by the balance of trade or by exporting to a greater value than it imported, it necessarily became the great object of political economy to diminish as much as possible the importation of foreign goods for home consumption and to increase as much as possible the exportation of the produce of domestic industry. Its two great engines for enriching the country, therefore, were restraints upon importation and encouragements to exportation.

The restraints upon importation were of two kinds.

First, Restraints upon the importation of such foreign goods for home consumption as could be produced at home, from whatever country they were imported.

Secondly, Restraints upon the importation of goods of almost all kinds from those particular countries with which the balance of trade was supposed to be disadvantageous.

Those different restraints consisted sometimes in high duties and sometimes in absolute prohibitions.

Exportation was encouraged sometimes by drawbacks, sometimes by bounties, sometimes by advantageous treaties of commerce with foreign states, and sometimes by the establishment of colonies in distant countries.

Drawbacks were given upon two different occasions. When the home manufactures were subject to any duty or excise, either the whole or a part of it was frequently drawn back upon their exportation; and when foreign goods liable to a duty were imported in order to be exported again, either the whole or a part of this duty was sometimes given back upon such exportation.

Bounties were given for the encouragement either of some beginning manufactures, or of such sorts of industry of other kinds as were supposed to deserve particular favor.

By advantageous treaties of commerce, particular privileges were procured in some foreign state for the goods and merchants of the country beyond what were granted to those of other countries.

By the establishment of colonies in distant countries, not only particular privileges, but a monopoly was frequently procured for the goods and merchants of the country which established them.

The two sorts of restraints upon importation above-mentioned, together with these four encouragements to exportation, constitute the six principal means by which the commercial system proposes to increase the quantity of gold and silver in any country by turning the balance of trade in its favor.

OF RESTRAINTS UPON THE IMPORTATION FROM FOREIGN COUNTRIES OF SUCH GOODS AS CAN BE PRODUCED AT HOME

By restraining, either by high duties, or by absolute prohibitions, the importation of such goods from foreign countries as can be produced at home, the monopoly of the home market is more or less secured to the domestic industry employed in producing them. Thus the prohibition of importing either live cattle or salt provisions from foreign countries secures to the graziers of Great Britain the monopoly of the home market for butcher's meat. The high duties upon the importation of corn, which in times of moderate plenty amount to a prohibition, give a like advantage to the growers of that commodity. The prohibition of the importation of foreign woolens is equally favorable to the woolen manufacturers. The silk manufacture, though altogether employed upon foreign materials, has lately obtained the same advantage. The linen manufacture has not yet obtained it but is making great strides toward it. Many other sorts of manufacturers have, in the same manner, obtained in Great Britain either altogether or very nearly a monopoly against their countrymen. The variety of goods of which the importation into Great Britain is prohibited, either absolutely or under certain circumstances, greatly exceeds what can easily be suspected by those who are not well acquainted with the laws of the customs.

That this monopoly of the home market frequently gives great encouragement to that particular species of industry which enjoys it, and frequently turns toward that employment a greater share of both the labor and stock of the society than would otherwise have gone to it, cannot be doubted. But whether it tends either to increase the general industry of the society or to give it the most advantageous direction is not, perhaps, altogether so evident.

The general industry of the society never can exceed what the capital of the society can employ. As the number of workmen that can be kept in employment by any particular person must bear a certain proportion to his capital, so the number of those that can be continually employed by all the members of a great society must bear a certain proportion to the whole capital of that society and never can exceed that proportion. No regulation of commerce can increase the quantity of industry in any society beyond what its capital can maintain. It can only divert a part of it into a direction into which it might not otherwise have gone; and it is by no means certain that this artificial direction is likely to be more advantageous to the society than that into which it would have gone of its own accord.

Every individual is continually exerting himself to find out the most advantageous employment for whatever capital he can command. It is his own advantage, indeed, and not that of society, which he has in view. But the study of his own advantage naturally or, rather, necessarily leads him to prefer that employment which is most advantageous to the society.

First, every individual endeavors to employ his capital as near home as he can and consequently as much as he can in the support of domestic industry, provided always that he can thereby obtain the ordinary or not a great deal less than the ordinary profits of stock. . . .

Secondly, every individual who employs his capital in the support of domestic industry necessarily endeavors so to direct that industry that its produce may be to the greatest possible value.

The produce of industry is what it adds to the subject or materials upon which it is employed. In proportion as the value of this produce is great or small, so will likewise be the profits of the employer. But it is only for the sake of profit that any man employs a capital in the support of industry; and he will always, therefore, endeavor to employ it in the support of that industry of which the produce is likely to be of the greatest value, or to exchange for the greatest quantity either of money or of other goods.

But the annual revenue for every society is always precisely equal to the exchangeable value of the whole annual produce of its industry, or rather is precisely the same thing with that exchangeable value. As every individual, therefore, endeavors as much as he can both to employ his capital in the support of domestic industry, and so to direct that industry that its produce may be of the greatest value, every individual necessarily labors to render the annual revenue of the society as great as he can. He generally, indeed, neither intends to promote the public interest nor knows how much he is promoting it. By preferring the support of domestic to that of foreign industry, he intends only his own security; and by directing that industry in such a manner as its produce may be of the greatest value, he intends only his own gain, and he is in this, as in many other cases, led by an invisible hand to promote an end which was no part of his intention. Nor is it always the worse for the society that it was no part of it. By pursuing his own interest, he frequently promotes that of the society more effectually than when he really intends to promote it. I have never known much good done by those who affected to trade for the public good. It is an affectation, indeed, not very common among merchants, and very few words need be employed in dissuading them from it.

What is the species of domestic industry which his capital can employ, and of which the produce is likely to be of the greatest value, every individual, it is evident, can, in his local situation, judge much better than any statesman or law-giver can do for him. The statesman, who should attempt to direct private people in what manner they ought to employ their capitals, would not only load himself with a most unnecessary attention but assume an authority which could safely be trusted not only to no single person but to no council or senate whatever, and which would nowhere be so dangerous as in the hands of a man who had folly and presumption enough to fancy himself fit to exercise it.

To give the monopoly of the home market to the produce of domestic industry, in any particular art of manufacture, is in some measure to direct private people in what manner they ought to employ their capitals and must, in almost all cases, be either a useless or a hurtful regulation. If the produce of domestic can be brought there as cheap as that of foreign industry, the regulation is evidently useless. If it cannot, it must generally be hurtful. It is the maxim of every prudent master of a family never to attempt to make at home what it will cost him more to make than to buy. The tailor does not attempt to make his own shoes but buys them of the shoemaker. The shoemaker does not attempt to make his own clothes but employs a tailor. The farmer attempts to make neither the one nor the other but employs those different artificers. All of them find it for their interest to employ their whole industry in a way in which they have some advantage over their neighbors and to purchase with a part of its produce, or what is the same thing, with the price of a part of it, whatever else they have occasion for.

What is prudence in the conduct of every private family can scarce be folly in that of a great kingdom. If a foreign country can supply us with a commodity cheaper than we ourselves can make it, better buy it of them with some part of the produce of our own industry, employed in a way in which we have some advantage. The general industry of the country, being always in proportion to the capital which employs it, will not thereby be diminished, no more than that of the above-mentioned artificers, but only left to find out the way in which it can be employed with the greatest advantage. It is certainly not employed to the greatest advantage when it is thus directed toward an object which it can buy cheaper than it can make. The value of its annual produce is certainly more or less diminished when it is thus turned away from producing commodities evidently of more value than the commodity which it is directed to produce. According to the supposition, that commodity could be purchased from foreign countries cheaper than it can be made at home. It could, therefore, have been purchased with a part only of the commodities or, what is the same thing, with a part only of the price of the commodities, which the industry employed by equal capital would have produced at home, had it been left to follow its natural course. The industry of the country, therefore, is thus turned away from a more, to a less, advantageous employment, and the exchangeable value of its annual produce, instead of being increased, according to the intention of the lawgiver, must necessarily be diminished by every such regulation. . . .

All systems either of preference or of restraint, therefore, being thus completely taken away, the obvious and simple system of natural liberty establishes itself of its own accord. Every man, as long as he does not violate the laws of justice, is left perfectly free to pursue his own interest his own way and to bring both his industry and capital into competition with those of any other man or order of men. The sovereign is completely discharged from a duty, in the attempting to perform which he must always be exposed to innumerable delusions, and for the proper performance of which no human wisdom or knowledge could ever be sufficient—the duty of superintending the industry of private people and of directing it toward the employments most suitable to the interest of the society. According to the system of natural liberty, the sovereign has only three duties to attend to; three duties of great importance, indeed, but plain and intelligible to common understandings: first, the duty of protecting the society from the violence and invasion of other independent societies; secondly, the duty of protecting, as far as possible, every member of the society from the injustice or oppression of every other member of it, or the duty of establishing an exact administration of justice; and, thirdly, the duty of erecting and maintaining certain public works and certain public institutions which it can never be for the interest of any individual, or small number of individuals, to erect and maintain, because the profit could never repay the expense to any individual or small number of individuals, though it may frequently do much more than repay it to a great society. . . .

The whole annual produce of the land and labor of every country, or what comes to the same thing, the whole price of that annual produce, naturally divides itself, it has already been observed, into three parts: the rent of land, the wages of labor, and the profits of stock; and constitutes a revenue to three different orders of people: to those who live by rent, to those who live by wages, and to those who live by profit. These are the three great, original, and constituent orders of every civilized society, from whose revenue that of every other order is ultimately derived.

The interest of the first of those three great orders, it appears from what has been just now said, is strictly and inseparably connected with the general interest of the society. Whatever either promotes or obstructs the one necessarily promotes or obstructs the other. When the public deliberates concerning any regulation of commerce or police, the proprietors of land never can mislead it, with a view to promote the interest of their own particular order; at least, if they have any tolerable knowledge of that interest. They are, indeed, too often defective in this tolerable knowledge. They are the only one of the three orders whose revenue costs them neither labor nor care but comes to them, as it were, of its own accord and independent of any plan or project of their own. That indolence, which is the natural effect of the ease and security of their situation, renders them too often not only ignorant but incapable of that application of mind which is necessary in order to foresee and understand the consequences of any public regulation.

The interest of the second order, that of those who live by wages, is as strictly connected with the interest of the society as that of the first. The wages of the laborer, it has already been shown, are never so high as when the demand for labor is continually rising, or when the quantity employed is every year increasing considerably.

When this real wealth of the society becomes stationary, his wages are soon reduced to what is barely enough to enable him to bring up a family or to continue the race of laborers. When the society declines, they fall even below this. The order of proprietors may, perhaps, gain more by the prosperity of the society than that of laborers; but there is no order that suffers so cruelly from its decline. But though the interest of the laborer is strictly connected with that of the society, he is incapable either of comprehending that interest or of understanding its connection with his own. His condition leaves him no time to receive the necessary information, and his education and habits are commonly such as to render him unfit to judge even though he was fully informed. In the public deliberations, therefore, his voice is little heard and less regarded, except upon some particular occasions, when his clamor is animated, set on, and supported by his employers, not for his, but their own particular purposes.

His employers constitute the third order—that of those who live by profit. It is the stock that is employed for the sake of profit which puts into motion the greater part of the useful labor of every society. The plans and projects of the employers of stock regulate and direct all the most important operations of labor, and profit is the end proposed by all those plans and projects. But the rate of profit does not, like rent and wages, rise with the prosperity and fall with the declension of the society. On the contrary, it is naturally low in rich, and high in poor countries, and it is always highest in the countries which are going fastest to ruin. The interest of this third order, therefore, has not the same connection with the general interest of the society as that of the other two. Merchants and master-manufacturers are, in this order, the two classes of people who commonly employ the largest capitals, and who by their wealth draw to themselves the greatest share of the public consideration. As during their whole lives they are engaged in plans and projects, they have frequently more acuteness of understanding than the greater part of country gentlemen. As their thoughts, however, are commonly exercised rather about the interest of their own particular branch of business than about that of the society, their judgment, even when given with the greatest candor (which it has not been upon every occasion), is much more to be depended upon with regard to the former of those two objects than with regard to the latter. Their superiority over the country gentlemen is not so much in their knowledge of the public interest as in their having a better knowledge of their own interest than he has of his. It is by this superior knowledge of their own interest that they have frequently imposed upon his generosity and persuaded him to give up both his own interest and that of the public from a very simple but honest conviction that their interest, and not his, was the interest of the public. The interest of the dealers, however, in any particular branch of trade or manufactures, is always in some respects different from, and even opposite to, that of the public. To widen the market and to narrow the competition is always the interest of the dealers. To widen the market may frequently be agreeable enough to the interest of the public; but to narrow the competition must always be against it and can serve only to enable the dealers, by raising their profits above what they naturally would be, to levy, for their own benefit, an absurd tax upon the rest of their fellow-citizens. The proposal of any new law or regulation of commerce which comes from this order ought always to be listened to with great precaution and ought never to be adopted till after having been long and carefully examined, not only with the most scrupulous, but with the most suspicious attention. It comes from an order of men whose interest is never exactly the same with that of the public, who have generally an interest to deceive and even to oppress the public, and who accordingly have, upon many occasions, both deceived and oppressed it. . . .

People of the same trade seldom meet together, even for merriment and diversion, but the conversation ends in a conspiracy against the public or in some contrivance to raise prices. It is impossible indeed to prevent such meetings, by any law which either could be executed, or would be consistent with liberty and justice. But though the law cannot hinder people of the same trade from sometimes assembling together, it ought to do nothing to facilitate such assemblies, much less to render them necessary.

A regulation which obliges all those of the same trade in a particular town to enter their names and places of abode in a public register facilitates such assemblies. It connects individuals who might never otherwise be known to one another and gives every man of the trade a direction where to find every other man of it.

A regulation which enables those of the same trade to tax themselves in order to provide for their poor, their sick, their widows and orphans, by giving them a common interest to manage, renders such assemblies necessary.

An incorporation not only renders them necessary but makes the act of the majority binding upon the whole. In a free trade an effectual combination cannot be established but by the unanimous consent of every single trader, and it cannot last longer than every single trader continues of the same mind. The majority of a corporation can enact a bylaw with proper penalties which will limit the competition more effectually and more durably than any voluntary combination whatever.

The pretense that corporations are necessary for the better government of the trade is without any foundation. The real and effectual discipline which is exercised over a workman is not that of his corporation but that of his customers. It is the fear of losing their employment which restrains his frauds and corrects his negligence. An exclusive corporation necessarily weakens the force of this discipline. A particular set of workmen must then be employed, let them behave well or ill. It is upon this account that in many large incorporated towns no tolerable workmen are to be found, even in some of the most necessary trades. If you would have your work tolerably executed, it must be done in the suburbs, where the workmen, have no exclusive privilege, have nothing but their character to depend upon, and you must them smuggle it into the town as well as you can.

It is in this manner that the policy of Europe, by restraining the competition in some employments to a smaller number than would otherwise be disposed to enter into them, occasions a very important inequality in the whole of the advantages and disadvantages of the different employments of labor and stock. . . .

Nothing, however, can be more absurd than this whole doctrine of the balance of trade, upon which not only these restraints but almost all the other regulations of commerce are founded. When two places trade with one another, this doctrine supposes that, if the balance be even, neither of them either loses or gains; but if it leans in any degree to one side, that one of them loses, and the other gains in proportion to its declension from the exact equilibrium. Both suppositions are false. A trade which is forced by means of bounties and monopolies may be, and commonly is, disadvantageous to the country in whose favor it is meant to be established, . . . But that trade which, without force or constraint, is naturally and regularly carried on between any two places is always advantageous, though not always equally so, to both.

By advantage or gain, I understand not the increase of the quantity of gold and silver but that of the exchangeable value of the annual produce of the land and labor of the country, or the increase of the annual revenue of its inhabitants. . . .

It is unnecessary, I imagine, to observe, how contrary such regulations are to the boasted liberty of the subject, of which we affect to be so very jealous; but which, in this case, is so plainly sacrificed to the futile interests of our merchants and manufacturers.

The laudable motive of all these regulations is to extend our

own manufactures, not by their own improvement, but by the depression
of those of all our neighbors, and by putting an end, as much as possible,
to the troublesome competition of such odious and disagreeable rivals.
Our master-manufacturers think it reasonable that they themselves
should have the monopoly of the ingenuity of all their countrymen.
Though by restraining, in some trades, the number of apprentices which
can be employed at one time, and by imposing the necessity of a long
apprenticeship in all trades, they endeavor, all of them, to confine the
knowledge of their respective employments to as small a number as
possible; they are unwilling, however, that any part of this small number should go abroad to instruct foreigners.

Consumption is the sole end and purpose of all production, and
the interest of the producer ought to be attended to only so far as it
may be necessary for promoting that of the consumer. The maxim is so
perfectly self-evident that it would be absurd to attempt to prove it.
But in the mercantile system, the interest of the consumer is almost
constantly sacrificed to that of the producer; and it seems to consider
production, and not consumption, as the ultimate end and object of all
industry and commerce.

In the restraints upon the importation of all foreign commodities which can come into competition with those of our own growth,
or manufacture, the interest of the home consumer is evidently sacrificed
to that of the producer. It is altogether for the benefit of the latter that
the former is obliged to pay that enhancement of price which this monopoly almost always occasions.

It is altogether for the benefit of the producer that bounties are
granted upon the exporation of some of his productions. The home consumer is obliged to pay, first, the tax which is necessary for paying
the bounty and, secondly, the still greater tax which necessarily arises
from the enhancement of the price of the commodity in the home
market.

By the famous treaty of commerce with Portugal, the consumer
is prevented by high duties from purchasing of a neighboring country
a commodity which our own climate does not produce but is obliged
to purchase it of a distant country, though it is acknowledged that the
commodity of the distant country is of a worse quality than that of the
near one. The home consumer is obliged to submit to this inconven-
iency, in order that the producer may import into the distant country
some of his productions upon more advantageous terms that he would
otherwise have been allowed to do. The consumer, too, is obliged to

pay whatever enhancement in the price of those very productions this forced exportation may occasion in the home market.

But in the system of laws which has been established for the management of our American and West Indian colonies, the interest of the home consumer has been sacrificed to that of the producer with a more extravagant profusion than in all our other commercial regulations. A great empire has been established for the sole purpose of raising up a nation of customers who should be obliged to buy from the shops of our different producers all the goods with which these could supply them. For the sake of that little enhancement of price which this monopoly might afford our producers, the home consumers have been burdened with the whole expense of maintaining and defending that empire. For this purpose, and for this purpose only, in the two last wars, more than two hundred millions have been spent, and a new debt of more than a hundred and seventy millions has been contracted over and above all that had been expended for the same purpose in former wars. The interest of this debt alone is not only greater than the whole extraordinary profit, which, it ever could be pretended, was made by the monopoly of the colony trade, but than the whole value of that trade, or than the whole value of the goods, which at an average have been annually exported to the colonies.

It cannot be very difficult to determine who have been the contrivers of this whole mercantile system; not the consumers, we may believe, whose interest has been entirely neglected; but the producers, whose interest has been so carefully attended to; and among this latter class our merchants and manufacturers have been by far the principal architects. In the mercantile regulations, which have been taken notice of in this chapter, the interest of our manufacturers has been most peculiarly attended to; and the interest, not so much of the consumers, as that of some other sets of producers, has been sacrificed to it.

2

◀ FRIEDRICH HAYEK* ▶

from

The Road to Serfdom (1944)

Although originally written for a British audience, Hayek's *The Road to Serfdom* gained immediate popularity in America. Because of the New Deal and the economic necessities of the second World War, the government's role in the economy had increased very rapidly during the 1930s and early 1940s. This alarmed conservative political leaders who feared the loss of home rule and laissez-faire economists who resisted the modification of the market system, which they felt the increasing role of the government implied. Hayek's prognosis of the evolution of capitalism served as a rallying point for these two groups, because it pointed to the economic and political dangers inherent in economic planning.

Hayek warns that economic planning will inevitably lead to totalitarianism. For him there is no compromise; it is an all or nothing proposition. Once economic planning starts it cannot be stopped short of complete loss of political freedom. Even though the leading advocates of planning may be men of good will, "from the saintly and single-minded idealist to the fanatic is often but a step."

Part of Hayek's fear that planning could not be stopped once it had been started stems from the definition of planning which he adopts. To him planning implies the central direction of "all economic activity according to a single plan." Thus once the planners gain a foothold in the government, they will move to implement a precon-

---

*Professor of Economics, University of Freiburg.

ceived plan which embraces all levels of economic activity. Here it is interesting to note that the American movement toward planning over the last thirty years seems to lack any underlying central objective. Policies are more likely to be tried on a hit-and-miss basis, very often with less than desirable consequences.

Hayek shows a lack of faith in the ability of the planners. According to him, "only the worst get on top," because to be elected to a governing position one must gain the support of the lower classes by appealing to their class hatreds. Hayek feels that the fact that these leaders are subject to democratic control is no guarantee that they will not be arbitrary rulers. While it is true that the lower stratum of society may hold the balance of political power, it is not true that they will necessarily desire inferior leaders. In fact, the choice of leaders depends upon the two major political parties, and it is they who must take the responsibility for the quality of leadership. Although democracy is no guarantee against arbitrary rule, modern liberals stress that neither is the market system, and consequently they emphasize that the action of the state can help those groups who have been denied their freedoms under the existing system.

For a further discussion of the connection between economic and political freedom, the reader is referred to the next article, by Milton Friedman. Friedman closely reflects Hayek's position on this issue. The important question as to whether or not planning is compatible with democracy remains an open one. Limited planning in England, France, and Sweden have not led to an erosion of political freedom. Although strong totalitarian tendencies do exist in the Soviet type societies, it is essential to note that unusual historical circumstances exerted a stronger influence on this development than did the economic planning system per se.

If Hayek's views on the political consequences of planning seem to be wide of the mark, he comes off slightly better on the economic issues. In the chapter from his book presented here, "The Inevitability of Planning," Hayek argues that the necessities of modern technology cannot be given as a reason for the growth of private monopolies. Basic to this belief is the view that achieving the lowest costs of production does not require giant size companies. The growth of monopolies, thus, is not a result of decreasing costs but of business collusion and encouragement by the government. Although Hayek admits that industrial societies have produced social problems, he denies that the solution to these problems requires planning. For Hayek, complex situations necessitate not more but less central planning. The answer to the problem of coordinating economic activity in a complex economy is to be found in the greater reliance on the market system which in turn necessitates moving toward a more competitive economic model.

Hayek places the blame for the movement toward planning on the conscious direction of the planners themselves, rather than on the inherent forces of technology. His views on this point should be compared with those of Schumpeter* and Galbraith.† It is clear that when Hayek talks about planning he is referring to governmental planning. However, the type of planning that characterizes the modern American economy is initiated not solely from the public sector, but from the private sector as well. As Galbraith and others show, it is the giant corporation that is the greatest planner in modern capitalism. The nature of Hayek's remarks indicates, however, that he would be just as opposed to this type of private planning as he would to public planning; for him neither is preferable to the market system. For Galbraith this is not the case. He views large size corporations as being a necessary condition for creating technological improvements. It must be said that economists are in disagreement over this point. Many argue that large size is neither a necessary nor a sufficient condition for the development of modern technology. Hayek's argument seems to indicate that he is in this latter camp. His conclusion that the growing complexity of an economy necessitates a greater reliance on the market mechanism is also interesting when viewed against recent Russian economic problems. As the economy became more developed the Soviets ran into problems which were difficult to solve with their highly centralized planning arrangements. These bottlenecks caused Soviet growth rates to slow down in the late 1950s. Russian planners came to realize that a greater reliance on "capitalist type" market techniques might help solve these problems. The limited adoption of some of these techniques led some Western observers to speculate on a possible convergence of the two systems. The reader should pay particular attention to the views of Heilbroner**, Galbraith†, and Harrington‡ on this point.

Although the limited Soviet experience might indicate the impracticability of planning "down to the last shoestring," it does not necessarily destroy the usefulness of planning on a broader level. Some argue that, as a method of mobilizing resources for given objectives, planning appears to be superior to the market. However, evidence at the present time seems to give some support to Hayek's view that a highly centralized, planned economy—like that of the Soviet Union— is not a very efficient way to operate an industrialized society. However, as many modern economies indicate, planning and the market system are not necessarily incompatible. To Hayek this is clearly not the case, for although planners might start out with limited objectives and good intentions there is an irresistible tendency to extend the scope of planning. Thus, even though more immediate gains may be achieved, in certain cases, by the use of planning, it should not be resorted to

---

*See chapter 7.
†See chapter 8.
**See chapter 10.
‡See chapter 15.

because of the long-term consequences. History has yet to show that Hayek's fears are valid or that a reversion from planning to the market system will provide the answers to complex modern economic problems.

—R. R.

from

*The Road to Serfdom**

We were the first to assert that the more complicated the forms assumed by civilization, the more restricted the freedom of the individual must become. —BENITO MUSSOLINI.

It is a revealing fact that few planners are content to say that central planning is desirable. Most of them affirm that we can no longer choose but are compelled by circumstances beyond our control to substitute planning for competition. The myth is deliberately cultivated that we are embarking on the new course not out of free will but because competition is spontaneously eliminated by technological changes which we neither can reverse nor should wish to prevent. This argument is rarely developed at any length—it is one of the assertions taken over by one writer from another until, by mere iteration, it has come to be accepted as an established fact. It is, nevertheless, devoid of foundation. The tendency toward monopoly and planning is not the result of any "objective facts" beyond our control but the product of opinions fostered and propagated for half a century until they have come to dominate all our policy.

Of the various arguments employed to demonstrate the inevitability of planning, the one most frequently heard is that technological changes have made competition impossible in a constantly increasing number of fields and that the only choice left to us is between control of production by private monopolies and direction by the government. This belief derives mainly from the Marxist doctrine of the "concentration of industry," although, like so many Marxist ideas, it is now found

---

*Reprinted from *The Road to Serfdom* by Friedrich Hayek, by permission University of Chicago Press. Copyright 1944 by University of Chicago. All rights reserved.

in many circles which have received it at third or fourth hand and do not know whence it derives.

The historical fact of the progressive growth of monopoly during the last fifty years and the increasing restriction of the field in which competition rules is, of course, not disputed—although the extent of the phenomenon is often greatly exaggerated.[1] The important question is whether this development is a necessary consequence of the advance of technology or whether it is simply the result of the policies pursued in most countries. We shall presently see that the actual history of this development strongly suggests the latter. But we must first consider in how far modern technological developments are of such a kind as to make the growth of monopolies in wide fields inevitable.

The alleged technological cause of the growth of monopoly is the superiority of the large firm over the small, owing to the greater efficiency of modern methods of mass production. Modern methods, it is asserted, have created conditions in the majority of industries where the production of the large firm can be increased at decreasing costs per unit, with the result that the large firms are everywhere underbidding and driving out the small ones; this process must go on until in each industry only one or at most a few giant firms are left. This argument singles out one effect sometimes accompanying technological progress; it disregards others which work in the opposite direction; and it receives little support from a serious study of the facts. We cannot here investigate this question in detail and must be content to accept the best evidence available. The most comprehensive study of the facts undertaken in recent times is that by the Temporary National Economic Committee on the *Concentration of Economic Power*. The final report of this committee (which certainly cannot be accused of an undue liberal bias) arrives at the conclusion that the view according to which the greater efficiency of large-scale production is the cause of the disappearance of competition "finds scant support in any evidence that is now at hand."[2] And the detailed monograph on the question which was prepared for the committee sums up the answer in this statement:

"The superior efficiency of large establishments has not been demonstrated; the advantages that are supposed to destroy competition

---

[1] For a fuller discussion of these problems see Professor Lionel Robbins' essay, "The Inevitability of Monopoly," *The Economic Basis of Class Conflict* (1939), pp. 45-80.

[2] *Final Report and Recommendations of the Temporary National Economic Committee* (77th Cong., 1st sess.; Senate Document No. 35 [1941]), p. 89.

have failed to manifest themselves in many fields. Nor do the economies of size, where they exist, invariably necessitate monopoly. . . . The size or the sizes of the optimum efficiency may be reached long before the major part of a supply is subjected to such control. The conclusions that the advantage of large-scale production must lead inevitably to the abolition of competition cannot be accepted. It should be noted, moreover, that monopoly is frequently the product of factors other than the lower costs of greater size. It is attained through collusive agreement and promoted by public policies. When these agreements are invalidated and when these policies are reversed, competitive conditions can be restored."[3]

An investigation of conditions in England would lead to very similar results. Anyone who has observed how aspiring monopolists regularly seek and frequently obtain the assistance of the power of the state to make their control effective can have little doubt that there is nothing inevitable about this development.

This conclusion is strongly supported by the historical order in which the decline of competition and the growth of monopoly manifested themselves in different countries. If they were the result of technological developments or a necessary product of the evolution of "capitalism," we should expect them to appear first in the countries with the most advanced economic system. In fact, they appeared first during the last third of the nineteenth century in what were then comparatively young industrial countries, the United States and Germany. In the latter country especially, which came to be regarded as the model country typifying the necessary evolution of capitalism, the growth of cartels and syndicates has since 1878 been systematically fostered by deliberate policy. Not only the instrument of protection but direct inducements and ultimately compulsion were used by the governments to further the creation of monopolies for the regulation of prices and sales. It was here that, with the help of the state, the first great experiment in "scientific planning" and "conscious organization of industry" led to the creation of giant monopolies, which were represented as inevitable growths fifty years before the same was done in Great Britain. It is largely due to the influence of German socialist theoreticians, particularly Sombart, generalizing from the experience of their country, that the inevitable development of the competitive system into "monopoly

---

[3]C. Wilcox, *Competition and Monopoly in American Industry* (Temporary National Economic Committee Monograph, No. 21 [1940]), p. 314.

capitalism" became widely accepted. That in the United States a highly protectionist policy made a somewhat similar development possible seemed to confirm this generalization. The development of Germany, however, more than that of the United States, came to be regarded as representative of a universal tendency; and it became a commonplace to speak—to quote a widely read political essay of recent date—of "Germany where all the social and political forces of modern civilization have reached their most advanced form."[4]

How little there was of inevitability in all this, and how much is the result of deliberate policy, becomes clear when we consider the position in England until 1931 and the development since that year in which Great Britain also embarked upon a policy of general protection. It is only a dozen years since, except for a few industries which had obtained protection earlier, British industry was on the whole as competitive as, perhaps, at any time in its history. And, although during the 1920s it suffered severely from incompatible policies followed with regard to wages and to money, at least the years up to 1929 compare with regard to employment and general activity not unfavorably with the 1930s. It is only since the transition to protection and the general change in British economic policy accompanying it that the growth of monopolies has proceeded at an amazing rate and has transformed British industry to an extent the public has scarcely yet realized. To argue that this development has anything to do with the technological progress during this period, that technological necessities which in Germany operated in the 1880s and 1890s, made themselves felt here in the 1930s, is not much less absurd than the claim, implied in a statement of Mussolini, that Italy had to abolish individual freedom before other European people because its civilization had marched so far in advance of the rest!

In so far as England is concerned, the thesis that the change in opinion and policy merely follows an inexorable change in the facts can be given a certain appearance of truth, just because the nation has followed at a distance the intellectual developments elsewhere. It could thus be argued that monopolistic organization of industry grew up in spite of the fact that public opinion still favored competition but that outside events frustrated their wishes. The true relation between theory and practice becomes, however, clear as soon as we look to the prototype of this development—Germany. That *there* the suppression of com-

---

[4]Reinhold Niebuhr, *Moral Man and Immoral Society* (1932).

petition was a matter of deliberate policy, that it was undertaken in the service of the ideal which we now call planning, there can be no doubt. In the progressive advance toward a completely planned society the Germans, and all the people who are imitating their example, are merely following the course which nineteenth-century thinkers, particularly Germans, have mapped out for them. The intellectual history of the last sixty or eighty years is indeed a perfect illustration of the truth that in social evolution nothing is inevitable but thinking makes it so.

The assertion that modern technological progress makes planning inevitable can also be interpreted in a different manner. It may mean that the complexity of our modern industrial civilization creates new problems with which we cannot hope to deal effectively except by central planning. In a sense this is true—yet not in the wide sense in which it is claimed. It is, for example, a commonplace that many of the problems created by a modern town, like many other problems caused by close contiguity in space, are not adequately solved by competition. But it is not these problems, like those of the "public utilities," etc., which are uppermost in the minds of those who invoke the complexity of modern civilization as an argument for central planning. What they generally suggest is that the increasing difficulty of obtaining a coherent picture of the complete economic process makes it indispensable that things should be co-ordinated by some central agency if social life is not to dissolve in chaos.

This argument is based on a complete misapprehension of the working of competition. Far from being appropriate only to comparatively simple conditions, it is the very complexity of the division of labor under modern conditions which makes competition the only method by which such co-ordination can be adequately brought about. There would be no difficulty about efficient control or planning were conditions so simple that a single person or board could effectively survey all the relevant facts. It is only as the factors which have to be taken into account become so numerous that it is impossible to gain a synoptic view of them that decentralization becomes imperative. But, once decentralization is necessary, the problem of co-ordination arises— a co-ordination which leaves the separate agencies free to adjust their activities to the facts which only they can know and yet brings about a mutual adjustment of their respective plans. As decentralization has become necessary because nobody can consciously balance all the considerations bearing on the decisions of so many individuals, the co-ordination can clearly be effected not by "conscious control" but only by arrangements which convey to each agent the information he must possess in order effectively to adjust his decisions to those of others. And because all the details of the changes constantly affecting the conditions of demand and supply of the different commodities can never be fully known, or quickly enough be collected and disseminated, by any one center, what is required is some apparatus of registration which automatically records all the relevant effects of individual actions and whose indications are at the same time the resultant of, and the guide for, all the individual decisions.

This is precisely what the price system does under competition, and which no other system even promises to accomplish. It enables entrepreneurs, by watching the movement of comparatively few prices, as an engineer watches the hands of a few dials, to adjust their activities to those of their fellows. The important point here is that the price system will fulfil this function only if competition prevails, that is, if the individual producer has to adapt himself to price changes and cannot control them. The more complicated the whole, the more dependent we become on that division of knowledge between individuals whose separate efforts are co-ordinated by the impersonal mechanism for transmitting the relevant information known by us as the price system.

It is no exaggeration to say that if we had had to rely on conscious central planning for the growth of our industrial system, it would never have reached the degree of differentiation, complexity, and flexibility it has attained. Compared with this method of solving the economic problem by means of decentralization plus automatic co-ordination, the more obvious method of central direction is incredibly clumsy, primitive, and limited in scope. That the division of labor has reached the extent which makes modern civilization possible we owe to the fact that it did not have to be consciously created but that man tumbled on a method by which the division of labor could be extended far beyond the limits within which it could have been planned. Any further growth of its complexity, therefore, far from making central direction more necessary, makes it more important than ever that we should use a technique which does not depend on conscious control.

There is yet another theory which connects the growth of monopolies with technological progress, and which uses arguments almost opposite to those we have just considered; though not often clearly stated, it has also exercised considerable influence. It contends not that modern technique destroys competition but that, on the contrary, it will be impossible to make use of many of the new technological possibilities unless protection against competition is granted, i.e., a monopoly is conferred. This type of argument is not necessarily fraudulent, as the critical reader will perhaps suspect: the obvious answer—that if a new technique for satisfying our wants is really better, it ought to be able to stand up against all competition—does not dispose of all instances to which this argument refers. No doubt in many cases it is used merely as a form of special pleading by interested parties. Even more often it is probably based on a confusion between technical excellence from a narrow engineering point of view and desirability from the point of view of society as a whole.

There remains, however, a group of instances where the argument has some force. It is, for example, at least conceivable that the British automobile industry might be able to supply a car cheaper and better than cars used to be in the United States if everyone in England were made to use the same kind of car or that the use of electricity for all purposes could be made cheaper than coal or gas if everybody could be made to use only electricity. In instances like these it is at least possible that we might all be better off and should prefer the new situation if we had the choice—but that no individual ever gets the choice, because the alternative is either that we should all use the same cheap car (or all should use only electricity) or that we should have the choice between these things with each of them at a much higher price. I do not know whether this is true in either of the instances given. But it must be admitted that it is possible that, by compulsory standardization or the prohibition of variety beyond a certain degree, abundance might be increased in some fields more than sufficiently to compensate for the restriction of the choice of the consumer. It is even conceivable that a new invention may be made some day whose adoption would seem unquestionably beneficial but which could be used only if many or all people were made to avail themselves of it at the same time.

Whether such instances are of any great or lasting importance, they are certainly not instances where it could be legitimately claimed that technical progress makes central direction inevitable. They would merely make it necessary to choose between gaining a particular advantage by compulsion and not obtaining it—or, in most instances, obtaining it a little later, when further technical advance has overcome the particular difficulties. It is true that in such situations we may have to sacrifice a possible immediate gain as the price of our freedom—but we avoid, on the other hand, the necessity of making future developments dependent upon the knowledge which particular people now possess. By sacrificing such possible present advantages, we preserve an important stimulus to further progress. Though in the short run the price we have to pay for variety and freedom of choice may sometimes be high, in the long run even material progress will depend on this very variety, because we can never predict from which of the many forms in which a good or service can be provided something better may develop. It cannot, of course, be asserted that the preservation of freedom at the expense of some addition to our present material comfort will be thus rewarded in all instances. But the argument for freedom is precisely that we ought to leave room for the unforeseeable free growth. It applies, therefore, no less when, on the basis of our present knowledge, compulsion would seem to bring only advantages, and although in a particular instance it may actually do no harm.

In much of the current discussion on the effects of technological progress this progress is presented to us as if it were something outside us which could compel us to use the new knowledge in a particular way. While it is true, of course, that inventions have given us tremendous power, it is absurd to suggest that we must use this power to destroy our most precious inheritance: liberty. It does mean, however, that if we want to preserve it, we must guard it more jealously than ever and that we must be prepared to make sacrifices for it. While there is nothing in modern technological developments which forces us toward comprehensive economic planning, there is a great deal in them which makes infinitely more dangerous the power a planning authority would possess.

While there can thus be little doubt that the movement toward planning is the result of deliberate action and that there are no external necessities which force us to it, it is worth inquiring why so large a proportion of the technical experts should be found in the front rank of the planners. The explanation of this phenomenon is closely connected with an important fact which the critics of the planners should always keep in mind: that there is little question that almost every one of the technical ideals of our experts could be realized within a comparatively short time if to achieve them were made the sole aim of humanity. There is an infinite number of good things, which we all agree are highly desirable as well as possible, but of which we cannot hope to achieve more than a few within our lifetime, or which we can hope to achieve only very imperfectly. It is the frustration of his ambitions in his own field which makes the specialist revolt against the existing order. We all find it difficult to bear to see things left undone which everybody must admit are both desirable and possible. That these things cannot all be done at the same time, that any one of them can be achieved only at the sacrifice of others, can be seen only by taking into account factors which fall outside any specialism, which can be appreciated only by a painful intellectual effort—the more painful as it forces us to see against a wider background the objects to which most of our labors are directed and to balance them against others which lie outside our immediate interest and for which, for that reason, we care less.

Every one of the many things which, considered in isolation, it would be possible to achieve in a planned society creates enthusiasts for planning who feel confident that they will be able to instil into the directors of such a society their sense of the value of the particular objective; and the hopes of some of them would undoubtedly be fulfilled, since a planned society would further some objectives more than is the case at present. It would be foolish to deny that the instances of planned or semiplanned societies which we know do furnish illustrations in point, good things which the people of these countries owe entirely to planning. The magnificent motor roads in Germany and Italy are an instance often quoted—even though they do not represent a kind of planning not equally possible in a liberal society. But it is equally foolish to quote such instances of technical excellence in particular fields as evidence of the general superiority of planning. It would be more correct to say that such extreme technical excellence out of line with general conditions is evidence of a misdirection of resources. Anyone who has driven along the famous German motor roads and found the amount of traffic on them less than on many a secondary road in England can have little doubt that, so far as peace purposes are concerned, there was little justification for them. Whether it was not a case where the planners decided in favor of "guns" instead of "butter" is another matter.[5] But by our standards there is little ground for enthusiasm.

The illusion of the specialist that in a planned society he would secure more attention to the objectives for which he cares most is a more general phenomenon than the term "specialist" at first suggests. In our predilections and interests we are all in some measure specialists. And we all think that our personal order of values is not merely personal but that in a free discussion among rational people we would

---

[5] But as I am correcting this the news comes that maintenance work on the German motor roads has been suspended!

convince the others that ours is the right one. The lover of the country-side who wants above all that its traditional appearance should be preserved and that the blots already made by industry on its fair face should be removed, no less than the health enthusiast who wants all the picturesque but insanitary old cottages cleared away, or the motorist who wishes the country cut up by big motor roads, the efficiency fanatic who desires the maximum of specialization and mechanization no less than the idealist who for the development of personality wants to preserve as many independent craftsmen as possible, all know that their aim can be fully achieved only by planning—and they all want planning for that reason. But, of course, the adoption of the social planning for which they clamor can only bring out the concealed conflict between their aims.

The movement for planning owes its present strength largely to the fact that, while planning is in the main still an ambition, it unites almost all the single-minded idealists, all the men and women who have devoted their lives to a single task. The hopes they place in planning, however, are the result not of a comprehensive view of society but rather of a very limited view and often the result of a great exaggeration of the importance of the ends they place foremost. This is not to underrate the great pragmatic value of this type of men in a free society like ours, which makes them the subject of just admiration. But it would make the very men who are most anxious to plan society the most dangerous if they were allowed to do so—and the most intolerant of the planning of others. From the saintly and single-minded idealist to the fanatic is often but a step. Though it is the resentment of the frustrated specialist which gives the demand for planning its strongest impetus, there could hardly be a more unbearable—and more irrational—world than one in which the most eminent specialists in each field were allowed to proceed unchecked with the realization of their ideals. Nor can "co-ordination," as some planners seem to imagine, become a new specialism. The economist is the last to claim that he has the knowledge which the co-ordinator would need. His plea is for a method which effects such co-ordination without the need for an omniscient dictator. But that means precisely the retention of some such impersonal, and often unintelligible, checks on individual efforts as those against which all specialists chafe.

3

◀ MILTON FRIEDMAN* ▶

from
Capitalism and Freedom (1962)

Milton Friedman is without doubt the most prominent advocate of conservatism within the ranks of professional economists. He has uncompromisingly advocated a free market approach in dealing with a wide variety of domestic and international economic problems; his advice has been eagerly solicited by several conservative political figures, including Senator Goldwater.

The main thrust of Friedman's critique is quite simple: the use of Keynesian-type fiscal and monetary policy—raising or lowering taxes, governmental spending, and the money supply, to offset fluctuations in the private sector—has exacerbated the country's economic difficulties. Moreover, a continual enlargement of the sphere of governmental activities tends, in Friedman's view, to destroy political freedom because it combines economic and political power. Friedman takes the position that economic freedom is a prerequisite for political freedom—a stand which is superficially in accord with that taken by the radicals. An important difference, however, stems from their differing definitions of economic freedom. Whereas the term connotes some notion of workers' control and (or) greater economic equality to the radical, Friedman employs the concept in a narrower perspective. To him, economic freedom means that each man can vote in a market for what he wants produced, choose how

*Professor of Economics, University of Chicago.

he will dispose of his labor, and enter into any business that he believes will promote his self-interest. Economic freedom is thus a buying and selling freedom. This definition clearly predisposes Friedman to arrive at the position that capitalism is the system most synonymous with individual freedom. To the radical, an important factor overlooked by Friedman is that even if one operates within the assumptions implied by the given institutional environment (for example, private property), economic freedom to the worker has meaning only in terms of available alternatives. If, for example, a labor surplus market exists, the worker's economic freedom, as measured by his ability to choose how he will dispose of his labor, is seriously compromised. Questionable also is the issue of whether there is a significant tendency for political freedom to be strengthened under capitalism, as Friedman implies. A society operating within a private enterprise framework appears to further the concentration of political power in a relatively small group. These questions are not directly considered in Friedman's simplified approach.

Friedman does, however, raise important and serious objections to the liberal's justifications of the government's countercyclical policy. He notes quite accurately that an increase in governmental expenditures relative to taxes is not necessarily expansionary (the "multiplier effect"), since this increase in the governmental sector may be offset by decreases in investment spending in the private business sector, and he says further that rising money incomes may be offset by rising prices. Friedman claimed that

> In fiscal policy as in monetary policy, all political considerations aside, we simply do not know enough to be able to use deliberate changes in taxation or expeditures as a sensitive stabilizing mechanism. In the process of trying to do so, we almost surely make matters worse.

As an antidote to the liberal's optimism concerning the use of countercyclical weapons, Friedman's warning is quite useful even though his statistical confirmation is debatable.

Friedman has attempted to rebuild the Quantity Theory of Money (changes in the money supply are viewed as an important cause of changes in price and output) as a counter to Keynesian theory. In this neoorthodox treatment, stable prices are viewed as a key prerequisite for a viable free enterprise system. Emphasis is placed on the demand for money, which Friedman regards as stable over time. Instead of allowing the Federal Reserve system to expand or contract the money supply, which Friedman believes is a strong destabilizing force, it is more effective, he says, to provide for a steady growth in the money stock roughly proportional to the growth in output. Price stability and full employment can be maintained if the money stock is increased by the proper amount. Friedman places the blame for the prolonged great depression of the 1930s on the monetary authorities;

they permitted a severe decline in the money supply—a fall of one-third from July 1929 to March 1933. "Had the money stock been kept from declining," says Friedman, "as it clearly could and should have been, the contraction would have been both shorter and far milder." His treatment contains no reference to the increasing inequality in the functional distribution of income in the late 1920s as evidenced by the rapidly growing gap between wages and propertied income. At the very least, these facts cast doubt on Friedman's purely monetary explanation of *the* major crisis in American economic history.

The problem of inequality disturbs Friedman much less than the problems of allocation of resources (efficiency) and the main-tenance of market freedom. All are allegedly related because "much of actual inequality derives from imperfections of the market," many of which are, in Friedman's opinion, created by governmental actions. In addition to chance and differences in natural ability, Friedman stresses the role of personal or social preferences as determinants of the degree of inequality, rather than the initial unequal distribution of wealth and the accompanying lack of early opportunities for the lowest economic strata. His approach harkens back to Malthus' theory that the poverty of the poor was essentially due to their own inferior choice making. His reasoning is that in a dynamically changing society with a high tendency for risk-taking ventures considerable inequality would (and perhaps should) be generated.

Closely related to this issue is Friedman's attempt to apply his competitive market model for dealing with such problems as educa-tion, discrimination, and welfare. He favors increased competition in the educational sector as a method of inducing higher quality. Parents, according to his scheme, would receive a voucher equal to a maximum sum per child per year which they would be free to spend on any "approved" educational service, private as well as public. "Our present school system," says Friedman, "far from equalizing opportunity, very likely does the opposite. It makes it all the harder for the exceptional few—and it is they who are the hope of the future—to rise above the poverty of their initial state." Although tinged with elitism, this approach is nondiscriminatory, at least on a formal level of analysis. According to Friedman, the judgment of the community ought to be the decisive determinant of what portion of their scarce resources to allocate to education, but he doesn't appear to be aware that com-munity judgments are affected by class factors. Although it is likely that Friedman's market-oriented educational methods would promote diversity, allow more personal choice, and perhaps improve the quality of education in some areas, it is hardly likely that such methods would offer more than token aid in dealing with the mass educational needs of today's low-income areas, particularly the black ghettos.

Friedman deals with discrimination in a similar manner. He notes, in the following article, that minority groups have a considerable stake in strengthening competitive capitalism, since an "impersonal market ... protects men from being discriminated against in their economic activities for reasons that are irrelevant to their productivity." Those who discriminate pay a price for so doing; their range of choice is limited and they pay higher prices or receive lower wages. This approach is oversimplified because, among other defects, it suffers from being a narrowly technical instead of a broader political economy. A more realistic analysis would focus on the short-run and long-run gains, as well as losses, for the various groups in our society for maintaining discrimination in the labor market. It would also deal with the intermeshing of economic and political elements.

Friedman almost studiously avoids an examination of the limitations of a system of free competition and individual freedom. The American experience lends weight to the view that concentration of power tends in time to grow out of operating an economy according to laissez faire tenets. It is doubtful whether an economy operating according to Friedman's rules of the game would experience less cyclical instability and less inequity even if one agreed with his unproved position that there would be more individual freedom. Despite the questionable quality of many of his laissez-faire proposals, Friedman should be given credit for aiding the thrust of economics toward better research techniques. His subtle and sophisticated questioning of Keynesian economics is also a salutary one even though an accurate appraisal of this critique is still forthcoming.

The mainstream of both liberal and radical thought tends to see Friedman's proposals as increasingly irrelevant for dealing with the crises of our twentieth-century industrial society, a society characterized by large power concentrations in both the business and the labor sectors and by price and wage structures that reflect this power. To many, Friedman has in the main structured elegant and logical models for a universe of limited applicability. Although they do not detract from his skills as an economist, his models do reflect political irrelevance.

————M. L.

from

Capitalism and Freedom*

INTRODUCTION

In a much quoted passage in his inaugural address, President Kennedy said, "Ask not what your country can do for you—ask what

*Reprinted from *Capitalism and Freedom* by Milton Friedman, by permission University of Chicago Press.

you can do for your country." It is a striking sign of the temper of our times that the controversy about this passage centered on its origin and not on its content. Neither half of the statement expresses a relation between the citizen and his government that is worthy of the ideals of free men in a free society. The paternalistic "what your country can do for you" implies that government is the patron, the citizen the ward, a view that is at odds with the free man's belief in his own responsibility for his own destiny. The organismic, "what you can do for your country" implies that government is the master or the deity, the citizen, the servant or the votary. To the free man, the country is the collection of individuals who compose it, not something over and above them. He is proud of a common heritage and loyal to common traditions. But he regards government as a means, an instrumentality, neither a grantor of favors and gifts, nor a master or god to be blindly worshipped and served. He recognizes no national goal except as it is the consensus of the goals that the citizens severally serve. He recognizes no national purpose except as it is the consensus of the purposes for which the citizens severally strive.

The free man will ask neither what his country can do for him nor what he can do for his country. He will ask rather "What can I and my compatriots do through government" to help us discharge our individual responsibilities, to achieve our several goals and purposes, and above all, to protect our freedom? And he will accompany this question with another: How can we keep the government we create from becoming a Frankenstein that will destroy the very freedom we establish it to protect? Freedom is a rare and delicate plant. Our minds tell us, and history confirms, that the great threat to freedom is the concentration of power. Government is necessary to preserve our freedom, it is an instrument through which we can exercise our freedom; yet by concentrating power in political hands, it is also a threat to freedom. Even though the men who wield this power initially be of good will and even though they be not corrupted by the power they exercise, the power will both attract and form men of a different stamp.

How can we benefit from the promise of government while avoiding the threat to freedom? Two broad principles embodied in our Constitution give an answer that has preserved our freedom so far, though they have been violated repeatedly in practice while proclaimed as precept.

First, the scope of government must be limited. Its major function must be to protect our freedom both from the enemies outside our gates and from our fellow-citizens: to preserve law and order, to enforce private contracts, to foster competitive markets. Beyond this major function, government may enable us at times to accomplish jointly what we would find it more difficult or expensive to accomplish severally. However, any such use of government is fraught with danger. We should not and cannot avoid using government in this way. But there should be a clear and large balance of advantages before we do. By relying primarily on voluntary co-operation and private enterprise, in both economic and other activities, we can insure that the private sector is a check on the powers of the governmental sector and an effective protection of freedom of speech, of religion, and of thought.

The second broad principle is that government power must be dispersed. If government is to exercise power, better in the county than in the state, better in the state than in Washington. If I do not like what my local community does, be it in sewage disposal, or zoning, or schools, I can move to another local community, and though few may take this step, the mere possibility acts as a check. If I do not like what my state does, I can move to another. If I do not like what Washington imposes, I have few alternatives in this world of jealous nations.

The very difficulty of avoiding the enactments of the federal government is of course the great attraction of centralization to many of its proponents. It will enable them more effectively, they believe, to legislate programs that—as they see it—are in the interest of the public, whether it be the transfer of income from the rich to the poor or from private to governmental purposes. They are in a sense right. But this coin has two sides. The power to do good is also the power to do harm; those who control the power today may not tomorrow; and, more important, what one man regards as good, another may regard as harm. The great tragedy of the drive to centralization, as of the drive to extend the scope of government in general, is that it is mostly led by men of good will who will be the first to rue its consequences.

The preservation of freedom is the protective reason for limiting and decentralizing governmental power. But there is also a constructive reason. The great advances of civilization, whether in architecture or painting, in science or literature, in industry or argiculture, have never come from centralized government. Columbus did not set out to seek a new route to China in response to a majority directive of a parliament, though he was partly financed by an absolute monarch. Newton and Leibnitz; Einstein and Bohr; Shakespeare, Milton, and Pasternak; Whitney, McCormick, Edison, and Ford; Jane Addams, Florence Nightingale, and Albert Schweitzer; no one of these opened new frontiers in human knowledge and understanding, in literature, in technical possibilities, or in the relief of human misery in response to governmental directives. Their achievements were the product of individual genius, of strongly held minority views, of a social climate permitting variety and diversity.

Government can never duplicate the variety and diversity of individual action. At any moment in time, by imposing uniform standards in housing, or nutrition, or clothing, government could undoubtedly improve the level of living of many individuals; by imposing uniform standards in schooling, road construction, or sanitation, central government could undoubtedly improve the level of performance in many local areas and perhaps even on the average of all communities. But in the process, government would replace progress by stagnation, it would substitute uniform mediocrity for the variety essential for that experimentation which can bring tomorrow's laggards above today's mean. . . .

It is extremely convenient to have a label for the political and economic viewpoint elaborated in this book. The rightful and proper label is liberalism. Unfortunately, "As a supreme, if unintended compliment, the enemies of the system of private enterprise have thought it wise to appropriate its label,"[1] so that liberalism has, in the United States, come to have a very different meaning than it did in the nineteenth century or does today over much of the Continent of Europe.

As it developed in the late eighteenth and early nineteenth centuries, the intellectual movement that went under the name of liberalism emphasized freedom as the ultimate goal and the individual as the ultimate entity in the society. It supported laissez faire at home as a means of reducing the role of the state in economic affairs and thereby enlarging the role of the individual; it supported free trade abroad as a means of linking the nations of the world together peacefully and democratically. In political matters, it supported the development of representative government and of parliamentary institutions, reduction in the arbitrary power of the state, and protection of the civil freedoms of individuals.

Beginning in the late nineteenth century, and especially after 1930 in the United States, the term liberalism came to be associated with a very different emphasis, particularly in economic policy. It came

---

[1] Joseph Schumpeter, *History of Economic Analysis* (New York: Oxford University Press, 1954), p. 394.

to be associated with a readiness to rely primarily on the state rather than on private voluntary arrangements to achieve objectives regarded as desirable. The catchwords become welfare and equality rather than freedom. The nineteenth-century liberal regarded an extension of freedom as the most effective way to promote welfare and equality; the twentieth-century liberal regards welfare and equality as either prerequisites of or alternatives to freedom. In the name of welfare and equality, the twentieth-century liberal has come to favor a revival of the very policies of state intervention and paternalism against which classical liberalism fought. In the very act of turning the clock back to seventeenth-century mercantilism, he is fond of castigating true liberals as reactionary!

The change in the meaning attached to the term liberalism is more striking in economic matters than in political. The twentieth-century liberal, like the nineteenth-century liberal, favors parliamentary institutions, representative government, civil rights, and so on. Yet even in political matters, there is a notable difference. Jealous of liberty, and hence fearful of centralized power, whether in governmental or private hands, the nineteenth-century liberal favored political decentralization. Committed to action and confident of the beneficence of power so long as it is in the hands of a government ostensibly controlled by the electorate, the twentieth-century liberal favors centralized government. He will resolve any doubt about where power should be located in favor of the state instead of the city, of the federal government instead of the state, and of a world organization instead of a national government.

Because of the corruption of the term liberalism, the views that formerly went under that name are now often labeled conservatism. But this is not a satisfactory alternative. The nineteenth-century liberal was a radical, both in the etymological sense of going to the root of the matter, and in the political sense of favoring major changes in social institutions. So too must be his modern heir. We do not wish to conserve the state interventions that have interfered so greatly with our freedom, though, of course, we do wish to conserve those that have promoted it. Moreover, in practice, the term conservatism has come to cover so wide a range of views, and views so incompatible with one another, that we shall no doubt see the growth of hyphenated designations, such as libertarian-conservative and aristocratic-conservative.

Partly because of my reluctance to surrender the term to proponents of measures that would destroy liberty, partly because I cannot find a better alternative, I shall resolve these difficulties by using the word liberalism in its original sense—as the doctrines pertaining to a free man.

THE RELATION BETWEEN ECONOMIC FREEDOM AND POLITICAL FREEDOM

It is widely believed that politics and economics are separate and largely unconnected; that individual freedom is a political problem and material welfare an economic problem; and that any kind of political arrangements can be combined with any kind of economic arrangements. The chief contemporary manifestation of this idea is the advocacy of "democratic socialism" by many who condemn out of hand the restrictions on individual freedom imposed by "totalitarian socialism" in Russia, and who are persuaded that it is possible for a country to adopt the essential features of Russian economic arrangements and yet to ensure individual freedom through political arrangements. The thesis of this chapter is that such a view is a delusion, that there is an intimate connection between economics and politics, that only certain combinations of political and economic arrangements are possible, and that in particular, a society which is socialist cannot also be democratic, in the sense of guaranteeing individual freedom.

Economic arrangements play a dual role in the promotion of a free society. On the one hand, freedom in economic arrangements is itself a component of freedom broadly understood, so economic freedom is an end in itself. In the second place, economic freedom is also an indispensable means toward the achievement of political freedom.

The first of these roles of economic freedom needs special emphasis because intellectuals in particular have a strong bias against regarding this aspect of freedom as important. They tend to express contempt for what they regard as material aspects of life, and to regard their own pursuit of allegedly higher values as on a different plane of significance and as deserving of special attention. For most citizens of the country, however, if not for the intellectual, the direct importance of economic freedom is at least comparable in significance to the indirect importance of economic freedom as a means to political freedom.

The citizen of Great Britain, who after World War II was not permitted to spend his vacation in the United States because of exchange control, was being deprived of an essential freedom no less than the citizen of the United States, who was denied the opportunity to spend his vacation in Russia because of his political views. The one was ostensibly an economic limitation on freedom and the other a political limitation, yet there is no essential difference between the two.

The citizen of the United States who is compelled by law to devote something like 10 per cent of his income to the purchase of a particular kind of retirement contract, administered by the government, is being deprived of a corresponding part of his personal freedom. How strongly this deprivation may be felt and its closeness to the deprivation of religious freedom, which all would regard as "civil" or "political" rather than "economic," were dramatized by an episode involving a group of farmers of the Amish sect. On grounds of principle, this group regarded compulsory federal old age programs as an infringement of their personal individual freedom and refused to pay taxes or accept benefits. As a result, some of their livestock were sold by auction in order to satisfy claims for social security levies. True, the number of citizens who regard compulsory old age insurance as a deprivation of freedom may be few, but the believer in freedom has never counted noses.

A citizen of the United States who under the laws of various states is not free to follow the occupation of his own choosing unless he can get a license for it, is likewise being deprived of an essential part of his freedom. So is the man who would like to exchange some of his goods with, say, a Swiss for a watch but is prevented from doing so by a quota. So also is the Californian who was thrown into jail for selling Alka-Seltzer at a price below that set by the manufacturer under so-called "fair trade" laws. So also is the farmer who cannot grow the amount of wheat he wants. And so on. Clearly, economic freedom, in and of itself, is an extremely important part of total freedom.

Viewed as a means to the end of political freedom, economic arrangements are important because of their effect on the concentration or dispersion of power. The kind of economic organization that provides economic freedom directly, namely, competitive capitalism, also promotes political freedom because it separates economic power from political power and in this way enables the one to offset the other.

Historical evidence speaks with a single voice on the relation between political freedom and a free market. I know of no example in time or place of a society that has been marked by a large measure of political freedom, and that has not also used something comparable to a free market to organize the bulk of economic activity.

Because we live in a largely free society, we tend to forget how limited is the span of time and the part of the globe for which there has ever been anything like political freedom: the typical state of mankind is tyranny, servitude, and misery. The nineteenth century and early twentieth century in the Western world stand out as striking exceptions to the general trend of historical development. Political freedom in this instance clearly came along with the free market and the development of capitalist institutions. So also did political freedom in the golden age of Greece and in the early days of the Roman era.

History suggests only that capitalism is a necessary condition for political freedom. Clearly it is not a sufficient condition. Fascist Italy and Fascist Spain, Germany at various times in the last seventy years, Japan before World Wars I and II, tzarist Russia in the decades before World War I—are all societies that cannot conceivably be described as politically free. Yet, in each, private enterprise was the dominant form of economic organization. It is therefore clearly possible to have economic arrangements that are fundamentally capitalist and political arrangements that are not free.

Even in those societies, the citizenry had a good deal more freedom than citizens of a modern totalitarian state like Russia or Nazi Germany, in which economic totalitarianism is combined with political totalitarianism. Even in Russia under the Tzars, it was possible for some citizens, under some circumstances, to change their jobs without getting permission from political authority, because capitalism and the existence of private property provided some check to the centralized power of the state.

The relation between political and economic freedom is complex and by no means unilateral. In the early nineteenth century, Bentham and the Philosophical Radicals were inclined to regard political freedom as a means to economic freedom. They believed that the masses were being hampered by the restrictions that were being imposed upon them, and that if political reform gave the bulk of the people the vote, they would do what was good for them, which was to vote for laissez faire. In retrospect, one cannot say that they were wrong. There was a large measure of political reform that was accompanied by economic reform in the direction of a great deal of laissez faire. An enormous increase in the well-being of the masses followed this change in economic arrangements.

The triumph of Benthamite liberalism in nineteenth-century England was followed by a reaction toward increasing intervention by government in economic affairs. This tendency to collectivism was greatly accelerated, both in England and elsewhere, by the two World Wars. Welfare rather than freedom became the dominant note in democratic countries. Recognizing the implicit threat to individualism, the intellectual descendants of the Philosophical Radicals—Dicey, Mises, Hayek, and Simons, to mention only a few—feared that a continued movement toward centralized control of economic activity would prove *The Road to Serfdom*, as Hayek entitled his penetrating analysis of the process. Their emphasis was on economic freedom as a means toward political freedom.

Events since the end of World War II display still a different relation between economic and political freedom. Collectivist economic planning has indeed interfered with individual freedom. At least in some countries, however, the result has not been the suppression of freedom, but the reversal of economic policy. England again provides the most striking example. The turning point was perhaps the "control of engagements" order which, despite great misgivings, the Labour party found it necessary to impose in order to carry out its economic policy. Fully enforced and carried through, the law would have involved centralized allocation of individuals to occupations. This conflicted so sharply with personal liberty that it was enforced in a negligible number of cases, and then repealed after the law had been in effect for only a short period. Its repeal ushered in a decided shift in economic policy, marked by reduced reliance on centralized "plans" and "programs," by the dismantling of many controls, and by increased emphasis on the private market. A similar shift in policy occurred in most other democratic countries.

The proximate explanation of these shifts in policy is the limited success of central planning or its outright failure to achieve stated objectives. However, this failure is itself to be attributed, at least in some measure, to the political implications of central planning and to an unwillingness to follow out its logic when doing so requires trampling rough-shod on treasured private rights. It may well be that the shift is only a temporary interruption in the collectivist trend of this century. Even so, it illustrates the close relation between political freedom and economic arrangements.

Historical evidence by itself can never be convincing. Perhaps it was sheer coincidence that the expansion of freedom occurred at the same time as the development of capitalist and market institutions. Why should there be a connection? What are the logical links between economic and political freedom? In discussing these questions we shall consider first the market as a direct component of freedom, and then the indirect relation between market arrangements and political freedom. A by-product will be an outline of the ideal economic arrangements for a free society.

As liberals, we take freedom of the individual, or perhaps the family, as our ultimate goal in judging social arrangements. Freedom as a value in this sense has to do with the interrelations among people; it has no meaning whatsoever to a Robinson Crusoe on an isolated island (without his Man Friday). Robinson Crusoe on his island is subject to "constraint," he has limited "power," and he has only a limited number of alternatives, but there is no problem of freedom in the sense that is relevant to our discussion. Similarly, in a society freedom has nothing to say about what an individual does with his freedom; it is not an all-embracing ethic. Indeed, a major aim of the liberal is to leave the ethical problem for the individual to wrestle with. The "really" important ethical problems are those that face an individual in a free society—what he should do with his freedom. There are thus two sets of values that a liberal will emphasize—the values that are relevant to relations among people, which is the context in which he assigns first priority to freedom; and the values that are relevant to the individual in the exercise of his freedom, which is the realm of individual ethics and philosophy.

The liberal conceives of men as imperfect beings. He regards the problem of social organization to be as much a negative problem of preventing "bad" people from doing harm as of enabling "good" people to do good; and, of course, "bad" and "good" people may be the same people, depending on who is judging them.

The basic problem of social organization is how to co-ordinate the economic activities of large numbers of people. Even in relatively backward societies, extensive division of labor and specialization of function is required to make effective use of available resources. In advanced societies, the scale on which co-ordination is needed, to take full advantage of the opportunities offered by modern science and technology, is enormously greater. Literally millions of people are involved in providing one another with their daily bread, let alone with their yearly automobiles. The challenge to the believer in liberty is to reconcile this widespread interdependence with individual freedom.

Fundamentally, there are only two ways of co-ordinating the economic activities of millions. One is central direction involving the use of coercion—the technique of the army and of the modern totalitarian state. The other is voluntary co-operation of individuals—the technique of the market place.

The possibility of co-ordination through voluntary co-operation rests on the elementary—yet frequently denied—proposition that both parties to an economic transaction benefit from it, *provided the transaction is bi-laterally voluntary and informed.*

Exchange can therefore bring about co-ordination without coercion. A working model of a society organized through voluntary exchange is a *free private enterprise exchange economy*—what we have been calling competitive capitalism.

In its simplest form, such a society consists of a number of independent households—a collection of Robinson Crusoes, as it were. Each household uses the resources it controls to produce goods and services that it exchanges for goods and services produced by other households, on terms mutually acceptable to the two parties to the bargain. It is thereby enabled to satisfy its wants indirectly by producing goods and services for others, rather than directly by producing goods for its own immediate use. The incentive for adopting this indirect route is, of course, the increased product made possible by division of labor and specialization of function. Since the household always has the alternative of producing directly for itself, it need not enter into any exchange unless it benefits from it. Hence, no exchange will take place unless both parties do benefit from it. Co-operation is thereby achieved without coercion.

Specialization of function and division of labor would not go far if the ultimate productive unit were the household. In a modern society, we have gone much farther. We have introduced enterprises which are intermediaries between individuals in their capacities as suppliers of service and as purchasers of goods. And similarly, specialization of function and division of labor could not go very far if we had to continue to rely on the barter of product for product. In consequence, money has been introduced as a means of facilitating exchange, and of enabling the acts of purchase and of sale to be separated into two parts.

Despite the important role of enterprises and of money in our actual economy, and despite the numerous and complex problems they raise, the central characteristic of the market technique of achieving co-ordination is fully displayed in the simple exchange economy that contains neither enterprises nor money. As in that simple model, so in the complex enterprise and money-exchange economy, co-operation is strictly individual and voluntary *provided*: (*a*) that enterprises are private, so that the ultimate contracting parties are individuals and (*b*) that individuals are effectively free to enter or not to enter into any particular exchange, so that every transaction is strictly voluntary.

It is far easier to state these provisos in general terms than to spell them out in detail, or to specify precisely the institutional arrangements most conducive to their maintenance. Indeed, much of technical economic literature is concerned with precisely these questions. The basic requisite is the maintenance of law and order to prevent physical coercion of one individual by another and to enforce contracts voluntarily entered into, thus giving substance to "private." Aside from this, perhaps the most difficult problems arise from monopoly—which inhibits effective freedom by denying individuals alternatives to the particular exchange—and from "neighborhood effects"—effects on third parties for which it is not feasible to charge or recompense them. . . .

So long as effective freedom of exchange is maintained, the central feature of the market organization of economic activity is that it prevents one person from interfering with another in respect of most of his activities. The consumer is protected from coercion by the seller because of the presence of other sellers with whom he can deal. The seller is protected from coercion by the consumer because of other consumers to whom he can sell. The employee is protected from coercion by the employer because of other employers for whom he can work, and so on. And the market does this impersonally and without centralized authority.

Indeed, a major source of objection to a free economy is precisely that it does this task so well. It gives people what they want instead of what a particular group thinks they ought to want. Underlying most arguments against the free market is a lack of belief in freedom itself.

The existence of a free market does not of course eliminate the need for government. On the contrary, government is essential both as a forum for determining the "rules of the game" and as an umpire to interpret and enforce the rules decided on. What the market does is to reduce greatly the range of issues that must be decided through political means, and thereby to minimize the extent to which government need participate directly in the game. The characteristic feature of action through political channels is that it tends to require or enforce substantial conformity. The great advantage of the market, on the other hand, is that it permits wide diversity. It is, in political terms, a system of proportional representation. Each man can vote, as it were, for the color of tie he wants and get it; he does not have to see what color the majority wants and then, if he is in the minority, submit.

It is this feature of the market that we refer to when we say that the market provides economic freedom. But this characteristic also has implications that go far beyond the narrowly economic. Political freedom means the absence of coercion of a man by his fellow men. The fundamental threat to freedom is power to coerce, be it in the hands of a monarch, a dictator, an oligarchy, or a momentary majority. The preservation of freedom requires the elimination of such concentration of power to the fullest possible extent and the dispersal and distribution of whatever power cannot be eliminated—a system of checks and balances. By removing the organization of economic activity from the control of political authority, the market eliminates this source of coercive power. It enables economic strength to be a check to political power rather than a reinforcement.

Economic power can be widely dispersed. There is no law of conservation which forces the growth of new centers of economic strength to be at the expense of existing centers. Political power, on the other hand, is more difficult to decentralize. There can be numerous small independent governments. But it is far more difficult to maintain numerous equipotent small centers of political power in a single large government than it is to have numerous centers of economic strength in a single large economy. There can be many millionaires in one large economy. But can there be more than one really outstanding leader, one person on whom the energies and enthusiasms of his countrymen are centered? If the central government gains power, it is likely to be at the expense of local governments. There seems to be something like a fixed total of political power to be distributed. Consequently, if economic power is joined to political power, concentration seems almost inevitable. On the other hand, if economic power is kept in separate hands from political power, it can serve as a check and a counter to political power.

The force of this abstract argument can perhaps best be demonstrated by example. Let us consider first, a hypothetical example that may help to bring out the principles involved, and then some actual examples from recent experience that illustrate the way in which the market works to preserve political freedom.

One feature of a free society is surely the freedom of individuals to advocate and propagandize openly for a radical change in the structure of the society—so long as the advocacy is restricted to persuasion and does not include force or other forms of coercion. It is a mark of the political freedom of a capitalist society that men can openly advocate and work for socialism. Equally, political freedom in a socialist society would require that men be free to advocate the introduction of capitalism. How could the freedom to advocate capitalism be preserved and protected in a socialist society?

In order for men to advocate anything, they must in the first place be able to earn a living. This already raises a problem in a socialist society, since all jobs are under the direct control of political authorities. It would take an act of self-denial whose difficulty is underlined by experience in the United States after World War II with the problem of "security" among Federal employees, for a socialist government to permit its employees to advocate policies directly contrary to official doctrine.

But let us suppose this act of self-denial to be achieved. For advocacy of capitalism to mean anything, the proponents must be able to finance their cause—to hold public meetings, publish pamphlets, buy radio time, issue newspapers and magazines, and so on. How could they raise the funds? There might and probably would be men in the socialist society with large incomes, perhaps even large capital sums in the form of government bonds and the like, but these would of necessity be high public officials. It is possible to conceive of a minor socialist official retaining his job although openly advocating capitalism. It strains credulity to imagine the socialist top brass financing such "subversive" activities.

The only recourse for funds would be to raise small amounts from a large number of minor officials. But this is no real answer. To tap these sources, many people would already have to be persuaded, and our whole problem is how to initiate and finance a campaign to do so. Radical movements in capitalist societies have never been financed this way. They have typically been supported by a few wealthy individuals who have become persuaded—by a Frederick Vanderbilt Field, or an Anita McCormick Blaine, or a Corliss Lamont, to mention a few names recently prominent, or by a Friedrich Engels, to go farther back. This is a role of inequality of wealth in preserving political freedom that is seldom noted—the role of the patron.

In a capitalist society, it is only necessary to convince a few wealthy people to get funds to launch any idea, however strange, and there are many such persons, many independent foci of support. And, indeed, it is not even necessary to persuade people or financial institutions with available funds of the soundness of the ideas to be propagated. It is only necessary to persuade them that the propagation can be financially successful; that the newspaper or magazine or book or other venture will be profitable. The competitive publisher, for example, cannot afford to publish only writing with which he personally agrees; his touchstone must be the likelihood that the market will be large enough to yield a satisfactory return on his investment.

In this way, the market breaks the vicious circle and makes it possible ultimately to finance such ventures by small amounts from many people without first persuading them. There are no such possibilities in the socialist society; there is only the all-powerful state.

Let us stretch our imagination and suppose that a socialist government is aware of this problem and is composed of people anxious to preserve freedom. Could it provide the funds? Perhaps, but it is difficult to see how. It could establish a bureau for subsidizing subversive propaganda. But how could it choose whom to support? If it gave to all who asked, it would shortly find itself out of funds, for socialism cannot repeal the elementary economic law that a sufficiently high price will call forth a large supply. Make the advocacy of radical causes sufficiently remunerative, and the supply of advocates will be unlimited.

Moreover, freedom to advocate unpopular causes does not require that such advocacy be without cost. On the contrary, no society could be stable if advocacy of radical change were costless, much less subsidized. It is entirely appropriate that men make sacrifices to advocate causes in which they deeply believe. Indeed, it is important to preserve freedom only for people who are willing to practice self-denial, for otherwise freedom degenerates into license and irresponsibility. What is essential is that the cost of advocating unpopular causes be tolerable and not prohibitive.

But we are not yet through. In a free market society, it is enough to have the funds. The suppliers of paper are as willing to sell it to the *Daily Worker* as to the *Wall Street Journal*. In a socialist society, it would not be enough to have the funds. The hypothetical supporter of capitalism would have to persuade a government factory making paper to sell to him, the government printing press to print his pamphlets, a government post office to distribute them among the people, a government agency to rent him a hall in which to talk, and so on.

Perhaps there is some way in which one could overcome these difficulties and preserve freedom in a socialist society. One cannot say it is utterly impossible. What is clear, however, is that there are very real difficulties in establishing institutions that will effectively preserve the possibility of dissent. So far as I know, none of the people who have been in favor of socialism and also in favor of freedom have really faced up to this issue, or made even a respectable start at developing the institutional arrangements that would permit freedom under socialism. By contrast, it is clear how a free market capitalist society fosters freedom.

A striking practical example of these abstract principles is the experience of Winston Churchill. From 1933 to the outbreak of World War II, Churchill was not permitted to talk over the British radio, which was, of course, a government monopoly administered by the British Broadcasting Corporation. Here was a leading citizen of his country, a Member of Parliament, a former cabinet minister, a man who was desperately trying by every device possible to persuade his countrymen to take steps to ward off the menace of Hitler's Germany. He was not permitted to talk over the radio to the British people because the BBC was a government monopoly and his position was too "controversial."

Another striking example, reported in the January 26, 1959 issue of *Time,* has to do with the "Blacklist Fadeout." Says the *Time* story,

> The Oscar-awarding ritual is Hollywood's biggest pitch for dignity, but two years ago dignity suffered. When one Robert Rich was announced as top writer for the *The Brave One,* he never stepped forward. Robert Rich was a pseudonym, masking one of about 150 writers ... blacklisted by the industry since 1947 as suspected Communists or fellow travelers. The case was particularly embarrassing because the Motion Picture Academy had barred any Communist or Fifth Amendment pleader from Oscar competition. Last week both the Communist rule and the mystery of Rich's identity were suddenly rescripted.
> Rich turned out to be Dalton (*Johnny Got His Gun*) Trumbo, one of the original "Hollywood Ten" writers who refused to testify at the 1947 hearings on Communism in the movie industry. Said producer Frank King, who had stoutly insisted that Robert Rich was "a young guy in Spain with a beard": "We have an obligation to our stockholders to buy the best script we can. Trumbo brought us *The Brave One* and we bought it." ...

In effect it was the formal end of the Hollywood black list.
For barred writers, the informal end came long ago. At
least 15 per cent of current Hollywood films are reportedly
written by blacklist members. Said Producer King, "There
are more ghosts in Hollywood than in Forest Lawn. Every
company in town has used the work of blacklisted people.
We're just the first to confirm what everybody knows."

One may believe, as I do, that communism would destroy all
of our freedoms, one may be opposed to it as firmly and as strongly as
possible, and yet, at the same time, also believe that in a free society
it is intolerable for a man to be prevented from making voluntary arrangements with others that are mutually attractive because he believes
in or is trying to promote communism. His freedom includes his freedom to promote communism. Freedom also, of course, includes the
freedom of others not to deal with him under those circumstances. The
Hollywood blacklist was an unfree act that destroys freedom because
it was a collusive arrangement that used coercive means to prevent
voluntary exchanges. It didn't work precisely because the market made
it costly for people to preserve the blacklist. The commercial emphasis,
the fact that people who are running enterprises have an incentive to
make as much money as they can, protected the freedom of the individuals who were blacklisted by providing them with an alternative form
of employment, and by giving people an incentive to employ them.

If Hollywood and the movie industry had been government
enterprises or if in England it had been a question of employment by
the British Broadcasting Corporation it is difficult to believe that the
"Hollywood Ten" or their equivalent would have found employment.
Equally, it is difficult to believe that under those circumstances, strong
proponents of individualism and private enterprise—or indeed strong
proponents of any view other than the status quo—would be able to
get employment.

Another example of the role of the market in preserving political freedom, was revealed in our experience with McCarthyism. Entirely
aside from the substantive issues involved, and the merits of the
charges made, what protection did individuals, and in particular government employees, have against irresponsible accusations and probings
into matters that it went against their conscience to reveal? Their appeal
to the Fifth Amendment would have been a hollow mockery without
an alternative to government employment.

Their fundamental protection was the existence of a private-market economy in which they could earn a living. Here again, the protection was not absolute. Many potential private employers were, rightly or wrongly, averse to hiring those pilloried. It may well be that there was far less justification for the costs imposed on many of the people involved than for the costs generally imposed on people who advocate unpopular causes. But the important point is that the costs were limited and not prohibitive, as they would have been if government employment had been the only possibility.

It is of interest to note that a disproportionately large fraction of people involved apparently went into the most competitive sectors of the economy—small business, trade, farming—where the market approaches most closely the ideal free market. No one who buys bread knows whether the wheat from which it is made was grown by a Communist or a Republican, by a constitutionalist or a Fascist, or, for that matter, by a Negro or a white. This illustrates how an impersonal market separates economic activities from political views and protects men from being discriminated against in their economic activities for reasons that are irrelevant to their productivity—whether these reasons are associated with their views or their color.

As this example suggests, the groups in our society that have the most at stake in the preservation and strengthening of competitive capitalism are those minority groups which can most easily become the object of the distrust and enmity of the majority—the Negroes, the Jews, the foreign-born, to mention only the most obvious. Yet, paradoxically enough, the enemies of the free market—the Socialists and Communists—have been recruited in disproportionate measure from these groups. Instead of recognizing that the existence of the market has protected them from the attitudes of their fellow countrymen, they mistakenly attribute the residual discrimination to the market.

FISCAL POLICY

Ever since the New Deal, a primary excuse for the expansion of governmental activity at the federal level has been the supposed necessity for government spending to eliminate unemployment. The excuse has gone through several stages. At first, government spending was needed to "prime the pump." Temporary expenditures would set the economy going and the government could then step out of the picture.

When the initial expenditures failed to eliminate unemployment and were followed by a sharp economic contraction in 1937–38,
the theory of "secular stagnation" developed to justify a permanently
high level of government spending. The economy had become mature,
it was argued. Opportunities for investment had been largely exploited
and no substantial new opportunities were likely to arise. Yet individuals would still want to save. Hence, it was essential for government
to spend and run a perpetual deficit. The securities issued to finance the
deficit would provide individuals with a way to accumulate savings
while the government expenditures provided employment. This view
has been thoroughly discredited by theoretical analysis and even more
by actual experience, including the emergence of wholly new lines for
private investment not dreamed of by the secular stagnationists. Yet
it has left its heritage. The idea may be accepted by none, but the government programs undertaken in its name, like some of those intended
to prime the pump, are still with us and indeed account for ever-growing
government expenditures.

        More recently, the emphasis has been on government expendi-
tures neither to prime the pump nor to hold in check the specter of
secular stagnation but as a balance wheel. When private expenditures
decline for any reason, it is said, governmental expenditures should rise
to keep total expenditures stable; conversely, when private expenditures
rise, governmental expenditures should decline. Unfortunately, the balance wheel is unbalanced. Each recession, however minor, sends a
shudder through politically sensitive legislators and administrators with
their ever present fear that perhaps it is the harbinger of another 1929-
33. They hasten to enact federal spending programs of one kind or
another. Many of the programs do not in fact come into effect until
after the recession has passed. Hence, insofar as they do affect total
expenditures, . . . they tend to exacerbate the succeeding expansion rather
than to mitigate the recession. The haste with which spending programs
are approved is not matched by an equal haste to repeal them or to
eliminate others when the recession is passed and expansion is under
way. On the contrary, it is then argued that a "healthy" expansion must
not be "jeopardized" by cuts in governmental expenditures. The chief
harm done by the balance-wheel theory is therefore not that it has failed
to offset recessions, which it has, and not that it has introduced an inflationary bias into governmental policy, which it has done too, but that it
has continuously fostered an expansion in the range of governmental
activities at the federal level and prevented a reduction in the burden of
federal taxes. . . .

If the balance-wheel theory has in practice been applied on the expenditure side, it has been because of the existence of other forces making for increased governmental expenditures; in particular, the widespread acceptance by intellectuals of the belief that government should play a larger role in economic and private affairs; the triumph, that is, of the philosophy of the welfare state. This philosophy has found a useful ally in the balance-wheel theory; it has enabled governmental intervention to proceed at a faster pace than would otherwise have been possible. ...

CONCLUSION

In the 1920s and the 1930s, intellectuals in the United States were overwhelmingly persuaded that capitalism was a defective system inhibiting economic well-being and thereby freedom, and that the hope for the future lay in a greater measure of deliberate control by political authorities over economic affairs. The conversion of the intellectuals was not achieved by the example of any actual collectivist society, though it undoubtedly was much hastened by the establishment of a communist society in Russia and the glowing hopes placed in it. The conversion of the intellectuals was achieved by a comparison between the existing state of affairs, with all its injustices and defects, and a hypothetical state of affairs as it might be. The actual was compared with the ideal.

At the time, not much else was possible. True, mankind had experienced many epochs of centralized control, of detailed intervention by the state into economic affairs. But there had been a revolution in politics, in science, and in technology. Surely, it was argued, we can do far better with a democratic political structure, modern tools, and modern science than was possible in earlier ages.

The attitudes of that time are still with us. There is still a tendency to regard any existing government intervention as desirable, to attribute all evils to the market, and to evaluate new proposals for government control in their ideal form, as they might work if run by able, disinterested men, free from the pressure of special interest groups. The proponents of limited government and free enterprise are still on the defensive.

Yet, conditions have changed. We now have several decades of experience with governmental intervention. It is no longer necessary to compare the market as it actually operates and government intervention as it ideally might operate. We can compare the actual with the actual.

If we do so, it is clear that the difference between the actual operation of the market and its ideal operation—great though it undoubtedly is—is as nothing compared to the difference between the actual effects of government intervention and their intended effects. Who can now see any great hope for the advancement of men's freedom and dignity in the massive tyranny and despotism that holds sway in Russia? Wrote Marx and Engels in *The Communist Manifesto*: "The proletarians have nothing to lose but their chains. They have a world to win." Who today can regard the chains of the proletarians in the Soviet Union as weaker than the chains of the proletarians in the United States, or Britain or France or Germany or any Western state?

Let us look closer to home. Which if any of the great "reforms" of past decades has achieved its objectives? Have the good intentions of the proponents of these reforms been realized?

Regulation of the railroads to protect the consumer quickly became an instrument whereby the railroads could protect themselves from the competition of newly emerging rivals—at the expense, of course, of the consumer.

An income tax initially enacted at low rates and later seized upon as a means to redistribute income in favor of the lower classes has become a facade, covering loopholes and special provisions that render rates that are highly graduated on paper largely ineffective. A flat rate of 23½ per cent on presently taxable income would yield as much revenue as the present rates graduated from 20 to 91 per cent. An income tax intended to reduce inequality and promote the diffusion of wealth has in practice fostered reinvestment of corporate earnings, thereby favoring the growth of large corporations, inhibiting the operation of the capital market, and discouraging the establishment of new enterprises.

Monetary reforms, intended to promote stability in economic activity and prices, exacerbated inflation during and after World War I and fostered a higher degree of instability thereafter than had ever been experienced before. The monetary authorities they established bear primary responsibility for converting a serious economic contraction into the catastrophe of the Great Depression from 1929-33. A system established largely to prevent bank panics produced the most severe banking panic in American history.

An agricultural program intended to help impecunious farmers and to remove what were alleged to be basic dislocations in the organization of agriculture has become a national scandal that has wasted public funds, distorted the use of resources, riveted increasingly heavy and detailed controls on farmers, interfered seriously with United States foreign policy, and withal has done little to help the impecunious farmer.

A housing program intended to improve the housing conditions of the poor, to reduce juvenile delinquency, and to contribute to the removal of urban slums, has worsened the housing conditions of the poor, contributed to juvenile delinquency, and spread urban blight.

In the 1930s, "labor" was synonymous with "labor union" to the intellectual community; faith in the purity and virtue of labor unions was on a par with faith in home and motherhood. Extensive legislation was enacted to favor labor unions and to foster "fair" labor relations. Labor unions waxed in strength. By the 1950s, "labor union" was almost a dirty word; it was no longer synonymous with "labor," no longer automatically to be taken for granted as on the side of the angels.

Social security measures were enacted to make receipt of assistance a matter of right, to eliminate the need for direct relief and assistance. Millions now receive social security benefits. Yet the relief rolls grow and the sums spent on direct assistance mount.

The list can easily be lengthened: the silver purchase program of the 1930s, public power projects, foreign aid programs of the postwar years, F.C.C., urban redevelopment programs, the stockpiling program—these and many more have had effects very different and generally quite opposite from those intended.

There have been some exceptions. The expressways crisscrossing the country, magnificent dams spanning great rivers, orbiting satellites are all tributes to the capacity of government to command great resources. The school systems, with all its defects and problems, with all the possibility of improvement through bringing into more effective play the forces of the market, has widened the opportunities available to American youth and contributed to the extension of freedom. It is a testament to the public-spirited efforts of the many tens of thousands who have served on local school boards and to the willingness of the public to bear heavy taxes for what they regarded as a public purpose. The Sherman antitrust laws, with all their problems of detailed administration, have by their very existence fostered competition. Public health measures have contributed to the reduction of infectious disease.

Assistance measures have relieved suffering and distress. Local authorities have often provided facilities essential to the life of communities.
Law and order have been maintained, though in many a large city the
performance of even this elementary function of government has been
far from satisfactory. As a citizen of Chicago, I speak feelingly.

If a balance be struck, there can be little doubt that the record
is dismal. The greater part of the new ventures undertaken by government in the past few decades have failed to achieve their objectives.
The United States has continued to progress; its citizens have become
better fed, better clothed, better housed, and better transported; class
and social distinctions have narrowed; minority groups have become
less disadvantaged; popular culture has advanced by leaps and bounds.
All this has been the product of the initiative and drive of individuals
co-operating through the free market. Government measures have
hampered not helped this development. We have been able to afford
and surmount these measures only because of the extraordinary fe-
cundity of the market. The invisible hand has been more potent for
progress than the visible hand of retrogression.

Is it an accident that so many of the government reforms of
recent decades have gone awry, that the bright hopes have turned to
ashes? Is it simply because the programs are faulty in detail?

I believe the answer is clearly in the negative. The central defect of these measures is that they seek through government to force
people to act against their own immediate interests in order to promote
a supposedly general interest. They seek to resolve what is supposedly
a conflict of interest, or a difference in view about interests, not by
establishing a framework that will eliminate the conflict, or by persuading people to have different interests, but by forcing people to act
against their own interest. They substitute the values of outsiders for
the values of participants; either some telling others what is good for
them, or the government taking from some to benefit others. These
measures are therefore countered by one of the strongest and most
creative forces known to man—the attempt by millions of individuals
to promote their own interests, to live their lives by their own values.
This is the major reason why the measures have so often had the
opposite of the effects intended. It is also one of the major strengths of
a free society and explains why governmental regulation does not
strangle it.

The interests of which I speak are not simply narrow self-
regarding interests. On the contrary, they include the whole range of
values that men hold dear and for which they are willing to spend

their fortunes and sacrifice their lives. The Germans who lost their lives opposing Adolf Hitler were pursuing their interests as they saw them. So also are the men and women who devote great effort and time to charitable, educational, and religious activities. Naturally, such interests are the major ones for few men. It is the virtue of a free society that it nonetheless permits these interests full scope and does not subordinate them to the narrow materialistic interests that dominate the bulk of mankind. That is why capitalist societies are less materialistic than collective societies.

Why is it, in light of the record, that the burden of proof still seems to rest on those of us who oppose new government programs and who seek to reduce the already unduly large role of government? Let Dicey answer: "The beneficial effect of State intervention, especially in the form of legislation, is direct, immediate, and, so to speak, visible, whilst its evil effects are gradual and direct, and lie out of sight. ... Nor ... do most people keep in mind that State inspectors may be incompetent, careless, or even occasionally corrupt ...; few are those who realize the undeniable truth that State help kills self-help. Hence the majority of mankind must almost of necessity look with undue favor upon governmental intervention. This natural bias can be counteracted only by the existence, in a given society, ... of a presumption or prejudice in favor of individual liberty, that is, of laissez-faire. The mere decline, therefore, of faith in self-help—and that such a decline has taken place is certain—is of itself sufficient to account for the growth of legislation tending towards socialism."[2]

The preservation and expansion of freedom are today threatened from two directions. The one threat is obvious and clear. It is the external threat coming from the evil men in the Kremlin who promise to bury us. The other threat is far more subtle. It is the internal threat coming from men of good intentions and good will who wish to reform us. Impatient with the slowness of persuasion and example to achieve the great social changes they envision, they are anxious to use the power of the state to achieve their ends and confident of their own ability to do so. Yet if they gained the power, they would fail to achieve their immediate aims and, in addition, would produce a collective state from which they would recoil in horror and of which they would be among the first victims. Concentrated power is not rendered harmless by the good intentions of those who create it.

---

[2] A. V. Dicey, *Lectures on the Relation Between Law and Public Opinion in England,* second edition (London: Macmillan, 1914), pp. 257–258.

The two threats unfortunately reinforce one another. Even if we avoid a nuclear holocaust, the threat from the Kremlin requires us to devote a sizable fraction of our resources to our military defense. The importance of government as a buyer of so much of our output, and the sole buyer of the output of many firms and industries, already concentrates a dangerous amount of economic power in the hands of the political authorities, changes the environment in which business operates and the criteria relevant for business success, and in these and other ways endangers a free market. This danger we cannot avoid. But we needlessly intensify it by continuing the present widespread governmental intervention in areas unrelated to the military defense of the nation and by undertaking ever new governmental programs—from medical care for the aged to lunar exploration.

As Adam Smith once said, "There is much ruin in a nation." Our basic structure of values and the interwoven network of free institutions will withstand much. I believe that we shall be able to preserve and extend freedom despite the size of the military programs and despite the economic powers already concentrated in Washington. But we shall be able to do so only if we awake to the threat that we face, only if we persuade our fellow men that free institutions offer a surer, if perhaps at times a slower, route to the ends they seek than the coercive power of the state. The glimmerings of change that are already apparent in the intellectual climate are a hopeful augury.

4

◀ MURRAY ROTHBARD* ▶

The Great Society: A Libertarian Critique (1967)

Rothbard represents an extreme right-wing mini-faction whose critique of present American society reveals astonishingly close kinship with that of many radicals, closer in fact than with his fellow conservatives. Although he is as strongly committed to a defense of laissez faire as other conservative figures (including those represented in this reader), his support of black power and his characterization of American foreign policy as "imperialistic" would be eagerly assented to by many thinkers usually associated with the political "left."

Rothbard's critique of the war in Vietnam and of American foreign policy in general is in striking contrast to that of other conservatives, and reveals more clearly than any other facet of his thinking the maverick quality of his philosophy. He is critical of cold war patriotism among the libertarian conservatives on the grounds that war accelerates the trend towards statism, the real enemy of liberty. He also claims that history indicates that the big businessman has been "one of the main driving forces of the statist dynamics of twentieth century America." He describes the American corporate state as a "tripartite rapprochement of big business, big unions, and big government." His view of the function of unions as disciplining the workers and integrating them into the burgeoning corporate state is embraced only by the far left, as is his claim that the function of our foreign aid

*Associate Professor of Economics, Polytechnic Institute of Brooklyn.

program is to provide a subsidy to both American business and the foreign clients of American business. This approach amounts to a broadside attack on both the liberal intelligentsia and conservatives for the combination welfare and warfare state that governs—and perhaps threatens—our lives.

Rothbard's closest intellectual kinship within the ranks of the conservatives is with Adam Smith. Like Smith, his sympathy is directed towards the lower ranks and his suspicions toward the privileged ranks, but unlike Smith he is writing in twentieth-century corporate, industrial America and therefore appears like King Canute trying to hold back the waves threatening the existence of the competitive vessel.

——M. L.

The Great Society: A Libertarian Critique*

The Great Society is the lineal descendant and the intensification of those other pretentiously named polities of twentieth-century America: the Square Deal, the New Freedom, the New Era, the New Deal, the Fair Deal, and the New Frontier. All of these assorted Deals constitute a basic and fundamental shift in American life—a shift from a relatively laissez-faire economy and minimal state to a society in which the state is unquestionably king.[1] In the previous century, the government could safely have been ignored by almost everyone; now we have become a country in which the government is the great and unending source of power and privilege. Once a country in which each man could by and large make the decisions for his own life, we have become a land where the state holds and exercises life-and-death power over every

---

*©Copyright 1967 by Random House, Inc. Reprinted from *The Great Society Reader,* edited by David Mermelstein and Marvin E. Gettleman, by permission of the publisher.

[1] Recent triumphal disclosures by economic historians that pure laissez faire did not exist in nineteenth century American are beside the point; no one ever claimed that it did. The point is that state power in society was minimal, relative to other times and countries, and that the general locus of decision making resided therefore in the individuals making up society rather than in the State. Cf. Robert Lively, "The American System," *Business History Review,* XXIX (1955), pp. 81–96.

person, group, and institution. The great Moloch government, once confined and cabined, has burst its feeble bonds to dominate us all.

The basic reason for this development is not difficult to fathom. It was best summed up by the great German sociologist Franz Oppenheimer; Oppenheimer wrote that there were fundamentally two, and only two, paths to the acquisition of wealth. One route is the production of a good or service and its voluntary exchange for the goods or services produced by others. This method—the method of the free market—Oppenheimer termed "the economic means" to wealth. The other path, which avoids the necessity for production and exchange, is for one or more persons to seize other people's products by the use of physical force. This method of robbing the fruits of another man's production was shrewdly named by Oppenheimer the "political means." Throughout history, men have been tempted to employ the "political means" of seizing wealth rather than expend effort in production and exchange. It should be clear that while the market process multiplies production, the political, exploitative means is parasitic and, as with all parasitic action, discourages and drains off production and output in society. To regularize and order a permanent system of predatory exploitation, men have created the state, which Oppenheimer brilliantly defined as "the organization of the political means."[2]

Every act of the state is necessarily an occasion for inflicting burdens and assigning subsidies and privileges. By seizing revenue by means of coercion and assigning rewards as it disburses the funds, the state creates ruling and ruled "classes" or "castes"; for one example, classes of what Calhoun discerned as net "taxpayers" and "tax-consumers," those who live off taxation.[3] And since by its nature, predation can only be supported out of the surplus of production above subsistence, the ruling class must constitute a minority of the citizenry.

---

[2]Franz Oppenheimer, *The State* (New York: 1926), pp. 24–27. Or, as Albert Jay Nock, heavily influenced by Oppenheimer's analysis, concluded: "The state claims and exercises the monopoly of crime" in its territorial area. Albert Jay Nock, *On Doing the Right Thing, and Other Essays* (New York: 1928), p. 143.

[3]See John C. Calhoun, *Disquisition on Government* . . . (Columbia, S. C.: 1850). On the distinction between this and the Marxian concept of the ruling class, see Ludwig von Mises, *Theory and History* (New Haven, Conn.: 1957), pp. 112 ff. Perhaps the earliest users of this kind of class analysis were the French libertarian writers of the Restoration period of the early nineteenth century, Charles Comte and Charles Dunoyer. Cf. Elie Halévy, *The Era of Tyrannies* (Garden City, N. Y.: 1965), pp. 23–34.

Since the state, nakedly observed, is a mighty engine of organized predation, state rule, throughout its many millennia of recorded history, could be preserved only by persuading the bulk of the public that its rule has not really been exploitative: that, on the contrary, it has been necessary, beneficent, even, as in the Oriental despotisms, divine. Promoting this ideology among the masses has ever been a prime function of intellectuals, a function that has created the basis for co-opting a corps of intellectuals into a secure and permanent berth in the state apparatus. In former centuries, these intellectuals formed a priestly caste that was able to wrap a cloak of mystery and quasi-divinity about the actions of the state for a credulous public; nowadays, the apologia for the state takes on more subtle and seemingly scientific forms. The process remains essentially the same.[4]

In the United States, a strong libertarian and antistatist tradition prevented the process of statization from taking hold at a very rapid pace. The major force in its propulsion has been that favorite theater of state expansionism, brilliantly identified by Randolph Bourne as "the health of the state": namely, war. For although in wartime various states find themselves in danger from one another, every state has found war a fertile field for spreading the myth among its subjects that they are the ones in deadly danger, from which their state is protecting them. In this way states have been able to dragoon their subjects into fighting and dying to save them under the pretext that the subjects were being saved from the dread Foreign Enemy. In the United States, the process of statization began in earnest under cover of the Civil War (conscription, military rule, income tax, excise taxes, high tariffs, national banking and credit expansion for favored businesses, paper money, land grants to railroads), and reached full flower as a result of World Wars I and II, to finally culminate in the Great Society.

The recently emerging group of "libertarian conservatives" in the United States have grasped a part of the recent picture of accelerated statism, but their analysis suffers from several fatal blind spots. One is their complete failure to realize that war, culminating in the present

---

[4]On various aspects of the alliance between intellectuals and the State, see George B. de Huszar, ed., *The Intellectuals* (Glencoe, Ill.: 1960); Joseph A. Schumpeter, *Capitalism, Socialism, and Democracy* (New York: 1942), pp. 143–55; Karl A. Wittfogel, *Oriental Despotism* (New Haven, Conn.: 1957); Howard K. Beale, "The Professional Historian: His Theory and Practice," *The Pacific Historical Review* (August, 1953), pp. 227–55; Martin Nicolaus, "The Professor, The Policeman and the Peasant," *Viet-Report* (June–July, 1966), pp. 15–19.

garrison state and military–industrial economy, has been the royal road to aggravated statism in America. On the contrary, the surge of reverent patriotism that war brings to conservative hearts, coupled with their eagerness to don buckler and armor against the "international Communist conspiracy," has made the conservatives the most eager and enthusiastic partisans of the Cold War. Hence their inability to see the enormous distortions and interventions imposed upon the economy by the enormous system of war contracts.[5]

Another conservative blind spot is their failure to identify which groups have been responsible for the burgeoning of statism in the United States. In the conservative demonology, the responsibility belongs only to liberal intellectuals, aided and abetted by trade unions and farmers. Big businessmen, on the other hand, are curiously exempt from blame (farmers are small enough businessmen, apparently, to be fair game for censure). How, then, do conservatives deal with the glaringly evident onrush of big businessmen to embrace Lyndon Johnson and the Great Society? Either by mass stupidity (failure to read the works of free-market economists), subversion by liberal intellectuals (e.g., the education of the Rockefeller brothers at Lincoln School), or craven cowardice (the failure to stand foursquare for free market principles in the face of governmental powers). Almost never is interest pinpointed as an overriding reason for statism among businessmen. This failure is all the more curious in the light of the fact that the laissez-faire liberals of the eighteenth and nineteenth centuries (e.g., the Philosophical Radicals in England, the Jacksonians in the United States) were never bashful about identifying and attacking the web of special privileges granted to businessmen in the mercantilism of their day.

In fact, one of the main driving forces of the statist dynamic of twentieth century America has been big businessmen, and this long before the Great Society. Gabriel Kolko, in his path-breaking *Triumph of Conservatism*,[6] has shown that the shift toward statism in the Progressive period was impelled by the very big business groups who were

---

[5]Thus, cf. H. L. Nieburg, *In the Name of Science* (Chicago: 1966); Seymour Melman, *Our Depleted Society* (New York: 1965); C. Wright Mills, *The Power Elite* (New York: 1956).

[6](New York: 1963). Also see Kolko's *Railroads and Regulation* (Princeton, N. J.: 1965). The laudatory reviews of the latter book by George W. Hilton *(American Economic Review)* and George W. Wilson *(Journal of Political Economy)* symbolize a potential alliance between "new left" and free-market historiography.

supposed, in the liberal mythology, to be defeated and regulated by the Progressive and New Freedom measures. Rather than a "people's movement" to check big business, the drive for regulatory measures, Kolko shows, stemmed from big businessmen whose attempts at monopoly had been defeated by the competitive market, and who then turned to the federal government as a device for compulsory cartellization. This drive for cartellization through government accelerated during the New Era of the 1920s and reached its apex in Franklin Roosevelt's NRA. Significantly, this exercise in cartellizing collectivism was put over by organized big business; after Herbert Hoover, who had done much to organize and cartellize the economy, had balked at an NRA as going too far toward an outright fascist economy, the U.S. Chamber of Commerce won a promise from FDR that he would adopt such a system. The original inspiration was the corporate state of Mussolini's Italy.[7]

The formal corporation of the NRA is long gone, but the Great Society retains much of its essence. The locus of social power has been emphatically assumed by the state apparatus. Furthermore, that apparatus is permanently governed by a coalition of big business, big labor groupings, groups that use the state to operate and manage the national economy. The usual tripartite rapprochement of big business, big unions, and big government symbolizes the organization of society by blocs, syndics, and corporations, regulated and privileged by the federal, state, and local governments. What this all amounts to in essence is the "corporate state," which during the 1920s served as a beacon light for big businessmen, big unions, and many liberal intellectuals as the economic system proper to a twentieth century industrial society.[8]

The indispensable intellectual role of engineering popular consent for state rule is played, for the Great Society, by the liberal intelligentsia, who provide the rationale of "general welfare," "humanity,"

---

[7]The national Recovery Administration, one of the most important creations of the early New Deal, was established by the National Industrial Recovery Act of June, 1933. It prescribed and imposed codes of "fair competition" upon industry. It was declared unconstitutional by the Supreme Court in 1935. For an analysis of the inception of the NRA, see my *America's Great Depression* (Princeton, N. J.: 1963).

[8]Part of this story has been told in John P. Diggins, "Flirtation with Fascism: American Pragmatic Liberals and Mussolini's Italy," *American Historical Review*, LXXI (January, 1966), pp. 487–506.

and the "common good" (just as the conservative intellectuals work the other side of the Great Society street by offering the rationale of "national security" and "national interest"). The liberals, in short, push the "welfare" part of our omnipresent welfare–warfare state, while the conservatives stress the warfare side of the pie. This analysis of the role of the liberal intellectuals puts into more sophisticated perspective the seeming "sellout" of these intellectuals as compared to their role during the 1930s. Thus, among numerous other examples, there is the seemingly anomaly of A. A. Berle and David Lilienthal, cheered and damned as flaming progressives in the thirties, now writing tomes hailing the new reign of big business. Actually, their basic views have not changed in the least. In the thirties, these theoreticians of the New Deal were concerned with condemning as "reactionaries" those big businessmen who clung to older individualist ideals and failed to understand or adhere to the new monopoly system of the corporate state. But now, in the 1950s and 1960s, this battle has been won, big businessmen are all eager to be privileged monopolists in the new dispensation, and hence they can now be welcomed by such theorists as Berle and Lilienthal as "responsible" and "enlightened," their "selfish" individualism a relic of the past.

The cruellest myth fostered by the liberals is that the Great Society functions as a great boon and benefit to the poor; in reality, when we cut through the frothy appearances to the cold reality underneath, the poor are the major victims of the welfare state. The poor are the ones to be conscripted to fight and die at literally slave wages in the Great Society's imperial war. The poor are the ones to lose their homes to the bulldozer of urban renewal, that bulldozer that operates for the benefit of real estate and construction interests to pulverize available low-cost housing.[9] All this, of course, in the name of "clearing the slums" and helping the aesthetics of housing. The poor are the welfare clientele whose homes are unconstitutionally but regularly invaded by government agents to ferret out sin in the middle of the night. The poor (e.g., Negroes in the South) are the ones disemployed by rising minimum wage floors, put in for the benefit of employers and unions in higher-wage areas (e.g., the North) to prevent industry from moving to the low-wage areas. The poor are cruelly victimized by an income tax that left and right alike misconstrue as an egalitarian program to soak the rich; actually, various tricks and exemptions insure

---

[9]See Martin Anderson, *The Federal Bulldozer* (Cambridge, Mass.: 1964).

that it is the poor and the middle classes who are hit the hardest.[10] The poor are victimized too by a welfare state of which the cardinal macro-economic tenet is perpetual if controlled inflation. The inflation and the heavy government spending favor the businesses of the military–industrial complex, while the poor and the retired, those on fixed pensions or Social Security, are hit the hardest. (Liberals have often scoffed at the anti-inflationists' stress on the "widows and orphans" as major victims of inflation, but these remain major victims nevertheless.) And the burgeoning of compulsory mass public education forces millions of unwilling youth off the labor market for many years, and into schools that serve more as houses of detention than as genuine centers of education.[11] Farm programs that supposedly aid poor farmers actually serve the large wealthy farmers at the expense of sharecropper and consumer alike; and commissions that regulate industry serve to cartellize it. The mass of workers is forced by governmental measures into trade unions that tame and integrate the labor force into the toils of the accelerating corporate state, there to be subjected to arbitrary wage "guidelines" and ultimate compulsory arbitration.

The role of the liberal intellectual and of liberal rhetoric is even more stark in foreign economic policy. Ostensibly designed to "help the underdeveloped countries," foreign aid has served as a gigantic subsidy by the American taxpayer of American export firms, a similar subsidy to American foreign investment through guarantees and subsidized government loans, an engine of inflation for the recipient country, and a form of massive subsidy to the friends and clients of U.S. imperialism in the recipient country.

The symbiosis between liberal intellectuals and despotic statism at home and abroad is, furthermore, no accident; for at the heart of the welfarist mentality is an enormous desire to "do good to" the mass of other people, and since people don't usually wish to be done good to, since they have their own ideas of what they wish to do, the liberal welfarist inevitably ends by reaching for the big stick with which to push the ungrateful masses around. Hence, the liberal ethos itself provides a powerful stimulant for the intellectuals to seek state power and ally themselves with the other rulers of the corporate state. The liberals

---

[10]Thus, see Gabriel Kolko, *Wealth and Power in America* (New York: 1962).
[11]Thus, see Paul Goodman, *Compulsory Mis-Education and The Community of Scholars* (New York: Vintage Books, 1966).

thus become what Harry Elmer Barnes has aptly termed "totalitarian liberals." Or, as Isabel Paterson put it a generation ago:

> The humanitarian wishes to be a prime mover in the lives of others. He cannot admit either the divine or the natural order, by which men have the power to help themselves. The humanitarian puts himself in the place of God.
> But he is confronted by two awkward facts; first, that the competent do not need his assistance; and second, that the majority of people ... positively do not want to be 'done good' by the humanitarian. ... Of course, what the humanitarian actually proposes is that he shall do what he thinks is good for everybody. It is at this point that the humanitarian sets up the guillotine.[12]

The rhetorical role of welfarism in pushing people around may be seen clearly in the Vietnam War, where American liberal planning for alleged Vietnamese welfare has been particularly prominent, e.g., in the plans and actions of Wolf Ladejinsky, Joseph Buttinger, and the Michigan State group. And the result has been very much of an American–operated "guillotine" for the Vietnamese people, North and South.[13] And even *Fortune* magazine invokes the spirit of humanitarian "idealism" as the justification for the United States' falling "heir to the onerous task of policing these shattered colonies" of Western Europe, and exerting its might all over the world. The will to make this exertion to the uttermost, especially in Vietnam and perhaps China, constitutes for *Fortune,* "the unending test of American idealism."[14] This liberal–welfarist syndrome may also be seen in the very different area of civil rights, in the terribly pained indignation of white liberals at the recent determination of Negroes to take the lead in helping themselves, rather than to keep deferring to the Lords and Ladies Bountiful of white liberalism.

In sum, the most important fact about the Great Society under which we live is the enormous disparity between rhetoric and content.

---

[12]Isabel Paterson, *The God of the Machine* (New York: 1943), p. 241.

[13]See John McDermott, "Welfare Imperialism in Vietnam," *The Nation* (July 25, 1966), pp. 76–88. Cf. readings 32 and 34.

[14]*Fortune* (August, 1965). As the right wing of the Great Society Establishment, Fortune presumably passes the Berle–Lilienthal test as spokesman for "enlightened" as opposed to narrowly "selfish" capitalism.

In rhetoric, America is the land of the free and the generous, enjoying the fused blessings of a free market tempered by and joined to accelerating social welfare, bountifully distributing its unstinting largesse to the less fortunate in the world. In actual practice, the free economy is virtually gone, replaced by an imperial corporate state Leviathan that organizes, commands, exploits the rest of society and, indeed, the rest of the world, for its own power and pelf. We have experienced, as Garet Garrett keenly pointed out over a decade ago, a "revolution within the form."[15] The old limited republic has been replaced by Empire, within and without our borders.

[15]Garet Garrett, *The People's Pottage* (Caldwell, Idaho: 1953).

BIBLIOGRAPHY

(In addition to the works included in the body of this section, the editors also recommend the following.)

Buckley, William. *The National Review.* New York: National Review, Inc., weekly.

Chamberlin, John. *The Roots of Capitalism.* Princeton, New Jersey: D. Van Nostrand Co., 1959.

Friedman, Milton and Heller, Walter. *Monetary vs. Fiscal Policy.* New York: W. W. Norton & Co., 1969.

Friedman, Milton. Weekly column in *Newsweek.*

Hazlitt, Henry. *The Failure of the "New Economics": An Analysis of the Keynesian Fallacies.* Princeton, New Jersey: D. Van Nostrand Co., 1959.

Kirk, Russell. *The Conservative Mind.* Chicago: H. Regnery & Co., Gateway Editions, 1960.

Knight, Frank. *Freedom and Reform.* New York: Harper and Brothers, 1947.

Rand, Ayn. *Capitalism: The Unknown Ideal.* New York: New American Library, Signet Books, 1967.

Ropke, Wilhelm. *The Humane Economy: The Social Framework of the Free Market.* Chicago: H. Regnery & Co., 1960.

Snyder, Carl. *Capitalism the Creator: The Economic Foundations of Modern Industrial Society.* New York: The Macmillan Co., 1940.

von Hayek, Friedrich. *Studies in Philosophy, Politics, and Economics.* New York: Simon and Schuster, 1967.

von Mises, Ludwig. *Human Action: A Treatise on Economics.* New Haven: Yale University Press, 1949.

————. *Socialism: An Economic and Sociological Analysis.* New Haven: Yale University Press, 1959.

Wallich, Henry C. *The Cost of Freedom.* New York: Collier Books, 1962.

Wright, David M. *Capitalism.* Chicago: H. Regnery & Co., Gateway Editions, 1962.

PART 2

THE LIBERAL VIEW

INTRODUCTION

Liberalism as used in this section is not the nineteenth-century liberalism described in Friedman's article. It can be regarded, however, as a reaction to that laissez-faire philosophy. The political economists of Adam Smith's day were concerned with unleashing the productive potential of the economy. They felt that this could be best accomplished under laissez-faire capitalism. In such a system each individual would be allowed to follow his basic psychological drive, the pursuit of his own self-interest. A key element in the system is that in doing so, he would also maximize the welfare of society. The role of the government, according to this philosophy, would have to be kept to a minimum, in fear that it would restrict individual freedom and thus the well-being of society. The idea of the existence of such a natural order in society, bolstered by the economic theories of David Ricardo and John Stuart Mill, became dominant in England during the first half of the nineteenth century. With Mill, however, a transition can be seen from the more fundamental philosophy of laissez-faire to one of a more aggressive role for government and other cooperative ventures, in order to correct the abuses developing during industrialization within the competitive market system. Recognizing the poor conditions of the working classes and the lack of concern shown by the industrialists, some writers broke from the traditional support of the laissez-faire system completely and predicted that the contradictions within capitalism would bring about its downfall. Most renowned among this group was, of course, Karl Marx. Others, however, were more concerned with preserving the basic institutions of capitalism but realized that they needed modification. These men became the "liberal reformers," and it is here that liberalism changes its meaning from one of support of the laissez-faire system to one of correcting its abuses. In England this feeling manifested itself in the passage of the Factory Acts and other regulatory measures for business in the second half of the nineteenth century, and the movement toward the welfare state in the twentieth century. In America, the movements of Progressivism, New Dealism, and the Great Society, are all examples of reform liberalism which aimed at ameliorating the ills of capitalism. In some cases, the force relied upon for reform was the social conscience of the businessman. Most often, however, it meant an increasing role for the government in controlling economic activity. From the thrust of the liberal movement, it can be seen that it is not an attempt to replace the capitalist system and its institutions but to correct its areas of malfunctioning. Liberal attempts to save capitalism from its own destruction have resulted in a mixed economy with the professed goals of providing for a more equitable distribution of income and of humanizing the competitive market system. Based on these objectives, the role of the government has been expanded to include the tasks of providing for full employment, economic growth, and a variety of social welfare programs. The underlying liberal position is that the laissez-faire economy, supported by modern conservatives, cannot or will not act to correct the problems of modern capitalism. The economic theories of Keynes have provided the basic insight necessary for modifying capitalism and have been accepted by the mainstream of liberal thought. Like conservatives, the liberals are concerned with individual freedom. But unlike them, they feel that competitive capitalism denies certain groups in society an equal economic and political role, and that the government can redress this imbalance by creating an environment in which each individual can make of himself all he is capable of being. Although such a philosophy often means curtailing the freedoms of some individuals, it is directed toward raising the total level of freedom and well-being in the society.

Intellectuals have played an important role in directing the movement toward a mixed economy. This is partially due to the fact that their technical expertise was needed and partially due to a strong "calling" which they undoubtedly felt. An insider's view of this benevolent spirit is given in Daniel P. Moynihan's article. The reader should also note the expectations of Schumpeter and Galbraith on the role of the intellectual in society. Their articles also provide an interesting contrast with Hayek's contention that a complex economy necessitates less, and not more, economic planning.

One of the forces that is seized upon by the liberals represented here as being instrumental in moving capitalism toward planning is the nature of technological change. Differing viewpoints on the impact of technological change and the availability of investment opportunities cause the authors presented here to come up with some interesting projections on the future of capitalism. Each feels in his own way that the advancing level of technology is somewhat destructive of the system which generates it and is incompatible with competitive capitalism. It is also instructive to compare the views of the liberals with those of such radicals as Marx and Veblen on the impact of technological change on the future of capitalism.

A close look at the liberal positions in this section will indicate that in general they agree that the government possesses the power to correct the problems which arise within capitalism without a radical change in its basic economic institutions. They show that capitalism will inevitably, and even desirably, move in the direction of greater federal management of the economy, a movement which most believe should be aided by enlightened intellectuals rather than the business community. Both Moynihan and Galbraith must be considered part of the elite eastern liberal establishment whose ideas have influenced the direction of the welfare state. Among this elite group, liberal political, and economic ideas usually converge. On lower levels, however, liberal economic objectives may conflict with more conservative feelings on such issues as civil rights or foreign policy. Even on economic and social issues, liberalism often extends about as far as the tolerance for paying taxes will allow it to. Thus not only is it difficult to classify an individual as a liberal or a nonliberal on the full range of problems, but it is increasingly evident that there is a large gap between the ideals of the liberal elite and the "lower classes." Although liberalism is undoubtedly the dominant tenor of opinion in America, the pace of change is likely to be slow since it depends on the evolution of thinking of the masses of the people and the willingness of the business community to adopt the reforms advocated by the liberals. The speed with which this transition is taking place is disturbing not only to the liberal elite, but to the conservatives, and the radicals as well.

——R. R.

5

◀ JOHN STUART MILL* ▶

from
The Principles of Political Economy (1848)

Brought up under the rigid standards of utilitarianism, which formed the psychological foundation of classical economic thought, John Stuart Mill later partially abandoned this faith in an attempt to effect a reconciliation between capitalism and socialism. On the one hand he was sympathetic to the cooperative, egalitarian ethic of a socialist society; he favored increasing land taxes as a step towards land nationalization, profit sharing as a step towards the formation of cooperative societies of producers, and severe limits on inheritance rights. On the other hand he saw considerable virtue in the competitive capitalist model; it supposedly tended to yield higher wages and lower consumer goods prices than would otherwise prevail, and provided a stimulus for economic activity. In the selection presented here Mill provides evidence of the overlapping convictions which make him a transitional figure in the shift from a laissez-faire economy to an interventionist government. Mill concluded that the socialist schemes developed during his period were "workable only by the elite of mankind. . . . However valuable as an ideal, and even as a prophecy of ultimate possibilities, [socialism] is not available as a present resource. . . . For a long period to come the principle of individual property will be in possession of the field."

Unlike the early classical economists, such as Smith, Ricardo, Say, and Malthus, Mill considered the right of private property as a qualified rather than an absolute one. Although the precise line of de-

---

*(1806–1873)

marcation is unclear in Mill's writings, he apparently believed that if legislation reduced the initial level of inequality, the social evils associated with private property would be significantly lessened. Mill believed that there was considerable room for integrating gradualistic reform measures within the framework of the market system. Unlike Marx he did not view class conflict as a necessary feature of a capitalist system. Still less did he see this conflict as an engine of revolutionary change. He said "where the rich are content with being rich and do not claim as such any political privileges, their interest and that of the poor are generally the same." This approach bypasses the important empirical question of whether in fact there has been a close connection between economic and political power. Most present day liberals and radicals would answer in the affirmative.

Mill's popular economic treatise, *Principles of Political Economy,* reflected not only his importance as a transitional thinker, but also served to sum up the thinking of the classical school; this book went on to become the leading text for over twenty-five years. Like Smith's other followers, Mill saw that profits had a tendency to decline in a competitive economy. He believed, however, that there were certain circumstances which counteracted the downward tendency of profits. These included technological improvements, which provided an outlet for absorbing the savings of businessmen, and the export of capital to colonies or foreign countries to seek higher profits than could be obtained at home. Mill thought that the latter method was crucially important in arresting the decline of profits in England. As an original extension of classical thought, Mill foresaw the day when continued capital accumulation would force the rate of profit down to a minimum and create a stationary state. The inevitability of such a state was due to the fact that Mill believed that the knowledge of physical laws of production had boundaries, and thus at some point in time technological change would cease. Mill viewed this state with aversion only if the country was in a backward stage of development. Otherwise the stationary state would result in the mental and moral improvement of the species, particularly since he expected it to be accompanied by a shortening of the workday and a lessening of mechanical drudgery. Mill did note, nevertheless, that birth control was a prerequisite for an improvement in the status of the working class. This represented a considerable change from Adam Smith who claimed that when a country attained a fully developed wealthy stage, competition would cause profits as well as wages to be very low.

In the excerpt presented here Mill describes the conditions that would exist under the stationary state. His projection of the future of capitalism is similar to that of Keynes' presented in the next selection. Perhaps because of this projection, and due to the fact that Mill astutely notes that the key economic problem faced by a country is related to its stage of development, he saw the distribution problem as coming more and more to the fore. "It is only in the backward countries of the world that increased production is still an important object; in those most advanced, what is economically needed is a better distribution . . ."

Today it is interesting to note that, although Mill saw nineteenth century England on the verge of pleasant stagnation, the ultimate limits of technological change do not seem to have been reached. In fact it is increasingly obvious that technological improvements grow at an exponential rate and that if capitalism does ultimately stagnate it is unlikely to do so for the lack of new technological frontiers.

———M. L.

from

The Principles of Political Economy

ON THE PROBABLE FUTURITY OF THE LABORING CLASSES

. . . A people who have once adopted the large system of production, either in manufactures or in agriculture, are not likely to recede from it; and when population is kept in due proportion to the means of support, it is not desirable that they should. Labor is unquestionably more productive on the system of large industrial enterprises; the produce, if not greater absolutely, is greater in proportion to the labor employed: the same number of persons can be supported equally well with less toil and greater leisure; which will be wholly an advantage, as soon as civilization and improvement have so far advanced, that what is a benefit to the whole shall be a benefit to each individual composing it. And in the moral aspect of the question, which is still more important than the economical, something better should be aimed at as the goal of industrial improvement, than to disperse mankind over the earth in single families, each ruled internally, as families now are, by a patriarchal despot, and having scarcely any community of interest, or necessary mental communion, with other human beings. The domination of the head of the family over the other members, in this state of things, is absolute; while the effect on his own mind tends towards concentration of all interests in the family, considered as an expansion of self, and absorption of all passions in that of exclusive possession, of all cares in those of preservation and acquisition. As a step out of the merely animal state into the human, out of reckless abandonment to brute instincts into prudential foresight and self-government, this moral condition may be seen without displeasure. But if public spirit, generous

sentiments, or true justice and equality are desired, association, not isolation, of interests, is the school in which these excellences are nurtured.
The aim of improvement should be not solely to place human beings
in a condition in which they will be able to do without one another,
but to enable them to work with or for one another in relations not
involving dependence. Hitherto there has been no alternative for those
who lived by their labor, but that of laboring either each for himself
alone, or for a master. But the civilizing and improving influences of
association, and the efficiency and economy of production on a large
scale, may be obtained without dividing the producers into two parties
with hostile interests and feelings, the many who do the work being
mere servants under the command of the one who supplies the funds,
and having no interest of their own in the enterprise except to earn
their wages with as little labor as possible. The speculations and discussions of the last fifty years, and the events of the last thirty, are
abundantly conclusive on this point. If the improvement which even
triumphant military despotism has only retarded, not stopped, shall
continue its course, there can be little doubt that the *status* of hired
laborers will gradually tend to confine itself to the description of work-
people whose low moral qualities render them unfit for anything more
independent: and that the relation of masters and workpeople will be
gradually superseded by partnership, in one of two forms: in some
cases, association of the laborers with the capitalist; in others, and perhaps finally in all, association of laborers among themselves. . . .

The form of association, however, which if mankind continue
to improve, must be expected in the end to predominate, is not that
which can exist between a capitalist as chief, and work-people without
a voice in the management, but the association of the laborers themselves on terms of equality, collectively owning the capital with which
they carry on their operations, and working under managers elected
and removable by themselves. . . .

When . . . co-operative societies shall have sufficiently multiplied,
it is not probable that any but the least valuable work-people will any
longer consent to work all their lives for wages merely; both private
capitalists and associations will gradually find it necessary to make the
entire body of laborers participants in profits. Eventually, and in perhaps a less remote future than may be supposed, we may, through the
co-operative principle, see our way to a change in society, which would
combine the freedom and independence of the individual, with the
moral, intellectual, and economical advantages of aggregate production; and which, without violence or spoliation, or even any sudden

disturbance of existing habits and expectations, would realize, at least in the industrial department, the best aspirations of the democratic spirit, by putting an end to the division of society into the industrious and the idle, and effacing all social distinctions but those fairly earned by personal services and exertions. Associations like those which we have described, by the very process of their success, are a course of education in those moral and active qualities by which alone success can be either deserved or attained. As associations multiplied, they would tend more and more to absorb all work-people, except those who have too little understanding, or too little virtue, to be capable of learning to act on any other system than that of narrow selfishness. As this change proceeded, owners of capital would gradually find it to their advantage, instead of maintaining the struggle of the old system with work-people of only the worst description, to lend their capital to the associations; to do this at a diminishing rate of interest, and at last, perhaps, even to exchange their capital for terminable annuities. In this or some such mode, the existing accumulations of capital might honestly, and by a kind of spontaneous process, become in the end the joint property of all who participate in their productive employment: a transformation which, thus effected, (and assuming of course that both sexes participate equally in the rights and in the government of the association), would be the nearest approach to social justice, and the most beneficial ordering of industrial affairs for the universal good, which it is possible at present to foresee.

I agree, then, with the Socialist writers in their conception of the form which industrial operations tend to assume in the advance of improvement; and I entirely share their opinion that the time is ripe for commencing this transformation, and that it should by all just and effectual means be aided and encouraged. But while I agree and sympathize with Socialists in this practical portion of their aims, I utterly dissent from the most conspicuous and vehement part of their teaching, their declamations against competition. With moral conceptions in many respects far ahead of the existing arrangements of society, they have in general very confused and erroneous notions of its actual working; and one of their greatest errors, as I conceive, is to charge upon competition all the economical evils which at present exist. They forget that wherever competition is not, monopoly is; and that monopoly, in all its forms, is the taxation of the industrious for the support of indolence, if not of plunder. They forget, too, that with the exception of competition among laborers, all other competition is for the benefit of the laborers, by cheapening the articles they consume; that competition even in the labor market is a source not of low but of high wages, wherever the competition *for* labor exceeds the competition *of* labor, as in America, in the colonies, and in the skilled trades; and never could be a cause of low wages, save by the overstocking of the labor market through the too great numbers of the laborer's families; while, if the supply of laborers is excessive, not even Socialism can prevent their remuneration from being low. Besides, if association were universal, there would be no competition between laborer and laborer; and that between association and association would be for the benefit of the consumers, that is, of the associations; of the industrious classes generally.

I do not pretend that there are no inconveniences in competition, or that the moral objections urged against it by Socialist writers, as a source of jealousy and hostility among those engaged in the same occupation, are altogether groundless. But if competition has its evils, it prevents greater evils. As M. Feugueray well says, "The deepest root of the evils and iniquities which fill the industrial world, is not competition, but the subjection of labor to capital, and the enormous share which the possessors of the instruments of industry are able to take from the produce. . . . If competition has great power for evil, it is no less fertile of good, especially in what regards the development of the individual faculties, and the success of innovations." It is the common error of Socialists to overlook the natural indolence of mankind; their tendency to be passive, to be the slaves of habit, to persist indefinitely in a course once chosen. Let them once attain any state of existence which they consider tolerable, and the danger to be apprehended is that they will thenceforth stagnate; will not exert themselves to improve, and by letting their faculties rust, will lose even the energy required to preserve them from deterioration. Competition may not be the best conceivable stimulus, but it is at present a necessary one, and no one can foresee the time when it will not be indispensable to progress. Even confining ourselves to the industrial department, in which, more than in any other, the majority may be supposed to be competent judges of improvements; it would be difficult to induce the general assembly of an association to submit to the trouble and inconvenience of altering their habits by adopting some new and promising invention, unless their knowledge of the existence of rival associations made them apprehend that what they would not consent to do, others would, and that they would be left behind in the race.

Instead of looking upon competition as the baneful and antisocial principle which it is held to be by the generality of Socialists, I conceive that, even in the present state of society and industry, every restriction of it is an evil, and every extension of it, even if for the time injuriously affecting some class of laborers, is always an ultimate good. To be protected against competition is to be protected in idleness, in mental dulness; to be saved the necessity of being as active and as intelligent as other people; and if it is also to be protected against being underbid for employment by a less highly paid class of laborers, this is only where old custom, or local and partial monopoly, has placed some particular class of artizans in a privileged position as compared with the rest; and the time has come when the interest of universal improvement is no longer promoted by prolonging the privileges of a few. If the slop-sellers and others of their class have lowered the wages of tailors, and some other artizans, by making them an affair of competition instead of custom, so much the better in the end. What is now required is not to bolster up old customs, whereby limited classes of laboring people obtain partial gains which interest them in keeping up the present organization of society, but to introduce new general practices beneficial to all; and there is reason to rejoice at whatever makes the privileged classes of skilled artizans feel that they have the same interests, and depend for their remuneration on the same general causes, and must resort for the improvement of their condition to the same remedies, as the less fortunately circumstanced and comparatively helpless multitude.

TENDENCY OF PROFITS TO A MINIMUM

... There is at every time and place some particular rate of profit, which is the lowest that will induce the people of that country and time to accumulate savings, and to employ those savings productively....

... This minimum rate of profit, less than which is not consistent with the further increase of capital, is lower in some states of society than in others; and I may add, that the kind of social progress characteristic of our present civilization tends to diminish it....

When a country has long possessed a large production, and a large net income to make savings from, and when, therefore, the means have long existed of making a great annual addition to capital; (the country not having, like America [1848], a large reserve of fertile land still unused;) it is one of the characteristics of such a country, that the rate of profit is habitually within, as it were, a hand's breadth of the

minimum, and the country therefore on the very verge of the stationary
state. By this I do not mean that this state is likely, in any of the great
countries of Europe, to be soon actually reached, or that capital does
not still yield a profit considerably greater than what is barely sufficient
to induce the people of those countries to save and accumulate. My
meaning is, that it would require but a short time to reduce profits to
the minimum, if capital continued to increase at its present rate, and no
circumstances having a tendency to raise the rate of profit occurred in
the meantime. The expansion of capital would soon reach its ultimate
boundary, if the boundary itself did not continually open and leave
more space. . . .

To fulfil the conditions of the hypothesis, we must suppose an
entire cessation of the exportation of capital for foreign investment.
No more capital sent abroad for railways or loans; no more emigrants
taking capital with them, to the colonies, or to other countries; no fresh
advances made, or credits given, by bankers or merchants to their foreign correspondents. We must also assume that there are no fresh loans
for unproductive expenditure, by the government, or on mortgage, or
otherwise; and none of the waste of capital which now takes place by
the failure of undertakings which people are tempted to engage in by
the hope of a better income than can be obtained in safe paths at the
present habitually low rate of profit. We must suppose the entire savings of the community to be annually invested in really productive
employment within the country itself; and no new channels opened
by industrial inventions, or by a more extensive substitution of the best
known processes for inferior ones.

Few persons would hesitate to say, that there would be great
difficulty in finding remunerative employment every year for so much
new capital, and most would conclude that there would be what used
to be termed a general glut; that commodities would be produced, and
remain unsold, or be sold only at a loss. But the full examination . . .
already given to this question, has shown that this is not the
mode in which the inconvenience would be experienced. The difficulty
would not consist in any want of a market. If the new capital were duly
shared among many varieties of employment, it would raise up a demand for its own produce, and there would be no cause why any part
of that produce should remain longer on hand than formerly. What
would really be, not merely difficult, but impossible, would be to employ
this capital without submitting to a rapid reduction of the rate of profit.

As capital increased, population either would also increase, or it would not. If it did not, wages would rise, and a greater capital would be distributed in wages among the same number of laborers. There being no more labor than before, and no improvements to render the labor more efficient, there would not be any increase of the produce; and as the capital, however largely increased, would only obtain the same gross return, the whole savings of each year would be exactly so much subtracted from the profits of the next and of every following year. It is hardly necessary to say that in such circumstances profits would very soon fall to the point at which further increase of capital would cease. An augmentation of capital, much more rapid than that of population, must soon reach its extreme limit, unless accompanied by increased efficiency of labor (through inventions and discoveries, or improved mental and physical education), or unless some of the idle people, or of the unproductive laborers, became productive.

If population did increase with the increase of capital and in proportion to it, the fall of profits would still be inevitable. Increased population implies increased demand for agricultural produce. In the absence of industrial improvements, this demand can only be supplied at an increased cost of production, either by cultivating worse land, or by a more elaborate and costly cultivation of the land already under tillage. The cost of the laborer's subsistence is therefore increased; and unless the laborer submits to a deterioration of his condition, profits must fall. In an old country like England, if, in addition to supposing all improvement in domestic agriculture suspended, we suppose that there is no increased production in foreign countries for the English market, the fall of profits would be very rapid. If both these avenues to an increased supply of food were closed, and population continued to increase, as it is said to do, at the rate of a thousand a day, all waste land which admits of cultivation in the existing state of knowledge would soon be cultivated, and the cost of production and price of food would be so increased, that, if the laborers received the increased money wages necessary to compensate for their increased expenses, profits would very soon reach the minimum. The fall of profits would be retarded if money wages did not rise, or rose in a less degree; but the margin which can be gained by a deterioration of the laborers' condition is a very narrow one: in general they *cannot* bear much reduction; when they can, they have also a higher standard of necessary requirements, and *will* not. On the whole, therefore, we may assume that in such a country as England, if the present annual amount of savings were to continue, without any of the counteracting circumstances which now keep in check the natural influence of those savings in reducing profit, the rate of profit would speedily attain the minimum, and all further accumulation of capital would for the present cease.

What, then, are these counteracting circumstances, which, in the existing state of things, maintain a tolerably equal struggle against the downward tendency of profits, and prevent the great annual savings which take place in this country from depressing the rate of profit much nearer to that lowest point to which it is always tending, and which, left to itself, it would so promptly attain? . . .

This brings us to [one] of the counter-agencies, namely, improvements in production. These evidently have the effect of extending . . . the field of employment, that is, they enable a greater amount of capital to be accumulated and employed without depressing the rate of profit: provided always that they do not raise, to a proportional extent, the habits and requirements of the laborer. If the laboring class gain the full advantage of the increased cheapness, in other words, if money wages do not fall, profits are not raised, nor their fall retarded. But if the laborers people up to the improvement in their condition, and so relapse to their previous state, profits will rise. All inventions which cheapen any of the things consumed by the laborers, unless their requirements are raised in an equivalent degree, in time lower money wages: and by doing so, enable a greater capital to be accumulated and employed, before profits fall back to what they were previously.

Improvements which only affect things consumed exclusively by the richer classes, do not operate precisely in the same manner. The cheapening of lace or velvet has no effect in diminishing the cost of labor; and no mode can be pointed out in which it can raise the rate of profit, so as to make room for a larger capital before the minimum is attained. It, however, produces an effect which is virtually equivalent; it lowers, or tends to lower, the minimum itself. In the first place, increased cheapness of articles of consumption promotes the inclination to save, by affording to all consumers a surplus which they may lay by, consistently with their accustomed manner of living and unless they were previously suffering actual hardships, it will require little self-denial to save some part at least of this surplus. In the next place, whatever enables people to live equally well on a smaller income, inclines them to lay by capital for a lower rate of profit. If people can live on an independence of 500*l.* a year in the same manner as they formerly could on one of 1000*l*., some persons will be induced to save in hopes of the one, who would have been deterred by the more remote prospect of the other. All improvements, therefore, in the production of almost any commodity, tend in some degree to widen the interval which has to be passed before arriving at the stationary state: but this effect belongs in a much greater degree to the improvements which affect the articles consumed by the laborer, since these conduce to it in two ways; they induce people to accumulate for a lower profit, and they also raise the rate of profit itself. . . .

This brings us to the [next] of the counter-forces which check the downward tendency of profits, in a country whose capital increases faster than that of its neighbours and whose profits are therefore nearer to the minimum. This is, the perpetual overflow of capital into colonies or foreign countries, to seek higher profits than can be obtained at home. I believe this to have been for many years one of the principal causes by which the decline of profits in England has been arrested. It has a twofold operation. In the first place, it does what a fire, or an inundation, or a commercial crisis would have done: it carries off a part of the increase of capital from which the reduction of profits proceeds. Secondly, the capital so carried off is not lost, but is chiefly employed either in founding colonies, which become large exporters of cheap agricultural produce, or in extending and perhaps improving the agriculture of older communities. It is to the emigration of English capital, that we have chiefly to look for keeping up a supply of cheap food and cheap materials for clothing, proportional to the increase of our population; thus enabling an increasing capital to find employment in the country, without reduction of profit, in producing manufactured articles with which to pay for this supply of raw produce. Thus, the exportation of capital is an agent of great efficacy in extending the field of employment for that which remains: and it may be said truly that, up to a certain point, the more capital we send away, the more we shall possess and be able to retain at home.

In countries which are further advanced in industry and population, and have therefore a lower rate of profit, than others, there is always, long before the actual minimum is reached, a practical minimum, viz., when profits have fallen so much below what they are elsewhere, that, were they to fall lower, all further accumulations would go abroad. In the present state of the industry of the world, when there is occasion, in any rich and improving country, to take the minimum of profits at all into consideration for practical purposes, it is only this practical minimum that need be considered. As long as there are old countries where capital increases very rapidly, and new countries where profit is still high, profits in the old countries will not sink to the rate which would put a stop to accumulation; the fall is stopped at the point which sends capital abroad. It is only, however, by improvements in production, and even in the production of things consumed by laborers, that the capital of a country like England is prevented from speedily reaching that degree of lowness of profit, which would cause all further savings to be sent to find employment in the colonies, or in foreign countries.

OF THE STATIONARY STATE

. . . In contemplating any progressive movement, not in its nature unlimited, the mind is not satisfied with merely tracing the laws of the movement; it cannot but ask the further question, to what goal? Towards what ultimate point is society tending by its industrial progress? When the progress ceases, in what condition are we to expect that it will leave mankind?

It must always have been seen, more or less distinctly, by political economists, that the increase of wealth is not boundless: that at the end of what they term the progressive state lies the stationary state, that all progress in wealth is but a postponement of this, and that each step in advance is an approach to it. We have now been led to recognise that this ultimate goal is at all times near enough to be fully in view; that we are always on the verge of it, and that if we have not reached it long ago, it is because the goal itself flies before us. The richest and most prosperous countries would very soon attain the stationary state, if no further improvements were made in the productive arts, and if there were a suspension of the overflow of capital from those countries into the uncultivated or ill-cultivated regions of the earth.

This impossibility of ultimately avoiding the stationary state— this irresistible necessity that the stream of human industry should finally spread itself out into an apparently stagnant sea—must have been, to the political economists of the last two generations, an unpleasing and discouraging prospect; for the tone and tendency of their speculations goes completely to identify all that is economically desirable with the progressive state, and with that alone. With Mr. M'Culloch, for example, prosperity does not mean a large production and a good distribution of wealth, but a rapid increase of it; his test of prosperity is high profits; and as the tendency of that very increase of wealth, which he calls prosperity, is towards low profits, economical progress, according to him, must tend to the extinction of prosperity. Adam Smith always assumes that the condition of the mass of the people, though it may not be positively distressed, must be pinched and stinted in a stationary condition of wealth, and can only be satisfactory in a progressive state. The doctrine that, to however distant a time incessant struggling may put off our doom, the progress of society must "end in shallows and in miseries," far from being, as many people still believe, a wicked invention of Mr. Malthus, was either expressly or tacitly affirmed by his most distinguished predecessors, and can only be successfully combated on his principles. Before attention had been directed to the principle of population as the active force in determining the remuneration of labor, the increase of mankind was virtually treated as a constant quantity; it was, at all events, assumed that in the natural and normal state of human affairs population must constantly increase, from which it followed that a constant increase of the means of support was essential to the physical comfort of the mass of mankind. The publication of Mr. Malthus' *Essay* is the era from which better views of this subject must be dated; and notwithstanding the acknowledged errors of his first edition, few writers have done more than himself, in the subsequent editions, to promote these juster and more helpful anticipations.

Even in a progressive state of capital, in old countries, a conscientious or prudential restraint on population is indispensable, to prevent the increase of numbers from outstripping the increase of capital, and the condition of the classes who are at the bottom of society from being deteriorated. Where there is not, in the people, or in some very large proportion of them, a resolute resistance to this deterioration —a determination to preserve an established standard of comfort—the condition of the poorest class sinks, even in a progressive state, to the lowest point which they will consent to endure. The same determination would be equally effectual to keep up their condition in the stationary state, and would be quite as likely to exist. Indeed, even now, the countries in which the greatest prudence is manifested in the regulating of population are often those in which capital increases least rapidly. Where there is an indefinite prospect of employment for increased numbers, there is apt to appear less necessity for prudential restraint. If it were evident that a new hand could not obtain employment but by displacing, or succeeding to, one already employed, the combined influences of prudence and public opinion might in some measure be relied on for restricting the coming generation within the numbers necessary for replacing the present.

I cannot, therefore, regard the stationary state of capital and wealth with the unaffected aversion so generally manifested towards it by political economists of the old school. I am inclined to believe that it would be, on the whole, a very considerable improvement on our present condition. I confess I am not charmed with the ideal of life held out by those who think that the normal state of human beings is that of struggling to get on; that the trampling, crushing, elbowing, and treading on each other's heels, which form the existing type of social life, are the most desirable lot of human kind, or anything but the disagreeable symptoms of one of the phases of industrial progress. It may be a necessary stage in the progress of civilization, and those European nations which have hitherto been so fortunate as to be preserved from it, may have it yet to undergo. It is an incident of growth, not a mark of decline, for it is not necessarily destructive of the higher aspirations and the heroic virtues; as America, in her great civil war, has proved to the world, both by her conduct as a people and by numerous splendid individual examples, and as England, it is to be hoped, would also prove, on an equally trying and exciting occasion. But it is not a kind of social perfection which philanthropists to come will feel any very eager desire to assist in realizing. Most fitting, indeed, is it, that while riches are power, and to grow as rich as possible the universal object of ambition, the path to its attainment should be open to all, without favour or partiality. But the best state for human nature is that in which, while no one is poor, no one desires to be richer, nor has any reason to fear being thrust back by the efforts of others to push themselves forward.

That the energies of mankind should be kept in employment by the struggle for riches, as they were formerly by the struggle of war, until the better minds succeed in educating the others into better things, is undoubtedly more desirable than that they should rust and stagnate. While minds are coarse they require coarse stimuli, and let them have them. In the meantime, those who do not accept the present very early stage of human improvement as its ultimate type, may be excused for being comparatively indifferent to the kind of economical progress which excites the congratulations of ordinary politicians; the mere increase of production and accumulation. For the safety of national independence it is essential that a country should not fall much behind its neighbours in these things. But in themselves they are of little importance, so long as either the increase of population or anything else prevents the mass of the people from reaping any part of the benefit of them. I know not why it should be matter of congratulation that persons who are already richer than any one needs to be, should have doubled their means of consuming things which give little or no pleasure except as representative of wealth; or that numbers of individuals should pass over, every year, from the middle classes into a richer class, or from the class of the occupied rich to that of the unoccupied. It is only in the backward countries of the world that increased production is still an important object: in those most advanced, what is economically needed is a better distribution, of which one indispensable means is a stricter restraint on population. Levelling institutions, either of a just or of an unjust kind, cannot alone accomplish it; they may lower the heights of society, but they cannot, of themselves, permanently raise the depths.

On the other hand, we may suppose this better distribution of property attained, by the joint effect of the prudence and frugality of individuals, and of a system of legislation favouring equality of fortunes, so far as is consistent with the just claim of the individual to the fruits, whether great or small, of his or her own industry. We may suppose, for instance . . . a limitation of the sum which any one person may acquire by gift or inheritance to the amount sufficient to constitute a moderate independence. Under this twofold influence society would exhibit these leading features: a well-paid and affluent body of laborers; no enormous fortunes, except what were earned and accumulated during a single lifetime; but a much larger body of persons than at present, not only exempt from the coarser toils, but with sufficient leisure, both physical and mental, from mechanical details, to cultivate freely the graces of life, and afford examples of them to the classes less favourably circumstanced for their growth. This condition of society, so greatly preferable to the present, is not only perfectly compatible with the stationary state, but, it would seem, more naturally allied with that state than with any other.

There is room in the world, no doubt, and even in old countries, for a great increase of population, supposing the arts of life to go on improving, and capital to increase. But even if innocuous, I confess I see very little reason for desiring it. The density of population necessary to enable mankind to obtain, in the greatest degree, all the advantages both of co-operation and of social intercourse, has, in all the most populous countries, been attained. A population may be too crowded, though all be amply supplied with food and raiment. It is not good for man to be kept perforce at all times in the presence of his species. A world from which solitude is extirpated is a very poor ideal. Solitude, in the sense of being often alone, is essential to any depth of meditation or of character; and solitude in the presence of natural beauty and grandeur, is the cradle of thoughts and aspirations which are not only good for the individual, but which society could ill do without. Nor is there much satisfaction in contemplating the world with nothing left to the spontaneous activity of nature; with every rood of land brought into cultivation, which is capable of growing food for human beings; every flowery waste or natural pasture ploughed up, all quadrupeds or birds which are not domesticated for man's use exterminated as his rivals for food, every hedgerow or superfluous tree rooted out, and scarcely a place left where a wild shrub or flower could grow without being eradicated as a weed in the name of improved agriculture. If the earth must lose that great portion of its pleasantness which it owes to things that the unlimited increase of wealth and population would extirpate from it, for the mere purpose of enabling it to support a larger, but not a better or happier population, I sincerely hope, for the sake of posterity, that they will be content to be stationary, long before necessity compels them to it.

It is scarcely necessary to remark that a stationary condition of capital and population implies no stationary state of human improvement. There would be as much scope as ever for all kinds of mental culture, and moral and social progress; as much room for improving the Art of Living, and much more likelihood of its being improved, when minds ceased to be engrossed by the art of getting on. Even the industrial arts might be as earnestly and as successfully cultivated, with this sole difference, that instead of serving no purpose but the increase of wealth, industrial improvements would produce their legitimate effect, that of abridging labor. Hitherto [1848] it is questionable if all the mechanical inventions yet made have lightened the day's toil of any human being. They have enabled a greater population to live the same life of drudgery and imprisonment, and an increased number of manufacturers and others to make fortunes. They have increased the comforts of the middle classes. But they have not yet begun to effect those great changes in human destiny, which it is in their nature and in their futurity to accomplish. Only when, in addition to just institutions, the increase of mankind shall be under the deliberate guidance of judicious foresight, can the conquests made from the powers of nature by the intellect and energy of scientific discoverers become the common property of the species, and the means of improving and elevating the universal lot.

6

◀ JOHN MAYNARD KEYNES* ▶

from

Essays in Persuasion

from

The General Theory of Employment, Interest, and Money (1936)

Keynes was undoubtedly the most influential economist of the twentieth century. He was responsible for redirecting the main thrust of economic thinking from a micro level, where the concern was with cost and price phenomena, to a macro level, where the concern was with levels of national income and employment. Keynes correctly claimed that the micro-oriented neo-classical economists assumed away the problems of business cycles through viewing a capitalist society as tending toward a norm of full employment. He posited the view that equilibrium could be at any level of employment, and that the effective demand of the businessman (as evidenced by his investment spending) and of the consumer (indicated by his expenditures) determined the level of employment and income. In order to maintain any given level of income and employment, it was necessary to find investment outlets for the abundant savings generated by rising

---

*(1883–1946)

117

incomes. This suggests that Keynesian economics has considerably more applicability for dealing with the economic problems of an advanced, industrial corporate society than it has for those of the typical underdeveloped country, where the critical problem is to raise the supply of savings in order to create the potential to overcome economic stagnation.

Keynes' rejection of neo-classical theory was influenced by the deep, prolonged depression of the 1930s. He observed that the most volatile element in a business enterprise society was private investment expenditures, determined primarily by profit expectations, and secondarily by the cost of borrowing (the rate of interest). Like Mill, Keynes asserted the possibility of falling profit rates and the stationary state. Keynes provided a rationale for rejecting laissez-faire in favor of a governmental interventionist approach. By demonstrating the small likelihood of unhampered private enterprise being able to sustain equilibrium at full employment, Keynes was able to show the importance of counter-cyclical governmental fiscal and monetary policy which aimed at offsetting undesirable fluctuations in the private sector. As a future projection, Keynes held that "a somewhat comprehensive socialization of investment [this would include all devices, including some public corporations, through which government investment projects would take place] will prove the only means of securing an approximation to full employment."

Despite many criticisms from both conservatives and radicals, this new school of Keynesian economics remains the mainstream of economic thought in the economically advanced countries. Keynesians believed that the price of tinkering with the system to make it more viable, and perhaps less inequitable, was less than the price paid through excessive devotion to laissez-faire principles. Writing in a period of growing political protest, Keynes represented the farsighted liberal view that reformism was the strategic key for preserving the basic features of the status quo. Keynesian economists have successfully checked some of the illusions of their predecessors. They have shown that yearly balancing of the budget can have a destabilizing effect—exacerbating both the expansions and contractions through increasing expenditures and reducing taxes in periods of expansion, and decreasing expenditures and increasing taxes in periods of contraction. They also cast doubt on the efficacy of reducing wages to stimulate employment by stressing that wages were a source of purchasing power to the consumer as well as a cost to the businessman.

The first two of the selections from Keynes are "non-Keynesian," inasmuch as they predate Keynes' sharp break with neoclassicism in his famous *General Theory of Employment, Interest and Money* which came out in 1936. They do, however, dimly foreshadow his later work. He was critical of laissez-faire more than a decade earlier. In pointing out the "tendency of big enterprise to socialize itself,"* he

---

*See the selection from Schumpeter, chapter 10, for an elaboration of this theme.

was the first economist to claim that the drive of corporate managers (as separate from the owners of capital) for stability and the proper corporate reputation was replacing the older, traditional aim of profit maximization. He also indicated in this early essay that some form of public coordination of savings and investment was desirable, a position in sharp contrast with the traditional defense of private enterprise. He searched for a method of reconciling individual initiative with the social controls that appeared to be necessary for dealing with actual problems. This is the hallmark of a pragmatist with a predilection for finding solutions within the framework of a market system. He said:

> I think that Capitalism, wisely managed, can probably be made more efficient for attaining economic ends than any alternative system yet in sight, but that in itself it is in many ways extremely objectionable. Our problem is to work out a social organization which shall be as efficient as possible without offending our notions of a satisfactory way of life.

One of the most important limitations of Keynesian analysis is the narrowness of its focus and assumptions. It is a short-run model which takes the level of technology as given. It is, therefore, not particularly well equipped for dealing with problems of economic development since changes in technology are crucial for dealing with such problems. While post-Keynesian theorists have extended the basic model to deal with the longer-run problems of economic growth in both developed and undeveloped countries, their attempt has been only partially successful. They focus primarily on technical economic growth factors while excluding the political economy of the development process—the distribution of wealth, the political and economic power of domestic and foreign capitalists, and above all the nature of the social system. Hence, the post-Keynesian models have greater manageability, but less realism. Furthermore, the basic rationale of Keynesian-oriented governmental spending is presented in terms of countering cyclical effects rather than in terms of welfare considerations. Here again, modern economic thinking has attempted to extend Keynesian analysis beyond this point, but the results are still inconclusive. Additional criticism of the Keynesian philosophy of governmental intervention is provided by Milton Friedman in chapter 3.

There is little doubt that the ideas of Keynes have had a monumental influence on the science of economics and on governmental economic policy. In the hands of skilled writers, Keynesian economics has been meshed with neoclassical analysis and presented in a form that the layman can readily understand. Keynes deserves credit for vastly enlarging the economist's macroeconomic kit of tools which is directly or indirectly responsible for the high level of precision that has been developed for dealing with the crucial problem of instability in a market system.

——M. L.

from
Essays in Persuasion*

Let us clear from the ground the metaphysical or general principles upon which, from time to time, laissez-faire has been founded.
It is *not* true that individuals possess a prescriptive "natural liberty" in
their economic activities. There is *no* "compact" conferring perpetual
rights on those who Have or on those who Acquire. The world is *not*
so governed from above that private and social interest always coincide.
It is *not* so managed here below that in practice they coincide. It
is *not* a correct deduction from the Principle of Economics that enlightened self-interest always operates in the public interest. Nor is it
true that self-interest generally *is* enlightened; more often individuals
acting separately to promote their own ends are too ignorant or too
weak to attain even these. Experience does *not* show that individuals,
when they make up a social unit, are always less clear-sighted than
when they act separately.

We cannot, therefore, settle on abstract grounds, but must
handle on its merits in detail, what Burke termed "one of the finest
problems in legislation, namely, to determine what the State ought to
take upon itself to direct by the public wisdom, and what it ought to
leave, with as little interference as possible, to individual exertion."
We have to discriminate between what Bentham, in his forgotten but
useful nomenclature, used to term *Agenda* and *Non-Agenda*, and to
do this without Bentham's prior presumption that interference, is at the
same time, "generally needless" and "generally pernicious."[1] Perhaps
the chief task of Economists at this hour is to distinguish afresh the
Agenda of Government from the *Non-Agenda*; and the companion
task of Politics is to devise forms of Government within a Democracy
which shall be capable of accomplishing the *Agenda*. I will illustrate
what I have in mind by two examples.

(1) I believe that in many cases the ideal size for the unit of
control and organisation lies somewhere between the individual and
the modern State. I suggest, therefore, that progress lies in the growth

---

*Reprinted from John Maynard Keynes, *Essays in Persuasion* (New York:
W. W. Norton, 1963).

[1]Bentham's *Manual of Political Economy*, published posthumously, in Bowring's
edition (1843).

and the recognition of semi-autonomous bodies within the State—
bodies whose criterion of action within their own field is solely the
public good as they understand it, and from whose deliberations motives
of private advantage are excluded, though some place it may still be
necessary to leave, until the ambit of men's altruism grows wider, to
the separate advantage of particular groups, classes, or faculties—
bodies which in the ordinary course of affairs are mainly autonomous
within their prescribed limitations, but are subject in the last resort to
the sovereignty of the democracy expressed through Parliament.

I propose a return, it may be said, towards mediaeval conceptions of separate autonomies. But, in England at any rate, corporations
are a mode of government which has never ceased to be important and
is sympathetic to our institutions. It is easy to give examples, from what
already exists, of separate autonomies which have attained or are
approaching the mode I designate—the Universities, the Bank of
England, the Port of London Authority, even perhaps the Railway
Companies.

But more interesting than these is the trend of Joint Stock
Institutions, when they have reached a certain age and size, to approxi-
mate to the status of public corporations rather than that of individualistic private enterprise. One of the most interesting and unnoticed
developments of recent decades has been the tendency of big enterprise
to socialise itself. A point arrives in the growth of a big institution—
particularly a big railway or big public utility enterprise, but also a big
bank or a big insurance company—at which the owners of the capital,
i.e. the shareholders, are almost entirely dissociated from the management, with the result that the direct personal interest of the latter in
the making of great profit becomes quite secondary. When this stage is
reached, the general stability and reputation of the institution are more
considered by the management than the maximum of profit for the
shareholders. The shareholders must be satisfied by conventionally
adequate dividends; but once this is secured, the direct interest of the
management often consists in avoiding criticism from the public and
from the customers of the concern. This is particularly the case if their
great size or semi-monopolistic position renders them conspicuous in
the public eye and vulnerable to public attack. The extreme instance,
perhaps, of this tendency in the case of an institution, theoretically the
unrestricted property of private persons, is the Bank of England. It is
almost true to say that there is no class of persons in the Kingdom of
whom the Governor of the Bank of England thinks less when he
decides on his policy than of his shareholders. Their rights, in excess

of their conventional dividend, have already sunk to the neighbourhood of zero. But the same thing is partly true of many other big institutions. They are, as time goes on, socialising themselves.

Not that this is unmixed gain. The same causes promote conservatism and a waning of enterprise. In fact, we already have in these cases many of the faults as well as the advantages of State Socialism. Nevertheless we see here, I think, a natural line of evolution. The battle of Socialism against unlimited private profit is being won in detail hour by hour. In these particular fields—it remains acute elsewhere—this is no longer the pressing problem. There is, for instance, no so-called important political question so really unimportant, so irrelevant to the reorganisation of the economic life of Great Britain, as the Nationalisation of the Railways.

It is true that many big undertakings, particularly public utility enterprises and other business requiring a large fixed capital, still need to be semi-socialised. But we must keep our minds flexible regarding the forms of this semi-socialism. We must take full advantage of the natural tendencies of the day, and we must probably prefer semi-autonomous corporations to organs of the Central Government for which Ministers of State are directly responsible.

I criticise doctrinaire State Socialism, not because it seeks to engage men's altruistic impulses in the service of Society, or because it departs from laissez-faire, or because it takes away from man's natural liberty to make a million, or because it has courage for bold experiments. All these things I applaud. I criticise it because it misses the significance of what is actually happening; because it is, in fact, little better than a dusty survival of a plan to meet the problems of fifty years ago, based on a misunderstanding of what some one said a hundred years ago. Nineteenth-century State Socialism sprang from Bentham, free competition, etc., and is in some respects a clearer, in some respects a more muddled, version of just the same philosophy as underlies nineteenth-century individualism. Both equally laid all their stress on freedom, the one negatively to avoid limitations on existing freedom, the other positively to destroy natural or acquired monopolies. They are different reactions to the same intellectual atmosphere.

(2) I come next to a criterion of *Agenda* which is particularly relevant to what it is urgent and desirable to do in the near future. We must aim at separating those services which are *technically social* from those which are *technically individual*. The most important *Agenda* of the State relate not to those activities which private individuals are already fulfilling, but to those functions which fall outside

the sphere of the individual, to those decisions which are made by *no one* if the State does not make them. The important thing for Government is not to do things which individuals are doing already, and to do them a little better or a little worse; but to do those things which at present are not done at all.

It is not within the scope of my purpose on this occasion to develop practical policies. I limit myself, therefore, to naming some instances of what I mean from amongst those problems about which I happen to have thought most.

Many of the greatest economic evils of our time are the fruits of risk, uncertainty, and ignorance. It is because particular individuals, fortunate in situation or in abilities, are able to take advantage of uncertainty and ignorance, and also because for the same reason big business is often a lottery, that great inequalities of wealth come about; and these same factors are also the cause of the Unemployment of Labor, or the disappointment of reasonable business expectations, and of the impairment of efficiency and production. Yet the cure lies outside the operations of individuals; it may even be to the interest of individuals to aggravate the disease. I believe that the cure for these things is partly to be sought in the deliberate control of the currency and of credit by a central institution, and partly in the collection and dissemination on a great scale of data relating to the business situation, including the full publicity, by law if necessary, of all business facts which it is useful to know. These measures would involve Society in exercising directive intelligence through some appropriate organ of action over many of the inner intricacies of private business, yet it would leave private initiative and enterprise unhindered. Even if these measures prove insufficient, nevertheless they will furnish us with better knowledge than we have now for taking the next step.

My second example relates to Savings and Investment. I believe that some co-ordinated act of intelligent judgment is required as to the scale on which it is desirable that the community as a whole should save, the scale on which these savings should go abroad in the form of foreign investments, and whether the present organisation of the investment market distributes savings along the most nationally productive channels. I do not think that these matters should be left entirely to the chances of private judgement and private profits, as they are at present.

My third example concerns Population. The time has already come when each country needs a considered national policy about what size of Population, whether larger or smaller than at present or the same, is most expedient. And having settled this policy, we must take steps to carry it into operation. The time may arrive a little later when the community as a whole must pay attention to the innate quality as well as to the mere numbers of its future members.

These reflections have been directed towards possible improvements in the technique of modern Capitalism by the agency of collective action. There is nothing in them which is seriously incompatible with what seems to me to be the essential characteristic of capitalism, namely the dependence upon an intense appeal to the money-making and money-loving instincts of individuals as the main motive force of the economic machine. Nor must I, so near to my end, stray towards other fields. Nevertheless, I may do well to remind you, in conclusion, that the fiercest contests and the most deeply felt divisions of opinion are likely to be waged in the coming years not round technical questions, where the arguments on either side are mainly economic, but round those which, for want of better words, may be called psychological or, perhaps, moral.

In Europe, or at least in some parts of Europe—but not, I think, in the United States of America—there is a latent reaction, somewhat widespread, against basing Society to the extent that we do upon fostering, encouraging, and protecting the money-motives of individuals. A preference for arranging our affairs in such a way as to appeal to the money-motive as little as possible, rather than as much as possible, need not be entirely *a priori,* but may be based on the comparison of experiences. Different persons, according to their choice of profession, find the money-motive playing a large or a small part in their daily lives, and historians can tell us about other phases of social organization in which this motive has played a much smaller part than it does now. Most religions and most philosophies deprecate, to say the least of it, a way of life mainly influenced by considerations of personal money profit. On the other hand, most men today reject ascetic notions and do not doubt the real advantages of wealth. Moreover it seems obvious to them that one cannot do without the money-motive, and that, apart from certain admitted abuses, it does its job well. In the result the average man averts his attention from the problem, and has no clear idea what he really thinks and feels about the whole confounded matter.

Confusion of thought and feeling leads to confusion of speech. Many people, who are really objecting to Capitalism as a way of life, argue as though they were objecting to it on the ground of its inefficiency in attaining its own objects. Contrariwise, devotees of Capitalism are often unduly conservative, and reject reforms in its technique, which might really strengthen and preserve it, for fear that they may prove to be first steps away from Capitalism itself. Nevertheless a time may be coming when we shall get clearer than at present as to when we are talking about Capitalism as an efficient or inefficient technique, and when we are talking about it as desirable or objectionable in itself. For my part, I think that capitalism, wisely managed, can probably be made more efficient for attaining economic ends than any alternative system yet in sight, but that in itself it is in many ways extremely objectionable. Our problem is to work out a social organisation which shall be as efficient as possible without offending our notions of a satisfactory way of life.

The next step forward must come, not from political agitation or premature experiments, but from thought. We need by an effort of the mind to elucidate our own feelings. At present our sympathy and our judgement are liable to be on different sides, which is a painful and paralysing state of mind. In the field of action reformers will not be successful until they can steadily pursue a clear and definite object with their intellects and their feelings in tune. There is no party in the world at present which appears to me to be pursuing right aims by right methods. Material Poverty provides the incentive to change precisely in situations where there is very little margin for experiments. Material Prosperity removes the incentive just when it might be safe to take a chance. Europe lacks the means, America the will, to make a move. We need a new set of convictions which spring naturally from a candid examination of our own inner feelings in relation to the outside facts.

Economic Possibilities for Our Grandchildren*

I

We are suffering just now from a bad attack of economic pessimism. It is common to hear people say that the epoch of enormous

---

*Reprinted from John Maynard Keynes, *Essays in Persuasion* (New York: W. W. Norton, 1963).

economic progress which characterised the nineteenth century is over; that the rapid improvement in the standard of life is now going to slow down—at any rate in Great Britain; that a decline in prosperity is more likely than an improvement in the decade which lies ahead of us.

I believe that this is a wildly mistaken interpretation of what is happening to us. We are suffering, not from the rheumatics of old age, but from the growing-pains of over-rapid changes, from the painfulness of readjustment between one economic period and another. The increase of technical efficiency has been taking place faster than we can deal with the problem of labor absorption; the improvement in the standard of life has been a little too quick; the banking and monetary system of the world has been preventing the rate of interest from falling as fast as equilibrium requires. . . .

The prevailing world depression, the enormous anomaly of unemployment in a world full of wants, the disastrous mistakes we have made, blind us to what is going on under the surface—to the true interpretation of the trend of things. For I predict that both of the two opposed errors of pessimism which now make so much noise in the world will be proved wrong in our own time—the pessimism of the revolutionaries who think that things are so bad that nothing can save us but violent change, and the pessimism of the reactionaries who consider the balance of our economic and social life so precarious that we must risk no experiments.

My purpose in this essay, however, is not to examine the present or the near future, but to disembarrass myself of short views and take wings into the future. What can we reasonably expect the level of our economic life to be a hundred years hence? What are the economic possibilities for our grandchildren?

From the earliest times of which we have record—back, say, to two thousand years before Christ—down to the beginning of the eighteenth century, there was no very great change in the standard of life of the average man living in the civilised centres of the earth. Ups and downs certainly. Visitations of plague, famine, and war. Golden intervals. But no progressive, violent change. Some periods perhaps 50 per cent better than others—at the utmost 100 per cent better—in the four thousand years which ended (say) in A.D. 1700.

This slow rate of progress, or lack of progress, was due to two reasons—to the remarkable absence of important technical improvements and to the failure of capital to accumulate.

The absence of important technical inventions between the prehistoric age and comparatively modern times is truly remarkable. Almost everything which really matters and which the world possessed at the commencement of the modern age was already known to man at the dawn of history. Language, fire, the same domestic animals which we have today, wheat, barley, the vine and the olive, the plough, the wheel, the oar, the sail, leather, linen and cloth, bricks and pots, gold and silver, copper, tin, and lead—and iron was added to the list before 1000 B.C.—banking, statecraft, mathematics, astronomy, and religion. There is no record of when we first possessed these things.

At some epoch before the dawn of history—perhaps even in one of the comfortable intervals before the last ice age—there must have been an era of progress and invention comparable to that in which we live today. But through the greater part of recorded history there was nothing of the kind.

The modern age opened, I think, with the accumulation of capital which began in the sixteenth century. I believe—for reasons with which I must not encumber the present argument—that this was initially due to the rise of prices, and the profits to which that led, which resulted from the treasure of gold and silver which Spain brought from the New World into the Old. From that time until today the power of accumulation by compound interest, which seems to have been sleeping for many generations, was re-born and renewed its strength. And the power of compound interest over two hundred years is such as to stagger the imagination. . . .

From the sixteenth century, with a cumulative crescendo after the eighteenth, the great age of science and technical inventions began, which since the beginning of the nineteenth century has been in full flood—coal, steam, electricity, petrol, steel, rubber, cotton, the chemical industries, automatic machinery and the methods of mass production, wireless, printing, Newton, Darwin, and Einstein, and thousands of other things and men too famous and familiar to catalogue.

What is the result? In spite of an enormous growth in the population of the world, which it has been necessary to equip with houses and machines, the average standard of life in Europe and the United States has been raised, I think, about fourfold. The growth of capital has been on a scale which is far beyond a hundredfold of what any previous age had known. And from now on we need not expect so great an increase of population.

If capital increases, say, 2 per cent per annum, the capital equipment of the world will have increased by a half in twenty years, and
seven and a half times in a hundred years. Think of this in terms of
material things—houses, transport, and the like.

At the same time technical improvements in manufacture and
transport have been proceeding at a greater rate in the last ten years
than ever before in history. In the United States factory output per head
was 40 per cent greater in 1925 than in 1919. In Europe we are held
back by temporary obstacles, but even so it is safe to say that technical
efficiency is increasing by more than 1 per cent per annum compound.
There is evidence that the revolutionary technical changes, which have
so far chiefly affected industry, may soon be attacking agriculture. We
may be on the eve of improvements in the efficiency of food production
as great as those which have already taken place in mining, manufacture, and transport. In quite a few years—in our own lifetimes I mean
—we may be able to perform all the operations of agriculture, mining,
and manufacture with a quarter of the human effort to which we have
been accustomed.

For the moment the very rapidity of these changes is hurting us
and bringing difficult problems to solve. Those countries are suffering
relatively which are not in the vanguard of progress. We are being
afflicted with a new disease of which some readers may not yet have
heard the name, but of which they will hear a great deal in the years
to come—namely, *technological unemployment.* This means unemployment due to our discovery of means of economising the use of labor
outrunning the pace at which we can find new uses for labor.

But this is only a temporary phase of maladjustment. All this
means in the long run *that mankind is solving its economic problem.*
I would predict that the standard of life in progressive countries one
hundred years hence will be between four and eight times as high as
it is today. There would be nothing surprising in this even in the light
of our present knowledge. It would not be foolish to contemplate the
possibility of a far greater progress still.

II

Let us, for the sake of argument, suppose that a hundred years
hence we are all of us, on the average, eight times better off in the
economic sense than we are today. Assuredly there need be nothing here
to surprise us.

Now it is true that the needs of human beings may seem to be insatiable. But they fall into two classes—those needs which are absolute in the sense that we feel them whatever the situation of our fellow human beings may be, and those which are relative in the sense that we feel them only if their satisfaction lifts us above, makes us feel superior to, our fellows. Needs of the second class, those which satisfy the desire for superiority, may indeed be insatiable; for the higher the general level, the higher still are they. But this is not so true of the absolute needs—a point may soon be reached, much sooner perhaps than we are all of us aware of, when these needs are satisfied in the sense that we prefer to devote our further energies to noneconomic purposes.

Now for my conclusion, which you will find, I think, to become more and more startling to the imagination the longer you think about it.

I draw the conclusion that, assuming no important wars and no important increase in population, the *economic problem* may be solved, or be at least within sight of solution, within a hundred years. This means that the economic problem is not—if we look into the future— *the permanent problem of the human race.*

Why, you may ask, is this so startling? It is startling because— if, instead of looking into the future, we look into the past—we find that the economic problem, the struggle for subsistence, always has been hitherto the primary, most pressing problem of the human race—not only of the human race, but of the whole of the biological kingdom from the beginnings of life in its most primitive forms.

Thus we have been expressly evolved by nature—with all our impulses and deepest instincts—for the purpose of solving the economic problem. If the economic problem is solved, mankind will be deprived of its traditional purpose.

Will this be a benefit? If one believes at all in the real values of life, the prospect at least opens up the possibility of benefit. Yet I think with dread of the readjustment of the habits and instincts of the ordinary man, bred into him for countless generations, which he may be asked to discard within a few decades.

To use the language of today—must we not expect a general "nervous breakdown"? We already have a little experience of what I mean—a nervous breakdown of the sort which is already common enough in England and the United States amongst the wives of the well-to-do classes, unfortunate women, many of them, who have been

deprived by their wealth of their traditional tasks and occupations—
who cannot find it sufficiently amusing, when deprived of the spur of
economic necessity, to cook and clean and mend, yet are quite unable
to find anything more amusing.

To those who sweat for their daily bread leisure is a longed-for
sweet—until they get it.

There is the traditional epitaph written for herself by the old
charwoman:—

Don't mourn for me, friends, don't weep for me never,
For I'm going to do nothing for ever and ever.

This was her heaven. Like others who look forward to leisure,
she conceived how nice it would be to spend her time listening-in—for
there was another couplet which occurred in her poem:—

With psalms and sweet music the heavens'll be ringing,
But I shall have nothing to do with the singing.

Yet it will only be for those who have to do with the singing
that life will be tolerable—and how few of us can sing!

Thus for the first time since his creation man will be faced with
his real, his permanent problem—how to use his freedom from pressing
economic cares, how to occupy the leisure, which science and compound
interest will have won for him, to live wisely and agreeably and well.

The strenuous purposeful money-makers may carry all of us
along with them into the lap of economic abundance. But it will be
those peoples, who can keep alive, and cultivate into a fuller perfection,
the art of life itself and do not sell themselves for the means of life,
who will be able to enjoy the abundance when it comes.

Yet there is no country and no people, I think, who can look
forward to the age of leisure and of abundance without a dread. For we
have been trained too long to strive and not to enjoy. It is a fearful problem for the ordinary person, with no special talents, to occupy himself,
especially if he no longer has roots in the soil or in custom or in the
beloved conventions of a traditional society. To judge from the behavior
and the achievements of the wealthy classes today in any quarter of the
world, the outlook is very depressing! For these are, so to speak, our
advance guard—those who are spying out the promised land for the
rest of us and pitching their camp there. For they have most of them
failed disastrously, so it seems to me—those who have an independent

income but no associations or duties or ties—to solve the problem which has been set them.

I feel sure that with a little more experience we shall use the new-found bounty of nature quite differently from the way in which the rich use it today, and will map out for ourselves a plan of life quite otherwise than theirs.

For many ages to come the old Adam will be so strong in us that everybody will need to do *some* work if he is to be contented. We shall do more things for ourselves than is usual with the rich today, only too glad to have small duties and tasks and routines. But beyond this, we shall endeavor to spread the bread thin on the butter—to make what work there is still to be done to be as widely shared as possible. Three-hour shifts or a fifteen-hour week may put off the problem for a great while. For three hours a day is quite enough to satisfy the old Adam in most of us!

There are changes in other spheres too which we must expect to come. When the accumulation of wealth is no longer of high social importance, there will be great changes in the code of morals. We shall be able to rid ourselves of many of the pseudo-moral principles which have hag-ridden us for two hundred years, by which we have exalted some of the most distasteful of human qualities into the position of the highest virtues. We shall be able to afford to dare to assess the money-motive at its true value. The love of money as a possession—as distinguished from the love of money as a means to the enjoyments and realities of life—will be recognised for what it is, a somewhat disgusting morbidity, one of those semi-criminal, semi-pathological propensities which one hands over with a shudder to the specialists in mental disease. All kinds of social customs and economic practices, affecting the distribution of wealth and of economic rewards and penalties, which we now maintain at all costs, however distasteful and unjust they may be in themselves, because they are tremendously useful in promoting the accumulation of capital, we shall then be free, at last, to discard.

Of course there will still be many people with intense, unsatisfied purposiveness who will blindly pursue wealth—unless they can find some plausible substitute. But the rest of us will no longer be under any obligation to applaud and encourage them. For we shall inquire more curiously than is safe today into the true character of this "purposiveness" with which in varying degrees nature has endowed almost all of us. For purposiveness means that we are more concerned with the remote future results of our actions than with their own quality or their immediate effects on our own environment. The "purposive" man is always trying to secure a spurious and delusive immortality for his acts by pushing his interest in them forward into time. He does not love his cat, but his cat's kittens; nor, in truth, the kittens, but only the kittens' kittens, and so on forward for ever to the end of cat-dom. For him jam is not jam unless it is a case of jam tomorrow and never jam today. Thus by pushing his jam always forward into the future, he strives to secure for his act of boiling it an immortality.

Let me remind you of the Professor in *Sylvie and Bruno*:—

"Only the tailor, sir, with your little bill," said a meek voice outside the door.

"Ah, well, I can soon settle *his* business," the Professor said to the children, "if you'll just wait a minute. How much is it, this year, my man?" The tailor had come in while he was speaking.

"Well, it's been a-doubling so many years, you see," the tailor replied, a little gruffly, "and I think I'd like the money now. Its two thousand pound, it is!"

"Oh, that's nothing!" the Professor carelessly remarked, feeling in his pocket, as if he always carried at least *that* amount about with him. "But wouldn't you like to wait just another year and make it *four* thousand? Just think how rich you'd be! Why, you might be a *king*, if you liked!"

"I don't know as I'd care about being a king," the man said thoughtfully. "But it *dew* sound a powerful sight o' money! Well, I think I'll wait——"

"Of course you will!" said the Professor. "There's good sense in *you*, I see. Good-day to you, my man!"

"Will you ever have to pay him that four thousand pounds?" Sylvie asked as the door closed on the departing creditor.

"*Never,* my child!" the Professor replied emphatically. "He'll go on doubling it till he dies. You see, it's *always* worth while waiting another year to get twice as much money!"

Perhaps it is not an accident that the race which did most to bring the promise of immortality into the heart and essence of our religions has also done most for the principle of compound interest and particularly loves this most purposive of human institutions.

I see us free, therefore, to return to some of the most sure and certain principles of religion and traditional virtue—that avarice is a vice, that the exaction of usury is a misdemeanour, and the love of money is detestable, that those walk most truly in the paths of virtue and sane wisdom who take least thought for the morrow. We shall once more value ends above means and prefer the good to the useful. We shall honour those who can teach us how to pluck the hour and the day virtuously and well, the delightful people who are capable of taking direct enjoyment in things, the lilies of the field who toil not, neither do they spin.

But beware! The time for all this is not yet. For at least another hundred years we must pretend to ourselves and to every one that fair is foul and foul is fair; for foul is useful and fair is not. Avarice and usury and precaution must be our gods for a little longer still. For only they can lead us out of the tunnel of economic necessity into daylight.

I look forward, therefore, in days not so very remote, to the greatest change which has ever occurred in the material environment of life for human beings in the aggregate. But, of course, it will happen gradually, not as a catastrophe. Indeed, it has already begun. The course of affairs will simply be that there will be ever larger and larger classes and groups of people from whom problems of economic necessity have been practically removed. The critical difference will be realised when this condition has become so general that the nature of one's duty to one's neighbour is changed. For it will remain reasonable to be economically purposive for others after it has ceased to be reasonable for oneself.

The *pace* at which we can reach our destination of economic bliss will be governed by four things—our power to control population, our determination to avoid wars and civil dissensions, our willingness to entrust to science the direction of those matters which are properly the concern of science, and the rate of accumulation as fixed by the margin between our production and our consumption; of which the last will easily look after itself, given the first three.

Meanwhile there will be no harm in making mild preparations for our destiny, in encouraging, and experimenting in, the arts of life as well as the activities of purpose.

But, chiefly, do not let us overestimate the importance of the economic problem, or sacrifice to its supposed necessities other matters of greater and more permanent significance. It should be a matter for specialists—like dentistry. If economists could manage to get themselves thought of as humble, competent people, on a level with dentists, that would be splendid!

from

The General Theory of Employment, Interest, and Money*

I

The outstanding faults of the economic society in which we live are its failure to provide for full employment and its arbitrary and inequitable distribution of wealth and incomes. The bearing of the foregoing theory on the first of these is obvious. But there are also two important respects in which it is relevant to the second.

Since the end of the nineteenth century significant progress towards the removal of very great disparities of wealth and income has been achieved through the instrument of direct taxation—income tax and surtax and death duties—especially in Great Britain. Many people would wish to see this process carried much further, but they are deterred by two considerations; partly by the fear of making skilful evasions too much worth while and also of diminishing unduly the motive towards risk-taking, but mainly, I think, by the belief that the growth of capital depends upon the strength of the motive towards individual saving and that for a large proportion of this growth we are dependent on the savings of the rich out of their superfluity. Our argument does not affect the first of these considerations. But it may considerably modify our attitude towards the second. For we have seen that, up to the point where full employment prevails, the growth of capital depends not at all on a low propensity to consume but is, on the contrary, held back by it; and only in conditions of full employment is a low propensity to consume conductive to the growth of capital. Moreover, experience suggests that in existing conditions saving by institutions and through sinking funds is more than adequate, and that measures for the redistribution of incomes in a way likely to raise the propensity to consume may prove positively favourable to the growth of capital.

*From The General Theory of Employment, Interest, and Money, by John Maynard Keynes. Reprinted by permission of Harcourt, Brace & World, Inc., the Trustees of the Estate of Lord Keynes, The Macmillan Company of Canada, Ltd., and Macmillan and Co., Ltd.

The existing confusion of the public mind on the matter is well illustrated by the very common belief that the death duties are responsible for a reduction in the capital wealth of the country. Assuming that the State applies the proceeds of these duties to its ordinary outgoings so that taxes on incomes and consumption are correspondingly reduced or avoided, it is, of course, true that a fiscal policy of heavy death duties has the effect of increasing the community's propensity to consume. But inasmuch as an increase in the habitual propensity to consume will in general (*i.e.* except in conditions of full employment) serve to increase at the same time the inducement to invest, the inference commonly drawn is the exact opposite of the truth.

Thus our argument leads towards the conclusion that in contemporary conditions the growth of wealth, so far from being dependent on the abstinence of the rich, as is commonly supposed, is more likely to be impeded by it. One of the chief social justifications of great inequality of wealth is, therefore, removed. I am not saying that there are no other reasons, unaffected by our theory, capable of justifying some measure of inequality in some circumstances. But it does dispose of the most important of the reasons why hitherto we have thought it prudent to move carefully. This particularly affects our attitude towards death duties; for there are certain justifications for inequality of incomes which do not apply equally to inequality of inheritances.

For my own part, I believe that there is social and psychological justification for signficant inequalities of incomes and wealth, but not for such large disparities as exist today. There are valuable human activities which require the motive of money-making and the environment of private wealth-ownership for their full fruition. Moreover, dangerous human proclivities can be canalised into comparatively harmless channels by the existence of opportunities for money-making and private wealth, which, if they cannot be satisfied in this way, may find their outlet in cruelty, the reckless pursuit of personal power and authority, and other forms of self-aggrandisement. It is better that a man should tryannise over his bank balance than over his fellow-citizens; and whilst the former is sometimes denounced as being but a means to the latter, sometimes at least it is an alternative. But it is not necessary for the stimulation of these activities and the satisfaction of these proclivities that the game should be played for such high stakes as at present. Much lower stakes will serve the purpose equally well, as soon as the players are accustomed to them. The task of transmuting human nature must not be confused with the task of managing it.

Though in the ideal commonwealth men may have been taught or inspired or bred to take no interest in the stakes, it may still be wise and prudent statesmanship to allow the game to be played, subject to rules and limitations, so long as the average man, or even a significant section of the community, is in fact strongly addicted to the money-making passion.

II

There is, however, a second, much more fundamental inference from our argument which has a bearing on the future of inequalities of wealth; namely, our theory of the rate of interest. The justification for a moderately high rate of interest has been found hitherto in the necessity of providing a sufficient inducement to save. But we have shown that the extent of effective saving is necessarily determined by the scale of investment and that the scale of investment is promoted by a *low* rate of interest, provided that we do not attempt to stimulate it in this way beyond the point which corresponds to full employment. Thus it is to our best advantage to reduce the rate of interest to that point relatively to the schedule of the marginal efficiency of capital at which there is full employment.

There can be no doubt that this criterion will lead to a much lower rate of interest than has ruled hitherto; and, so far as one can guess at the schedules of the marginal efficiency of capital corresponding to increasing amounts of capital, the rate of interest is likely to fall steadily, if it should be practicable to maintain conditions of more or less continuous full employment—unless, indeed, there is an excessive change in the aggregate propensity to consume (including the State).

I feel sure that the demand for capital is strictly limited in the sense that it would not be difficult to increase the stock of capital up to a point where its marginal efficiency had fallen to a very low figure. This would not mean that the use of capital instruments would cost almost nothing, but only that the return from them would have to cover little more than their exhaustion by wastage and obsolescence together with some margin to cover risk and the exercise of skill and judgment. In short, the aggregate return from durable goods in the course of their life would, as in the case of short-lived goods, just cover their labor-costs of production *plus* an allowance for risk and the costs of skill and supervision.

Now, though this state of affairs would be quite compatible with some measure of individualism, yet it would mean the euthanasia of the rentier, and, consequently, the euthanasia of the cumulative oppressive power of the capitalist to exploit the scarcity-value of capital. Interest today rewards no genuine sacrifice, any more than does the rent of land. The owner of capital can obtain interest because capital is scarce, just as the owner of land can obtain rent because land is scarce. But whilst there may be intrinsic reasons for the scarcity of land, there are no intrinsic reasons for the scarcity of capital. An intrinsic reason for such scarcity, in the sense of a genuine sacrifice which could only be called forth by the offer of a reward in the shape of interest, would not exist, in the long run, except in the event of the individual propensity to consume proving to be of such a character that net saving in conditions of full employment comes to an end before capital has become sufficiently abundant. But even so, it will still be possible for communal saving through the agency of the State to be maintained at a level which will allow the growth of capital up to the point where it ceases to be scarce.

I see, therefore, the rentier aspect of capitalism as a transitional phase which will disappear when it has done its work. And with the disappearance of its rentier aspect much else in it besides will suffer a sea-change. It will be, moreover, a great advantage of the order of events which I am advocating, that the euthansia of the rentier, of the functionless investor, will be nothing sudden, merely a gradual but prolonged continuance of what we have seen recently in Great Britain, and will need no revolution.

Thus we might aim in practice (there being nothing in this which is unattainable) at an increase in the volume of capital until it ceases to be scarce, so that the functionless investor will no longer receive a bonus; and at a scheme of direct taxation which allows the intelligence and determination and executive skill of the financier, the entrepreneur *et hoc genus omne* (who are certainly so fond of their craft that their labor could be obtained much cheaper than at present), to be harnessed to the service of the community on reasonable terms of reward.

At the same time we must recognise that only experience can show how far the common will, embodied in the policy of the State, ought to be directed to increasing and supplementing the inducement to invest; and how far it is safe to stimulate the average propensity to consume, without forgoing our aim of depriving capital of its scarcity-value within one or two generations. It may turn out that the propensity to consume will be so easily strengthened by the effects of a falling rate of interest, that full employment can be reached with a rate of accumulation little greater than at present. In this event a scheme for the higher taxation of large incomes and inheritances might be open to the objection that it would lead to full employment with a rate of accumulation which was reduced considerably below the current level. I must not be supposed to deny the possibility, or even the probability, of this outcome. For in such matters it is rash to predict how the average man will react to a changed environment. If, however, it should prove easy to secure an approximation to full employment with a rate of accumulation not much greater than at present, an outstanding problem will at least have been solved. And it would remain for separate decision on what scale and by what means it is right and reasonable to call on the living generation to restrict their consumption, so as to establish, in course of time, a state of full investment for their successors.

III

In some other respects the foregoing theory is moderately conservative in its implications. For whilst it indicates the vital importance of establishing certain central controls in matters which are now left in the main to individual initiative, there are wide fields of activity which are unaffected. The State will have to exercise a guiding influence on the propensity to consume partly through its scheme of taxation, partly by fixing the rate of interest, and partly, perhaps, in other ways. Furthermore, it seems unlikely that the influence of banking policy on the rate of interest will be sufficient by itself to determine an optimum rate of investment. I conceive, therefore, that a somewhat comprehensive socialisation of investment will prove the only means of securing an approximation to full employment; though this need not exclude all manner of compromises and of devices by which public authority will co-operate with private initiative. But beyond this no obvious case is made out for a system of State Socialism which would embrace most of the economic life of the community. It is not the ownership of the instruments of production which it is important for the State to assume. If the State is able to determine the aggregate amount of resources devoted to augmenting the instruments and the basic rate of reward to those who own them, it will have accomplished all that is necessary. Moreover, the necessary measures of socialisation can be introduced gradually and without a break in the general traditions of society.

Our criticism of the accepted classical theory of economics has consisted not so much in finding logical flaws in its analysis as in pointing out that its tacit assumptions are seldom or never satisfied, with the result that it cannot solve the economic problems of the actual world. But if our central controls succeed in establishing an aggregate volume of output corresponding to full employment as nearly as is practicable, the classical theory comes into its own again from this point onwards. If we suppose the volume of output to be given, *i.e.* to be determined by forces outside the classical scheme of thought, then there is no objection to be raised against the classical analysis of the manner in which private self-interest will determine what in particular is produced, in what proportions the factors of production will be combined to produce it, and how the value of the final product will be distributed between them. Again, if we have dealt otherwise with the problem of thrift, there is no objection to be raised against the modern classical theory as to the degree of consilience between private and public advantage in conditions of perfect and imperfect competition respectively. Thus, apart from the necessity of central controls to bring about an adjustment between the propensity to consume and the inducement to invest, there is no more reason to socialise economic life than there was before.

To put the point concretely, I see no reason to suppose that the existing system seriously misemploys the factors of production which are in use. There are, of course, errors of foresight; but these would not be avoided by centralising decisions. When 9,000,000 men are employed out of 10,000,000 willing and able to work, there is no evidence that the labor of these 9,000,000 men is misdirected. The complaint against the present system is not that these 9,000,000 men ought to be employed on different tasks, but that tasks should be available for the remaining 1,000,000 men. It is in determining the volume, not the direction, of actual employment that the existing system has broken down.

Thus I agree with Gesell that the result of filling in the gaps in the classical theory is not to dispose of the "Manchester System," but to indicate the nature of the environment which the free play of economic forces requires if it is to realise the full potentialities of production. The central controls necessary to ensure full employment will, of course, involve a large extension of the traditional functions of government. Furthermore, the modern classical theory has itself called attention to various conditions in which the free play of economic forces may need to be curbed or guided. But there will still remain a wide field for the exercise of private initiative and responsibility. Within this field the traditional advantages of individualism will still hold good.

Let us stop for a moment to remind ourselves what these advantages are. They are partly advantages of efficiency—the advantages of decentralisation and of the play of self-interest. The advantage to

efficiency of the decentralization of decisions and of individual responsibility is even greater, perhaps, than the nineteenth century supposed;
and the reaction against the appeal to self-interest may have gone too
far. But, above all, individualism, if it can be purged of its defects and
its abuses, is the best safeguard of personal liberty in the sense that,
compared with any other system, it greatly widens the field for the
exercise of personal choice. It is also the best safeguard of the variety
of life, which emerges precisely from this extended field of personal
choice, and the loss of which is the greatest of all the losses of the
homogeneous or totalitarian state. For this variety preserves the traditions which embody the most secure and successful choices of former
generations; it colors the present with the diversification of its fancy;
and, being the handmaid of experiment as well as of tradition and of
fancy, it is the most powerful instrument to better the future.

Whilst, therefore, the enlargement of the functions of government, involved in the task of adjusting to one another the propensity
to consume and the inducement to invest, would seem to a nineteenth-
century publicist or to a contemporary American financier to be a ter-
rific encroachment on individualism, I defend it, on the contrary, both
as the only practicable means of avoiding the destruction of existing
economic forms in their entirety and as the condition of the successful
functioning of individual initiative.

For if effective demand is deficient, not only is the public
scandal of wasted resources intolerable, but the individual enterpriser
who seeks to bring these resources into action is operating with the
odds loaded against him. The game of hazard which he plays is furnished with many zeros, so that the players *as a whole* will lose if they
have the energy and hope to deal all the cards. Hitherto the increment
of the world's wealth has fallen short of the aggregate of positive individual savings; and the difference has been made up by the losses of
those whose courage and initiative have not been supplemented by
exceptional skill or unusual good fortune. But if effective demand is
adequate, average skill and average good fortune will be enough.

The authoritarian state systems of today seem to solve the problem of unemployment at the expense of efficiency and of freedom. It
is certain that the world will not much longer tolerate the unemployment which, apart from brief intervals of excitement, is associated—
and, in my opinion, inevitably associated—with present-day capitalistic
individualism. But it may be possible by a right analysis of the problem
to cure the disease whilst preserving efficiency and freedom.

IV

I have mentioned in passing that the new system might be more favourable to peace than the old has been. It is worth while to repeat and emphasize that aspect.

War has several causes. Dictators and others such, to whom war offers, in expectation at least, a pleasurable excitement, find it easy to work on the natural bellicosity of their peoples. But, over and above this, facilitating their task of fanning the popular flame, are the economic causes of war, namely, the pressure of population and the competitive struggle for markets. It is the second factor, which probably played a predominant part in the nineteenth century, and might again, that is germane to this discussion.

I have pointed out in the preceding chapter that, under the system of domestic laissez-faire and an international gold standard such as was orthodox in the latter half of the nineteenth century, there was no means open to a government whereby to mitigate economic distress at home except through the competitive struggle for markets. For all measures helpful to a state of chronic or intermittent under-employment were ruled out, except measures to improve the balance of trade on income account.

Thus, whilst economists were accustomed to applaud the prevailing international system as furnishing the fruits of the international division of labor and harmonising at the same time the interests of different nations, there lay concealed a less benign influence; and those statesmen were moved by common sense and a correct apprehension of the true course of events, who believed that if a rich, old country were to neglect the struggle for markets its prosperity would droop and fail. But if nations can learn to provide themselves with full employment by their domestic policy (and, we must add, if they can also attain equilibrium in the trend of their population), there need be no important economic forces calculated to set the interest of one country against that of its neighbours. There would still be room for the international division of labor and for international lending in appropriate conditions. But there would no longer be a pressing motive why one country need force its wares on another or repulse the offerings of its neighbour, not because this was necessary to enable it to pay for what it wished to purchase, but with the express object of upsetting the equilibrium of payments so as to develop a balance of trade in its own favour. International trade would cease to be what it is, namely, a desperate expedient to maintain employment at home by forcing sales on foreign markets and restricting purchases, which, if successful, will merely shift the problem of unemployment to the neighbour which is worsted in the struggle, but a willing and unimpeded exchange of goods and services in conditions of mutual advantage.

V

Is the fulfilment of these ideas a visionary hope? Have they insufficient roots in the motives which govern the evolution of political society? Are the interests which they will thwart stronger and more obvious than those which they will serve?

I do not attempt an answer in this place. It would need a volume of a different character from this one to indicate even in outline the practical measures in which they might be gradually clothed. But if the ideas are correct—an hypothesis on which the author himself must necessarily base what he writes—it would be a mistake, I predict, to dispute their potency over a period of time. At the present moment people are unusually expectant of a more fundamental diagnosis; more particularly ready to receive it; eager to try it out, if it should be even plausible. But apart from this contemporary mood, the ideas of economists and political philosophers, both when they are right and when they are wrong, are more powerful than is commonly understood. Indeed the world is ruled by little else. Practical men, who believe themselves to be quite exempt from any intellectual influences, are usually the slaves of some defunct economist. Madmen in authority, who hear voices in the air, are distilling their frenzy from some academic scribbler of a few years back. I am sure that the power of vested interests is vastly exaggerated compared with the gradual encroachment of ideas. Not, indeed, immediately, but after a certain interval; for in the field of economic and political philosophy there are not many who are influenced by new theories after they are twenty-five or thirty years of age, so that the ideas which civil servants and politicians and even agitators apply to current events are not likely to be the newest. But, soon or late, it is ideas, not vested interests, which are dangerous for good or evil.

7

◀ JOSEPH A. SCHUMPETER* ▶

from

Capitalism, Socialism, and Democracy (1942)

It is difficult to place Schumpeter into any of the three categories set up in this volume. He is classified as a liberal only because he seems to fit less comfortably into either of the other two categories. While not an advocate of laissez-faire, neither did he look forward to the transformation of capitalism into socialism, which he predicted would eventually occur. He does not fit squarely into the liberal camp either, since he was critical of reformist attempts to tinker with capitalism. Schumpeter characterized himself as an objective scientist who looked at the forces of change within capitalism and regrettably predicted its eventual demise. "Prognosis," Schumpeter said, "does not imply anything about the desirability of the course of events that one predicts." The difficulty of placing Schumpeter into any school of economic thought should serve as an indication to the reader that he must not be arbitrary about categorization.

Even though he tended to be critical of Keynesian economics, and the growing role of government that it brought on, Schumpeter had a great deal of influence over American liberal thinking. This influence is especially evident in the work, presented later in this volume, of John Kenneth Galbraith. In the selection presented here, Schumpeter draws a correlation between large size firms and technological change. To him the misallocation of resources resulting from highly concentrated industries in static equilibrium was offset by the

---

* (1883–1950)

competition (quality rather than price) which arose from the innovations produced by the firms in those industries. In contrast to those who extol the virtues of competitive capitalism, Schumpeter held large corporations responsible for America's high standard of living. The reaffirmation of the link between size and progressiveness in Galbraith's *New Industrial State** has caused an outcry from those economists who see the economic and political dangers inherent in accepting this form of technological determinism.

Perhaps Schumpeter's greatest achievement is the rich insight he provided into the operation of capitalist institutions through his broad approach to economic problems. Schumpeter goes beyond the bounds of pure economics and examines the long-run psychological and social changes which are involved in the evolutionary process. In the study of business cycles for instance, Schumpeter shows how the three elements that he believes are chiefly responsible for economic development (the entrepreneur, innovation, and credit) combine to cause fluctuations in economic activity. The reason for the cyclical pattern of economic growth under capitalism was the dynamic nature of technology; Schumpeter believed that technological breakthroughs came in clusters or waves. When a new discovery was made, a few entrepreneurs, followed by a flood of imitators, came into the market in search of profits. Eventually this led to a secondary wave of innovations, opportunities for which were opened up by the original discovery. Entrepreneurs financed the development of the new innovations with private bank credit provided by the capitalist system. The combination of innovations, entrepreneurial ability, and credit expansion caused an increase in business activity which gradually produced its own doom. The resulting downswing was partially due to the rising prices and costs associated with economic expansion. But Schumpeter was not critical of capitalism on this point, for he acknowledged that business cycles were the price that had to be paid for economic development. The fact that he saw the seeds of the downswing inherent in the expansion of business activity is indicative of his entire approach to the evolution of capitalism.

Schumpeter underscored the necessary and important role of the entrepreneur and the process of innovation in economic development. His analysis, however, led him to conclude that these key elements were gradually being replaced by a "depersonalized" bureaucratic routine. Schumpeter believed that as a result of this evolutionary process capitalism was losing its dynamic spirit and thus giving way to some form of socialism. Although routine might lessen the instability of capitalism, it replaced the traditional defenses of the system. Schumpeter thus predicted the demise of capitalism but, unlike Marx, he

---

*See chapter 8.

claimed that the end was due to the successes and not the failures of the system. In the article presented here he shows how the defenses of capitalism, including the aristrocracy, the bourgeois family, and the small businessman, were being broken down, and how forces hostile to the system were growing. A crucial source of hostility was an idle class of intellectuals who became critical of capitalist institutions and who infiltrated the labor union movement to form a solid base for political change. The interests of the government were thus directed into anti-capitalist techniques such as the nationalization of industry. If one accepts the contentions of Galbraith and others on the increasing socialization of industry, some of Schumpeter's predictions seem to be bearing fruit; however, as liberals have pointed out, this tendency is not likely to result in nationalization. It seems upon closer examination that Schumpeter has overstated the radical tendencies of the intellec-tuals and their influence within the labor movement. The opinions of those who influence the public, as well as of the general citizenry, are molded by the goals of corporate capitalism (à la Galbraith), and the American unions do not seem as interested in political affairs as some more radical intellectuals would want them. However, modern social-ists, such as Michael Harrington, still feel the hope for the future lies in a coalition of trade unions and intellectuals. The lack of a movement toward it is a painful reminder to socialists that America is a country that has thus far psychologically resisted such a coalition.

————R. R.

from

Capitalism, Socialism, and Democracy*

PROLOGUE

Can capitalism survive? No. I do not think it can. But this opinion of mine, like that of every other economist who has pro-nounced upon the subject, is in itself completely uninteresting. What counts in any attempt at social prognosis is not the Yes or No that sums up the facts and arguments which lead up to it but those facts

*Abridged from pp. 61–2, 81–6, 87–91, 106, 132–4, 138–42, 143, 145–7, 152–5, 161–3 in Capitalism, Socialism, and Democracy, Third Edition, by Joseph A. Schumpeter. Copyright 1942, 1947 by Joseph A. Schumpeter. Reprinted by per-mission of Harper and Row, Publishers, and George Allen and Unwin Ltd.

and arguments themselves. They contain all that is scientific in the final result. Everything else is not science but prophecy. Analysis, whether economic or other, never yields more than a statement about the tendencies present in an observable pattern. And these never tell us what *will* happen to the pattern but only what *would* happen if they continued to act as they have been acting in the time interval covered by our observation and if no other factors intruded. "Inevitability" or "necessity" can never mean more than this.

What follows must be read with that proviso. But there are other limitations to our results and their reliability. The process of social life is a function of so many variables many of which are not amenable to anything like measurement that even mere diagnosis of a given state of things becomes a doubtful matter quite apart from the formidable sources of error that open up as soon as we attempt prognosis. These difficulties should not be exaggerated, however. We shall see that the dominant traits of the picture clearly support certain inferences which, whatever the qualifications that may have to be added, are too strong to be neglected on the ground that they cannot be proved in the sense in which a proposition of Euclid's can.

. . . The thesis I shall endeavor to establish is that the actual and prospective performance of the capitalist system is such as to negative the idea of its breaking down under the weight of economic failure, but that its very success undermines the social institutions which protect it, and "inevitably" creates conditions in which it will not be able to live and which strongly point to socialism as the heir apparent. My final conclusion therefore does not differ, however much my argument may, from that of most socialist writers and in particular from that of all Marxists. But in order to accept it one does not need to be a socialist. Prognosis does not imply anything about the desirability of the course of events that one predicts. If a doctor predicts that his patient will die presently, this does not mean that he desires it. One may hate socialism or at least look upon it with cool criticism, and yet foresee its advent. Many conservatives did and do.

Nor need one accept this conclusion in order to qualify as a socialist. One may love socialism and ardently believe in its economic, cultural and ethical superiority but nevertheless believe at the same time that capitalist society does not harbor any tendency toward self-destruction. There are in fact socialists who believe that the capitalist order is gathering strength and is entrenching itself as time goes on, so that it is chimerical to hope for its breakdown. . . .

THE PROCESS OF CREATIVE DESTRUCTION

The theories of monopolistic and oligopolistic competition and their popular variants may in two ways be made to serve the view that capitalist reality is unfavorable to maximum performance in production. One may hold that it always has been so and that all along output has been expanding in spite of the secular sabotage perpetrated by the managing bourgeoisie. Advocates of this proposition would have to produce evidence to the effect that the observed rate of increase can be accounted for by a sequence of favorable circumstances unconnected with the mechanism of private enterprise and strong enough to overcome the latter's resistance. . . . However, those who espouse this variant at least avoid the trouble about historical fact that the advocates of the alternative proposition have to face. This avers that capitalist reality once tended to favor maximum productive performance, or at all events productive performance so considerable as to constitute a major element in any serious appraisal of the system; but that the later spread of monopolist structures, killing competition, has by now reversed that tendency.

First, this involves the creation of an entirely imaginary golden age of perfect competition that at some time somehow metamorphosed itself into the monopolistic age, whereas it is quite clear that perfect competition has at no time been more of a reality than it is at present. Secondly, it is necessary to point out that the rate of increase in output did not decrease from the nineties from which, I suppose, the prevalence of the largest-size concerns, at least in manufacturing industry, would have to be dated; that there is nothing in the behavior of the time series of total output to suggest a "break in trend"; and, most important of all, that the modern standard of life of the masses evolved during the period of relatively unfettered "big business." If we list the items that enter the modern workman's budget and from 1899 on observe the course of their prices not in terms of money but in terms of the hours of labor that will buy them—i.e., each year's money prices divided by each year's hourly wage rates—we cannot fail to be struck by the rate of the advance which, considering the spectacular improvement in qualities, seems to have been greater and not smaller than it ever was before. If we economists were given less to wishful thinking and more to the observation of facts, doubts would immediately arise as to the realistic virtues of a theory that would have led us to expect a very different result. Nor is this all. As soon as we go into details

and inquire into the individual items in which progress was most conspicuous, the trail leads not to the doors of those firms that work under
conditions of comparatively free competition but precisely to the doors
of the large concerns—which, as in the case of agricultural machinery,
also account for much of the progress in the competitive sector—and a
shocking suspicion dawns upon us that big business may have had more
to do with creating that standard of life than with keeping it down. . . .

The essential point to grasp is that in dealing with capitalism
we are dealing with an evolutionary process. It may seem strange that
anyone can fail to see so obvious a fact which moreover was long ago
emphasized by Karl Marx. Yet that fragmentary analysis which yields
the bulk of our propositions about the functioning of modern capitalism
persistently neglects it. Let us restate the point and see how it bears
upon our problem.

Capitalism, then, is by nature a form or method of economic
change and not only never is but never can be stationary. And this
evolutionary character of the capitalist process is not merely due to the
fact that economic life goes on in a social and natural environment
which changes and by its change alters the data of economic action;
this fact is important and these changes (wars, revolutions and so on)
often condition industrial change, but they are not its prime movers.
Nor is this evolutionary character due to a quasi-automatic increase in
population and capital or to the vagaries of monetary systems of which
exactly the same thing holds true. The fundamental impulse that sets
and keeps the capitalist engine in motion comes from the new consumers' goods, the new methods of production or transportation, the
new markets, the new forms of industrial organization that capitalist
enterprise creates.

. . . The contents of the laborer's budget, say from 1760 to 1940,
did not simply grow on unchanging lines but they underwent a process
of qualitative change. Similarly, the history of the productive apparatus
of a typical farm, from the beginnings of the rationalization of crop
rotation, plowing and fattening to the mechanized thing of today—
linking up with elevators and railroads—is a history of revolutions.
So is the history of the productive apparatus of the iron and steel industry from the charcoal furnace to our own type of furnace, or the
history of the apparatus of power production from the overshot water
wheel to the modern power plant, or the history of transportation from
the mailcoach to the airplane. The opening up of new markets, foreign
or domestic, and the organizational development from the craft shop

and factory to such concerns as U. S. Steel illustrate the same process of industrial mutation—if I may use that biological term—that incessantly revolutionizes[1] the economic structure *from within,* incessantly destroying the old one, incessantly creating a new one. This process of Creative Destruction is the essential fact about capitalism. It is what capitalism consists in and what every capitalist concern has got to live in. This fact bears upon our problem in two ways.

First, since we are dealing with a process whose every element takes considerable time in revealing its true features and ultimate effects, there is no point in appraising the performance of that process *ex visu* of a given point of time; we must judge its performance over time, as it unfolds through decades or centuries. A system—any system, economic or other—that at *every* given point of time fully utilizes its possibilities to the best advantage may yet in the long run be inferior to a system that does so at *no* given point of time, because the latter's failure to do so may be a condition for the level or speed of long-run performance.

Second, since we are dealing with an organic process, analysis of what happens in any particular part of it—say, in an individual concern or industry—may indeed clarify details of mechanism but is inconclusive beyond that. Every piece of business strategy acquires its true significance only against the background of that process and within the situation created by it. It must be seen in its role in the perennial gale of creative destruction; it cannot be understood irrespective of it or, in fact, on the hypothesis that there is a perennial lull.

But economists who, *ex visu* of a point of time, look for example at the behavior of an oligopolist industry—an industry which consists of a few big firms—and observe the well-known moves and countermoves within it that seem to aim at nothing but high prices and restrictions of output are making precisely that hypothesis. They accept the data of the momentary situation as if there were no past or future to it and think that they have understood what there is to understand if they interpret the behavior of those firms by means of the principle of maximizing profits with reference to those data. The usual theorist's paper and the usual government commission's report practically never try to

---

[1] Those revolutions are not strictly incessant; they occur in discrete rushes which are separated from each other by spans of comparative quiet. The process as a whole works incessantly, however, in the sense that there always is either revolution or absorption of the results of revolution, both together forming what are known as business cycles.

see that behavior, on the one hand, as a result of a piece of past history
and, on the other hand, as an attempt to deal with a situation that is
sure to change presently—as an attempt by those firms to keep on their
feet, on ground that is slipping away from under them. In other words,
the problem that is usually being visualized is how capitalism adminis-
ters existing structures, whereas the relevant problem is how it creates
and destroys them. As long as this is not recognized, the investigator
does a meaningless job. As soon as it is recognized, his outlook on capitalist practice and its social results changes considerably.[2]

The first thing to go is the traditional conception of the *modus
operandi* of competition. Economists are at long last emerging from
the stage in which price competition was all they saw. As soon as quality
competition and sales effort are admitted into the sacred precincts of
theory, the price variable is ousted from its dominant position. However, it is still competition within a rigid pattern of invariant conditions, methods of production and forms of industrial organization in
particular, that practically monopolizes attention. But in capitalist
reality as distinguished from its textbook picture, it is not that kind of
competition which counts but the competition from the new commodity, the new technology, the new source of supply, the new type of
organization (the largest-scale unit of control for instance)—competition which commands a decisive cost or quality advantage and which
strikes not at the margins of the profits and the outputs of the existing
firms but at their foundations and their very lives. This kind of competition is as much more effective than the other as a bombardment is
in comparison with forcing a door, and so much more important that
it becomes a matter of comparative indifference whether competition
in the ordinary sense functions more or less promptly; the powerful
lever that in the long run expands output and brings down prices is in
any case made of other stuff.

It is hardly necessary to point out that competition of the kind
we now have in mind acts not only when in being but also when it is
merely an ever-present threat. It disciplines before it attacks. The businessman feels himself to be in a competitive situation even if he is

---

[2]It should be understood that it is only our appraisal of economic performance
and not our moral judgment that can be so changed. Owing to its autonomy,
moral approval or disapproval is entirely independent of our appraisal of social
(or any other) results, unless we happen to adopt a moral system such as utilitarianism which makes moral approval and disapproval turn on them *ex defi-
nitione.*

alone in his field or if, though not alone, he holds a position such that investigating government experts fail to see any effective competition between him and any other firms in the same or a neighboring field and in consequence conclude that his talk, under examination, about his competitive sorrows is all make-believe. In many cases, though not in all, this will in the long run enforce behavior very similar to the perfectly competitive pattern.

Many theorists take the opposite view which is best conveyed by an example. Let us assume that there is a certain number of retailers in a neighborhood who try to improve their relative position by service and "atmosphere" but avoid price competition and stick as to methods to the local tradition—a picture of stagnating routine. As others drift into the trade that quasi-equilibrium is indeed upset, but in a manner that does not benefit their customers. The economic space around each of the shops having been narrowed, their owners will no longer be able to make a living and they will try to mend the case by raising prices in tacit agreement. This will further reduce their sales and so, by successive pyramiding, a situation will evolve in which increasing potential supply will be attended by increasing instead of decreasing prices and by decreasing instead of increasing sales.

Such cases do occur, and it is right and proper to work them out. But as the practical instances usually given show, they are fringe-end cases to be found mainly in the sectors furthest removed from all that is most characteristic of capitalist activity.[3] Moreover, they are transient by nature. In the case of retail trade the competition that matters arises not from additional shops of the same type, but from the department store, the chain store, the mail-order house and the supermarket which are bound to destroy those pyramids sooner or later.[4] Now a theoretical

---

[3]This is also shown by a theorem we frequently meet with in expositions of the theory of imperfect competition, viz., the theorem that, under conditions of imperfect competition, producing or trading businesses tend to be irrationally small. Since imperfect competition is at the same time held to be an outstanding characteristic of modern industry we are set to wondering what world these theorists live in, unless, as stated above, fringe-end cases are all they have in mind.

[4]The mere threat of their attack cannot, in the particular conditions, environmental and personal, of small-scale retail trade, have its usual disciplining influence, for the small man is too much hampered by his cost structure and, however well he may manage within his inescapable limitations, he can never adapt himself to the methods of competitors who can afford to sell at the price at which he buys.

construction which neglects this essential element of the case neglects all that is most typically capitalist about it; even if correct in logic as well as in fact, it is like *Hamlet* without the Danish prince.

MONOPOLISTIC PRACTICES

...We have...seen that, both as a fact and as a threat, the impact of new things—new technologies for instance—on the existing structure of an industry considerably reduces the long-run scope and importance of practices that aim, through restricting output, at conserving established positions and at maximizing the profits accruing from them. We must now recognize the further fact that restrictive practices of this kind, as far as they are effective, acquire a new significance in the perennial gale of creative destruction, a significance which they would not have in a stationary state or in a state of slow and balanced growth. In either of these cases restrictive strategy would produce no result other than an increase in profits at the expense of buyers except that, in the case of balanced advance, it might still prove to be the easiest and most effective way of collecting the means by which to finance additional investment.[5] But in the process of creative destruction, restrictive practices may do much to steady the ship and to alleviate temporary difficulties....

Practically any investment entails, as a necessary complement of entrepreneurial action, certain safeguarding activities such as insuring or hedging. Long-range investing under rapidly changing conditions, especially under conditions that change or may change at any moment under the impact of new commodities and technologies, is like shooting at a target that is not only indistinct but moving—and moving jerkily at that. Hence it becomes necessary to resort to such protecting

---

[5]Theorists are apt to look upon anyone who admits this possibility as guilty of gross error, and to prove immediately that financing by borrowing from banks or from private savers or, in the case of public enterprise, financing from the proceeds of an income tax is much more rational than is financing from surplus profits collected through a restrictive policy. For some patterns of behavior they are quite right. For others they are quite wrong. I believe that both capitalism and communism of the Russian type belong in the latter category. But the point is that theoretical considerations, especially theoretical considerations of the short-run kind, cannot solve, although they contribute to the solution of, the problem.

devices as patents or temporary secrecy of processes or, in some cases, long-period contracts secured in advance. But these protecting devices which most economists accept as normal elements of rational management[6] are only special cases of a larger class comprising many others which most economists condemn although they do not differ fundamentally from the recognized ones.

If for instance a war risk is insurable, nobody objects to a firm's collecting the cost of this insurance from the buyers of its products. But that risk is no less an element in long-run costs, if there are no facilities for insuring against it, in which case a price strategy aiming at the same end will seem to involve unnecessary restriction and to be productive of excess profits. Similarly, if a patent cannot be secured or would not, if secured, effectively protect, other means may have to be used in order to justify the investment. Among them are a price policy that will make it possible to write off more quickly than would otherwise be rational, or additional investment in order to provide excess capacity to be used only for aggression or defense. Again, if long-period contracts cannot be entered into in advance, other means may have to be devised in order to tie prospective customers to the investing firm.

In analyzing such business strategy *ex visu* of a given point of time, the investigating economist or government agent sees price policies that seem to him predatory and restrictions of output that seem to him synonymous with loss of opportunities to produce. He does not see that restrictions of this type are, in the conditions of the perennial gale, incidents, often unavoidable incidents, of a long-run process of expansion which they protect rather than impede. There is no more of paradox in this than there is in saying that motorcars are traveling faster than they otherwise would *because* they are provided with brakes.

This stands out most clearly in the case of those sectors of the economy which at any time happen to embody the impact of new things and methods on the existing industrial structure. The best way of getting a vivid and realistic idea of industrial strategy is indeed to visualize the behavior of new concerns or industries that introduce new commodities or processes (such as the aluminum industry) or else reor-

---

[6] Some economists, however, consider that even those devices are obstructions to progress which, though perhaps necessary in capitalist society, would be absent in a socialist one. There is some truth in this. But that does not affect the proposition that the protection afforded by patents and so on is, in the conditions of a profit economy, on balance a propelling and not an inhibiting factor.

ganize a part or the whole of an industry (such as, for instance, the old Standard Oil Company).

As we have seen, such concerns are aggressors by nature and wield the really effective weapon of competition. Their intrusion can only in the rarest of cases fail to improve total output in quantity or quality, both through the new method itself—even if at no time used to full advantage—and through the pressure it exerts on the preexisting firms. But these aggressors are so circumstanced as to require, for purposes of attack and defense, also pieces of armor other than price and quality of their product which, moreover, must be strategically manipulated all along so that at any point of time they seem to be doing nothing but restricting their output and keeping prices high.

On the one hand, largest-scale plans could in many cases not materialize at all if it were not known from the outset that competition will be discouraged by heavy capital requirements or lack of experience, or that means are available to discourage or checkmate it so as to gain the time and space for further developments. Even the conquest of financial control over competing concerns in otherwise unassailable positions or the securing of advantages that run counter to the public's sense of fair play—railroad rebates—move, as far as long-run effects on total output alone are envisaged, into a different light;[7] they *may* be methods for removing obstacles that the institution of private property puts in the path of progress. In a socialist society that time and space would be no less necessary. They would have to be secured by order of the central authority.

On the other hand, enterprise would in most cases be impossible if it were not known from the outset that exceptionally favorable situa-

---

[7]The qualification added removes, I think, any just cause for offense that the above proposition might conceivably cause. In case that qualification is not explicit enough, I beg leave to repeat that the moral aspect is in this case, as it must be in every case, entirely unaffected by an economic argument. For the rest, let the reader reflect that even in dealing with indubitably criminal actions every civilized judge and every civilized jury take account of the ulterior purpose in pursuit of which a crime has occurred and of the difference it makes whether an action that is a crime has or has not also effects they consider socially desirable.

Another objection would be more to the point. If an enterprise can succeed only by such means, does not that prove in itself that it cannot spell social gain? A very simple argument can be framed in support of this view. But it is subject to a severe *ceteris paribus* proviso. That is to say, it holds for conditions which are just about equivalent to excluding the process of creative destruction—capitalist reality. On reflection, it will be seen that the analogy of the practices under discussion with patents is sufficient to show this.

tions are likely to arise which if exploited by price, quality and quantity manipulation will produce profits adequate to tide over exceptionally unfavorable situations provided these are similarly managed. Again this requires strategy that in the short run is often restrictive. In the majority of successful cases this strategy just manages to serve its purpose. In some cases, however, it is so successful as to yield profits far above what is necessary in order to induce the corresponding investment. These cases then provide the baits that lure capital on to untried trails. Their presence explains in part how it is possible for so large a section of the capitalist world to work for nothing: in the midst of the prosperous twenties just about half of the business corporations in the United States were run at a loss, at zero profits, or at profits which, if they had been foreseen, would have been inadequate to call forth the effort and expenditure involved.

Our argument however extends beyond the cases of new concerns, methods and industries. Old concerns and established industries, whether or not directly attacked, still live in the perennial gale. Situations emerge in the process of creative destruction in which many firms may have to perish that nevertheless would be able to live on vigorously and usefully if they could weather a particular storm. Short of such general crises or depressions, sectional situations arise in which the rapid change of data that is characteristic of that process so disorganizes an industry for the time being as to inflict functionless losses and to create avoidable unemployment. Finally, there is certainly no point in trying to conserve obsolescent industries indefinitely; but there is point in trying to avoid their coming down with a crash and in attempting to turn a rout, which may become a center of cumulative depressive effects, into orderly retreat. Correspondingly there is, in the case of industries that have sown their wild oats but are still gaining and not losing ground, such a thing as orderly advance.[8]

---

[8]A good example illustrative of this point—in fact of much of our general argument—is the postwar history of the automobile and the rayon industry. The first illustrates very well the nature and value of what we might call "edited" competition. The bonanza time was over by about 1916. A host of firms nevertheless crowded into the industry afterwards, most of which were eliminated by 1925. From a fierce life and death struggle three concerns emerged that by now account for over 80 percent of total sales. They are under competitive pressure inasmuch as, in spite of the advantages of an established position, an elaborate sales and service organization and so on, any failure to keep up and improve the quality of their products or any attempt at monopolistic combination would call in new competitors. Among themselves, the three concerns behave in a way which should be called corespective rather than competitive: they refrain from

All this is of course nothing but the tritest common sense. But it is being overlooked with a persistence so stubborn as sometimes to raise the question of sincerity. And it follows that, within the process of creative destruction, all the realities of which theorists are in the habit of relegating to books and courses on business cycles, there is another side to industrial self-organization than that which these theorists are contemplating. "Restraints of trade" of the cartel type as well as those which merely consist in tacit understandings about price competition may be effective remedies under conditions of depression. As far as they are, they may in the end produce not only steadier but also greater expansion of total output than could be secured by an entirely uncontrolled onward rush that cannot fail to be studded with catastrophes. Nor can it be argued that these catastrophes occur in any case. We know what has happened in each historical case. We have a very imperfect idea of what might have happened, considering the tremendous pace of the process, if such pegs had been entirely absent.

Even as now extended however, our argument does not cover all cases of restrictive or regulating strategy, many of which no doubt have that injurious effect on the long-run development of output which is uncritically attributed to all of them. And even in the cases our argument does cover, the net effect is a question of the circumstances and of the way in which and the degree to which industry regulates itself in each individual case. It is certainly as conceivable that an all-pervading cartel system might sabotage all progress as it is that it might realize, with smaller social and private costs, all that perfect competition is supposed to realize. This is why our argument does not amount to a case against state regulation. It does show that there is no general case for indiscriminate "trust-busting" or for the prosecution of everything

---

certain aggressive devices (which, by the way, would also be absent in perfect competition); they keep up with each other and in doing so play for points at the frontiers. This has now gone on for upwards of fifteen years and it is not obvious that if conditions of theoretically perfect competition had prevailed during that period, better or cheaper cars would now be offered to the public, or higher wages and more or steadier employment to the workmen. The rayon industry had its bonanza time in the twenties. It presents the features incident to introducing a commodity into fields fully occupied before and the policies that impose themselves in such conditions still more clearly than does the automobile industry. And there are a number of other differences. But fundamentally the case is similar. The expansion in quantity and quality of rayon output is common knowledge. Yet restrictive policy presided over this expansion at each individual point of time.

that qualifies as a restraint of trade. Rational as distinguished from vindictive regulation by public authority turns out to be an extremely delicate problem which not every government agency, particularly when in full cry against big business, can be trusted to solve.[9] But our argument, framed to refute a prevalent *theory* and the inferences drawn therefrom about the relation between modern capitalism and the development of total output, only yields another *theory,* i.e., another outlook on facts and another principle by which to interpret them. For our purpose that is enough. For the rest, the facts themselves have the floor. . . .

Thus it is not sufficient to argue that because perfect competition is impossible under modern industrial conditions—or because it always has been impossible—the large-scale establishment or unit of control must be accepted as a necessary evil inseparable from the economic progress which it is prevented from sabotaging by the forces inherent in its productive apparatus. What we have got to accept is that it has come to be the most powerful engine of that progress and in particular of the long-run expansion of total output not only in spite of, but to a considerable extent through, this strategy which looks so restrictive when viewed in the individual case and from the individual point of time. In this respect, perfect competition is not only impossible but inferior, and has no title to being set up as a model of ideal efficiency. It is hence a mistake to base the theory of government regulation of industry on the principle that big business should be made to work as the respective industry would work in perfect competition. And socialists should rely for their criticisms on the virtues of a socialist economy rather than on those of the competitive model.

CRUMBLING WALLS

THE OBSOLESCENCE OF THE ENTREPRENEURIAL FUNCTION

. . . [There exists] the possibility that the economic wants of humanity might some day be so completely satisfied that little motive

---

[9]Unfortunately, this statement is almost as effective a bar to agreement on policy as the most thoroughgoing denial of any case for government regulation could be. In fact it may embitter discussion. Politicians, public officers and economists can stand what I may politely term the whole hog opposition of "economic royalists." Doubts about their competence, such as crowd upon us particularly when we see the legal mind at work, are much more difficult for them to stand.

would be left to push productive effort still further ahead. Such a state of satiety is no doubt very far off even if we keep within the present scheme of wants; and if we take account of the fact that, as higher standards of life are attained, these wants automatically expand and new wants emerge or are created,[10] satiety becomes a flying goal, particularly if we include leisure among consumers' goods. However, let us glance at that possibility, assuming, still more unrealistically, that methods of production have reached a state of perfection which does not admit of further improvement.

A more or less stationary state would ensue. Capitalism, being essentially an evolutionary process, would become atrophic. There would be nothing left for entrepreneurs to do. They would find themselves in much the same situation as generals would in a society perfectly sure of permanent peace. Profits and along with profits the rate of interest would converge toward zero. The bourgeois strata that live on profits and interest would tend to disappear. The management of industry and trade would become a matter of current administration, and the personnel would unavoidably acquire the characteristics of a bureaucracy. Socialism of a very sober type would almost automatically come into being. Human energy would turn away from business. Other than economic pursuits would attract the brains and provide the adventure.

For the calcuable future this vision is of no importance. But all the greater importance attaches to the fact that many of the effects on the structure of society and on the organization of the productive process that we might expect from an approximately complete satisfaction of wants or from absolue technological perfection can also be expected from a development that is clearly observable already. Progress itself may be mechanized as well as the management of a stationary economy, and this mechanization of progress may affect entrepreneurship and capitalist society nearly as much as the cessation of economic progress would. In order to see this it is only necessary to restate, first, what the entrepreneurial function consists in and, secondly, what it means for bourgeois society and the survival of the capitalist order.

. . . The function of entrepreneurs is to reform or revolutionize the pattern of production by exploiting an invention or, more generally, an untried technological possibility for producing a new commodity or producing an old one in a new way, by opening up a new source of

---

[10]Wilhelm Wundt called this Heterogony of Aims (*Heterogonie der Zwecke*).

supply of materials or a new outlet for products, by reorganizing an industry and so on. Railroad construction in its earlier stages, electrical power production before the First World War, steam and steel, the motorcar, colonial ventures afford spectacular instances of a large genus which comprises innumerable humbler ones—down to such things as making a success of a particular kind of sausage or toothbrush. This kind of activity is primarily responsible for the recurrent "prosperities" that revolutionize the economic organism and the recurrent "recessions" that are due to the disequilibrating impact of the new products or methods. To undertake such new things is difficult and constitutes a distinct economic function, first, because they lie outside of the routine tasks which everybody understands and, secondly, because the environment resists in many ways that vary, according to social conditions, from simple refusal either to finance or to buy a new thing, to physical attack on the man who tries to produce it. To act with confidence beyond the range of familiar beacons and to overcome that resistance requires aptitudes that are present in only a small fraction of the population and that define the entrepreneurial type as well as the entrepreneurial function. This function does not essentially consist in either inventing anything or otherwise creating the conditions which the enterprise exploits. It consists in getting things done.

This social function is already losing importance and is bound to lose it at an accelerating rate in the future even if the economic process itself of which entrepreneurship was the prime mover went on unabated. For, on the one hand, it is much easier now than it has been in the past to do things that lie outside familiar routine—innovation itself is being reduced to routine. Technological progress is increasingly becoming the business of teams of trained specialists who turn out what is required and make it work in predictable ways. The romance of earlier commercial adventure is rapidly wearing away, because so many more things can be strictly calculated that had of old to be visualized in a flash of genius.

On the other hand, personality and will power must count for less in environments which have become accustomed to economic change—best instanced by an incessant stream of new consumers' and producers' goods—and which, instead of resisting, accept it as a matter of course. The resistance which comes from interests threatened by an innovation in the productive process is not likely to die out as long as the capitalist order persists. It is, for instance, the great obstacle on the road toward mass production of cheap housing which presupposes radical mechanization and wholesale elimination of inefficient methods of work on the plot. But every other kind of resistance—the resistance, in particular, of consumers and producers to a new kind of thing because it is new—has well-nigh vanished already.

Thus, economic progress tends to become depersonalized and automatized. Bureau and committee work tends to replace individual action. . . .

Now a similar social process—in the last analysis the same social process—undermines the role and, along with the role, the social position of the capitalist entrepreneur. His role, though less glamorous than that of medieval warlords, great or small, also is or was just another form of individual leadership acting by virtue of personal force and personal responsibility for success. His position, like that of warrior classes, is threatened as soon as this function in the social process loses its importance, and no less if this is due to the cessation of the social needs it served than if those needs are being served by other, more impersonal, methods. . . .

. . . If capitalist evolution—"progress"—either ceases or becomes completely automatic, the economic basis of the industrial bourgeoisie will be reduced eventually to wages such as are paid for current administrative work excepting remnants of quasi-rents and monopoloid gains that may be expected to linger on for some time. Since capitalist enterprise, by its very achievements, tends to automatize progress, we conclude that it tends to make itself superfluous—to break to pieces under the pressure of its own success. The perfectly bureaucratized giant industrial unit not only ousts the small or medium-sized firm and "expropriates" its owners, but in the end it also ousts the entrepreneur and expropriates the bourgeoisie as a class which in the process stands to lose not only its income but also what is infinitely more important, its function. The true pacemakers of socialism were not the intellectuals or agitators who preached it but the Vanderbilts, Carnegies and Rockefellers. This result may not in every respect be to the taste of Marxian socialists, still less to the taste of socialists of a more popular (Marx would have said, vulgar) description. But so far as prognosis goes, it does not differ from theirs.

The Destruction of the Protecting Strata

. . . Barring . . . exceptional conditions, the bourgeois class is ill equipped to face the problems, both domestic and international, that have normally to be faced by a country of any importance. The bourgeois themselves feel this in spite of all the phraseology that seems to deny it, and so do the masses. Within a protecting framework not made of bourgeois material, the bourgeoisie may be successful, not only in the political defensive but also in the offensive, especially as an opposition. For a time it felt so safe as to be able to afford the luxury of attacking the protective frame itself; such bourgeois opposition as there was in imperial Germany illustrates this to perfection. But without protection by some non-bourgeois group, the bourgeoisie is politically helpless and unable not only to lead its nation but even to take care of its particular class interest.

But the capitalist process, both by its economic mechanics and by its psycho-sociological effects, did away with this protecting master or, as in this country, never gave him, or a substitute for him, a chance to develop. The implications of this are strengthened by another consequence of the same process. Capitalist evolution eliminates not only the king *Dei Gratia* but also the political entrenchments that, had they proved tenable, would have been formed by the village and the craft guild. Of course, neither organization was tenable in the precise shape in which capitalism found it. But capitalist policies wrought destruction much beyond what was unavoidable. They attacked the artisan in reservations in which he could have survived for an indefinite time. They forced upon the peasant all the blessings of early liberalism—the free and unsheltered holding and all the individualist rope he needed in order to hang himself.

In breaking down the pre-capitalist framework of society, capitalism thus broke not only barriers that impeded its progress but also flying buttresses that prevented its collapse. That process, impressive in its relentless necessity, was not merely a matter of removing institutional deadwood, but of removing partners of the capitalist stratum, symbiosis with whom was an essential element of the capitalist schema. Having discovered this fact which so many slogans obscure, we might well wonder whether it is quite correct to look upon capitalism as a social form *sui generis* or, in fact, as anything else but the last stage of the decomposition of what we have called feudalism. On the whole, I am inclined to believe that its peculiarities suffice to make a type and to accept that symbiosis of classes which owe their existence to different epochs and processes as the rule rather than as an exception—at least it has been the rule these 6000 years, i.e., ever since primitive tillers of the soil became the subjects of mounted nomads. But there is no great objection that I can see against the opposite view alluded to.

The Destruction of the Institutional Framework of Capitalist Society

. . . The capitalist process in much the same way in which it destroyed the institutional framework of feudal society also undermines its own. . . .

. . . The very success of capitalist enterprise paradoxically tends to impair the prestige or social weight of the class primarily associated with it and . . . the giant unit of control tends to oust the bourgeoisie from the function to which it owed that social weight. The corresponding change in the meaning, and the incidental loss in vitality, of the institutions of the bourgeois world and of its typical attitudes are easy to trace.

On the one hand, the capitalist process unavoidably attacks the economic standing ground of the small producer and trader. What it did to the pre-capitalist strata it also does—and by the same competitive mechanism—to the lower strata of capitalist industry. Here of course Marx scores. It is true that the facts of industrial concentration do not quite live up to the ideas the public is being taught to entertain about it. . . . The process has gone less far and is less free from setbacks and compensatory tendencies than one would gather from many a popular exposition. In particular, large-scale enterprise not only annihilates but also, to some extent, creates space for the small producing, and especially trading firm. Also, in the case of the peasants and farmers, the capitalist world has at last proved both willing and able to pursue an expensive but on the whole effective policy of conservation. In the long run, however, there can be little doubt about the fact we are envisaging, or about its consequences. Outside of the agrarian field, moreover, the bourgeoisie has shown but little awareness of the problem[11] or its importance for the survival of the capitalist order. The profits to be made by rationalizing the organization of production and especially by cheapening the tortuous way of commodities from the factory to the ultimate consumer are more than the mind of the typical businessman can resist.

Now it is important to realize precisely what these consequences consist in. A very common type of social criticism . . . laments the "decline of competition" and equates it to the decline of capitalism because

---

[11]Although some governments did; the government of imperial Germany did much to fight this particular kind of rationalization, and there is now a strong tendency to do the same in this country.

of the virtues it attributes to competition and the vices it attributes to modern industrial "monopolies." In this schema of interpretation, monopolization plays the role of arteriosclerosis and reacts upon the fortunes of the capitalist order through increasingly unsatisfactory economic performance. We have seen the reasons for rejecting this view. Economically neither the case for competition nor the case against concentration of economic control is anything like as strong as this argument implies. And, whether weak or strong, it misses the salient point. Even if the giant concerns were all managed so perfectly as to call forth applause from the angels in heaven, the political consequences of concentration would still be what they are.

The political structure of a nation is profoundly affected by the elimination of a host of small and medium-sized firms the owner-managers of which, together with their dependents, henchmen and connections, count quantitatively at the polls and have a hold on what we may term the foreman class that no management of a large unit can ever have; the very foundation of private property and free contracting wears away in a nation in which its most vital, most concrete, most meaningful types disappear from the moral horizon of the people.

On the other hand, the capitalist process also attacks its own institutional framework—let us continue to visualize "property" and "free contracting" as *partes pro toto*—within the precincts of the big units. Excepting the cases that are still of considerable importance in which a corporation is practically owned by a single individual or family, the figure of the proprietor and with it the specifically proprietary interest have vanished from the picture. There are the salaried executives and all the salaried managers and submanagers. There are the big stockholders. And then there are the small stockholders. The first group tends to acquire the employee attitude and rarely if ever identifies itself with the stockholding interest even in the most favorable cases, i.e., in the cases in which it identifies itself with the interest of the concern as such. The second group, even if it considers its connection with the concern as permanent and even if it actually behaves as financial theory would have stockholders behave, is at one remove from both the functions and the attitudes of an owner. As to the third group, small stockholders often do not care much about what for most of them is but a minor source of income and, whether they care or not, they hardly ever bother, unless they or some representatives of theirs are out to exploit their nuisance value; being often very ill used and still more often thinking themselves ill used, they almost regularly drift into an attitude hostile to "their" corporations, to big business in general and, particularly when things look bad, to the capitalist order as such. No element of any of those three groups into which I schematized the typical situation unconditionally takes the attitude characteristic of that curious phenomenon, so full of meaning and so rapidly passing, that is covered by the term Property.

Freedom of contracting is in the same boat. In its full vitality it meant individual contracting regulated by individual choice between an indefinite number of possibilities. The stereotyped, unindividual, impersonal and bureaucratized contract of today—this applies much more generally, but *a potiori* we may fasten upon the labor contract—which presents but restricted freedom of choice and mostly turns on a *c'est à prendre ou à laisser*, has none of the old features the most important of which become impossible with giant concerns dealing with other giant concerns or impersonal masses of workmen or consumers. The void is being filled by a tropical growth of new legal structures—and a little reflection shows that this could hardly be otherwise.

Thus the capitalist process pushes into the background all those institutions, the institutions of property and free contracting in particular, that expressed the needs and ways of the truly "private" economic activity. Where it does not abolish them, as it already has abolished free contracting in the labor market, it attains the same end by shifting the relative importance of existing legal forms—the legal forms pertaining to corporate business for instance as against those pertaining to the partnership or individual firm—or by changing their contents or meanings. The capitalist process, by substituting a mere parcel of shares for the walls of and the machines in a factory, takes the life out of the idea of property. It loosens the grip that once was so strong— the grip in the sense of the legal right and the actual ability to do as one pleases with one's own; the grip also in the sense that the holder of the title loses the will to fight, economically, physically, politically, for "his" factory and his control over it, to die if necessary on its steps. And this evaporation of what we may term the material substance of property—its visible and touchable reality—affects not only the attitude of holders but also that of the workmen and of the public in general. Dematerialized, defunctionalized and absentee ownership does not impress and call forth moral allegiance as the vital form of property did. Eventually there will be *nobody* left who really cares to stand for it—nobody within and nobody without the precincts of the big concerns.

GROWING HOSTILITY

The Social Atmosphere of Capitalism

. . . The capitalist process, so we have seen, eventually decreases the importance of the function by which the capitalist class lives. We have also seen that it tends to wear away protective strata, to break down its own defenses, to disperse the garrisons of its entrenchments. And we have finally seen that capitalism creates a critical frame of mind which, after having destroyed the moral authority of so many other institutions, in the end turns against its own; the bourgeois finds to his amazement that the rationalist attitude does not stop at the credentials of kings and popes but goes on to attack private property and the whole scheme of bourgeois values.

The bourgeois fortress thus becomes politically defenseless. Defenseless fortresses invite aggression especially if there is rich booty in them. Aggressors will work themselves up into a state of rationalizing hostility[12]—aggressors always do. No doubt it is possible, for a time, to buy them off. But this last resource fails as soon as they discover that they can have all. In part, this explains what we are out to explain. So far as it goes—it does not go the whole way of course—this element of our theory is verified by the high correlation that exists historically between bourgeois defenselessness and hostility to the capitalist order: there was very little hostility on principle as long as the bourgeois position was safe, although there was then much more reason for it; it spread *pari passu* with the crumbling of the protecting walls. . . .

In order to realize what all this means for the efficiency of the capitalist engine of production we need only recall that the family and the family home used to be the mainspring of the typically bourgeois kind of profit motive. Economists have not always given due weight to this fact. When we look more closely at their idea of the self-interest of entrepreneurs and capitalists we cannot fail to discover that the results it was supposed to produce are really not at all what one would expect from the rational self-interest of the detached individual or the childless couple who no longer look at the world through the windows

---

[12]It is hoped that no confusion will arise from my using the verb "to rationalize" in two different meanings. An industrial plant is being "rationalized" when its productive efficiency per unit of expenditure is being increased. We "rationalize" an action of ours when we supply ourselves and others with reasons for it that satisfy our standard of values regardless of what our true impulses may be.

of a family home. Consciously or unconsciously they analyzed the behavior of the man whose views and motives are shaped by such a home
and who means to work and to save primarily for wife *and children.*
As soon as these fade out from the moral vision of the businessman, we
have a different kind of *homo oeconomicus* before us who cares for
different things and acts in different ways. For him and from the standpoint of his individualistic utilitarianism, the behavior of that old type
would in fact be completely irrational. He loses the only sort of romance
and heroism that is left in the unromantic and unheroic civilization of
capitalism—the heroism of *navigare necesse est, vivere non necesse est.*[13]
And he loses the capitalist ethics that enjoins working for the future
irrespective of whether or not one is going to harvest the crop oneself.

The last point may be put more tellingly. . . . The capitalist order
entrusts the long-run interests of society to the upper strata of the bourgeoisie. They are really entrusted to the family motive operative in
those strata. The bourgeoisie worked primarily in order to invest, and
it was not so much a standard of consumption as a standard of accumulation that the bourgeoisie struggled for and tried to defend against
governments that took the short-run view.[14] With the decline of the
driving power supplied by the family motive, the businessman's time-
horizon shrinks, roughly, to his life expectation. And he might now
be less willing than he was to fulfill that function of earning, saving
and investing even if he saw no reason to fear that the results would
but swell his tax bills. He drifts into an anti-saving frame of mind and
accepts with an increasing readiness anti-saving *theories* that are indicative of a short-run *philosophy.*

But anti-saving theories are not all that he accepts. With a
different attitude to the concern he works for and with a different
scheme of private life he tends to acquire a different view of the values
and standards of the capitalist order of things. Perhaps the most striking
feature of the picture is the extent to which the bourgeoisie, besides
educating its own enemies, allows itself in turn to be educated by them.
It absorbs the slogans of current radicalism and seems quite willing to
undergo a process of conversion to a creed hostile to its very existence.
Haltingly and grudgingly it concedes in part the implications of that

---

[13]"Seafaring is necessary, living is not necessary." Inscription on an old house in
Bremen.
[14]It has been said that in economic matters "the state can take the longer view."
But excepting certain matters outside of party politics such as conservation of
natural resources, it hardly ever does.

creed. This would be most astonishing and indeed very hard to explain were it not for the fact that the typical bourgeois is rapidly losing faith in his own creed. And this again becomes fully understandable as soon as we realize that the social conditions which account for its emergence are passing.

This is verified by the very characteristic manner in which particular capitalist interests and the bourgeoisie as a whole behave when facing direct attack. They talk and plead—or hire people to do it for them; they snatch at every chance of compromise; they are ever ready to give in; they never put up a fight under the flag of their own ideals and interests—in this country there was no real resistance anywhere against the imposition of crushing financial burdens during the last decade or against labor legislation incompatible with the effective management of industry. . . . I am far from overestimating the political power of either big business or the bourgeoisie in general. Moreover, I am prepared to make large allowances for cowardice. But still, means of defense were not entirely lacking as yet and history is full of examples of the success of small groups who, believing in their cause, were resolved to stand by their guns. The only explanation for the meekness we observe is that the bourgeois order no longer makes any sense to the bourgeoisie itself and that, when all is said and nothing is done, it does not really care.

Thus the same economic process that undermines the position of the bourgeoisie by decreasing the importance of the functions of entrepreneurs and capitalists, by breaking up protective strata and institutions, by creating an atmosphere of hostility, also decomposes the motor forces of capitalism from within. Nothing else shows so well that the capitalist order not only rests on props made of extra-capitalist material but also derives its energy from extra-capitalist patterns of behavior which at the same time it is bound to destroy. . . .

THE SOCIOLOGY OF THE INTELLECTUAL

. . . Neither the opportunity of attack nor real or fancied grievances are in themselves sufficient to produce, however strongly they may favor, the emergence of active hostility against a social order. For such an atmosphere to develop it is necessary that there be groups to whose interest it is to work up and organize resentment, to nurse it, to voice it and to lead it. . . . The mass of people never develops definite opinions on its own initiative. Still less is it able to articulate them and to turn them into consistent attitudes and actions. All it can do is to follow or refuse to follow such group leadership as may offer itself. Until we have discovered social groups that will qualify for that role our theory of the atmosphere of hostility to capitalism is incomplete.

Broadly speaking, conditions favorable to general hostility to a social system or specific attack upon it will in any case tend to call forth groups that will exploit them. But in the case of capitalist society there is a further fact to be noted: unlike any other type of society, capitalism inevitably and by virtue of the very logic of its civilization creates, educates and subsidizes a vested interest in social unrest. . . .[15]

. . . Intellectuals are not a social class in the sense in which peasants or industrial laborers constitute social classes; they hail from all the corners of the social world, and a great part of their activities consist in fighting each other and in forming the spearheads of class interests not their own. Yet they develop group attitudes and group interests sufficiently strong to make large numbers of them behave in the way that is usually associated with the concept of social classes. Again, they cannot be simply defined as the sum total of all the people who have had a higher education; that would obliterate the most important features of the type. Yet anyone who had—and, save exceptional cases, nobody who had not—is a potential intellectual; and the fact that their minds are all similarly furnished facilitates understanding between them and constitutes a bond. Nor would it serve our purpose to make the concept coextensive with the membership of the liberal professions; physicians or lawyers for instance are not intellectuals in the relevant sense unless they talk or write about subjects outside of their professional competence which no doubt they often do—particularly the lawyers. Yet there is a close connection between the intellectuals and the professions. For *some* professions—especially if we count in journalism—actually do belong almost wholly to the domain of the intellectual type; the members of *all* professions have the opportunity of becoming intellectuals; and many intellectuals take to some profession for a living. . . .

---

[15]Every social system is sensitive to revolt and in every social system stirring up revolt is a business that pays in case of success and hence always attracts both brain and brawn. It did in feudal times—very much so. But warrior nobles who revolted against their superiors attacked individual persons or positions. They did not attack the feudal system as such. And feudal society as a whole displayed no tendencies to encourage—intentionally or unintentionally—attacks upon its own social system as a whole.

. . . Intellectuals are in fact people who wield the power of the spoken and the written word, and one of the touches that distinguish them from other people who do the same is the absence of direct responsibility for practical affairs. This touch in general accounts for another—the absence of that first-hand knowledge of them which only actual experience can give. The critical attitude, arising no less from the intellectual's situation as an onlooker—in most cases also as an outsider —than from the fact that his main chance of asserting himself lies in his actual or potential nuisance value should add a third touch. . . .

. . . One of the most important features of the later stages of capitalist civilization is the vigorous expansion of the educational apparatus and particularly of the facilities for higher education. This development was and is no less inevitable than the development of the largest-scale industrial unit,[16] but, unlike the latter, it has been and is being fostered by public opinion and public authority so as to go much further than it would have done under its own steam. Whatever we many think of this from other standpoints and whatever the precise causation, there are several consequences that bear upon the size and attitude of the intellectual group.

First, inasmuch as higher education thus increases the supply of services in professional, quasi-professional and in the end all "white-collar" lines beyond the point determined by cost-return considerations, it may create a particularly important case of sectional unemployment.

Second, along with or in place of such unemployment, it creates unsatisfactory conditions of employment—employment in substandard work or at wages below those of the better-paid manual workers.

Third, it may create unemployability of a particularly disconcerting type. The man who has gone through a college or university easily becomes psychically unemployable in manual occupations without necessarily acquiring employability in, say, professional work. . . .

All those who are unemployed or unsatisfactorily employed or unemployable drift into the vocations in which standards are least definite or in which aptitudes and acquirements of a different order count.

---

[16] At present this development is viewed by most people from the standpoint of the ideal of making educational facilities of any type available to all who can be induced to use them. This ideal is so strongly held that any doubts about it are almost universally considered to be nothing short of indecent, a situation not improved by the comments, all too often flippant, of dissentients. Actually, we brush here against a set of extremely complex problems of the sociology of education and educational ideals which we cannot attack within the limits of this sketch. . . .

They swell the host of intellectuals in the strict sense of the term
whose numbers hence increase disproportionately. They enter it in a
thoroughly discontented frame of mind. Discontent breeds resentment.
And it often rationalizes itself into that social criticism which . . . is
in any case the intellectual spectator's typical attitude toward men,
classes and institutions especially in a rationalist and utilitarian civilization. Well, here we have numbers; a well-defined group situation of
proletarian hue; and a group interest shaping a group attitude that will
much more realistically account for hostility to the capitalist order than
could the theory—itself a rationalization in the psychological sense—
according to which the intellectual's righteous indignation about the
wrongs of capitalism simply represents the logical inference from out-
rageous facts and which is no better than the theory of lovers that their
feelings represent nothing but the logical inference from the virtues of
the beloved.[17] Moreover our theory also accounts for the fact that this
hostility increases, instead of diminishing, with every achievement of
capitalist evolution.

Of course, the hostility of the intellectual group—amounting to
moral disapproval of the capitalist order—is one thing, and the general
hostile atmosphere which surrounds the capitalist engine is another
thing. The latter is the really significant phenomenon; and it is not
simply the product of the former but flows partly from independent
sources, some of which have been mentioned before; so far as it does,
it is raw material for the intellectual group to work on. There are give-
and-take relations between the two which it would require more space
to unravel than I can spare. The general contours of such an analysis
are however sufficiently obvious and I think it safe to repeat that the role
of the intellectual group consists primarily in stimulating, energizing,
verbalizing and organizing this material and only secondarily in adding to it. Some particular aspects will illustrate the principle.

Capitalist evolution produces a labor movement which obviously is not the creation of the intellectual group. But it is not surprising
that such an opportunity and the intellectual demiurge should find each
other. Labor never craved intellectual leadership but intellectuals in-

---

[17]The reader will observe that any such theories would be unrealistic even if
the facts of capitalism or the virtues of the beloved were actually all that the
social critic or the lover believes them to be. It is also important to note that in
the overwhelming majority of cases both critics and lovers are obviously sincere:
neither psycho-sociological nor psycho-physical mechanisms enter as a rule into
the limelight of the Ego, except in the mask of sublimations.

vaded labor politics. They had an important contribution to make: they verbalized the movement, supplied theories and slogans for it—class war is an excellent example—made it conscious of itself and in doing so changed its meaning. In solving this task from their own standpoint, they naturally radicalized it, eventually imparting a revolutionary bias to the most bourgeois trade-union practices, a bias most of the non-intellectual leaders at first greatly resented. But there was another reason for this. Listening to the intellectual, the workman is almost invariably conscious of an impassable gulf if not of downright distrust. In order to get hold of him and to compete with non-intellectual leaders, the intellectual is driven to courses entirely unnecessary for the latter who can afford to frown. Having no genuine authority and feeling always in danger of being unceremoniously told to mind his own business, he must flatter, promise and incite, nurse left wings and scowling minorities, sponsor doubtful or submarginal cases, appeal to fringe ends, profess himself ready to obey—in short, behave toward the masses as his predecessors behaved first toward their ecclesiastical superiors, later toward princes and other individual patrons, still later toward the collective master of bourgeois complexion. Thus, though intellectuals have not created the labor movement, they have yet worked it up into something that differs substantially from what it would be without them.

The social atmosphere, for the theory of which we have been gathering stones and mortar, explains why public policy grows more and more hostile to capitalist interests, eventually so much so as to refuse on principle to take account of the requirements of the capitalist engine and to become a serious impediment to its functioning. The intellectual group's activities have however a relation to anti-capitalist policies that is more direct than what is implied in their share in verbalizing them. Intellectuals rarely enter professional politics and still more rarely conquer responsible office. But they staff political bureaus, write party pamphlets and speeches, act as secretaries and advisers, make the individual politician's newspaper reputation which, though it is not everything, few men can afford to neglect. In doing these things they to some extent impress their mentality on almost everything that is being done.

The actual influence exerted varies greatly with the state of the political game from mere formulation to making a measure politically possible or impossible. But there is always plenty of scope for it. When we say that individual politicians and parties are exponents of class interests we are at best emphasizing one-half of the truth. The other half, just as important if not more so, comes into view when we consider that politics is a profession which evolves interests of its own— interests that may clash with as well as conform to the interests of the groups that a man or party "represents."[18] Individual and party opinion is, more than anything else, sensitive to those factors in the political situation that directly affect the career or the standing of the individual or party. Some of these are controlled by the intellectual group in much the same sense as is the moral code of an epoch that exalts the cause of some interests and puts the cause of others tacitly out of court.

Finally, that social atmosphere or code of values affects not only policies—the spirit of legislation—but also administrative practice. But again there is also a more direct relation between the intellectual group and bureaucracy. The bureaucracies of Europe are of pre- and extra-capitalist origin. However much they may have changed in composition as the centuries rolled on, they never identified themselves wholly with the bourgeoisie, its interests or its scheme of values, and never saw much more in it than an asset to be managed in the interest of the monarch or of the nation. Except for inhibitions due to professional training and experience, they are therefore open to conversion by the modern intellectual with whom, through a similar education, they have much in common, while the tinge of gentility that in many cases used to raise a barrier has been fading away from the modern civil servant during the last decades. Moreover, in times of rapid expansion of the sphere of public administration, much of the additional personnel required has to be taken directly from the intellectual group. . . .

We have rediscovered what from different standpoints and, so I believe, on inadequate grounds has often been discovered before: there is inherent in the capitalist system a tendency toward self-destruction which, in its earlier stages, may well assert itself in the form of a tendency toward retardation of progress.

I shall not stay to repeat how objective and subjective, economic and extra-economic factors, reinforcing each other in imposing accord, contribute to that result. Nor shall I stay to show . . . that those factors make not only for the destruction of the capitalist but for the emergence of a socialist civilization. They all point in that direction. The capitalist

---

[18]This of course is just as true of the intellectuals themselves with respect to the class from which they come or to which, economically and culturally, they belong. . . .

process not only destroys its own institutional framework but it also creates the conditions for another. Destruction may not be the right word after all. Perhaps I should have spoken of transformation. The outcome of the process is not simply a void that could be filled by whatever might happen to turn up; things and souls are transformed in such a way as to become increasingly amenable to the socialist form of life. With every peg from under the capitalist structure vanishes an impossibility of the socialist plan. In both these respects Marx's *vision* was right. We can also agree with him in linking the particular social transformation that goes on under our eyes with an economic process as its prime mover. What our analysis, if correct, disproves is after all of secondary importance, however essential the role may be which it plays in the socialist credo. In the end there is not so much difference as one might think between saying that the decay of capitalism is due to its success and saying that it is due to its failure.

But our answer to the question that heads this part posits far more problems than it solves. . . . The reader should bear in mind:

First, that so far we have not learned anything about the kind of socialism that may be looming in the future. For Marx and for most of his followers—and this was and is one of the most serious short-comings of their doctrine—socialism meant just one definite thing. But the definiteness really goes on further than nationalization of industry would carry us and with this an indefinite variety of economic and cultural possibilities will be seen to be compatible.

Secondly, that similarly we know nothing as yet about the precise way by which socialism may be expected to come except that there must be a great many possibilities ranging from a gradual bureaucratization to the most picturesque revolution. Strictly speaking we do not even know whether socialism will actually come to stay. For to repeat: perceiving a tendency and visualizing the goal of it is one thing and predicting that this goal will actually be reached and that the resulting state of things will be workable, let alone permanent, is quite another thing. Before humanity chokes (or basks) in the dungeon (or paradise) of socialism it may well burn up in the horrors (or glories) of imperialist wars.[19]

Third, that the various components of the tendency we have been trying to describe, while everywhere discernible, have as yet nowhere fully revealed themselves. Things have gone to different lengths

[19]Written in the summer of 1935.

in different countries but in no country far enough to allow to say with any confidence precisely how far they will go, or to assert that their "underlying trend" has grown too strong to be subject to anything more serious than temporary reverses. Industrial integration is far from being complete. Competition, actual and potential, is still a major factor in any business situation. Enterprise is still active, the leadership of the bourgeois group still the prime mover of the economic process. The middle class is still a political power. Bourgeois standards and bourgeois motivations though being increasingly impaired are still alive. Survival of traditions—and family ownership of controlling parcels of stock—still make many an executive behave as the owner-manager did of old. The bourgeois family has not yet died; in fact, it clings to life so tenaciously that no responsible politician has as yet dared to touch it by any method other than taxation. From the standpoint of immediate practice as well as for the purposes of short run forecasting—and in these things, a century is a "short run"[20]—all this surface may be more important than the tendancy toward another civilization that slowly works deep down below.

---

[20]This is why the facts and arguments . . . do not invalidate my reasoning about the possible economic results of another fifty years of capitalist evolution. The thirties may well turn out to have been the last gasp of capitalism—the likelihood of this is of course greatly increased by the current war. But again they may not. In any case there are no *purely economic* reasons why capitalism should not have another successful run which is all I wished to establish.

8

◀ JOHN KENNETH GALBRAITH* ▶

from

The New Industrial State (1967)

John Kenneth Galbraith is in many ways the epitome of the American liberal establishment and is no doubt today's most popularly read economist. One of the Kennedy entourage of intellectuals, he served as Ambassador to India from 1961 to 1963, and is, at the time of this writing, chairman of the Americans for Democratic Action, a liberal political organization. Galbraith's three major works, *American Capitalism* (1952), *The Affluent Society* (1958), and *The New Industrial State* (1967), are all concerned with the balance of power in American capitalism and have established him as one of America's most prominent social critics.

The first of these works attempts to show that even though the competitive market has been broken down as a regulating force, due to the high concentration in manufacturing industries, the allocation of resources is not as distorted as the traditional economic models would lead one to suspect. This is because a new self-regulating force, countervailing power, has grown up. Galbraith sees the growth of large companies in the sellers' market as breeding large power blocks on the opposite side of the market. Thus the big three of the automobile industry must deal with the big four of the tire

---

*Professor of Economics, Harvard University.

industry, or with the large labor unions, in purchasing their inputs. These countervailing powers tend to neutralize the monopolist power of large sellers with the resulting prices and wages more closely approximating those which would prevail under more traditionally competitive (same side of the market competition) market conditions. This insight of Galbraith's does have some validity in American capitalism; however, it has a number of limitations. For one thing this type of self-regulating force is not universally present, and even where it may potentially operate it tends to break down if any degree of collusion exists between the two opposing power blocks. In addition, Galbraith even concedes the point that during periods of inflation, when high levels of aggregate demand are present, producers may be willing to give in to the high wage demands of unions because the additional cost can be passed on to the consumer, through higher product prices, without hurting sales. Also if firms are vertically integrated and supply their own inputs, or where recriprocal buying arrangements exist, countervailing forces tend to break down.

In *The Affluent Society* Galbraith shifts his attention from the balance of power among giant producers in the market to the allocation of resources between the public and private sectors of the economy. To Galbraith business advertising, the unwillingness of Americans to increase taxes, and persistent inflation, all tend to result in an overproduction of private goods and an underproduction of public goods. This has created, according to Galbraith, a serious "social imbalance" in America. His book is a plea for a future expansion of public services in order to increase the quality of life. In relation to public policy, the need for a better balance of public vs. private goods has led some liberals, including Galbraith, to favor increases in government spending over tax cuts as a means of countering business recessions. The acceptance of Galbraith's position necessitates a greater role for government in the economy, a basic tenet of American liberalism.

In the selection presented here, the essential message of Galbraith's book, *The New Industrial State,* is put forth.* This time the line between the public and private sectors of the economy becomes blurred by the massive power of giant corporations. Galbraith pictures a major segment of the American economy as planed but where the planning organization is the corporation rather than the state, and where corporate sovereignty has replaced consumer sovereignty. According to him, "modern highly technical processes and products and [the] associated requirements of capital and time lead inevitably to planning—to the management of markets by those who supply them," and in order to carry out this planning, corporations must be large. Gone are the countervailing forces which Galbraith once believed kept monop-

---

*This article originally appeared in *The Atlantic Monthly* and is Galbraith's own condensation of his book.

olistic power in check, and in their place is the subjection of both the consumer and the state to the goals of the mature corporation and its ruling "technostructure." Galbraith does not view these developments completely with disdain, for he feels that they are the inevitable (and even desirable) result of the imperatives of modern technology. If society is to continue to advance, large-size corporations are necessary in order to achieve operational efficiency, innovation, and economic stability. It is on these points that Galbraith has been most severely criticized by economists. Many are not willing to accept his position that giant corporations are a necessary condition for efficiency and progress, or that technology destroys the usefulness of the market. The argument of Hayek* may be thought of as a counter to Galbraith's brand of technological determinism.

As the following article shows, Galbraith is often critical of traditional economists for not accepting his proposition that for the largest part of the American economy the market system is no longer viable. As a counter, Galbraith's peers have often regarded him as a poor theoretician and a generalizer who can't support his arguments with facts. But criticism is not limited to the academic community; businessmen are often critical of his view of them as manipulators of the market, and the public is suspicious of his seemingly ambitious programs which they see as increasing the tax burden. In fact Galbraith is an intellectual who is willing to go beyond the boundaries of traditional economics to try to arrive at a more realistic picture of the operation of American capitalism. He is a great admirer of American big business and demonstrates both in his writings and in his personal actions that he values the welfare of society above all else. What is perhaps his greatest weakness was pointed out by his admirer Robert Heilbroner. In a review of *The New Industrial State* Heilbroner points out that Galbraith's "grand outline is weakened by an unwillingness to press home his analysis to its bitter conclusion." Heilbroner states, and with some validity, that Galbraith lacks "the courage to carry his theoretical model into the future, whatever its course." Concerning the implications of Galbraith's system for the future of capitalism, "rather than producing clear judgment, the moral power of his argument is, finally, dissipated in wit." In an article presented later in this volume, Heilbroner himself attempts to be more adventurous.**

Galbraith does not wish to see Americans becoming slaves to the goals of the military–industrial complex, but his call for the scientific and educated elite to direct the government, to maintain an aesthetic balance, has thus far been a futile one.

——R. R.

---

*See chapter 2.
**See reading 10.

from

The New Industrial State*†

PLANNING AND THE MODERN CORPORATION

Few things so firmly establish one's grasp on the commonplace as to list the changes that have occurred in economic life in the last half century. Machines have, of course, extensively replaced crude manpower. Increasingly, one machine instructs other machines in the process called automation. Industrial corporations have become very, very large. They are no longer directed as a matter of right by their owners; they are guided impersonally by their management. They deploy large amounts of capital, much of which they derive from their own earnings. These earnings are now by far the most important source of savings—income that is needed for industrial expansion is no longer allowed to get into the hot and eager hands of those who might choose to use it for their personal consumption.

Economic well-being has also greatly increased—at least in the fortunate countries of Europe and North America. And the market has changed. In the world described by Alfred Marshall, the great English economist of the early decades of this century, prices were established, as he said, by the "higgling and bargaining" of the market after having been, as he also said, "tossed hither and thither like a shuttlecock." Now, in the world of the large corporation, they are set by the corporation, and they often remain fixed for long periods of time. These companies are also at considerable pains to persuade the customer on what he should buy. Everyone, including all economists, agrees on consumer sovereignty in principle, but no one wants to trust it unduly in practice.

Finally, even in countries such as the United States, where, as we all agree, faith in free enterprise is one of the minor branches of theology, the state plays a large and increasing role in economic affairs.

*The New Industrial State Copyright © 1967 by John Kenneth Galbraith reprinted by permission of the publisher Houghton Mifflin Company.
†From The New Industrial State Copyright © 1967 by J. K. Galbraith (Hamish Hamilton, London).

It stabilizes purchasing power—what economists call aggregate demand; it underwrites expensive technology such as modern weaponry and the supersonic transports; it restrains, or anyhow seeks to restrain, wages and prices to prevent inflation; it educates the technical and specialized manpower that modern industry requires; and the state buys upwards of a fifth of all that the modern industrial community produces. In the presumptively capitalist economy of the United States, one is charmed to reflect, the state plays a very much larger role in almost every facet of economic activity than it does in the avowedly planned and socialist economy of, say, India.

I want to show . . . that the changes just mentioned are part of an interrelated complex, or matrix, as economists say. And I want to show also that the result is larger than the sum of the parts, that specifically there have been three great consequences. The first is rather comprehensive economic planning; which is to say, producers extensively manage the lives of those whom they are assumed to serve. And they must. By its nature, the modern industrial economy is a planned economy.

The second consequence is that there are strongly convergent tendencies, as there are in all industrial societies. This is despite their very different billing as capitalist or socialist or Communist by those who act as the custodians of our official ideology.

The third consequence is that to a far greater extent than we imagine, our beliefs and cultural attitudes are accommodated to the needs and goals of the industrial mechanism by which we are supplied. These serve the convenience of modern industry. Industrial societies differ not in the fact but in the method by which ideas are patterned to industrial convenience and need.

Let me begin by showing how technology, time, and capital shape the modern economy.

On June 15, 1903, after some months of preparation, the Ford Motor Company was formed in Detroit, Michigan, for the manufacture of automobiles. The first car reached the market that *same* October. The firm had an authorized capital of $150,000, although only $100,000 worth was issued and only $28,500 was for cash. Although it does not bear on the present discussion, the company made a handsome profit that year and did not fail to make a very large profit for many years thereafter. In 1903 Ford employed 125 men.

In the spring of 1964, the Ford Motor Company introduced what is now called a new automobile. In accordance with current fashion, it was named, one hopes inappropriately, a "Mustang"—a mustang is a very roughriding animal, as all close students of television are aware. Preparations for the Mustang required three and a half years. From late in the autumn of 1962, when the design was settled, until the spring of 1964, there was a fairly firm commitment to the particular car that eventually emerged. Engineering, "styling," and development costs were nearly $60 million.[1] In 1964, employment in the Ford Motor Company averaged 317,000 men. Assets in 1964 were approximately $6 billion.

Nearly all of the effects of industrial change are revealed in one way or another by these comparisons. Let me list them.

First. With increasingly sophisticated knowledge there is an increasing lapse of time between the beginning and the completion of a task. Technology means the systematic application of scientific or other organized knowledge to practical tasks. It is applied not to the manufacture of a car as a whole. It is brought to bear on very small elements of its manufacture—on the qualities of particular steels or the methods of machining a particular part. Then knowledge is applied to the combination of these parts, and then on assembly, and thus on to final completion. The process of manufacture stretches back in time as the root system of a plant stretches down into the ground, and the longest of these filaments, as it were, sets the total time required in production. The first Ford needed only ordinary steel, obtained from the warehouse in the morning and worked that afternoon. The provision of steel for the Mustang, in contrast, reached back to specifications prepared by the designers, to tests in the laboratory, then to design of the appropriate metalworking machinery, and to production and installation of these tools. Years thus elapse between the beginning of work on a car and its appearance.

Second. There is a great increase in the amount of capital that is committed to production. This is partly the result of the increased elapse of time, for that means increased investment in the work that is in process. But the knowledge which is applied to the various elements of the task also costs money. And so does machinery, which is the most characteristic manifestation of technology.

---

[1] I am grateful to Mr. Walter T. Murphy of the Ford Motor Company for providing these details. I have also drawn on earlier help from Robert McNamara which he gave when he was still an executive of Ford. Details on the early history of Ford are mostly from Allan Nevins, *Ford: The Times, the Man, the Company* (Charles Scribner's Sons, 1954).

Only very simple machinery was used in the manufacture of the first Ford. No trained engineers were employed. The frame of the car was moved manually, and it could be lifted by two men. The modern auto factory, in contrast, is itself a complex and closely articulated machine. Nothing is done by muscular effort. Computers control the flow of parts and components to the assembly line. Only the recurrent hideousness of the product remains to remind one that human beings are involved. Thus (along with increased output, of course) the increase in capitalization of Ford to $6 billion.

Third. With increasing technology, time and capital tend to be committed ever more inflexibly to a particular task. Organized knowledge is used to improve the performance of a specific task. That task must be precisely defined before it is divided and subdivided into its component parts. Knowledge and equipment are then brought to bear on these fractions. But they are applied only to the fractions of the task as it was initially conceived. If that task is changed, new knowledge and new equipment will have to be mobilized for each part. So once a decision is made on what to produce, it is very difficult to alter it.

The engine and chassis of the original Ford were made by the Dodge Brothers (who eventually also made an automobile themselves). Their machine shop could have worked as well on bicycles, steam engines, or carriages, and in point of fact, it had been so employed. Had Ford and his associates decided at any point to shift from gasoline to steam power as a source of power for the vehicle, the machine shop could have accommodated itself to this considerable change by modern standards in a few hours.

By contrast, all parts of the Mustang, the tools and equipment that worked on these parts, and the steel and the other materials going into these parts were designed for this car and this car almost alone. The manufacture of a Barracuda, which differs mostly in having an even more bizarre name, would have required a very different tooling up. So would a "Serpent," a "Roach," or a "Locust"—if one may look ahead on automobile nomenclature.

Fourth. Technology requires specialized manpower. Not surprisingly, organized knowledge can be brought to bear only by those who possess such knowledge. However, technology is not the only thing that requires specialized manpower; so does the planning, which I will come to in a moment. And so does organization, for it takes specialists in organization to manage the organization which results from specialization.

This does not mean that the talent required for modern industry is necessarily more demanding, on some absolute scale of intelligence, than that of an earlier and technically less advanced era. Modern industrial man is not some species of superman; he must be helped to resist the temptation so to regard himself.

Indeed, the makers of the original Ford were men of considerable talent. The Dodge Brothers had previously invented a bicycle and a steam launch. Detroit legend also celebrated their remarkable exuberance when drunk. James Couzens, who was Ford's partner and who almost certainly had more to do with the early success of the enterprise than Henry Ford himself, went on to be a police commissioner and mayor of Detroit and then to the Senate to become, as a Republican, a brilliant and undeviating supporter of Franklin D. Roosevelt. Not even Robert McNamara has shown more reach. What the members of the modern company do have is a much deeper knowledge of the specialized matters for which they are responsible. It is, like all others, a great assemblage of such specialists.

Fifth. Specialization obviously requires organization. Only thus is the work of specialists brought to a coherent result. It is obvious that if there are many specialists, this coordination will be a major task in itself. Next only to machinery, massive and complex organizations are the most visible manifestations of a world of advanced technology. Its manifestation in the case of Ford is the growth from 125 to 317,000 men.

Finally, from the time and capital that must be committed and the rigidity of these commitments comes the inevitability of planning. Tasks must be so performed that they are right not for the time that they are undertaken but for the time in the distant future when they are completed. Developments, occurring between the time of initiation and the time of accomplishment, must be anticipated. The effect, if adverse, must be neutralized. Or the events must be prevented.

In the early days of the Ford Motor Company, the future was very close at hand. What was raw material today would be a car next week. To fail to anticipate adverse contingencies was not fatal; anything that went unexpectedly wrong could be quickly remedied. Many things did go wrong. The earliest vehicles, as they came to the market, would have worried Ralph Nader. The cooling system did not always cool, the brakes did not reliably brake, and the carburetor did not always feed fuel to the engine. Once a Los Angeles dealer sent a message that when the cars he was receiving were steered, the "front wheels turn wrong." But these defects, though not minor, could be promptly remedied. Such faults in the Mustang would have been highly unpleasant and both time-consuming and costly to repair. Similarly, the original Ford used materials, labor, and components of a highly unspecialized character that were available in the open market. A shortage could be remedied by sending someone out to buy what was needed. A failure in delivery for the specialized machinery, materials, or components required for the modern vehicle would be subject to no such remedy. And the situation is the same with labor. In the days of the first Ford, an ordinary laborer or even a first-rate operative could be hired in the nearest saloon. A systems engineer cannot be so recruited. Nor can other specialized talent.

Here I come to a point of great importance. Technology—and associated change—not only requires planning, but also impairs and even destroys the usefulness of the market. Simple things can be bought and sold on the market. Complex things cannot. The farmer can find the things he needs for production in the next town. The automobile manufacturer cannot. There was an open market for muskets in their day. There is not, fortunately, for missiles. Orville Wright was able to buy most of what he needed for the first airplane in Dayton, Ohio. The market will not supply the materials, parts, systems, and engineering talent required for a modern spacecraft. These must be foreseen, and the supply and price arranged months and years in advance.

The modern automobile, by which I have illustrated the foregoing tendencies, is, by many standards, an elementary product. For more sophisticated products, time, capital, inflexibility of commitment, specialization, organization, and planning are all greatly increased. This is remarkably so for, among other things, modern weaponry.

When Philip II settled on the redemption of England at the end of March, 1587, he was not unduly troubled by the circumstance that Spain had no navy. Some men-of-war were available from newly conquered Portugal; but, in the main, merchant ships would suffice. In other words, a navy could be had from the market. At Cadiz three weeks later Sir Francis Drake destroyed quite a few of these vessels. But this was not a fatal blow; more could be bought or quickly built. Accordingly, and despite what historians have always described as unconscionable inefficiency, the Armada sailed in a strength of 130 ships a little over a year later on May 18, 1588. The cost, though it was certainly considerable, was well within the resources of the Spanish Empire.

To create a modern fleet of the numerical size of the Armada, comprising aircraft carriers and an appropriate complement of aircraft, nuclear submarines, Polaris missiles, destroyers, auxiliary and supporting craft, and bases and communications, would take a first-rate industrial power a minimum of twenty years. Though modern Spain is rich beyond the dreams of its monarchs in its most expansive age, it could not for a moment contemplate such an enterprise. In World War II, no combat plane that had not been substantially designed before the outbreak of hostilities saw actual service. Since then, the lead time for comparable weaponry has become very much greater. No one in late middle age stands in any danger of weapons now being designed; they are a menace to the unborn and the unconceived.

It is a commonplace of modern technology that we know that problems have solutions before there is knowledge of how they are to be solved. It is reasonably certain that a man can be landed on the moon within the next five years. However, numerous technical details of this journey remain to be worked out. It is known that air can be made breathable and water drinkable for those who must remain behind; but there is still much uncertainty as to the best methods of cleaning up the atmosphere and the lakes and streams.

If methods of performing a specified task have been fully worked out, the cost in time and money of bringing organized intelligence to bear on the task will be much less than if the methods are still uncretain. Uncertainty about the properties of the metal to be used for the skin of a supersonic transport, uncertainty therefore about the proper way of handling and working the metal, and uncertainty therefore about the character and design of the equipment required all can add extravagantly to the time and cost of obtaining such a vehicle. This problem-solving, with its high costs in time and money, is a recognized feature of modern technology. It graces all modern economic discussion under the cachet of industrial research and development.

The need for planning arises from the long period of time that elapses during the production process, the high investment that is involved, the inflexible commitment of that investment to the particular task, and the failure of the market when there is high technology. Where methods are unknown or uncertain, and where, accordingly, there must be this expenditure for research and development, planning is even more essential. It is also more demanding. The time that is involved, the money that is at risk, and the number of things, accordingly, that can go wrong and the magnitude of the possible ensuing disaster all increase. The cost and risk may be beyond the resources of a private firm.

An obvious solution is to have the state absorb the major risks under such circumstances. This is becoming established practice. It can guarantee a market for the weapon, airplane, or other similar technical product. Or it can underwrite the costs of development; if these increase beyond expectation, the firms will not have to carry them. The drift of this argument will be evident. Technology leads to planning. And in its higher manifestations, technology puts the problems of planning beyond the reach of the individual industrial firm. The compulsions of technology, not ideology or political wile, then require the firm to seek the help and the proctection of the state. This is true under what has always been called capitalism. It is true, as a matter of course, in the formally planned and Communist economies. Technology and associated change require planning by the producing firm. Both impose a broadly similar role on the state.

But in the Western economies, it is a mistake to think of the state as the main planning instrument. Rather it is the large corporation. This is not without paradox. Large corporations, we were all taught from our prenatal days, are the very essence of unplanned capitalism.

A market economy is an arrangement by which people sally forth and by their purchases make clear what they want or do not want. Their market behavior, in turn, is an instruction to producers in regard to what they should or should not produce. The initiative lies with the individual. He is sovereign. There is something admirably libertarian and democratic about this process. It is not hard to understand why, among the devout, the market, no less than Christianity and Zen Buddhism, evokes such formidable spiritual feeling.

But in the case of the Mustang, the initiatve came not from the consumer but the producer. It was not the consumer who established the price in the market. The price was set by the manufacturer. The consumer had no idea that he needed this blessing before it was unveiled, although indubitably he welcomed it thereafter. Nor was he left with a free choice of his purchase. On the contrary, considerable thought was given to the means of ensuring that he would want it and buy it.

When initiative lies with the consumer, we agree that we have a market economy. When it passes to the producer—and the consumer is accommodated to the needs and convenience of the producer—it is commonly and correctly said that we have a planned economy.

The planning may be imperfect. The consumer retains the right to resist persuasion or otherwise contract out of the management to which he or she is subject. There will be Edsels as well as Mustangs, and the latter may much exceed planned totals. Nevertheless, imperfect or otherwise, there is planning. The modern large corporation can be understood only as an adaptation to the needs of modern technology, related capital requirements, and of organization and the resulting planning.

Successful planning requires that the planning authority be able to control or sufficiently influence the various contingencies which bear upon the results it seeks. And it must not be subject to the power of those who might frustrate its plans either by ill-considered interference or even by carefully considered interference which reflects other and alien objectives. The modern large business corporation possesses the principal requisites of successful planning. What it cannot do is done by the state.

The modern corporation achieves much of the requisite authority merely by being very large. This enables it to possess and control large amounts of capital and to mobilize and direct the large number of specialists that modern technology requires. Also, if the firm is large, contingencies that cannot be perfectly controlled can be absorbed or offset. If planning for a particular product by General Motors or General Dynamics goes sour, there are other products to offset this misfortune.

A plausible consequence of these advantages of size is that the modern industrial enterprise will be very large. And so it is. In 1962 the five largest industrial corporations in the United States, with combined assets in excess of $36 billion, possessed over 12 percent, almost one eighth, of all the assets used by all companies in manufacturing. The 50 largest firms had over a third of all manufacturing resources. The 500 largest, a number whose presidents could be seated in a moderate-sized theater, had well over two thirds.[2] In the mid-nineteen-fifties, 23 corporations provided 15 per cent of all the employment in manufacturing.

We have difficulty in thinking of the private firm as a planning instrument because we associate planning with the state. But the mod-

---

[2] Data on the concentration of industrial activity in the hands of large firms, and especially any that seem to show an increase in concentration, sustain a controversy in the United States that at times reaches mildly pathological proportions. The reason is that much of the argument between those who see the market as a viable institution and those who feel that it is succumbing to monopolistic influences has long turned on these figures. These figures are defended or attacked according to predilection. However, the orders of magnitude given here are not subject to serious question.

ern industrial enterprise operates on a scale that is far more nearly comparable with that of government than that of old-fashioned market-oriented activity. In 1965 three American industrial corporations, General Motors, Standard Oil of New Jersey, and Ford Motor Company, together had more gross income than all the farms in the United States. The income of General Motors alone about equaled that of the three million smallest farmers in the country. The gross revenues of each of these three corporations far exceeded those of any single state of the American Union. The revenues of General Motors in 1963 were fifty times those of the state of Nevada, eight times those of the state of New York, and slightly less than one-fifth those of the federal government.

Economists have anciently quarreled over the reason for the great size of the modern corporation. Is it because size is essential in order to reap the economies of modern large-scale production? Is it, more insidiously, because the big firm wishes to exercise monopoly power in its markets? There is a little truth in the answers to both of these shopworn questions. The firm must be large enough to carry the large capital commitments of modern technology. It must also be large enough to control its markets. But the modern firm is larger than either of these purposes requires. General Motors is not only large enough to afford the best size of automobile plant but is large enough to afford a dozen of the best size. And it is large enough, in addition, to produce a host of other things as diverse as aircraft engines and refrigerators. Why is this? And why, although it is large enough to have the market power associated with monopoly, do consumers not complain excessively about exploitation? We have here the answer. The great size of a modern corporation allows economies not possible for the small firm and permits the control of markets, to be sure; but its primary advantage lies in the service it renders to its planning. And for this planning— the control of supply, control of demand, control of capital supply, absorption of risk or minimization of risk where risk cannot be avoided —there is no clear upper limit to the desirable size. It could be that the bigger the better.

A prime requirement of the planning authority is control over its own decisions. This autonomy has, in fact, a double purpose. It is indispensable if the authority is to pursue the objectives of its planning. I shall have more to say on this later. It is also a vitally necessary aspect of decision-making under conditions of advanced technology. I must digress here for a special word about this.

As technology becomes increasingly sophisticated and as it leads

on to specialization and planning, decisions in the business enterprise
cease to come from individuals. They come necessarily, inescapably,
from groups. The groups, as often informal as formal, and subject to
constant change in composition, contain the men possessed of the information or with access to the information that bears on the particular
decision. They contain also those whose skills consist in extracting and
testing this information and obtaining a conclusion. It is through such
groups that men act successfully on matters where no single person,
however exalted or intelligent, has more than a fraction of the necessary knowledge. It is such groups that make modern business possible,
and in other contexts, also make modern government possible.

Effective participation in such decision-making is not closely
related to the individual's nominal rank in the formal hierarchy of the
company or corporation. This is something that takes an effort of mind
to grasp. Everyone is influenced by the stereotyped organization chart
of the business enterprise. At the top is the board of directors, the
chairman, the president, and the principal executive officer, thereafter
the department or divisional heads. Power is assumed to pass down
from this pinnacle. Those at the top give orders; those below relay
them on or respond.

Power is employed in this way only in very simple organizations—in the peacetime drill of the National Guard or in a troop of
Boy Scouts moving out on Saturday maneuvers. Elsewhere decisions
require information, and some power will then pass to the person or
persons who have this information. If this knowledge is highly particular to themselves, as in the case of sophisticated technology, their power
becomes very great. At Los Alamos, New Mexico, during the development of the atomic bomb, Enrico Fermi rode a bicycle up the hill to
his work; Major General Leslie Groves presided in grandeur over the
entire Manhattan District. Fermi, in company with a handful of others,
could, at various stages, have brought the entire enterprise to an end.
They were also irreplaceable. No such power rested with General
Groves at the top. At any moment he could have been replaced by
any one of one hundred others without any loss.

When power is exercised in this fashion by a group, not only
does it pass into the organization but it passes into the organization
irrevocably. If an individual has taken a decision, he can be called
before another individual, who is his superior in the hierarchy, and
his information can be extracted and examined, and his decision can
then be reversed by the greater wisdom or experience of the superior.
But if the decision requires the combined information of a group, it

cannot be safely reversed by another individual. The individual will have to get the judgment of other specialists. This returns the power once more to the organization.

The modern large business corporation is admirably equipped to protect the autonomy on which the group decision required by technology and planning so deeply depends. The corporate charter accords a large area of independent action to the firm in the conduct of its affairs. And this freedom of conduct is defended as a sacred right. In our business attitudes nothing is held to be so iniquitous as government interference in the internal affairs of the corporation. And attitudes in other countries are similar if somewhat less choleric. There is equally vehement resistance to any invasion by trade unions of the prerogatives of managment.

But interference from those who own or supply capital would be equally damaging to the planning of the firm and to the quality of its decisions. The modern firm exempts itself from interference from those who supply current capital requirements first of all by having its own source of capital. The use of earnings returned from profits is wholly at the discretion of those who run the firm. If funds must come from a banker, his views must be treated with respect. He can also intervene. If he isn't needed and the funds aren't coming from him, only politeness is in order.

Few things have resulted in a greater shift in power than the ability of the large modern firm to supply itself with capital. Few things have more altered the character of capitalism. It is hardly surprising that retained earnings of corporations have become such an overwhelmingly important source of capital.

The stockholder too has been separated from all effective power in the large corporation. Many things have led to this result. With the passage of time and the ineluctable effects of distribution by inheritance, of estate taxes, of philanthropy, of alimony, and of the other enjoyments of nonfunctional heirs, even the largest holdings are dispersed. It is next to impossible to get any considerable number of stockholders together for an action in opposition to management. Instead, the board of directors meets in solemn conclave to select the management, which previously selected that board. The electoral rituals of the modern large company are among our most elaborate exercises in popular and self illusion.

But the exercise of authority by the modern enterprise is also protected by the technical complexity of its decisions. Some forty years ago it was discovered that Colonel Robert W. Stewart, who was then the head of the Standard Oil Company of Indiana, was transferring an appreciable share of the revenues of the company, at least temporarily, to his own pocket. With colleagues he had arranged to have the firm buy crude petroleum from a Canadian company, which he partly owned and which existed for the sole purpose of buying the oil in Texas and marking up the price to sell it to (among others) Colonel Stewart's firm. It was an admirable business. There were no costs at all, and Colonel Stewart got the profit. He later explained that he intended to return the bonds in which he put these profits to Standard Oil of Indiana, but had carelessly allowed them to remain in his safe-deposit box for many years and even more carelessly had clipped some of the coupons. The Rockefellers, who owned about 15 percent of the stock of the company, were able, though not without effort and expense, to throw the colonel out. It might not have been possible without the great prestige of John D. Rockefeller, Jr., and it was only possible because the colonel was engaged in a simple and very comprehensible form of skulduggery. Modern malfeasance or misfeasance would turn on some complicated problem of patents, procurement, royalties, government contracts, or the like in the technology of petrochemicals. It would not seem nearly so safe for outsiders to intervene in so difficult a matter, nor would the remedy be so unambiguous. I have said that modern group decision-making requires the exclusion of uninformed interference. This works both ways. The nature of the decision also excludes interference by owners.

One thing does make the autonomy of the modern corporation vulnerable. That is a failure of earnings. Then the corporation has no source of earnings, so it must turn to banks and other outside investors for savings. The latter, since the firm is doing badly, will have prying tendencies. And the stockholders who are not being rewarded may also be moved to do something about it. In modern times virtually all proxy battles in major companies have occurred when the firm was doing poorly. We may lay it down as a rule that a management which is making money is secure in its autonomy. One which is losing money is not. We should expect, as a final characteristic of the large corporation, that it would take care to protect its autonomy by always making money.

Here too our expectations are fulfilled. Economists have not yet noticed how completely they are fulfilled.

In the year 1957, a year of mild recession in the United States, not one of the hundred largest industrial corporations failed to return a profit. Only one of the largest two hundred finished the year in the red. Seven years later, in 1964, which was a prosperous year by general agreement, all of the first hundred again made money; only two among the first two hundred had losses, and only seven among the first five hundred. None of the fifty largest merchandising trading firms failed to return a profit. Nor did any one of the fifty largest utilities. And among the fifty largest transportation companies, only three railroads, together with the temporarily troubled Eastern Airlines, failed to make money.

Business liturgy has long intoned that profits and losses are symmetrical. One gets the profits at the price of risking losses. "The American competitive enterprise system is an acknowledged profit and loss system, the hope of profits being the incentive and the fear of loss being the spur." This is not true of that part of the economy in which the firm is able to protect its profits by planning. It isn't true of the United States Steel Corporation, author of the sentence just cited, which has not had losses for a quarter of a century.

Such is the corporation as a planning authority. It rivals in size the state itself. It has authority extending over and uniting the capital and organized talent that modern technology requires. Its authority extends on to its supply of capital. And its power is safely removed and protected from the extraneous or conflicting authority of either the state or its own owners or creditors.

[Next] I propose to examine how the corporation as a planning authority manages its environment—more especially, its prices and customers—and how it relates itself to the state.

MARKET PLANNING AND THE ROLE OF GOVERNMENT

In fact since Adam and as a matter of settled doctrine since Adam Smith, the businessman has been assumed to be subordinate to the market. . . . [I have shown that] modern highly technical processes and products and associated requirements of capital and time lead inevitably to planning—to the management of markets by those who supply them. It is technology, not ideology, that brings this result. The market serves admirably to supply simple things. But excellent as it may be on muskets, it is very bad on missiles. And not even the supply of components for the modern automobile can be trusted to the market; neither is it safe to assume that the market will absorb the necessary production at a remunerative price. There must be planning here as well.

The principal planning instrument in the modern economy is the large corporation. Within broad limits, it determines what the consumer shall have and at what price he shall have it. And it foresees the need for and arranges the necessary supply of capital, machinery, and materials.

The modern corporation is the direct descendant of the entrepreneur. This has kept us from seeing it in its new role. Had the corporation been an outgrowth of the state, which we readily associate with planning, we would not be in doubt. The modern corporation has, in fact, moved into a much closer association with the state than most of us imagine. And its planning activities are extensively and systematically supplemented by those of the state.

Let us consider first the regulation of prices in the modern economy and the means by which public behavior is accommodated to plan. Here, I should warn, we encounter some of the more deeply entrenched folk myths of our time, including a certain vested interest in error on the part of both economists and businessmen. If one takes faith in the market away from the economist, he is perilously barren of belief. So, he defends the market to defend his stock of knowledge. And the large corporate enterprise needs the concept of the market as a cover for the authority it exercises. It has great influence over our material existence and also our beliefs. But accepted doctrine holds that in all of its behavior it is subordinate to the market. It is merely an automaton responding to instructions therefrom. Any complaint as to the use or misuse of power can be met by the answer that there is none.

Control of prices is an intrinsic feature of all planning. And it is made urgent by the special vagaries of the market for highly technical products. In the formally planned economies—that of the Soviet Union, for example—price control is a forthright function of the state, although there has been some tendency in recent times to allow some of the power over prices to devolve on the socialist firm. In the Western-type economies, comprehensive systems of price control have come about by evolution and adaptation. Nobody willed them. They were simply required by circumstance.

The power to set minimum industrial prices exists whenever a small number of firms share a market. The innocent at the universities have long been taught that small numbers of firms in the market —oligopoly, as it is known—accord to sellers the same power in imperfect form that has anciently been associated with monopoly. The principal difference is the imperfect nature of this monopoly power. It does not permit the exploitation of the consumer in quite such efficient fashion as was possible under the patents of monopoly accorded by the first Elizabeth to her favorites or by John D. Rockefeller to himself.

But in fact, the modern market shared by a few large firms is combined, in one of the more disconcerting contradictions of economic theory, with efficient production, expansive output, and prices that are generally thought rather favorable to the public. The consequences of oligopoly (few sellers) are greatly condemned in principle as being like those of monopoly but greatly approved in practice. Professor Paul Samuelson, the most distinguished of contemporary economists, warns in his famous textbook on economics that "to reduce the imperfections of competition" (by which he means markets consisting of a small number of large firms or oligopoly) "a nation must struggle perpetually and must ever maintain vigilance." Since American markets are now dominated by a very small number of large firms, the struggle, obviously, has been a losing one and is now lost. But the result is that the economy functions very well. Samuelson himself concludes that man-hour efficiency in the United States "can hardly help but grow at the rate of three per cent or more, even if we do not rouse ourselves." A similar conflict between the inefficiency of oligopoly and the efficiency of an economy composed thereof is present in every well-regarded economic textbook. Samuelson agrees that technology and associated capital use are what improve efficiency. But these are precisely what require that there be planning and price control.

And here we have the answer. Prices in the modern economy are controlled not for the purposes of monopolistic exploitation. They are controlled for purposes of planning. This comes about as an effortless consequence of the development of that economy. Modern industrial planning both requires and rewards great size. This means, in turn, that a comparatively small number of large firms will divide the production of most (though not all) products. Each, as a matter of ordinary prudence, will act with full consideration of its own needs and of the common need. Each must have control of its own prices. Each will recognize this to be a requirement of others. Each will foreswear any action, and notably any sanguinary or competitive price-cutting, which would be prejudicial to the common interest in price control. This control is not difficult either to achieve or to maintain. Additionally, one firm's prices are another firm's costs. So, stability in prices means stability in costs.

The fact of control is far more important than the precise level at which prices are established. In 1964 in the United States, the big automobile companies had profits on their sales ranging from 5 percent to over 10 percent. There was security against collapse of prices and earnings for firms at either level. Planning was possible at either level of return. All firms could function satisfactorily. But none could have functioned had the price of a standard model fluctuated, depending on whim and reaction to the current novelties, from, say, $1800 to $3600, with steel, glass, chrome, plastics, paint, tires, stereo music, and labor moving over a similar range.

However, the level of prices is not unimportant. And from time to time, in response to major changes in cost—often when the renegotiation of a wage contract provides a common signal to all firms in the industry—prices must be changed. The prices so established will reflect generally the goals of those who guide the enterprise, not of the owners but of those who make the decisions. Security of earnings will be a prime objective. This is necessary for autonomy—for freedom from interference by shareholders and creditors. The next most important goal will be the growth of the firm. This is almost certainly more important than maximum profits. The professional managers and technicians who direct and guide the modern firm do not themselves get the profits. These accrue mainly to the shareholders. But the managers and technicians do get the benefits of expansion. This brings the prestige which is associated with a larger firm and which is associated with growth as such. And as a very practical matter, it opens up new executive jobs, new opportunities for promotion, and better excuses for higher pay.

Prices, accordingly, will be set with a view to attracting customers and expanding sales. When price control is put in the context of planning, the contradiction between expectation of monopolistic exploitation and expectation of efficiency, which pervades all textbook discussion, disappears. Planning calls for stability of prices and costs, security of return, and expansion. With none of these is the consumer at odds. Reality has, by its nature, advantages of internal consistency.

I must mention here one practical consequence of this argument, namely, its bearing on legal action against monopoly. There is a remarkable discrimination in which such measures, notably the antitrust laws, are now applied. A great corporation wielding vast power over its markets is substantially immune. It does not appear to misuse its power; accordingly, it is left alone. And in any case, to declare all large corporations illegal is, in effect, to declare the modern economy illegal. That is rather impractical—and would damage any President's consensus. But if two small firms making the same product seek to unite, this corporate union will be meticulously scrutinized. And very possibly, it will be forbidden. This may be so even though the merged firm is miniscule in size or market power as compared with the giant that is already a giant.

The explanation is that the modern antimonopoly and anti-trust laws are substantially a charade. Their function is not to prevent exploitation of the public. If great size and great market power led to such exploitation, our case would long since have been hopeless. Their function is to persuade people, liberal economists in particular, that the market still exists, for here is the state vigilantly standing guard. It does so by exempting the larger firms and swatting those that seek to become larger.

The French, Germans, and Japanese either do not have or do not enforce such laws. That is because they are not impelled similarly to worship at the altar of the market. They quietly accept the logic of planning and its requirements in size for effective market control. There is no indication that they suffer in consequence.

When prices for a particular product are set by a few large firms, there is little danger of price-cutting. This part of the control is secure. There does remain a danger of uncontrolled price increases.

In particular, when a few large firms bargain with a strong union, conflict can be avoided by acceding to union demands. And there is not much incentive to resist. There is a common understanding among the firms that all will raise their prices to compensate for such a settlement. If demand is strong enough to keep the economy near full employment, it will be strong enough to make such price increases feasible. These price increases, in turn, set in motion demands for further wage increases. Thus, the familiar upward spiral of wages and prices proceeds. And this too is prejudicial to planning. The individual firm, moreover, cannot prevent such price increases; they are beyond its control as a planning unit.

So here, more and more we follow the practice of the formally planned economies. We rely on the state to set maximum wages and prices. In the United States as in Britain this is done with great caution, circumspection, and diffidence, somewhat in the manner of a Victorian spinster viewing an erotic statue. Such action is held to be unnatural and temporary. Economists accord it little or no standing in economic policy. They say it interferes with the market. Unions also dislike it: they say it interferes with free collective bargaining. Businessmen disapprove: they say it interferes with their natural freedom of decision on prices. And what everyone opposes in principle, all advanced countries end up doing in practice. The answer once more is clear. In a market economy, such ceilings would be unnecessary. But they are an indispensable counterpart of economic planning and of the minimum price control that already exists.

This price- and wage-setting by the state could be dispensed with by having such a shortage of demand that it would be impossible for firms to raise prices and unions to raise wages. That is to say, we could do without such controls by rehabilitating the market for labor and industrial products. It would not then be possible to raise wages in response to prices or prices in response to wages. But that would mean unemployment or greater uncertainty of employment, and it would mean greater market uncertainty for producers—for businessmen. Despite everyone's affection for the market, almost no one wants these results. So we have strong demand, small unemployment, reliable purchases, and the maximum price and wage controls that these require. And we try to avert our eyes from this result. It would be simpler were we to recognize that we have planning and that this control is an indispensable aspect.

This leads to another subject, the management of what people buy at the controlled prices.

The key to the management of demand is effective influence over the purchases of final consumers. The latter include both private individuals and the state. If all such purchases are under effective control, there will then be a reliable demand throughout the system for raw materials, parts, machinery, and other items going into the ultimate product. If the demand for its automobiles is secure, an automobile company can accord its suppliers the certainty of long-term contracts for *their* planning. And, even in the absence of such contracts, there will still be a reliable and predictable flow of orders. How, then, are the individual consumers managed?

As so often happens, change in modern industrial society has made possible what change requires. The need to control consumer behavior arises from the exigencies of planning. Planning, in turn, is made necessary by extensive use of advanced technology and the time and capital this requires. This is an efficient way of producing goods; the result is a very large volume of production. As a further consequence in the economically advanced countries, goods that serve elementary physical sensation—that prevent hunger, protect against cold, provide shelter, suppress pain—include only a small and diminishing part of what people consume. Only a few goods serve needs that are made known to the individual by the palpable discomfort or pain that is experienced in their absence. Most are enjoyed because of some psychic or aesthetic response to their possession or use. They give the individual a sense of personal achievement; they accord him a feeling of equality with his neighbors; they make him feel superior; or they divert his mind from thought or the absence of thought; or they promote or satisfy sexual aspiration; or they promise social acceptability; or they enhance his subjective feelings of health, well-being, and adequate peristalsis; or they are thought to contribute to personal beauty.

Thus it comes about that as the industrial system develops to where it has need for planning and the management of the consumer that this requires, we find it serving wants which are psychological in origin. And these are admirably subject to appeal to the psyche. Hence they can be managed. A man whose stomach is totally empty cannot be persuaded that his need is for entertainment. Physical discomfort will tell him he needs food more. But though a hungry man cannot be persuaded to choose between bread and a circus, a well-fed man can. And he can be persuaded to choose between different circuses and different foods.

By giving a man a ration card or distributing to him the specific commodities he is to consume, the individual can be required to consume in accordance with plan. But this is an onerous form of control, and is ill adapted to differences in personality. In advanced industrial societies, it is considered acceptable only in times of great stress or for the very poor. (Even in the formally planned economies—the Soviet Union and the Eastern European states—the ration card is a manifestation of failure.) It is easier, and if less precise, still sufficient, to manage people by persuasion rather than by fiat.

Though advertising will be thought of as the central feature of this persuasion, and is certainly important, it is but a part of a much larger apparatus for the management of demand. Nor does this consist alone in devising a sales strategy for a particular product. It often means devising a product, or features of a product, around which a sales strategy can be built. Product design, model change, packaging, and even performance reflect the need to provide what are called strong selling points. They are as much a part of the process of demand management as the advertising campaign.

The first step in this process, generally speaking, is to ensure a loyal or automatic corps of customers. This is known as building customer loyalty and brand recognition. If successful, it means that the firm has a stable body of customers who are secure against any large-scale defection. Being thus reliable and predictable, they allow planning.

A purely defensive strategy will not, however, suffice. In line with the goals of its directing organization, the firm will want to expand sales. And such effort is necessary to hold a given position. The same will be true of others. Out of these efforts, from firms that have the resources to play the game (another advantage of size), comes a crude equilibrating process which accords to each participant a reasonably reliable share of the market.

Specifically, when a firm is enjoying a steady patronage by its existing customers and recruiting new ones at what seems a satisfactory rate, the existing strategy for consumer management—advertising, selling methods, product design—will be considered satisfactory. The firm will not quarrel with success. However, if sales are stationary or slipping, this will call for a change in selling methods—in advertising, product design, or even in the product itself. Testing and experiment are possible. And sooner or later, a formula providing a suitable response is obtained. This will lead, in turn, to countering action by the firms that are then failing to make gains. And out of this process a rough but reliable equilibrium between the participants is achieved.

It does not always work. There are Edsels. But it is the everyday assumption of those who engage in management of demand that if sales of a product are slipping, a new selling formula can be found that will correct the situation. By and large, the assumption is justified. Means, in other words, can almost always be found to keep the exercise of consumer discretion within safe or planned limits.

Management of the consumer on the scale that I have just outlined requires that there be some comprehensive, repetitive, and compelling communication between the managers of demand and those who are managed. It must be possible to win the attention of those who are being managed for considerable periods of time without great effort on their part.

Technology, once again, solved the problem it created. Coincidentally with rising mass incomes came first radio and then television. In their capacity to hold effortless interest, their accessibility over the entire cultural spectrum, and their independence of any educational qualification, these were superbly suited to mass persuasion. Television was especially serviceable. Not since the invention of speech has any medium of communication appeared which is so readily accommodated to the whole spectrum of mental capacity.

There is an insistent tendency among social scientists, including economists, to think that any institution which features singing commercials, shows the human intestinal tract in full or impaired operation, equates the effortless elimination of human whiskers with the greatest happiness of man, and implies that exceptional but wholesome opportunities for seduction are associated with a particular make of automobile is inherently trivial. This is a great mistake. The modern industrial system is profoundly dependent on this art. What is called progress makes it increasingly so.

And the management of demand so provided is in all respects an admirably subtle arrangement in social design. It works not on the individual but on the mass. An individual of will and determination can, in principle, contract out from under its influence. This being the case, no individual compulsion in the purchase of any product can ever be established. To all who object there is a natural answer: You are at liberty to leave! Yet there is no danger that enough people will ever assert this choice—will ever leave—to impair the management of mass behavior.

In the nonsocialist economy, the modern large corporation is, to repeat, the basic planning unit. For some planning tasks, we see that it is exceedingly competent. It can fix minimum prices. It can sufficiently manage consumer wants. And it can extract from revenues the savings it needs for its own growth and expansion. But some things it cannot do. Though the modern corporation can set and maintain minimum prices, it cannot, we have seen, set maximum prices and wages; it cannot prevent wages from forcing up prices and prices from forcing up wages in the familiar spiral. And while it can manage the demand for individual products, it cannot control total demand—it cannot ensure that total purchasing power in the economy will be equal, or approximately equal, to the supply of goods that can be produced by the current working force.

There are two other planning tasks that the large corporation cannot perform. It cannot supply the specialized manpower that modern technology and complex organization and planning require. It can train, but on the whole, it cannot educate. And it cannot absorb the risks and costs that are associated with very advanced forms of scientific and technical development—with the development of atomic power, or supersonic air transports, or antimissile defenses, or weapons systems to pierce these defenses, or the like requirements of modern civilized living.

This leads to a conclusion of great importance. The shortcomings of the large corporation as a planning instrument define the role of the modern state in economic policy. Wherever the private corporation cannot plan, the state comes in and performs the required function. Wherever the modern corporation can do the job, as in setting minimum prices or managing consumer demand, the state must remain out, usually as a matter of principle. But the corporation cannot fix maximum prices, so we have the state establishing wage and price guideposts or otherwise limiting wage and price increases. The private firm cannot control aggregate demand, so the state comes in to manipulate taxes, public spending, and bank lending—to implement what we call modern Keynesian policy. The private firm cannot supply specialized manpower, so we have a great expansion in publicly supported education. Private firms cannot afford to underwrite supersonic aircraft. So governments— British, French, or American—come in to do so and with no taint of socialism.

Our attitudes on the proper role of the state are firmly fixed by what the private corporation can or cannot do. The latter can set minimum prices for cigarettes, persuade people to buy a new and implausible detergent, or develop a more drastic laxative. This being so, such planning activity is naturally held to be sacred to private enterprise.

The planning functions of the state are somewhat less sacred. Some still have an improvised or *ad hoc* aspect. Thus, restraints on wages and prices are perpetual emergency actions; though fully accepted. Keynesian regulation of aggregate demand is thought to be occasioned by the particular imperatives of full employment and growth; the expansion of education is regarded as a result of a new enlightenment following World War II; the underwriting of especially expensive technology is a pragmatic response to the urgent social need for faster travel, emigration to the moon, bigger explosions, and competition with the Soviet Union.

So to regard matters is to fail to see the nature of modern planning. It is to yield unduly to the desire to avert our eyes from the reality of economic life. The planning functions of the state are not *ad hoc* or separate developments. They are a closely articulated set of functions which supplement and fill the gaps in the planning of the modern large firm. Together these provide a comprehensive planning apparatus. It decides what people should have and then arranges that they will get it and that they will want it. Not the least of its achievements is in leaving them with the impression that the controlling decisions are all theirs.

The Keynesian regulation of aggregate demand also requires only a word. The need for it follows directly from modern industrial planning. As we have seen, corporations decide authoritatively what they will reserve from earnings for reinvestment and expansion. But in the non-Soviet economies, there is no mechanism that ensures that the amounts so withheld for investment will be matched in the economy as a whole by what is invested. So there must be direct action by the state to equate the two. This it does primarily by manipulating private investment (principally in housing) and public spending and taxation. The need to equate the planned savings and the planned investment of the large corporation is not, of course, the only reason for such action. Savings and investment elsewhere in the economy must also be matched. But savings and investment by the large planning corporations are by far the most important in the total.

The successful regulation of demand requires that the quantitative role of the state in the modern economy be relatively large. That is because demand is regulated primarily by increasing or decreasing the expenditures of the state or decreasing or increasing the taxes it collects. Only when the state is large and its revenues are substantial will these changes be large enough to serve. One effective way of ensuring the requisite scale of state activity is to have it underwrite modern technology, which is admirably expensive. Such is the case with modern weaponry, space exploration, even highway and airport design. Though technology helps destroy the market, it does make possible the planning that replaces the market.

The next function of the state is to provide the specialized and trained manpower which the industrial system cannot supply to itself. This has led in our time to a very great expansion in education, especially in higher education, as has been true in all of the advanced countries. In 1900, there were 24,000 teachers in colleges and universities in the United States; in 1920, there were 49,000; by 1970, three years hence, there will be 480,000. This is rarely pictured as an aspect of modern economic development; it is the vanity of educators that they consider themselves the moving force in a new enlightenment. But it may be significant that when industry, at a little earlier stage, required mostly unlettered proletarians, that is what the educational system supplied. As it has come to need engineers, sales executives, copywriters, computer programmers, personnel managers, information retrieval specialists, product planners, and executive panjandrums, these are what the educational system has come to provide.

Once the community or nation that wanted more industry gave first thought to its capital supply and how to reassure the bankers on its reliability. Now it gives first thought to its educational system.

We cannot be altogether happy about education that is so motivated. There is danger that it will be excessively vocational and that we shall have a race of men who are strong on telemetry and space communications but who cannot read anything but a blueprint or write anything but a computer program. There is currently some uneasiness about liberal education in the modern industrial society. But so far this has manifested itself only in speeches by university presidents. In this segment of society, unfortunately a solemn speech is regularly considered a substitute for action.

Much the most interesting of the planning functions of the state is the underwriting of expensive technology. Few changes in economic life have ever proceeded with such explosive rapidity. Few have so undermined conventional concepts of public and private enterprise. In 1962, the U.S. government spent an estimated $10.6 billion on research and development. This was more than its total dollar outlay for all purposes, military or civilian, before World War II. But this function also includes the underwriting of markets—the provision of a guaranteed demand for billions of dollars worth of highly technical products, from aircraft to missiles to electronic gear to space vehicles. Nearly all of this expenditure, some 80 to 85 percent, goes to the large corporation, which is to say that it is to the planned sector of the American economy. It also brings the modern large corporation into the most intimate association with the state. In the case of such public agencies as NASA, the Atomic Energy Commission, or the Air Force, and the corporations serving them, it is no longer easy to say where the public sector ends and the private sector begins. Individuals and organizations are intimately associated. The private sector becomes, in effect, an extended arm of the public bureaucracy. However, the banner of private enterprise can be quite aggressively flaunted by the firm that does 75 percent of its business with the government and yearns to do more.

In the past, Keynesians have argued that there is nothing very special about government business. Relying to standard Marxian charges that capitalism depends excessively on armaments, they have pointed out that spending for housing, theaters, automobiles, highways to allow more automobiles to exist, and for radios to supply more automobiles to amuse more people while they are sitting in the resulting traffic jams, and for other of the attributes of gracious living will serve to sustain demand just as well as spending on arms. This, we now see, is not the whole story. The expenditures I have just mentioned would not serve to underwrite techonology. And this underwriting is beyond the reach of private planning. Replacement of military spending, with its emphasis on underwriting advanced technology, must be by other equally technical outlays if it is to serve the same purpose. Otherwise, technical development will have to be curtailed to that level where corporate planning units can underwrite on their own. And this curtailment under present circumstances would be very, very drastic.

This analysis makes a considerable case for the space race. It is not that exploring the moon, Mars, or even Saturn is of high social urgency. Rather, the space race allows for an extensive underwriting of advanced technology. And it does this in a field of activity where spending is large and where, in contrast with weapons and weapons systems, competition with the Soviets is comparatively safe and benign. At the same time, as in the case of competitive athletics, everyone can easily be persuaded that it is absolutely vital to win.

We now see the modern corporation, in the technological aspects of its activities, moving into a very close association with the state. The state is the principal customer for such technology and the underwriter of major risk. In the planning of tasks and missions, the mapping of development work, and the execution of contracts, there is nowadays a daily and intimate association between the bureaucracy and the large so-called private firm. But one thing, it will be said, keeps them apart. The state is in pursuit of broad national goals, whatever these may be And the private firm seeks to make money—in the more solemn language of economics, to maximize profits. This difference in goals, it will be said, sufficiently differentiates the state from private enterprise.

But here again reality supplies that indispensable thread of consistency. For power . . . has passed from the owners of the corporation to the managers and scientists and technicians. The latter now exercise largely autonomous power, and not surprisingly, they exercise it in *their* own interest. And this interest differs from that of the owners. As noted, security of return is more important that the level of total earnings. When earnings fail, the autonomy of the decision-makers is threatened. And growth is more important to managers and technicians than maximum earnings.

But a further and important conclusion follows, for economic security and growth are also prime goals of the modern state. Nothing has been more emphasized in modern economic policy than the prevention of depression or recession. Politicians promise it automatically and without perceptible thought. And no test of social achievement is so completely and totally accepted as the rate of economic growth. It is the common measure of accomplishment of all the economic systems. Transcending political faith, religion, occupation, or all except eccentric philosophical persuasion, it is something on which Americans, Russians, Englishmen, Frenchmen, Germans, Italians, and Yugoslavs, and even Irishmen, all agree.

We have seen that as an aspect of its planning, the modern industrial enterprise accommodates the behavior and beliefs of the individual consumer to its needs. It is reasonable to assume that it has also accommodated our social objectives and associated beliefs to what it needs. In any case, there has been an interaction between state and firm which has brought a unity of goals.

A somber thought will occur to many here. We have seen that the state is necessary for underwriting the technology of modern industrial enterprise. Much of this it does within the framework of military expenditure. In the consumer goods economy, the wants and beliefs of the consumer, including his conviction that happiness is associated all but exclusively with the consumption of goods, are accommodated, in greater or less measure, to producer need. Is this true also of the state? Does it respond in its military procurement to what the supplying firms need to sell—and the technology that they wish to have underwritten? Are images of foreign policy in the planned industrial communities— in the United States, the Soviet Union, Western Europe—shaped by industrial need? Do we have an image of conflict because that serves technological and therewith planning need?

We cannot exclude that possibility; on the contrary, it is most plausible. It is a conclusion that was reached, perhaps a bit more intuitively, by President Eisenhower while he was President of the United States. In his famous valedictory, he warned of the influence on public

policy resulting from the "conjunction of an immense military establishment and a large arms industry." This will not be an agreeable thought
for those for whom the mind is an instrument for evading reality.
Others will see the possibility of a two-way flow of influence. Presumably it will be true of any planned economy, East or West. The image
of the foreign policy affects the demand of the state on industry. But
the needs of economic planning expressed in the intimate association
between industry and the state will affect the state's view of military
requirements and of foreign policy. It is a matter where we had best be
guided by reality. . . .

CAPITALISM, SOCIALISM, AND THE FUTURE OF THE INDUSTRIAL STATE

By its nature the direction of the modern large corporation is
a collective, not an individual, function. Decisions are made by groups,
not by individuals. That is because technology, planning, and organization all require specialized knowledge. The knowledge of specialists
must be combined, and the result is collective authority. It is the authority of amorphous and changing combinations of specialized talent. . . .
I want to look a little more broadly at this group authority, to show how
it manifests itself not in the firm with capitalist antecedents but in the
socialist enterprise. Is it inevitable there? And does it mean that under
socialism or Communism one will tend to find the same general structure of organization as in the United States and Western Europe? And
where, in this industrial development, are we headed?

We may agree at the outset that since technology and planning
and organization are what accord power to the group as distinct from the
individual, the group will have a decisive authority wherever technology, planning, and organization are features of the productive process.
This is a technical matter; ideology is not involved. If decisions require
the information of several or many people, power will pass to the several
or many, whatever the proclaimed form of the system.

In the nonsocialist economies, as the firm develops, it becomes
necessary to exclude uninformed authority. This, as I have shown in
earlier articles, includes the owners. In the 1920s and 1930s and on into
the war years, the first Henry Ford insisted on exercising his authority
as the sole owner of the Ford Motor Company. It was disasterous. Losses
were enormous; the firm very nearly failed. During the war there was
discussion in Washington of having Ford taken over and managed by

Studebaker. In the same period, Montgomery Ward suffered somewhat less severely from the similar effort of its chairman, Mr. Sewell Avery. And the creditors of TWA a few years ago made it a condition of their loans that Howard Hughes, the then owner, not exercise his prerogatives as owner. Ford, Avery, and Hughes were not notably stupid men; it was rather that all of these firms had reached the size and technical complexity where group decision-making had to be protected from such interference. Capitalism at its highest development requires there be no capitalist interference. One would expect that a public corporation of similar size and complexity would suffer from similar intervention by cabinet members, politicians, or bureaucrats. But if the latter must be excluded, it means that socialism, similarly, must be without social control. Experience bears out this expectation.

The British, who have a superior instinct for administration, have recognized the need for autonomy for the nationalized industries. These were considerably expanded in number by the Attlee government following World War II. A decisive issue was that of parliamentary questions and comment. If these were allowed on the decisions of nationalized industries, ministers would have to be informed of such decisions in advance. Otherwise they would confess ignorance and imply neglect of duty. But important decisions, those which Parliament would be most likely to be concerned with, turn on complex and technical information. So, if the minister were to exercise informed judgment, he would need the help of a technical staff. All this being so, responsibility would be removed from the nationalized firm to the ministry. The cost in delayed decision would also be high. So, only if parliamentary intervention were excluded could the firm, and therein the decision-making specialists, act responsibly on questions requiring specialized information. All important questions do. Coal, electricity, gas, road transport, the airlines, and the other publicly owned industries were, in consequence, all accorded such autonomy.

This autonomy is even more necessary for large decisions than for small. And it is large decisions that we call policy decisions. The choice between molecular and atomic reactions for the generation of electricity is a policy decision. It is also grounded in a variety of scientific, technical, economic, and planning judgments. Only a committee, or more precisely, a complex of committees, can combine the knowledge, training, and experience that such a decision requires. So also with the question of whether the North Atlantic should be flown by American or British aircraft. So, in only slightly less measure, the question of how wage scales are to be revised or the railways rationalized. These are the questions on which Parliament would most expect to be consulted. They are among the ones from which it is most decisively excluded. Some years ago Mr. C. A. R. Crosland, the economist and present Minister of Education in the Wilson government, observed that "the public corporation in Britain has not up to the present been in any real sense accountable to Parliament, whose function has been limited to fitful, fragmentary, and largely ineffective *ex post facto* criticism." This is as one would expect.

For most socialists the purpose of socialism is control of productive enterprise by the society. And for democratic socialists this means the legislature. None, or not many, seek socialism so that power can be exercised by an autonomous and untouchable corporation, and yet this is as it must be. It does not matter that the capitalist, the ancient target of the socialist, suffers from the same exclusion and must, like the Rockefellers, Kennedys, and Harrimans, go into politics in order to have power. Not all admit to this change in capitalism. They observe only how little difference nationalization of an industry seems to mean. As A. M. F. Palmer, a socialist commentator, referring to Britain put it a few years ago, "If an intelligent observer from Mars or Venus should come and examine all large contemporary industrial concerns—public or private—as *working enterprises,* he would notice, I suspect, only their overwhelming sameness."

One result is that a large number of socialists have come to feel that public corporations are, by their nature, and again in Mr. Crosland's words, "remote, irresponsible bodies, immune from public scrutiny or democratic control." And in further consequences, a considerable number have given up the fight for public ownership or accord it only lip service. They have agreed, though few have yet recognized it, that democratic socialism, like vintage capitalism, is the natural victim of modern technology and associated organization and planning.

There have been experiments with more aggressive public control which serve to show that this is not an alternative. In India and Ceylon, and also in some of the new African countries, public enterprises have not, as in Britain, been accorded autonomy. Here the democratic socialist prerogative has, in effect, been fully asserted. The right to examine budgets and expenditures, to review policies, and in particular, to question management through the responsible minister on all actions of the public corporation has been reserved to the legislature.

And here, as elsewhere, if the minister is to be questioned, he must have knowledge. He cannot plead that he is uninformed without admitting to being a nonentity, a common enough condition in the politics of all countries but one which can never be treated with candor. Technical personnel in these countries are less experienced than in the countries which were industrialized earlier. Organization is less mature. This leads to error, and it further suggests to parliamentarians and civil servants the need for careful review of decisions by higher and presumably wiser authority. India, in particular, as a legacy of colonial administration has an illusion of official omnipotence which extends to highly technical decisions. Moreover, poverty makes nepotism and favoritism in letting contracts both more tempting and more culpable than in the rich country where jobs are more plentiful and business is easier to come by. This also seems to call for further review. Rigid personnel and civil service requirements may prevent the easy constitution and reconstitution of groups with information relevant to changing problems.

The effect in these countries of this denial of autonomy has been exceedingly inefficient operations by the public firms. Delay occasioned by review of decisions has added its special dimensions of cost. In business operations a wrong decision can often be reversed at little cost when the error becomes evident. But the cost of a delayed decision—in terms of men and capital that stand idle awaiting the decision—can never be retrieved.

Social control naturally bears with particular effect on two decisions which are of great popular interest—on the prices to be charged to the public and the wages to be paid to workers. Its effect is to keep prices lower and wages higher than the more authoritarian corporations in the advanced countries would ever allow. This is no good fortune. It eliminates net earnings and therewith this source of savings. The poor country, which most needs capital, is thus denied the source of capital on which the rich countries most rely. In India and Ceylon nearly all publicly owned corporations operate at a loss. The situation is similar in other new countries. (One of the sometime exceptions, it is interesting to notice, is the publicly owned airline. It usually claims for itself an autonomy that other public corporations do not have. One possible reason is that public officials are among the principal clients and sense the personal danger in denying airline management the requisite autonomy.)

The poor showing of democratic socialism has, on the whole, been one of the great disappointments of these last years in countries where there has been a concern for industrial development. And the reason rests not with socialism as such, but with the effort to combine socialist industrial management with democracy. It is part of the modern faith that democracy is both good and omnipotent. Like the family, truth, and sound personal hygiene, it is always above doubt. But it cannot be brought to bear on the decisions of the modern large-scale industrial enterprise. By its nature, this is an autarchy of its managers and technicians.

If autonomy is necessary for the effective performance by the firm, it should be needed also in the Soviet-type economies. The requirement begins with the need to combine the specialized information of different men. This need, to repeat, cannot be dispensed with by any ideology.

The need for autonomy in the Soviet firm could, however, be somewhat less, for its functions are far fewer than those of an American enterprise of comparable size in a similar industry. That is because many of the planning functions performed by the American or European firm are, in the Soviet-type economy, performed by the state. The large American corporation sets its prices, organizes the demand for its products, establishes or negotiates prices for its raw materials and components, takes steps to ensure supply, and establishes or negotiates rates for various categories of trained and specialized employees. In the U.S.S.R. these tasks are all performed by the state planning apparatus. Production and investment targets, which are established by the American firm for itself, are also given to the Soviet firm, though with some flexibility in application, by the state.

In consequence, the organization of the Soviet firm is far simpler than that of its American or British counterpart. There are no comparable sales, merchandising, dealer relations, product planning, procurement planning, or industrial relations departments. Most of the top positions are held by engineers. This is in keeping with the much greater preoccupation of the Soviet Union with technical as distinct from planning functions.

Nonetheless, the Soviet firm sets considerable and increasing store by its autonomy. There are two major sources of outside interference in the Soviet Union—the state planning apparatus and the Communist Party.[3] Soviet economic literature recurrently warns against bureaucratic interference with the operations of the firm. As Professor

---

[3] I have drawn here not only on the vast literature of Soviet planning but on fairly extensive firsthand observation, in the spring of 1959 and more briefly in the summer of 1964. I am extensively grateful to Soviet economists and plant managers for help and hospitality.

Ely Devons, a noted British authority, concluded in an article in *The Listener* in 1957:

> The Russians have learnt by experience that you cannot
> have responsible and efficient action at the level of the firm
> with continuous intervention and instruction from numer-
> ous outside authorities. Conflicting instructions from out-
> side give the manager innumerable excuses for failure;
> waste and inefficiency may result from a serious attempt to
> run the firm from a distance. Every argument for delega-
> tion, decentralization, and devolution used in discussions
> about business administration in the West is echoed,
> although in a different jargon, in Russia. And the case for
> such devolution has been pressed with increasing emphasis
> as Russian industry has grown and become more complex.

Soviet plant managers, from my own experience, do not hesitate
to stress both their need for autonomy and also their past difficulties in
this regard. And on the other side, managements, especially those of
large firms, have often been condemned for excessive independence—
for behaving as "feudal lords" above the law. In the Soviet Union the
most important medium of social comment after poetry is the novel;
one of the half dozen most discussed works since World War II has been
Vladimir Dudintsev's defense of the small, independent inventor against
the mindless bureaucracy of the great metal *combinat* in his book *Not
by Bread Alone.* The author's affections are in close harmony with those
of the American who, in the tradition of Brandeis, argues for the genius
of the small entrepreneur as against the solid, unimaginative behavior
of the great corporation. Both have more support from humane instinct than reality. Neither sees that modern technology makes essential
the machinery for mobilizing specialized knowledge. It might also be
added that Dudintsev's inventor would never have got the Soviet astro-
nauts into space.

    The position of the Communist Party Secretary—the second
source of interference—is also predictably difficult. This man enters the
plant hierarchy horizontally, as a member of the staff or working force,
and is still subject to the external authority of the Party. If he partici-
pates as a member of the decision-making group, he naturally becomes
responsible for its decisions, and therefore he is no longer the independent agent of the Party. If he does not participate, he no longer knows
what is going on. If he is too good a source of information, and here I
quote from a distinguished authority, Professor Joseph S. Berliner, "He

may be raised in party rank but . . . then he will not be able to find out what is going on in the plant. Nobody will have any confidence in him." Professor David Granick, another authority, concludes that the relationship of the party officials is "an uneasy compromise." Given the imperatives of group decision and the group's need to protect itself from outside intervention, we see that this is the plausible result.

So, it seems likely that the Soviet resolution of the problem of authority in the industrial enterprise is not so different from that in the West. Like that of the shareholder in the United States or Britain, the authority of the people and party is celebrated in public ritual. They are pictured as paramount, as the stockholder is with us. But in practice, as with us, extensive and increasing power of final decision is vested in the enterprise.

The trend to decentralization, so called, in the Soviet and other Eastern European countries reflects this growing autonomy. It accords to the firm greater authority over prices, individual wage rates, production targets, investment, and other uses of its earnings. Among the more eager or anxious friends of the price system in the United States, this trend has been widely hailed as reflecting a return to the market. The celebration is premature. The large Soviet firm is not being made subject to uncontrolled prices, unmanaged demand, or to the market prices for its labor or raw materials. Given the level of technology, the related commitment of time and capital, this would no more be possible in the U.S.S.R. than in the United States. The Soviet firm through decentralizations is being given some of the planning functions that Western corporations have long performed. This reflects the need of the Soviet firm to have more of the instruments for successful operation under its own authority. There is no tendency for the Soviet and the Western systems to converge under the authority of the market. Both have outgrown that. What exists is a very important convergence to the same form of planning under the authority of the business firm. I want now to reflect on the meaning of this development—on the question, Where does all this lead?

For some of these consequences—the effect on government, education, urban life, the prospect for leisure and toil, the future of the unions, the evolution of what I have called the educational and scientific estate, and the effect of fewer workers and more educators on politics—I must refer the reader to *The New Industrial State,* . . . But though I cannot be exhaustive, I must sketch some broad conclusions here.

In the latter part of the last century and the early decades of

this, no subject was more discussed than the future of capitalism. Economists, men of unspecific wisdom, political philosophers, knowledgeable
ecclesiastics, and George Bernard Shaw all contributed their personal
revelation. All agreed that the economic system was in a state of development and in time would transform itself into something hopefully
better but certainly different. Socialists drew strength from the belief
that theirs was the plausible next step in the natural process of change.

Now the future of the modern industrial economy is not much
discussed. The prospect for agriculture is still subject to debate; it is
assumed to be in a process of transition. So are the chances for the small
businessman. But General Motors is an ultimate achievement. One does
not wonder where he is going if he has already arrived. That there will
be no further change in institutions that are themselves a result of such
vast change is highly implausible. The future of the modern industrial
system is not discussed, partly because of the influence it exercises over
our belief. We agree that unions, the churches, airplanes, and the Congress lack absolute perfection. The modern corporation, however, is a
perfected structure. So it has won exemption from speculation as to how
it might be improved.

Additionally, to consider its future is to fix attention on where
it already is. Among the least attractive phrases in the American business lexicon are planning, government control, and socialism. To consider the chance for these in the future is to bring home the extent to
which they are already a fact. The government influences industrial
prices and wages, regulates demand, supplies the decisive factor of
production, which is trained manpower, underwrites much technology,
and provides the markets for products of highest technical sophistication. In the formally planned economies of Eastern Europe, the role
of the state is not startlingly different. And these things have arrived,
at a minimum with the acquiescence, and at the maximum at the
demand, of private enterprise itself.

The next step will be a general recognition of the convergent
tendencies of modern industrial systems, even though differently billed
as socialism or capitalism. And we must also assume that this is a good
thing. In time it will dispose of the notion of inevitable conflict based
on irreconcilable difference. This difference is still cherished by the
ideologists on both sides. To Marxists, the evolution here described, and
most notably the replacement of capitalist power by that of technical
organization, is unacceptable. Marx did not foresee it, and Marx has
always been required by his disciples to have had the supernatural power

of foreseeing everything for all time—although some alterations are allowed on occasion in what he is thought to have seen. And ideologists in the West who speak for the unbridgeable gulf that divides the free from the Communist world are protected by a similar theology, supported in many cases by a rather proud immunity to intellectual influences. But these positions can survive the evidence only for a time. Men lose their resistance when they realize that they are coming to look retarded or old-fashioned. Vanity is a great force for intellectual modernization.

The modern planned economy requires that the state underwrite its more sophisticated and risky technology. The weapons competition provides the rationale for much of this underwriting at the present time. This competition depends, in its turn, on the notion of irreconcilable hostility based on irreconcilable difference between economic systems. But the fact is convergence. The conclusion follows and by no especially elaborate chain of reasoning. The difference between economic systems, from which the assumption of hostility and conflict derives, does not exist. What exists is an image adhered to on both sides that serves the underwriting of technology. And very obviously, there are other ways of underwriting technology.

To bring the weapons competition to an end will not be easy. But it contributes to this goal, one trusts, to realize that the economic premises on which it rests are not real. None of this disposes of different attitudes on intellectual and cultural freedom and the First Amendment. I set rather high store by these. But these have been thought to be partially derivative of the economic systems.

Private enterprise has anciently been so described because it was subordinate to the market and those in command derived their power from the ownership of private property. The modern corporation is no longer subordinate to the market; those who guide it no longer depend on ownership for their authority. They must have autonomy within a framework of goals. But this allows them to work intimately with the public bureaucracy and, indeed, to perform tasks for the bureaucracy that it cannot do, or cannot do as well, for itself. In consequence, for tasks of technical sophistication, there is a close fusion, as we have seen, of the modern industrial system with the state. As I have earlier observed, the line that now divides public from so-called private organization in military procurement, space exploration, and atomic energy is so indistinct as to be nearly imperceptible. Men move easily across the line. Technicians from government and corporations work constantly together. On retirement, admirals and generals and high civil servants go more or less automatically to government-related industries. One close and experienced observer, Professor Murray L. Weidenbaum, a former employee of Boeing, has called this the "seminationalized" branch of the economy.

He is speaking of firms which do all or a large share of their business with the government. But most large firms do a substantial share of their business with the state. And they are as dependent on the state as the weapons firms for the other supports to their planning. It requires no great exercise of imagination to suppose that the mature corporation, as it develops, will eventually become a part of the larger administrative complex with the state. In time the line between the two will largely disappear. Men will marvel at the thin line that once caused people to refer to General Electric, Westinghouse, or Boeing as *private* business.

Although this recognition will not be universally welcomed, it will be healthy. And if the mature corporation is recognized to be part of the state or some penumbra of the state, it cannot plead its inherently private character, or its subordination to the market, as cover for the pursuit of goals of primary interest to its own guiding organization. It can be expected to accept public goals in matters of aesthetics, health and safety, and general social tranquillity that are not inconsistent wth its survival. The public bureaucracy has an unquestioned tendency to pursue its own goals and reflect its own interest and convenience. But it cannot plead this as a right. So with the corporation as its essentially public character comes to be accepted.

Other changes can be imagined. As the public character of the mature corporation comes to be recognized, attention will doubtless focus on the position of the shareholder. This is already anomalous. A shareholder is a passive and functionless figure, remarkable only in his capacity to participate, without effort or even, given the planning, without risk, in the gains of the growth by which the directing organization now measures its success. No grant of feudal privilege in history ever equaled, for effortless return, that of the American grandparent who thoughtfully endowed his descendants with a thousand shares each of General Motors and IBM. But I do not need to pursue these matters here. Questions of equity as between the accidentally rich have their own special expertise.

Some will insist that the world of the modern large firms is not the whole economy. At the opposite pole from General Motors and

Standard Oil is the world of the independent shopkeeper, farmer, shoe repairman, bookmaker, narcotics peddler, pizza merchant, streetwalker, and owner of the car and dog laundry. Here prices are not controlled. Here the consumer is sovereign. Here pecuniary motivation is unimpaired. Here technology is simple, and there is no research or development to make it otherwise. Here there are no government contracts; independence from the state, the narcotics trade and prostitution possibly apart, is a reality. But one should cherish his critics and protect them where possible from foolish error. The tendency of the great corporation in the modern industrial system to become part of the administrative complex of the state cannot be refuted by appeal to the contrary tendencies of the miniscule enterprise.

The two questions most asked about an economic system are whether it serves man's physical needs and whether it is consistent with his liberty and general happiness. There is little doubt as to the ability of the modern industrial system to supply man with goods—it is able to manage consumer demand only because it supplies it so abundantly. Wants would not be subject to management or manipulation had they not been first dulled by sufficiency. In the United States, as in other advanced countries, there are many poor people. But they are not to be found within the part of the economy with which we are here concerned. That [this] article [does] not deal with poverty does not mean, incidentally, that I am unaware of its existence.

The prospect for liberty is far more interesting. It has always been imagined, especially by conservatives, that to associate all, or a large part, of economic activity with the state is to endanger freedom. The individual in one way or another will be sacrificed to the convenience of the political and economic power so conjoined. As the modern industrial system evolves into a penumbra of the state, the question of its relation to liberty thus arises in urgent form. In recent years in the Soviet Union and in the Soviet-type economies, there has been a poorly concealed conflict between the state and the intellectuals. It has been between those who speak for the needs of the state and its disciplines, as economic planner and producer of goods, and those who assert the higher claims of intellectual and artistic expression. Is this a warning to us?

The instinct which warns of dangers in this association of economic and public power is quite sound. Unhappily, those who warn look in the wrong place. They have feared that the state might reach out and destroy the vigorous moneymaking entrepreneur. They have not noticed that, all the while, the successors to this vintage hero have been uniting themselves ever more closely with the state and rejoicing in the result. With equal enthusiasm, they have been accepting drastic abridgement of their own freedom. This is partly the price of organized activity. But they were also losing freedom in the precise pattern of classical expectation. The officers of Republic Aviation, which does all of its business with the United States government, are no more likely in public to speak critically of some nonsense perpetrated by the Air Force than is the head of a Soviet *combinat* of the ministry to which he reports. No Ford executive will ever fight Washington as did Henry I. No head of Montgomery Ward will ever again breathe defiance of a President as did Sewell Avery in the age of Roosevelt. Manners may be involved here. But most would state the truth: "Too much is now at stake!"

But the problem is not the freedom of the businessman. It can be laid down as a general rule that those who speak most of liberty least use what they have. The businessman who praises it most is a disciplined organization man. The retired general who now lectures on the threat of Communist regimentation was invariably a martinet who relished an existence in accordance with military regulations. The Secretary of State who speaks most feelingly of the free world most admires the fine conformity of his own thought.

The greater danger is in the subordination of belief to the needs of the modern industrial system. As this persuades us on the goods we buy, and as it persuades us on the public policies that are necessary for its planning, so it also accommodates us to its goals and values. These are that technology is always good; that economic growth is always good; that firms must always expand; that consumption of goods is the principal source of happiness; that idleness is wicked; and that nothing should interfere with the priority we accord to technology, growth, and increased consumption.

If we continue to believe that the goals of the modern industrial system and the public policies that serve these goals are coordinate with all of life, then all of our lives will be in the service of these goals. What is consistent with these ends we shall have or be allowed; all else will be off limits. Our wants will be managed in accordance with the needs of the industrial system; the state in civilian and military policy will be heavily influenced by industrial need; education will be adapted to similar need; the discipline required by the industrial system will be the conventional morality of the community. All other goals will be made to seem precious, unimportant, or antisocial. We will be the mentally indentured servants of the industrial system. This will be the benign servitude of the household retainer who is taught to love her master and mistress and believe that their interests are her own. But it is not exactly freedom.

If, on the other hand, the industrial system is seen to be only a part, and as we grow wealthier, a diminishing part, of life, there is much less occasion for concern. Aesthetic goals will have pride of place; those who serve them will not be subject to the goals of the industrial system; the industrial system itself will be subordinate to the claims of larger dimensions of life. Intellectual preparation will be for its own sake and not merely for the better service to the industrial system. Men will not be entrapped by the belief that apart from the production of goods and income by progressively more advanced technical methods there is nothing much in life. Then, over time, we may come to see industrial society as a technical arrangement for providing convenient goods and services in adequate volume. Those who rise through its hierarchy will so see themselves. And the public consequences will be in keeping. For if economic goals are the only goals of the society, the goals of the industrial system will dominate the state. If industrial goals are not the only goals, other purposes will be pursued.

Central among these other purposes is the aesthetic dimension of life. It is outside the scope of the modern industrial system. And that is why the industrial system tends to dismiss aesthetic considerations as precious and impractical and to condemn their proponents as "aesthetes."

The conflict arises in three forms. First and simply, there is the conflict between beauty and industrial efficiency. It is cheaper to have power lines march across the fields; to have highways take the most direct route through countryside or villages or towns or cities; or to allow jet aircraft to ignore the tranquillity of those below; or to pour industrial refuse into the air or into the water.

Next, there is a conflict between the artist and organization. Scientists and engineers can specialize; artists cannot. Accordingly, the organization which accommodates the specialist, though right for the engineer or scientist, is wrong for the artist. The artist does badly as an organization man; the organization does badly by the artist. So the artist tends to stand outside the modern industrial system; and it responds, naturally enough, by minimizing the importance of the aesthetic concerns it cannot easily embrace.

Finally, some important forms of artistic expression require a framework of order. This is notably true of structural and landscape architecture and urban design. It is order rather than the intrinsic merit of their buildings which accounts for the charm of Georgetown or Bloomsbury or Haussman's boulevards. Not even the Taj Mahal would be terribly attractive between two gasoline stations and surrounded by neon signs. Individuals, nevertheless, could have served better their economic interest by rejecting Haussman's designs or by getting a Shell franchise adjacent to the Taj.

The need is to subordinate economic to aesthetic goals—to sacrifice efficiency, including the efficiency of organization, to beauty. Nor must there be any nonsense about beauty paying in the long run. It need not pay. The requisite order will also require strong action by the state. Because of the abdication of this function in the interest of economic goals, no city, some noncommercial capitals apart, built since the Industrial Revolution attracts any particular admiration. And millions flock to admire ancient and medieval cities where, as a matter of course, such order was provided. The liberalism which allowed every individual and every entrepreneur to build as he wished was faster, more adaptable, and more efficient, and accommodated site better to need, than anything that could be provided under a "controlled" environment. But the aesthetic effect was at best undistinguished, and more often it was ghastly.

The change in goals and values which is here required is aided by the fact that the modern industrial system is intellectually demanding. It brings into existence, to serve its technical and scientific and other intellectual needs, a very large community of educated men and women. Hopefully this community will, in turn, reject the monopoly of social purpose by the industrial system.

But the rewards of time and understanding can also be hastened and enlarged by energetic political action. It is through the state that the society must assert the superior claims of aesthetic over economic goals and particularly of environment over cost. It is to the state that we must look for freedom of individual choice as to toil; for a balance between liberal education and the technical training that primarily serves the industrial system; and it is for the state to reject images of international politics that underwrite technology but at the price of unacceptable danger. If the state is to serve these ends, the scientific and educational estate and larger intellectual community must be aware of their power and their opportunity and they must use them. There is no one else.

9

◀ DONALD N. MICHAEL* ▶

Cybernation: The Silent Conquest (1962)

AND

◀ ROBERT THEOBALD† ▶

from

The Guaranteed Income (1967)

One of the chief concerns of economists and social philosophers since Adam Smith's time has been the relationship between technological change and employment. Smith emphasized the salutary effects of technological change which served to expand the market by lowering product prices. This in turn permitted a greater division of labor, which resulted in economic growth and an increasing demand for labor services. In general, Smith's followers were optimistic

---

*Professor of Psychology, University of Michigan.

†Former economic consultant to the United Nations.

about the social and economic impact of technological change. They viewed the dislocation of labor as a temporary phenomenon. Marx's position stands in striking contrast. He asserted that technological change and capital accumulation, spurred on by a profit-driven capitalist system, caused mass unemployment and disrupted the functioning of the society.

Today the debate continues over the impact of technological change (as represented by automation or cybernation which includes the combination of computers and automated machinery) on the employment of labor and on the future of the economy. Economists are divided into at least two groups on this point. Some feel that the pace of technological change is becoming so rapid that it is displacing more jobs than it is creating. This implies that some time in the future labor may work fewer hours, have more leisure time, and perhaps eventually face the prospect of no jobs at all. The two selections which follow fit into this general trend of thinking. While the opposing group concedes that some temporary structural unemployment may result from a rapid rate of technological change, they point to the fact that automation has always opened up more job opportunities than it has displaced and that it will continue to do so in the future. This group is in the majority and in fact argues that the pace of technological change and the level of employment have very little relationship. To those who have learned their Keynesian economics well, the level of employment is dependent on aggregate demand, not on the rate of technological advance. Thus, at least theoretically, it is always possible to generate full employment by stimulating total spending to the desired level. The question of whether automation creates more or fewer jobs than it displaces thus becomes irrelevant, for the level of employment can be regulated by the proper use of monetary and fiscal policies. Although most of the economists who hold this position are willing to admit the possibility of a small amount of technological unemployment, which may require manpower retraining programs, in general they agree that aggregate demand can be adjusted to compensate for any foreseeable rate of technological change. Since the productivity of labor, measured in terms of output per man-hour (a fair approximation of the rate of technological change), may be increasing, as long as demand keeps pace with the enlarged capacity no unemployment need result. The fact that the average work week has steadily declined, and will, no doubt, continue to do so, prompts the majority of economists to view this as an indication that consumers place a greater value on increased leisure than they do on increased work; therefore, the decreasing work week is not primarily the result of technological necessity.

The articles by Michael and Theobald indicate a somewhat contrary view. To them the nature of the cybernetic revolution is so vastly different from technological advances of past eras that contemporary economic analysis is inapplicable. Their articles are attempts to enlighten the public on the social and economic problems they believe it will have to face in the future. Both emphasize the necessity of recognizing the movement toward a cybernetic era in the hopes that we will be able to cope with its effects and not become slaves to its requirements. Michael's description of the process of change is followed by Theobald's policy for dealing with it. Theobald's view of the impact of cybernation on employment has changed noticeably. The high rates of unemployent in the early 1960s led him to believe that we were entering a new era where structural unemployment was more prevalant and where traditional governmental policies to deal with this problem would be ineffective. Against this background his rather extreme views on the impact of cybernation led him to issue statements such as, "cybernation will make full employment infeasible in the near future," and "unemployment will rise substantially during the sixties." At this time Theobald doubted whether aggregate demand would be able to keep pace with productive capacity. He pointed out that demand would fall as people lost their jobs and therefore their source of income. As a solution to the problem Theobald advocated a guaranteed annual income. This would not only maintain the high levels of demand necessary for increasing production, but would allow man, for the first time in history, to achieve the highest level of development of which he is capable, irrespective of his ability to compete in the market. The success of economic policy in lowering the rate of unemployment during the sixties has caused Theobald to modify his view somewhat. In the article presented here he admits that Keynesian economics has made it possible to keep aggregate demand expanding as fast as capacity, but he still maintains that sometime in the future the number of conventional jobs will not expand fast enough to allow for full employment. It is clear that Theobald really represents a separate wing of liberal thinking. Like the conservatives, he has often been critical of Keynesian economics and a burdensome federal bureaucracy. But unlike them, he rejects the idea that the market system is in all regards compatible with the needs of the future. His arguments represent a case for a further modification of capitalism in order to deal with a society of abundance rather than one of scarcity. His support for a guaranteed annual income is, thus, still linked to the long-run effect of cybernation. However, his proposal of minimum income guarantees as a short-run objective is linked to the more traditional view that it is a way to eliminate poverty. It is through this route that the guaranteed annual income has become part of "the liberals'" socioeconomic program.

The support of the principle of minimum income guarantees by liberals as well as certain conservatives (Milton Friedman suggested a negative income tax be used), has led to the point where some form of this potentially revolutionary concept is almost certain to be implemented in the near future. The reasons for the support of such a program vary from Theobald's belief that cybernation will eventually necessitate it, to Friedman's position that it ought to replace what he calls the "rag bag" of present welfare programs. Replacing a variety of complicated governmental programs with one simple and, hopefully, efficient program is therefore not totally inconsistent with Friedman's conservative philosophy. But if the principle of a minimum income is eventually accepted it is most likely to be based on the poverty issue rather than on the position of Friedman or the long-run objectives of Theobald. Liberals, however, do seem to be worried that the electorate might be enticed into thinking of and supporting Friedman's scheme for a single program as a cure-all for the poverty problem.

Even though the views of Michael and Theobald must be considered extreme positions on the probable impact of automation and technological change, they are nevertheless interesting additions to the list of speculations on the future of American capitalism. Whether they have finally predicted the outcome is debatable; at least their analysis underlines what has been and what is likely to be one of the major forces of change, not only on the economic system but on society as a whole.

—R. R.

Cybernation: The Silent Conquest*

INTRODUCTION

Both optimists and pessimists often claim that automation is simply the latest stage in the evolution of technological means for removing the burdens of work. The assertion is misleading. There is a very good possibility that automation is so different in degree as to be a profound difference in kind, and that it will pose unique problems for society, challenging our basic values and the ways in which we

---

*Donald Michael, *Cybernation: The Silent Conquest* (Santa Barbara: Center for the Study of Democratic Institutions, 1962). Used by permission.

express and enforce them.[1]

In order to understand what both the differences and the problems are and, even more, will be, we have to know something of the nature and use of automation and computers. There are two important classes of devices. One class, usually referred to when one speaks of "automation," is made up of devices that automatically perform sensing and motor tasks, replacing or improving on human capacities for performing these functions. The second class, usually referred to when one speaks of "computers," is composed of devices that perform, very rapidly, routine or complex logical and decision-making tasks, replacing or improving on human capacities for performing these functions.

Using these machines does not merely involve replacing men by having machines do tasks that men did before. It is, as John Diebold says, a way of "thinking as much as it is a way of doing. . . . It is no longer necessary to think in terms of individual machines, or even in terms of groups of machines; instead, for the first time, it is practical to look at an entire production of information-handling process as an integrated system and not as a series of individual steps."[2] For example, if the building trades were to be automated, it would not mean inventing machines to do the various tasks now done by men; rather, buildings would be redesigned so that they could be built by machines. One might invent an automatic bricklayer, but it is more likely that housing would be designed so that bricks would not be laid. Automation of the electronic industry was not brought about through the invention of automatic means for wiring circuits but through the invention of essentially wireless—i.e., printed—circuits (though today there are automatic circuit wirers as well).

The two classes of devices overlap. At one pole are the automatic producers of material objects and, at the other, the sophisticated analyzers and interpreters of complex data. In the middle zone are the

---

[1] This paper makes the following assumptions in looking on the next twenty years or so: 1) international relations will derive from the same general conditions that pertain today; 2) the weapons systems industries will continue to support a major share of our economy; 3) major discoveries will be made and applied in other technologies, including psychology and medicine; 4) trends in megalopolis living and in population growth will continue; 5) no major shifts in underlying social attitudes and in public and private goals will take place.

[2] John Diebold, *Automation: Its Impact on Business and Labor,* National Planning Association, Planning Pamphlet No. 106, Washington, D. C., May, 1959, p. 3.

mixed systems, in which computers control complicated processes, such as the operations of an oil refinery, on the basis of interpretations that they make of data automatically fed to them about the environment. Also in this middle zone are those routine, automatic, data-processing activities which provide men with the bases for controlling, or at least understanding, what is happening to a particular environment. Processing of social security data and making straightforward tabulations of census information are examples of these activities.[3]

Cybernated systems perform with a precision and a rapidity unmatched in humans. They also perform in ways that would be impractical or impossible for humans to duplicate. They can be built to detect and correct errors in their own performance and to indicate to men which of their components are producing the error. They can make judgments on the basis of instructions programmed into them. They can remember and search their memories for appropriate data, which either has been programmed into them along with their instructions or has been acquired in the process of manipulating new data. Thus, they can learn on the basis of past experience with their environment. They can receive information in more codes and sensory modes than men can. They are beginning to perceive and to recognize.

As a result of these characteristics, automation is being used to make and roll steel, mine coal, manufacture engine blocks, weave cloth, sort and grade everything from oranges to bank checks. More versatile fabricators are becoming available, too.

> U.S. Industries announced . . . that it had developed what was termed the first general-purpose automation machine available to manufacturers as standard "off-the-shelf" hardware. . . . The new machine, called a TransfeRobot, sells for $2,500. . . . The Westclox Company of La Salle, Ill., has been using a TransfeRobot to oil clock assemblies as they pass on a conveyor belt. The machine oils eight pre-

---

[3]In order to eliminate the awkwardness of repeating the words "automation" and "computers" each time we wish to refer to both at the same time, and in order to avoid the semantic difficulties involved in using one term or the other to mean both ends of the continuum, we invent the term "cybernation" to refer to *both* automation and computers. The word is legitimate at least to the extent that it derives from "cybernetics," a term invented by Norbert Wiener to mean the processes of communication and control in man and machines. He derived it from the Greek word for "steersman." The theory and practice of cybernetics underlie all systematic design and application of automation and computers.

cision bearings simultaneously in a second. At the Underwood Corporation typewriter plant in Hartford, the robot picks up, transfers and places a small typewriter component into a close-fitting nest for an automatic machine operation. In an automobile plant the device feeds partly fabricated parts of a steering assembly to a trimming press and controls the press. The device consists basically of an arm and actuator that can be fitted with many types of fingers and jaws. All are controlled by a self-contained electronic brain.[4]

At the other end of the continuum, computers are being used rather regularly to analyze market portfolios for bankers; compute the best combination of crops and livestock for given farm conditions; design and "fly" under typical and extreme conditions rockets and airplanes before they are built; design, in terms of costs and traffic-flow characteristics, the appropriate angles and grades for complex traffic interchanges; keep up-to-date inventory records and print new stock orders as automatically computed rates of sales and inventory status indicate. Computers have also been programmed to write mediocre TV dramas (in manipulating segments of the plot), write music, translate tolerably if not perfectly from one language to another, and simulate some logical brain processes (so that the machine goes about solving puzzles—and making mistakes in the process—in the ways people do). Also, computers are programmed to play elaborate "games" by themselves or in collaboration with human beings. Among other reasons, these games are played to understand and plan more efficiently for the conduct of war and the procedures for industrial and business aggrandizement. Through such games, involving a vast number of variables, and contingencies within which these variables act and interact, the best or most likely solutions to complex problems are obtained.

The utility and the applicability of computers are being continually enhanced. For example, after a few hours of training, non-specialists can operate the smaller computers without the aid of programmers simply by plugging in pre-recorded instruction tapes that tell the computer how to do specific tasks. Instruction-tape libraries can supply pre-programmed computer directions for everything from finding the cube root of a number to designing a bridge. When the machine is

---

[4]"Multi-Purpose Automation Unit is Sold 'Off the Shelf,'" *New York Times*, June 23, 1961, p. 44.

through with one task, its circuits can be easily cleared so that a new set of pre-programmed instructions can be plugged in by its businessman operator.

But the capabilities of computers already extend well beyond even these applications. Much successful work has been done on computers that can program themselves. For example, they are beginning to operate the way man appears to when he is exploring ways of solving a novel problem. That is, they apply and then modify, as appropriate, previous experiences with and methods of solution for what appear to be related problems. Some of the machines show originality and unpredictability. To take one example from a recent paper of Norbert Wiener:

> The present level of these learning machines is that they play a fair amateur game at chess but that in checkers they can show a marked superiority to the player who has programmed them after from 10 to 20 playing hours of working and indoctrination. They thus most definitely escape from the completely effective control of the man who has made them. Rigid as the repertory of factors may be which they are in a position to take into consideration, they do unquestionably—and so say those who have played with them—show originality, not merely in their tactics, which may be quite unforeseen, but even in the detailed weighting of their strategy.[5]

Another example of a machine the behavior of which is not completely controllable or predictable is the Perceptron, designed by Dr. Frank Rosenblatt. This machine can learn to recognize what it has seen before and to teach itself generalizations about what it recognizes. It can also learn to discriminate, and thereby to identify shapes similar to those it has seen before. Future versions will hear as well as see. It is not possible to predict the degree and quality of recognition that the machine will display as it is learning. It is designed to learn and discriminate in the same way that it is believed man may learn and discriminate; it has its own pace and style of learning, of refining its discriminations, and of making mistakes in the process.

It is no fantasy, then, to be concerned with the implications of the thinking machines. There is every reason to believe that within the next two decades machines will be available outside the laboratory

---

[5]Norbert Wiener, "Some Moral and Technical Consequences of Automation," *Science,* Vol. 131, No. 3410, May 6, 1960, p. 1356.

that will do a credible job of original thinking, certainly as good think-ing as that expected of most middle-level people who are supposed to "use their minds." There is no basis for knowing where this process will stop, nor, as Wiener has pointed out, is there any comfort in the assertion that, since man built the machine, he will always be smarter or more capable than it is.

> It may be seen that the result of a programming technique of [cybernation] is to remove from the mind of the designer and operator an effective understanding of many of the stages by which the machine comes to its conclusions and of what the real tactical intentions of many of its operations may be. This is highly relevant to the problem of our being able to foresee undesired consequences outside the frame of the strategy of the game while the machine is still in action and while intervention on our part may prevent the occur-rence of these consequences. Here it is necessary to realize that human action is a feedback action. To avoid a dis-astrous consequence, it is not enough that some action on our part should be sufficient to change the course of the machine, because it is quite possible that we lack informa-tion on which to base consideration of such an action.[6]

The capabilities and potentialities of these devices are unlimited. They contain extraordinary implications for the emancipation and enslavement of mankind.

The opportunities for man's enhancement through the benefits of cybernation are generally more evident and more expected, especially in view of our proclivity to equate technological advances with progress and happiness. In the words of the National Association of Manufac-turers:

> For the expanding, dynamic economy of America, the sky is indeed the limit. Now more than ever we must have confidence in America's capacity to grow. Guided by elec-tronics, powered by atomic energy, geared to the smooth, effortless workings of automation, the magic carpet of our free economy heads for distant and undreamed horizons. Just going along for the ride will be the biggest thrill on earth![7]

---

[6]Ibid, p. 1357.
[7]*Calling All Jobs,* National Association of Manufacturers, New York, October, 1957, p. 21.

But the somber and complex difficulties produced by cybernation, which already are beginning to plague some aspects of our society and economy, are only beginning to be recognized. Thus, although this paper will describe, first, the advantages of cybernation, which make its ever expanding application so compelling, it will, on the whole, emphasize the less obvious, sometimes acutely uncomfortable aspects of this development with which we must successfully contend if we are to enjoy the benefits of both cybernation and democracy.

THE ADVANTAGES OF CYBERNATION

In recent years deteriorating sales prospects, rising production costs, increased foreign competition, and lower profits have led business management to turn to our national talent for technological invention as the most plausible means of reducing costs and increasing productivity, whether the product is an engine block or tables of sales figures. And the government, faced with the need to process and understand rapidly increasing masses of numerical facts about the state of the nation and the world, is already using 524 computers and is the major customer for more of them.

What are the advantages of cybernated systems that make government and private enterprise turn to them to solve problems?

In the first place, in a competitive society a successfully cybernated organization often has economic advantages over a competitor using people instead of machines. As *U.S. News and World Report* says:

> In one line of business after another, the trend is the same. Companies are spending millions of dollars to mechanize their operations, boost output and cut costs. . . . Says an official of a big electric company: "It is no longer a question of whether or not to automate, but rather it is how far to go and how fast to proceed. If you don't, your competition will."[8]

Not only must many organizations automate to compete, but the same principle probably holds for competing nations. We are by no means the only semi-cybernated society. Europe and Russia are well

---

[8]"When Machines Have Jobs—and Workers Do Not," *U.S. News and World Report,* Vol. 50, No. 6, February 6, 1961, p. 76.

under way, and their machines and products compete with ours here and in the world market. The U.S.S.R. is making an all-out effort to cybernate as much of its planning-economic-industrial operation as it can.

In the second place, reducing the number of personnel in an organization reduces the magnitude of management's human relations tasks, whether these be coping with over-long coffee breaks, union negotiations, human errors, or indifference.

In the third place, cybernation permits much greater rationalization of managerial activities. The computers can produce information about what is happening now, as well as continuously up-dated information about what will be the probable consequences of specific decisions based on present and extrapolated circumstances. The results are available in a multitude of detailed or simplified displays in the forms of words, tables of figures, patterns of light, growth and decay curves, dial readings, etc. In many situations, built-in feedback monitors the developing situation and deals with routine changes, errors, and needs with little or no intervention by human beings. This frees management for attention to more basic duties. There is, for example,

> . . . an automatic lathe . . . which gauges each part as it is produced and automatically resets the cutting tools to compensate for tool wear. In addition, when the cutting tools have been worn down to a certain predetermined limit, the machine automatically replaces them with sharp tools. The parts are automatically loaded onto the machine and are automatically unloaded as they are finished. These lathes can be operated for 5 to 8 hours without attention, except for an occasional check to make sure that parts are being delivered to the loading mechanism.[9]

Another example, combining built-in feedback with a display capability, adds further illumination:

> The Grayson-Robinson apparel chain, which has more than 100 stores throughout the country, receives print-punch tags daily from its stores and converts them to full-

[9]From statement by Walter Reuther before the Subcommittee on Economic Stabilization of the Joint Committee on the Economic Report, U. S. Congress; *Automation and Technological Change,* 84th Congress, First Session, USGPO, 1955, p. 99.

size punchcards. The complete merchandise and inventory control function is then handled on a computer. What styles are to be processed first are determined at the computer center. During any given week about 60 per cent of the sales data are received and summarized. On the following Monday morning the remaining 40 per cent of the sales data are received. The computer can then begin running style reports immediately after the tickets have been converted to cards. By this time the company can run up style reports by departments and price lines in order to obtain the necessary merchandising information. The entire reporting job is completed by Wednesday afternoon of each week, including reports on all inactive stockpiles.[10]

Freeing management from petty distractions in these ways permits more precise and better substantiated decisions, whether they have to do with business strategy, government economic policy, equipment system planning, or military strategy and tactics. Thus, management in business or government can have much better control both over the system as it operates and over the introduction of changes into future operations. Indeed, the changes themselves may be planned in conformity with, and guided by, a strategy that is derived from a computer analysis of the future environment.

In the fourth place, cybernation allows government and industry much greater freedom in locating their facilities efficiently in relation to the accessibility of raw products, markets, transportation, and needed (or cheaper) human and material resources. Distance is no longer a barrier to control and coordination. The computers that control automated processes need not be near the factories nor the data-processing computers near their sources of information or users if other considerations are more pressing. Widely dispersed installations can be coordinated and controlled from still another place, and the dispersed units can interact with each other and affect one another's performance as easily, in many cases, as if they were all in the same place.

In the fifth place some degree of cybernation is necessary to meet the needs of our larger population and to maintain or increase the rate

---

[10] From statement of James A. Suffridge, President, Retail Clerks International Association, before the Subcommittee on Automation and Energy Resources of the Joint Economic Committee, U. S. Congress; *New Views on Automation,* 86th Congress, Second Session, USGPO, 1960, p. 591.

of growth of the Gross National Product. An estimated 80,000,000 persons will be added to our population in the next twenty years. Beyond increases in productivity per man hour to be expected from the projected 20 per cent growth in the labor force during this same period, productive growth will have to be provided by machines.

If the criteria are control, understanding, and profits, there are strong reasons why government and business should want to, and indeed would have to, expand cybernation as rapidly as they can. The versatility of computers and automation is becoming better understood all the time by those who use them, even, though, as with the human brain, most present users are far from applying their full potential. Cheap and general purpose computers or modular components applicable to many types of automatic production and decision-making are now being manufactured. In good part, they are cheap because they themselves are produced by automated methods. Techniques for gathering the field data that serve as the "inputs" to the machines are being refined and themselves automated or semi-automated. For example, a large shoe distributor is planning to attach a pre-punched IBM card to each shoe box. When a sale is made, the card is returned to a central facility to guide inventory adjustment, reordering, and sales recording and analysis. Techniques for quickly implementing the "outputs" from the machines are also being invented. Methods are being developed for systematically establishing the precise kind and degree of cybernation required in specific situations as well as the changes needed in the rest of the institution or organization using cybernation.

These are the advantages for management, for government, and for those parts of the work force whose status has been enhanced because of cybernation. But as cybernation advances, new and profound problems will arise for our society and its values. Cybernation presages changes in the social system so vast and so different from those with which we have traditionally wrestled that it will challenge to their roots our current perceptions about the viability of our way of life. If our democratic system has a chance to survive at all, we shall need far more understanding of the consequences of cybernation. Even the job of simply preserving a *going* society will take a level of planning far exceeding any of our previous experiences with centralized control.

The balance of this paper will point out some of the implications of cybernation that we must recognize in our task of developing a society and institutions in which man may be allowed to reach his full capacities.

THE PROBLEMS OF CYBERNATION

Unemployment and Employment

Blue-Collar Adults

In the highly automated chemical industry, the number
of production jobs has fallen 3% since 1956 while output
has soared 27%. Though steel capacity has increased 20%
since 1955, the number of men needed to operate the industry's plants—even at full capacity—has dropped 17,000.
Auto employment slid from a peak of 746,000 in boom
1955 to 614,000 in November. . . . Since the meat industry's 1956 employment peak, 28,000 workers have lost
their jobs despite a production increase of 3%. Bakery jobs
have been in a steady decline from 174,000 in 1954 to
163,000 last year. On the farm one man can grow enough
to feed 24 people; back in 1949 he could feed only 15.[11]

Further insight into the problem of declining employment for
the blue-collar worker comes from union statements to the effect that
the number of these employees in manufacturing has been reduced by
1,500,000 in the last six years. As one example from the service industries, automatic elevators have already displaced 40,000 operators in
New York.

Another disturbing aspect of the blue-collar displacement problem is its impact on employment opportunities for Negroes. There is
already an increasingly lopsided Negro-to-white unemployment ratio
as the dock, factory, and mine operations where Negroes have hitherto
found their steadiest employment are cybernated. This, plus the handi-
caps of bias in hiring and lack of educational opportunity, leaves
Negroes very few chances to gain new skills and new jobs. Continued
widespread and disproportionate firings of Negroes, if accompanied by
ineffectual reemployment methods, may well produce a situation that
will increase disenchantment abroad and encourage discontent and
violence here.

Service Industries

It is commonly argued that, with the growth of population,
there will always be more need for people in the service industries. The

[11]"The Automation Jobless . . . Not Fired, Just Not Hired," *Time,* Vol. 77, No. 9,
February 24, 1961, p. 69.

assumption is that these industries will be able to absorb the displaced, retrained blue-collar labor force; that automation will not seriously displace people who perform service functions; and that the demand for engineers and scientists will be so great as to provide employment for any number of the young people who graduate with engineering training. (Indeed, some of this demand is expected to arise from the needs of cybernetic systems themselves.)

It is all very well to speak glowingly of the coming growth in the service industries and the vast opportunities for well-paid jobs and job-upgrading that these activities will provide as blue-collar opportunities diminish. But is the future as bright and simple as this speculation implies? In the first place, service activities will also tend to displace workers by becoming self-service, by becoming cybernated, and by being eliminated. Consider the following data: The U.S. Census Bureau was able to use fifty statisticians in 1960 to do the tabulations that required 4,100 in 1950. Even where people are not being fired, service industries can now carry on a vastly greater amount of business without hiring additional personnel; for example, a 50 per cent increase in the Bell System's volume of calls in the last ten years with only a 10 per cent increase in personnel.

Automation frequently permits the mass production of both cheap items and items of adequate to superior quality. It frequently uses methods of fabrication that make replacement of part or all of the item more efficient or less bother than repairing it. As automation results in more leisure time, certainly some of this time will be used by more and more do-it-yourselfers to replace worn-out or faulty components in home appliances that are now repaired by paid service personnel. Nor is it clear that repairing computers will be big business. Computer design is in the direction of microminiaturized components: when there is a failure in the system, the malfunctioning part is simply unplugged or pulled out, much as a drawer from a bureau, and replaced by a new unit. Routine procedures determine which component is malfunctioning, so routine that the larger computers now indicate where their own troubles are, so routine that small computers could be built to troubleshoot others. This does not mean that clever maintenance and repair people will be completely unnecessary, but it does mean that a much more careful estimate is required of the probable need for these skills in home-repair work or in computer-repair work.

Drip-dry clothes, synthetic fabrics, plus self-service dry and wet cleaning facilities, probably will outmode this type of service activity.

Identification by fingerprints, instantly checked against an up-to-date nation-wide credit rating (performed by a central computer facility), could eliminate all service activities associated with processing based on identification (for example, bank tellers). A computer that can identify fingerprints does not yet exist, but there is no reason to believe it will not be invented in the next two decades.

If people cost more than machines—either in money or because of the managerial effort involved—there will be growing incentives to replace them in one way or another in most service activities where they perform routine, predefined tasks. It is possible, of course, that eventually people will not cost more than machines, because there may be so many of them competing for jobs, including a growing number of working women. But will service people be this cheap? As union strength is weakened or threatened through reductions in blue-collar membership, unions will try, as they have already begun to do, to organize the white-collar worker and other service personnel more completely in order to help them to protect their jobs from managements willing to hire those who, having no other work to turn to, would work for less money. Former blue-collar workers who, through retraining, will join the ranks of the service group may help to produce an atmosphere conducive to such unionizing. But how many service organizations will accept the complications of union negotiations, strikes, personnel services, and higher wages in preference to investing in cybernation?

It is possible that as automation and computers are applied more widely an attitude of indifference to personalized service will gradually develop. People will not demand it and organizations will not provide it. The family doctor is disappearing; clerks of all sorts in stores of all sorts are disappearing as well. For example:

> The R. H. Macy Co. is trying out its first electronic sales girl. This machine is smart enough to dispense 36 different items in 10 separate styles and sizes. It accepts one- and five-dollar bills in addition to coins and returns the correct change plus rejecting counterfeit currency.[12]

People either get used to this or, as in the case of the self-service supermarket, seem to prefer it.

---

[12]From statement by Howard Coughlin, President, Office Employees International Union, AFL-CIO, before the Subcommittee on Automation and Energy Resources of the Joint Economic Committee, U. S. Congress; *New Views on Automation,* 86th Congress, Second Session, USGPO, 1960, p. 513.

It is already the rare sales clerk who knows the "real" differences between functionally similar items; indeed, in most stores, sales clerks as such are rare. Thus, the customer is almost forced to do much of his own selecting and to know at least as much about or to be at least as casual about the differences between competing items as the clerk. As automation increases, the utility of the sales clerk will further diminish. With some products, automation will permit extensive variation in design and utility. With others, especially if our society follows its present course, automation will encourage the needless proliferation of items only marginally different from one other. In either event there is no reason to believe that the clerk or salesman will become more knowledgeable about an even larger variety of competing items. Finally, it is obvious that the remaining tasks of the clerk, such as recording the sale and insuring that the item is paid for, can be cybernated without difficulty.

The greater the indifference to personalized service by both buyers and sellers, the greater the opportunity, of course, to remove human judgments from the system. Cybernation may well encourge acceptance of such depersonalization, and this, in turn, would encourage further reductions in opportunities for service jobs.

Middle Management

The blue-collar worker and the relatively menial service worker will not be the only employment victims of cybernation.

> . . . Broadly, our prognostications are along the following lines:
> 1) Information technology should move the boundary between planning and performance upward. Just as planning was taken from the hourly worker and given to the industrial engineer, we now expect it to be taken from a number of middle managers and given to as yet largely nonexistent specialists: "operation researchers," perhaps, or "organizational analysts." Jobs at today's middle-management level will become highly structured. Much more of the work will be programmed, *i.e.*, covered by sets of operating rules governing the day-to-day decisions that are made.
> 2) Correlatively, we predict that large industrial organizations will recentralize, that top managers will take on an

ever larger proportion of the innovating, planning, and other "creative" functions than they have now.

3) A radical reorganization of middle-management levels should occur with *certain classes* of middle-management jobs moving downward in status and compensation (because they will require less autonomy and skill), while other classes move upward into the top-management group.

4) We suggest, too, that the line separating the top from the middle of the organization will be drawn more clearly and impenetrably than ever, much like the line drawn in the last few decades between hourly workers and first-line supervisors.

. . . Information technology promises to allow fewer people to do more work. The more it can reduce the number of middle managers, the more top managers will be willing to try it. . . . One can imagine major psychological problems arising from the depersonalization of relationships within management and the greater distance between people at different levels. . . . In particular, we may have to reappraise our traditional notions about the worth of the individual as opposed to the organization, and about the mobility rights of young men on the make. This kind of inquiry may be painfully difficult, but will be increasingly necessary.[13]

As cybernation moves into the areas now dominated by middle management in government and in business—and this move is already beginning—growing numbers of middle managers will find themselves displaced. Perhaps the bulk of displaced members of the blue-collar and service work force might be trained "up" or "over" to other jobs with, generally speaking, little or no decline in status. But the middle manager presents a special and poignant problem. Where can he go? To firms that are not as yet assigning routine liaison, analysis, and minor executive tasks to machines? This may take care of some of the best of the displaced managers and junior executives, but if these firms are to have a future, the chances are that they will have to computerize eventually in order to compete. To the government? Again, some could join it, but the style and format of governmental operations may require readjustments that many junior executives would be unable to make. And, in any case, government too, as we have seen, is turning to com-

---

[13]Harold J. Leavitt and Thomas L. Whisler, "Management in the 1980's," *Harvard Business Review,* Nov.-Dec. 1958, pp. 41–48.

puters, and it is entirely possible that much of the work of *its* middle management will be absorbed by the computers. Up into top management? A few, of course, but necessarily only a few. Into the service end of the organization, such as sales? Some here, certainly, if they have the talent for such work. If computers and automation lead to an even greater efflorescence of marginally differentiated articles and services, there will be a correspondingly greater emphasis on sales in an effort to compete successfully. But can this be an outlet for a truly significant portion of the displaced? And at what salary? Overseas appointments in nations not yet using cybernation at the management level? Again, for a few, but only for those with the special ability to fit into a different culture at the corresponding level from which they came.

Middle management is the group in the society with the most intensive emotional drive for success and status. Their family and social life is molded by these needs, as the endless literature on life in suburbia and exurbia demonstrate. They stand to be deeply disturbed by the threat and fact of their replacement by machines. One wonders what the threat will do to the ambitions of those who will still be students and who, as followers of one of the pervasive American dreams, will have aspired to the role of middle manager "on the way up."

With the demise or downgrading of this group, changes in consumption levels and patterns can also be expected. These people, although they are not the only consumers of products of the sort advertised in *The New Yorker, Holiday,* and the like, are certainly among the largest of such consumers. They are the style-setters, the innovators, and the experimenters with new, quality products. With their loss of status and the loss of their buying power, one can imagine changes in advertising, or at least changes in the "taste" that this advertising tries to generate. It is possible that the new middle élite, the engineers, operations researchers, and systems analysts, will simply absorb the standards of the group they will have replaced. But they may be different enough in outlook and motives to have different styles in consumption.

Overworked Professionals

There are service jobs, of course, that require judgments about people by people. (We are not including here the "personalized service" type of salesmanship.) The shortage of people with these talents is evidenced by the 60-hour and more work-weeks of many professionals. But these people are the products of special education, special motives, and special attitudes that are not shared to any great degree by those who turn to blue-collar or routine service tasks. Increasing the proportion of citizens with this sort of professional competence would require systematic changes in attitudes, motives, and levels of education, not to mention more teachers, a professional service already in short supply. Alterations of this magnitude cannot be carried out overnight or by casual advertising campaigns or minor government appropriations. It is doubtful indeed, in our present operating context, that they can be done fast enough to make a significant difference in the employment picture for professional services in the next decade or two. Values become imbedded early in life. They are subject to change, to be sure, but we are not, as a democratic society, adept at or inclined to change them deliberately and systematically.

Even if the teachers and the appropriate attitudes already existed, service needs at the professional level might not be great enough to absorb a large share of the potentially unemployed. Much of the work that now takes up the time of many professionals, such as doctors and lawyers, could be done by computers—just as much of the time of teachers is now taken up by teaching what could be done as well by machines.

The development of procedures for medical diagnosis by machine is proceeding well. A completely automatic analysis of data can produce just as good a diagnosis of brain malfunction as that done by a highly trained doctor. Cybernated diagnosis will be used in conjunction with improved multi-purpose antibiotics and with microminiaturized, highly sensitive, and accurate telemetering equipment (which can be swallowed, imbedded in the body, or affixed to it) in order to detect, perhaps at a distance, significant symptoms.[14] All of these developments are likely to change the nature of a doctor's time-consuming tasks. In the field of law successful codification, so that searches and evaluations can be automatic, as well as changes in legal procedures, will probably make the lawyer's work substantially different from what it is today, at least in terms of how he allocates his time.

Computers probably will perform tasks like these because the shortage of professionals will be more acute at the time the computers acquire the necessary capabilities. By then, speeded-up data processing and interpretation will be necessary if professional services are to be

---

[14]See, for example, Howard Rusk, "New Tools in Medicine," *New York Times,* July 23, 1961.

rendered with any adequacy. Once the computers are in operation, the need for additional professional people may be only moderate, and those who are needed will have to be of very high calibre indeed. Probably only a small percentage of the population will have the natural endowments to meet such high requirements. A tour of the strongholds of science and engineering and conversations with productive scientists and engineers already lead to the conclusion that much of what now appears to be creative, barrier-breaking "research and development" is in fact routine work done by mediocre scientists and engineers. We lose sight of the fact that not everybody with dirty hands or a white coat is an Einstein or a Steinmetz. Many first-class scientists in universities will testify that one consequence of the increasingly large federal funds for research is that many more mediocre scientists doing mediocre work are being supported. No doubt for some time to come good use can be made by good professionals of battalions of mediocre professionals. But battalions are not armies. And sooner or later one general of science or engineering will be able to fight this war for knowledge more effectively with more push-buttons than with more intellectual foot-soldiers.

Untrained Adolescents

Altogether the United States will need 13,500,000 more jobs in the Sixties merely to keep abreast of the expected growth in the labor force. This means an average of 25,000 new jobs each week, on top of those required to drain the reservoir of present unemployment and to replace jobs made superfluous by improved technology. In the last year, despite the slackness of employment opportunities, 2,500,000 more people came into the job scramble than left it through death, age, sickness or voluntary withdrawal. This was more than double the 835,000 average annual growth in the working population in the last ten years. By the end of this decade, 3,000,000 youngsters will be starting their quest for jobs each year, as against 2,000,000 now. This almost automatically guarantees trouble in getting the over-all unemployment rate down to 4 per cent because the proportion of idleness among teen-age workers is always far higher than it is among their elders.[15]

[15]A. H. Raskin, "Hard-Core Unemployment a Rising National Problem," *New York Times*, April 6, 1961, p. 18.

The Labor Department estimates that 26,000,000 adolescents will seek work in the Sixties. If present performance is any indicator, in the decade ahead 30 per cent of adolescents will continue to drop out before completing high school and many who could go to college won't. The unemployment rate for such drop-outs is about 30 per cent now. Robert E. Iffert, of the Department of Health, Education, and Welfare, concluded in a 1958 study that approximately one-fourth of the students who enter college leave after their freshman year never to return. Figures compiled since then lead him to conclude that there has been no significant change, in spite of the National Defense Education Act, which was supposed to help reduce this figure.[16]

If some figures recently given by James B. Conant turn out to be typical, at least one situation is much more serious than the average would imply. He found that in one of our largest cities, in an almost exclusively Negro slum of 125,000, 70 per cent of the boys and girls between 16 and 21 were out of school and unemployed. In another city, in an almost exclusively Negro slum, in the same age group, 48 per cent of the high school graduates were unemployed and 63 per cent of the high school drop-outs were unemployed.[17] These adolescents would in the normal course join the untrained or poorly trained work force, a work force that will be more and more the repository of untrainable or untrained people displaced from their jobs by cybernation. These adolescents will have the following choices: they can stay in school, for which they are unsuited either by motivation or by intelligence; they can seek training that will raise them out of the untrained work force; they can compete in the growing manpower pool of those seeking relatively unskilled jobs; or they can loaf.

If they loaf, almost inevitably they are going to become delinquent. Thus, without adequate occupational outlets for these youths, cybernation may contribute substantially to further social disruption.

Threatened institutions often try forcibly to repress groups demanding changes in the *status quo*. Imagine the incentives to use force that would exist in a nation beset by national and international frustrations and bedeviled by anarchic unemployed-youth movements.

---

[16]In conversation with Mr. Iffert. See also Robert E. Iffert, *Retention and Withdrawal of College Students,* Bulletin No. 1, Department of Health, Education, and Welfare, 1958.

[17]James B. Conant, "Social Dynamite in Our Large Cities," *Vital Speeches,* #18, July 1, 1961, p. 554 ff.

Imagine, too, the incentives to use force in view of the reserves of volunteer "police" made up of adults who can vent their own unemployment-based hostility in a socially approved way by punishing or disciplining these "children."

A constructive alternative, of course, is to provide appropriate training for these young people in tasks that are not about to be automated. But this implies an elaborate, costly program of research and planning to recruit teachers, to apply advanced teaching machine methods as a supplement to teachers, and to stimulate presently unmotivated youngsters to learn. The program would also require intensive cooperation among business, labor, education, local social service agencies, and the government. And all this must begin *now* in order for it to be ready when it will be needed.

None of this is easily met. Persuading drop-outs to stay in school will not be easy. Teachers will not be easy to recruit unless they are well paid. There is already a shortage of teachers. And let no one suggest that an easy source of teachers would be displaced workers. There is no reason to believe that they have the verbal and social facility to teach, and most of them would have nothing to teach but skills that have become obsolete. Some, of course, might be taught to teach, though this would add obvious complications to the whole effort.

Knowing what to teach will depend on knowing what types of jobs are likely to exist when the student finishes his training. This will require knowledge about the trends and plans of local industry, if that is where the youths are to work (and if that is where industry plans to stay!), and of industries in other localities, if the youths are willing to move. Such knowledge often does not exist in a rapidly changing world or, if it exists, may not be forthcoming from businesses more concerned with competition than with the frustrated "delinquents" of their community. As of now, in the words of Dr. Conant, "unemployment of youth is literally nobody's affair."

Some Proposed Solutions

Retraining is often proposed as if it were also the cure-all for coping with adults displaced by cybernation as well as young people. In some circumstances it has worked well for some people, especially with office personnel who have been displaced by data-processing computers and have learned other office jobs, including servicing the computers. But in other cases, especially with poorly educated blue-collar workers, retraining has not always been successful, nor have new jobs based on that retraining always been available. Max Horton, Michigan's Director of Employment Security, says:

> "I suppose that is as good as any way for getting rid of the unemployed—just keeping them in retraining. But how retrainable are the mass of these unskilled and semi-skilled unemployed? Two-thirds of them have less than a high school education. Are they interested in retraining? But most important, is there a job waiting for them when they have been retrained?" The new California Smith-Collier Act retraining program drew only 100 applicants in six months.[18]

A. H. Raskin's survey of the situation leads him to conclude:

> The upgrading task will be a difficult, and perhaps impossible, one for those whose education and general background do not fit them for skilled work. The outlook is especially bleak for miners, laborers and other unskilled workers over 40, who already make up such a big chunk of the hard core of joblessness.[19]

Moreover, management has not always been willing to institute retraining programs. People are either fired outright in some cases or, more often, simply are not rehired after a layoff.

> Labor and management have been slow to face the problem over the bargaining table. Harry Bridges' West Coast longshoremen's union recently agreed to give shippers a free hand to mechanize cargo handling—in exchange for a guarantee of present jobs, plus early retirement and liberal death benefits. In Chicago this week, President Clark Kerr of the University of California, one of the top labor economists, will preside over a company-union committee meeting at Armour & Co. to draw up a plan for the rapidly automating meat industry. A similar committee is at work at Kaiser Steel Co. But many authorities think such efforts are far

[18]"The Automation Jobless . . . Not Fired, Just Not Hired," *Time,* Vol. 77, No. 9, February 24, 1961, p. 69.
[19]A. H. Raskin, "Fears About Automation Overshadowing Its Boons," *New York Times,* April 7, 1961, p. 16.

too few, that management must do more. E. C. Schulze, acting area director of Ohio's state employment service, says: "I've yet to see an employer's group willing to take a look at this problem and seek solutions. They refuse to recognize their responsibility. They talk about long-term trends—but nobody talks about the immediate problem of jobless, needy people."[20]

The problem of retraining blue-collar workers is formidable enough. But, in view of the coming role of cybernation in the service industries, the retraining problem for service personnel seems insuperable. No one has seriously proposed what service tasks this working group could be retrained *for*—to say nothing of training them for jobs that would pay high enough wages to make them good consumers of the cornucopia of products manufactured by automation.

Another proposal for coping with the unemployment-via-cybernation problem is shorter hours for the same pay. This approach is intended to maintain the ability of workers to consume the products of cybernation and, in the case of blue-collar workers, to maintain the strength of unions. This would retain the consumer purchasing capacity for x workers in those situations where the nature of the cybernation process is such that x men would do essentially the same work as x plus y men used to do. But when the task itself is eliminated or new tasks are developed that need different talents, shorter shifts clearly will not solve the problem. The latter conditions are the more likely ones as cybernation becomes more sophisticated.

Proponents of cybernation claim that it should reduce the price of products by removing much of the cost of labor and increasing consumer demand. Whether the price of beef, or milk, or rent will be reduced in phase with the displaced worker's lowered paycheck remains to be seen. So far this has not happened. Whether the price of TV sets, cars, refrigerators, etc., will be reduced substantially depends in part on how much product cost goes into larger advertising budgets aimed at differentiating the product from the essentially same one produced last year or from the practically identical one produced on some other firm's automated production line.

An obvious solution to unemployment is a public works program. If our understanding of the direction of cybernation is correct, the government will probably be faced for the indefinite future with the

---

[20]*Time, loc. cit.*

need to support part of the population through public works. There is no dearth of public work to be done, and it is not impossible that so much would continue to be needed that an appropriately organized public works program could stimulate the economy to the point that a substantial portion of the work force could be re-absorbed into the private sector. That is, although the proportion of workers needed for any particular task will be reduced through the use of cybernation, the total number of tasks that need to be done could equal or exceed the absolute number of people available to do them. It is not known whether this situation would obtain for enough tasks in enough places so that the portion of the population working on public projects would be relatively small. However, if it should turn out that this felicitous state of affairs could be realized in principle, clearly it could only be realized and sustained if there were to be considerable and continuous centralized planning and control of financing, the choice of public projects, and the places where they were to be done. If, for whatever reasons, this situation could not be achieved, the public works payroll would remain very large indeed.

What would be the effects on the attitudes and aspirations of a society, and particularly of its leadership, when a significant part of it is overtly supported by governmental public works programs? ("Overtly" is used because much of the aerospace industry in particular and of the weapons systems industry in general is subsidized by the government right now: they literally live off cost plus fixed fee contracts, and there is no other comparable market for their products.) Whatever else the attitudes might be, they certainly would not be conducive to maintaining the spirit of a capitalistic economy. This shift in perspective may or may not be desirable, but those who think it would be undesirable should realize that encouraging the extension of cybernation, in the interests of free enterprise and better profits, may be self-defeating.

The inherent flexibility of cybernated systems, which permits great latitude in their geographic location, is the inspiration for the proposal that if jobs are lost through cybernation, the unemployed could be moved to another area where jobs exist. It is said that a governmental agency similar to the Agricultural Resettlement Administration, which moved farmers from the Dust Bowl to cities, could be used. However, two important differences between that situation and this one would complicate this effort: the contemporary cause of the unemployment would not be the result of an act of God; and it is not immediately evident that these unemployed people could find jobs in other areas, which might be suffering from a similar plethora of useless workers.

Herbert Striner has suggested that a more extreme approach would be to export blue-collar and white-collar workers and their families to nations needing their talents. The problem of whether or how the salary differential might be made up is one of several difficulties with this proposal. Yet, if such emigration could be carried out, it might be a better solution than letting the workers atrophy here. The economic history of former colonial powers and their colonization techniques indicate that "dumping" of excess personnel into foreign lands would not be a radically new innovation.

Another possible long-run approach might be curtailment of the birth rate. In times of depression the rate falls off naturally—which may be the way the process would be accomplished here if enough people became unemployed or marginally employed (although the effects of the lowered birth rate would only follow after the economic and social changes had been made). Of course, the government could encourage birth control by reducing the income tax dependency deduction or other tax means.

Finally, there is the proposal to reduce the working population by increasing the incentives for early retirement. Government could do this by reducing the retirement age for social security, and unions and management could use their collective ingenuity to provide special retirement incentives. Naturally, this would increase the already large percentage of retired elderly people. Along with the other familiar problems associated with this group is the poignant one we shall face in more general form in the next section: how are all these people to be kept happily occupied in their leisure?

Whether any of these proposed solutions is adequate to the challenge of unemployment is not known to us or, we gather, to those who have proposed one solution or another. But even if, in principle, some combination of them would be adequate, in order to put them into effect a considerable change would be necessary in the attitudes and voting behavior of Congress and our tax-paying citizens. Preconceptions about the virtues and vices of work, inflation, the national debt, and government control run deeply and shift slowly.

Not all of these dire threats would come to pass, of course, if cybernation reduced consumer buying power through unemployment and, thereby, the financial capability of industry and business to introduce or profit from cybernation. In this way we might all be saved from the adverse effects of unemployment from this source. But the economy would still be faced with those threats to its well-being which, as were pointed out earlier, make the need to cybernate so compelling.

Cybernation is by nature the sort of process that will be introduced selectively by organization, industry, and locality. The ill-effects will be felt at first only locally and, as a result, will not be recognized by those who introduce it—and perhaps not even by the government—as a *national* problem with many serious implications for the whole social system. Also, because one of the chief effects of cybernation on employment is not hire rather than to fire, the economic-social consequences will be delayed and will at any time be exacerbated or ameliorated by other economic and social factors such as the condition of our foreign markets, which also are being changed and challenged by European and Russian cybernation. By the time the adverse effects of cybernation are sufficiently noticeable to be ascribed to cybernation, the equipment will be in and operating.

Once this happens, the costs of backtracking may be too great for private enterprise to sustain. For, in addition to the costs of removing the equipment, there will be the costs of building a pre-cybernation system of operations. But which firms will voluntarily undertake such a job if they are unsure whether their competitors are suffering the same setback—or indeed if their competitors are going to decybernate at all? And, if not voluntarily, how would the government enforce, control, and pay for the change-over?

ADDITIONAL LEISURE

It is generally recognized that sooner or later automation and computers will mean shorter working hours and greater leisure for most if not all of the American people. It is also generally, if vaguely, recognized that there probably are problems connected with the use of leisure that will take time to work out.

Two stages need to be distinguished: the state of leisure over the next decade or two, when our society will still be in transition to a way of life based on the widespread application of cybernation; and the relatively stable state some time in the future when supposedly everybody will have more leisure time than today and enough security to enjoy it. The transitional stage is our chief concern, for the end is far enough off to make more than some general speculations about it footless. At this later time people's behavior and attitudes will be conditioned as much by presently unforeseeable social and technological developments as by the character and impact of cybernation itself.

During the transition there will be four different "leisure" classes: 1) the unemployed, 2) the low-salaried employees working short hours, 3) the adequately paid to high-salaried group working short hours, and 4) those with no more leisure than they now have— which in the case of many professionals means very few hours of leisure indeed.

Leisure Class One

Today, most of the unemployed are from low educational backgrounds where leisure has always been simply a respite from labor. No particular aspirations to or positive attitudes about the creative use of leisure characterize this group. Since their main concern is finding work and security, what they do with their leisure is a gratuitous question; whatever they do, it will hardly contribute to someone else's profits.

It is worth speculating that one thing they might do is to participate in radical organizations through which they could vent their hostility over being made insecure and useless. Another thing they could do, if so motivated and if the opportunity were available, would be to learn a skill not likely to be cybernated in the near future, although, as we have seen, the question arises of what this would be. Another thing would be to move to areas where there is still a demand for them. But breaking community ties is always difficult, especially during periods of threat when the familiar social group is the chief symbol of security. And who would pay for their move and who would guarantee a job when they got where they were going?[21]

As cybernation expands its domain, the unemployed "leisure" class will not consist only of blue-collar workers. The displaced service worker will also swell the ranks of the unemployed, as well as the relatively well-trained white-collar workers until they can find jobs or displace from jobs the less well-trained or less presentable, like the college graduate filling-station attendant of not so many years ago. It is doubtful that during their unemployed period these people will look upon that time as "leisure" time. For the poorly educated, watching television, gossiping, and puttering around the house will be low-cost time-fillers between unemployment checks; for the better educated, efforts at self-improvement, perhaps, as well as reading, television,

---

[21]Perhaps an indication of things to come is to be found in the recent Federal Court ruling that employees have an "earned and vested right" of seniority and that this cannot be "denied unilaterally" or affected by a change in the location of their employer. "Court Bars Firing in Plant Move," *Washington Post,* July 7, 1961.

and gossip; for many, it will be time spent in making the agonizing shift in style of living required of the unemployed. These will be more or less individual tragedies representing at any given time a small portion of the work force of the nation, statistically speaking. They will be spread over the cities and suburbs of the nation, reflecting the consequences of actions taken by particular firms. If the spirit of the day grows more statistical than individualistic, as this paper suggests later that it well might, there is a real question of our capacity to make the necessary organized effort in order to anticipate and cope with these "individual" cases.

The free time of some men will be used to care for their children while their wives, in an effort to replace lost income, work at service jobs. But this arrangement is incompatible with our image of what properly constitutes man's role and man's work. The efforts of this use of "leisure" on all family members will be corrosive rather than constructive and will contribute to disruption of the family circle. "Leisure" for this group of people may well acquire a connotation that will discourage for a long time to come any real desire to achieve it or any effort to learn how to use it creatively.

One wonders, too, what women, with their growing tendency to work—to combat boredom as well as for money—will do as the barriers to work become higher, as menial white-collar jobs disappear under the impact of cybernation, and as the competition increases for the remaining jobs. If there are jobs, 6,000,000 more women are expected to be in the labor force in 1970 than were in it in 1960. Out of a total labor force of 87,000,000 at that time, 30,000,000 would be women. To the extent that women who want jobs to combat boredom will not be able to get them, there will be a growing leisure class that will be untrained for and does not want the added leisure. As for those women who have a source of adequate income but want jobs because they are bored, they will have less and less to do at home as automated procedures further routinize domestic chores.

Leisure Class Two

A different kind of leisure problem will exist for the low-income group working shorter hours. This group will be composed of people with the attitudes and behavior traditionally associated with this class, as well as some others who will have drifted into the group as a result of having been displaced by cybernation. What evidence there is indicates that now and probably for years to come, when members of this group have leisure time as a result of fewer working hours, the tendency will be to take another job.[22] It is reasonable to believe that the general insecurity inevitably arising from changing work arrangements and the over-all threat of automation would encourage "moonlighting" rather than the use of free time for recreation. If these people cannot find second jobs, it is hard to imagine their doing anything different with their free time from what they do now, since they will not have the money, the motives, or the knowledge to search out different activities.

If the shorter hours are of the order of four eight-hour days, potentially serious social problems will arise. For example, a father will be working fewer hours than his children do in school. What he will do "around the house" and what adjustments he, his wife, and children will have to make to each other will certainly add very real difficulties to the already inadequate, ambiguous, and frustrating personal relationships that typify much of middle-class family life.

Leisure Class Three

Workers with good or adequate income employed for shorter hours are the group usually thought of when one talks about the positive opportunities for using extra leisure in a cybernated world. Its members for the most part will be the professional, semi-professional, or skilled workers who will contribute enough in their social role to command a good salary but who will not be so rare as to be needed for 40 hours a week. These people already value learning and learning to learn. Given knowledge about, money for, and access to new leisure-time activities, they are likely to make use of them. They could help to do various desirable social service tasks in the community, tasks for which there is not enough money to attract paid personnel of high enough quality. They could help to teach, and, by virtue of their own intimate experiences with cybernation, they would be able to pass on the attitudes and knowledge that will be needed to live effectively in a cybernated world. It is likely, too, that this group will be the chief repository of creative, skilled manual talents. In a nation living off mass-produced, automatically produced products, there may be a real if limited demand for hand-made articles. (We may become again in part a nation of small shopkeepers and craftsmen.) In general, this

---

[22]Harvey Swados, "Less Work—Less Leisure," *Mass Leisure,* ed. Eric Larrabee and Rolf Meyersohn, The Free Press, Glencoe, Ill., 1958, p. 353.

group of people will probably produce and consume most of its own leisure-time activities.

Leisure Class Four

The fourth group consists of those who probably will have little or no more leisure time than they now have except to the extent permitted by additions to their ranks and by the services of cybernation. But extrapolations for the foreseeable future indicate insufficient increases in the class of presently overworked professionals and executives. Computers should be able to remove many of the more tedious aspects of their work in another few years, but for some time to come these people will continue to be overburdened. Some of this relatively small proportion of the population may manage to get down to a 40-hour week, and these lucky few should find no difficulty in using their leisure as productively and creatively as those in the third group.

Thus, during the transition period, it is the second group, the low-salaried workers who cannot or will not find another job, that presents the true leisure problem, as distinct from the unemployment problem. Here is where the multiple problems connected with private and public make-play efforts may prove very difficult indeed. We have some knowledge about relatively low-income workers who become voluntarily interested in adult education and adult play sessions, but we have had no real experience with the problems of how to stimulate the interests and change the attitudes of a large population that is forced to work shorter hours but is used to equating work and security, that will be bombarded with an advertising *geist* praising consumption and glamorous leisure, that will be bounded closely on one side by the unemployed and on the other by a relatively well-to-do community to which it cannot hope to aspire. Boredom may drive these people to seek new leisure-time activities if they are provided and do not cost much. But boredom combined with other factors may also make for frustration and aggression and all the social and political problems these qualities imply.

DECISIONS AND PUBLIC OPINION

Privileged Information

The government must turn to computers to handle many of its major problems simply because the data involved are so massive and the factors so complex that only machines can handle the material fast enough to allow timely action based on understanding of the facts. In the nature of the situation, the decisions made by the government with the help of computers would be based in good part on computers that have been programmed with more or less confidential information —and privileged access to information, at the time it is needed, is a sufficient if not always necessary condition for attaining and maintaining power. There may not be any easy way to insure that decisions based on computers could not become a threat to democratic government.

Most of the necessary inputs for the government's computer systems are available only to the government, because it is the only institution with sufficiently extensive facilities for massive surveys (whether they be photographic, observational, paper and pencil, or electronic in nature). Also, the costs of these facilities and their computer installations are so great that buying and maintaining such a system is sensible only if one has the decision-making needs of a government and the data required to feed the machines. Other organizations, with other purposes, would not need this kind of installation. These machines can provide more potent information than merely rapidly produced summaries and tabulations of data. They can quickly provide information on relationships among data, which may be appreciated as significant only by those already having privileged information based on a simpler level of analysis or on other non-quantified intelligence to which the user is privy.[23] Computers can also provide information in the form of extrapolations of the consequences of specific strategies and the probabilities that these consequences will arise. This information can be based on exceedingly complex contingencies. The utility and applicability of these extrapolations will be fully understandable only to those knowing the particular assumptions that went into the programming of the machines.

The Inevitability of Ignorance

It may be impossible to allow much of the government, to say nothing of the public, access to the kind of information we have been discussing here. But let us assume that somehow the operation of the government has been reorganized so that procedures are enforced to permit competing political parties and other private organizations to

---

[23]Lawrence E. Davies, "Data Retriever to Help the CIA. Finds One Page in Millions in Only a Few Seconds," *New York Times,* July 12, 1961.

have access to the government's raw data, to have parallel systems for the processing of data as well as to have access to the government's computer programs. Even then, most people will be incapable of judging the validity of one contending computer program compared to another, or whether the policies based on them are appropriate.

This condition exists today about military postures. These are derived in good part from computer analyses and computer-based games that produce probabilities based on programmed assumptions about weapon systems and our and the enemy's behavior. Here the intellectual ineffectualness of the layman is obscured by the secrecy that keeps him from finding out what he probably would not be able to understand anyway. If this sounds condescending, it only needs to be pointed out that there are large areas of misunderstanding and misinterpretation among the military too. At any given time, some of these people do not fully appreciate the relationships between the programs used in the computers and the real world in which the consequences are supposed to follow. As it is now, the average intelligent man has little basis for judging the differing opinions of economists about the state of the economy or even about the reasons for a past state. He also has little basis for appraising the conflicting opinions among scientists and engineers about the costs and results of complex scientific developments such as man in space. In both examples, computers play important roles in the esoteric arguments involved.

Thus, even if people may have more leisure time to attend more closely to politics, they may not have the ability to contribute to the formulation of policy. Some observers feel that the middle class does not now take a strong interest in voting and is alienated in its responsibility for the conduct of government. Leisure may not change this trend, especially when government becomes in large part the complex computer operation that it must necessarily become.

Significant public opinion may come from only a relatively small portion of the public: a) those who are able to follow the battles of the computers and to understand the implications of their programs; and b) those who are concerned with government policy but who are outside of or unfamiliar with the computer environment.

For this segment of the voting population, differences over decisions that are made or should be made might become more intense and more irreconcilable. Already there is a difference of opinion among intelligent men about the problem of the proper roles in American foreign policy of military weapons, arms control, and various levels of disarmament. One side accuses its opponents of naïveté or ignorance about the "facts" (computer-based), and the other side objects to the immorality or political insensibilities of its opponents. Many aspects of the problem involve incommensurables; most are too complex to stand simplification in order to appeal to the larger public or to an unsophisticated Congressman. Yet the arguments *are* simplified for these purposes and the result is fantastic confusion. The ensuing frustration leads to further efforts to make the case black or white and to further efforts by one contingent to provide ever more impressive computer-based analyses and by the other side to demonstrate that they are beside the point.

This is only one example of the problems that will arise from the existence of sophisticated computers. Will the problems create greater chasms between the sophisticated voter and the general public, and within the sophisticated voting group itself?

Personnel and Personalities

As for the selection of the men who are to plan or make policy, a computerized government will require different training from that which executive personnel in most governmental agencies has today. Certainly, without such training (and perhaps with it) there is bound to be a deepening of the split between politics and facts. For example, it is evident that the attitudes of many Congressmen toward space activities are motivated more by politics and conventional interpretations of reality than by engineering facts or the realities of international relations.

The same schisms will be compounded as computers are used more and more to plan programs in the Department of Health, Education, and Welfare, urban development, communications, transportation, foreign aid, and the analysis of intelligence data of all sorts.

In business and industry the shift has already begun toward recruiting top management from the cadre of engineering and laboratory administration, for these are the people who understand the possibilities of and are sympathetic to computer-based thinking. In government the trend has not been as clear-cut, but it is noteworthy that the scientist, as high-level adviser, is a recent innovation and one clearly here to stay. Sometimes unhappily and sometimes enthusiastically, the scientists, scientist-administrator, and engineer acknowledge that their role of adviser is frequently confused with that of policymaker. As people with this training come more to influence policy and those chosen to make it, changes in the character and attitudes of the men responsible for the conduct of government will inevitably occur.

For reasons of personality as well as professional perspective, many operations researchers and systems analysts have great difficulty in coping with the more ambiguous and less "logical" aspects of society.[24] Their temperaments, training, and sympathies may not incline them to indulge the slow, ponderous, illogical, and emotional tendencies of democratic processes. Or they may ignore the extra-logical nature of man. Emphasis on "logic," in association with the other factors we have mentioned, may encourage a trend toward the recruitment of authoritarian personalities. There is no necessary correlation between the desire to apply scientific logic to problems and the desire to apply democratic principles to daily, or even to professional scientific, life.

Mass vs. the Individual

The psychological influence of computers is overwhelming: they symbolize and reenforce the potency of America's belief in the utility of science and technology. There is a sense of security in nicely worked-up curves and complex displays of information which are the products of almost unimaginably intricate and elegant machinery. In general, the influence of computers will continue to be enhanced if those who use them attend chiefly to those components of reality which can be put into a computer and processed by it, and the important values will become those which are compatible with this approach to analyzing and manipulating the world. For example, the influence of computers has already been sufficiently strong to seduce military planners and civil defense planners *away* from those aspects of their problems which are not now subject to data processing. Most of the planning for survival following nuclear attack has to do with those parts of the situation which can be studied by computers. Crucial aspects of psychological and social reorganization have been pushed into the background simply because they cannot be handled statistically with convenience or with the demonstrated "expertness" of the specialist in computers. Thus, the nature of the post-attack situation is argued learnedly but spuriously by those who have the attention of leadership, an attention stimulated by the glamor of computers, the prestige of their scientist-keepers, and the comfort of their "hard facts."

---

[24]Donald N. Michael, "Some Factors Tending to Limit the Utility of the Social Scientist in Military Systems Analysis," *Operations Research*, Vol. 5, No. 1, February, 1957, pp. 90–96.

Computers are especially useful for dealing with social situations that pertain to people in the mass, such as traffic control, financial transactions, mass-demand consumer goods, allocation of resources, etc. They are so useful in these areas that they undoubtedly will help to seduce planners into inventing a society with goals that can be dealt with in the mass rather than in terms of the individual. In fact, the whole trend toward cybernation can be seen as an effort to remove the variabilities in man's on-the-job behavior and off-the-job needs which, because of their non-statistical nature, complicate production and consumption. Thus, somewhere along the line, the idea of the individual may be completely swallowed up in statistics. The planner and those he plans for may become divorced from one another, and the alienation of the individual from his government and individual from individual within government may grow ever greater.

Computers will inevitably be used to plan employment for those displaced by cybernation. This may lead to a more rationalized society than could otherwise be invented, with a more adequate allocation of jobs. But one wonders whether it will not also lead, on a national scale, to an attitude in the planner of relative indifference to the individual, an indifference similar to that shown by many managers of large self-service institutions who find an occasional complaint too much trouble to cope with individually because the influence of the individual on the operation of the system is too negligible to warrant attention.

What will be the consequences for our relations with underdeveloped nations of a government that sees the world through computers? With our general public alienated from its own productive and governmental processes and our leadership seemingly successful through its use of computer-based planning and control, our government may well become more and more incapable of recognizing the differences between the needs, aspirations, and customs of these nations and those of our own country. In these nations, productive and governmental processes will still be very human activities, with all the non-statistical variabilities that implies. Our decision to race U.S.S.R. to the moon is an initial indication of our incapacity as an advanced technological nation to appreciate what our acts look like to other nations with different attitudes.

On the other hand, the emphasis on human behavior as a statistical reality may encourage revisions in the temporal scale of government planning and programs. Time is a statistical property in cybernated systems: it takes time for variables to average out, to rise

or fall in their effects, and the time period usually is not a fiscal year
or some small multiple thereof. Thus, perhaps, we can hope for more
sensible long-range planning in government as a result of the computer's need for long time periods in which to make its statistical models
work out. If this should come about, of course, it will require vast
changes in the conduct of government and in the devices that government, and especially the Congress, uses for controlling its activities. It
may also result in extending the present trend of turning over governmental policy-planning and, in effect, policy-making responsibilities
to private organizations and their human and machine computers such
as RAND. For unless the rules for Congressional elections are also
changed, some of the responsibility that Congressmen now take for
programs, when they vote relatively short-term appropriations, will no
doubt be transferred to the machines that invented the plans if Congressmen should be faced with passing on appropriations and programs
that would extend far beyond the time of their incumbencies.

Decisions for Business

The implications of the concentration of decision-making within
business firms as a result of cybernation are not as clear-cut as the effects
for government. In principle, both big and small business will be able
to know much more about the nature of their markets and of their
organizational operations through cybernation. Whether or not this
will help both big and small proportionately is far from clear. Big
business will undoubtedly have better facilities for information and
decisions, but small business may be able to get what it needs by buying
it from service organizations that will come into existence for this purpose. Big organizations will be able to afford high-priced personnel for
doing the thinking beyond that done by machines. If quality of thinking is always related to price, the big organizations will be able to put
their small competitors out of business. But the big organizations, precisely because of their size, may have relatively little maneuverability,
and some of the best minds may find the little organizations a more
exciting game. Whether the little organizations could stay afloat is moot,
but one can anticipate some exciting entrepreneurial maneuvers among
the small firms while they last.

One thing is clear: among the small organizations, and probably among the big ones too, we can expect disastrous mistakes as a result
of poor machine programming or inaccurate interpretations of the
directives of the machines. These will be greatest during the early period

when it will be faddish to plan via machine and when few organizations will have the brainpower and organization to do so intelligently. Thus, added to the unemployment ranks in the decade or so ahead will be those who have been put out of jobs because their firms have misused computers.

THE CONTROL OF CYBERNATION

TIME AND PLANNING

Time is crucial in any plan to cope with cybernation. Ways of ameliorating its adverse effects require thinking farther ahead than we ever do. In a society in the process of becoming cybernated, education and training for work as well as education and training for leisure must begin early in life. Shifts in behavior, attitudes, and aspirations take a long time to mature. It will be extraordinarily difficult to produce appropriate "culture-bearers," both parents and teachers, in sufficient numbers, distribution, and quality in the relatively brief time available. It is hard to see, for example, how Congress, composed in good part of older men acting from traditional perspective and operating by seniority, could recognize soon enough and then legislate well enough to produce the fundamental shifts needed to meet the complexities of cybernation. It is hard to see how our style of pragmatic making-do and frantic crash programs can radically change in the next few years. This is especially hard to visualize when the whole cybernation situation is such that we find it impossible to determine the consequences of cybernation even in the medium long run. The differences expressed in the public statements of business and labor demonstrate that any reconciliation of interests will be a very long-range effort indeed. "Drastic" actions to forestall or eliminate the ill-effects of cybernation will not be taken in time unless we change our operating style drastically.

EDUCATION: OCCUPATIONS AND ATTITUDES

Among the many factors contributing to the stability of a social system are two intimately intertwined ones: the types of tasks that are performed; and the nature of the relationship between the attitudes of the members of the society toward these tasks and their opinions about the proper goals of the individual members of the society and the right ways of reaching them.

The long-range stability of the social system depends on a population of young people properly educated to enter the adult world of tasks and attitudes. Once, the pace of change was slow enough to permit a comfortable margin of compatibility between the adult world and the one children were trained to expect. This compatibility no longer exists. Now we have to ask: What should be the education of a population more and more enveloped in cybernation? What are the appropriate attitudes toward the training for participation in government, the use of leisure, standards of consumption, particular occupations?

Education must cope with the transitional period when the disruption among different socio-economic and occupational groups will be the greatest; and the latter, relatively stable period, if it ever comes to exist, when most people would have adequate income and shorter working hours. The problem involves looking ahead, five, ten, twenty years to see what are likely to be the occupational and social needs and attitudes of those future periods; planning the intellectual and social education of each age group in the numbers needed; motivating young people to seek certain types of jobs and to adopt the desirable and necessary attitudes; providing enough suitable teachers; being able to alter all of these as the actualities in society and technology indicate; and directing the pattern of cybernation so that it fits with the expected kinds and distribution of abilities and attitudes produced by home and school.

To what extent education and technology can be coordinated is not at all clear, if only because we do not know, even for today's world, the criteria for judging the consonance or dissonance in our educational, attitudinal, and occupational systems. We think that parts of the social system are badly out of phase with other parts and that, as a whole, the system is progressively less capable of coping with the problems it produces. But there is little consensus on the "causes" and even less on what can be done about them. All we have at present is the hope that most people can be educated for significant participation in such a world as we have foreseen here—we have no evidence that it can be done.

If we do not find the answers to these questions soon, we will have a population in the next ten or twenty years more and more out of touch with national and international realities, ever more the victims of insecurity on the one hand and ennui on the other, and more and more mismatched to the occupational needs of the day. If we fail to find the answers, we can bumble along, very probably heading into disaster, or we can restrict the extension of cybernation, permitting it only where necessary for the national interest. But judging the national interest and distinguishing it from private interests would confront us with most of the problems that we have outlined in this paper.

Perhaps time has already run out. Even if our style somehow should shift to long-range planning, it would not eliminate the inadequate training and inadequate values of much of our present adolescent and pre-adolescent population, as well as of those adults who will be displaced or remain unhired as a result of cybernation in the next decade. Only a partial solution exists in this case: Begin now a program of economic and social first aid for these people.

A MORATORIUM ON CYBERNATION?

Can we control the effects of cybernation by making it illegal or unprofitable to develop cybernation technology? No, not without virtually stopping the development of almost all of new technology and a good part of the general development of scientific knowledge. The accumulation of knowledge in many areas of science depends on computers. To refine computers and make them more versatile requires research in almost every scientific area. It also requires the development of a technology, usually automated, to produce the articles needed to build new computers. As long as we choose to compete with other parts of the world, we shall have to develop new products and new means for producing them better. Cybernation is the only way to do it on a significant scale. As long as we choose to live in a world guided by science and its technology we have no choice but to encourage the development of cybernation. If we insist on this framework, the answers to coping with its effects must be found elsewhere than in a moratorium on its development.

CONTROL: PUBLIC OR PRIVATE?

There has always been tension between big industry, with its concern for profit and market control, and government, with its concern for the national interest. The tension has increased as big business has become so large as to be quasi-governmental in its influence and as government has had to turn to and even subsidize parts of business in order to meet parts of the national interest within a free-enterprise framework. Under these circumstances we can expect strong differences between government and business as to when and where it is socially legitimate to introduce automation.

Sufficient governmental control over who can cybernate, when, and where would not come easily. In the first place, decisions about control would have to be based on the intentions of local business and industry as well as on the national picture. For example, the effects on Congressional seating of shifts in populations as a result of cybernation-based industrial relocation would presumably enter the calculations. Longer-run consequences would have to be balanced against short-run profits or social dislocations. Implications for our military posture and for international trade would be significant. Moreover, it would be difficult for the government to make a case for control of private organizations on the basis of ambiguous estimates of the effects of automation on hiring policy. In any particular case, it becomes clear only well after the fact of cybernation whether increases or changes in production resulted in a corresponding increase in man-hours of work sufficient to compensate the economy for the jobs lost or the people unhired.

Finally, it must be kept in mind that the power of some of the largest unions is seriously threatened by automation. In a relatively short time they may not have the leverage they now have. Thus, a crucial counterbalance to the pressures from business may be absent when it is most needed. It is possible that the crisis that will arouse the government to exert control will not be evident until the blue-collar work force has been so eroded as to have weakened the unions irreparably.

Yet some sort of control is going to be necessary. There are, of course, the federal regulatory agencies. However, they have never been distinguished for applying their powers with the vigor sometimes allowed by their mandates, and there is no reason to suppose that their traditional weaknesses would suddenly disappear and that an agency created to cope with cybernation would be effective. Nor is there any reason to believe that an agency with the very wide-ranging powers that it would need would be approved before the crisis that it was supposed to avert was upon us.

In theory, control could be exercised by private enterprise. But in the unlikely case that competitors could see their mutual interests clearly enough to join forces, the very act of cooperative control would be incompatible with our anti-trust laws. Whether the government or some alter-government comprised of business, labor, and industry were to do the controlling, either group would have to undertake a degree of national planning and control thoroughly incompatible with the way in which we look upon the management of our economic and social system today.

AFTER THE TAKE-OVER

In twenty years, other things being equal, most of the routine blue-collar and white-collar tasks that can be done by cybernation will be. Our schools will probably be turning out a larger proportion of the population better educated than they are today, but most of our citizens will be unable to understand the cybernated world in which they live. Perhaps they will understand the rudiments of calculus, biology, nuclear physics, and the humanities. But the research realm of scientists, the problems of government, and the interplay between them will be beyond the ken even of our college graduates. Besides, most people will have had to recognize that, when it comes to logic, the machines by and large can think better than they, for in that time reasonably good thinking computers should be operating on a large scale.

There will be a small, almost separate, society of people in rapport with the advanced computers. These cyberneticians will have established a relationship with their machines that cannot be shared with the average man any more than the average man today can understand the problems of molecular biology, nuclear physics, or neuropsychiatry. Indeed, many scholars will not have the capacity to share their knowledge or feeling about this new man-machine relationship. Those with the talent for the work probably will have to develop it from childhood and will be trained as intensively as the classical ballerina.

Some of the remaining population will be productively engaged in human-to-human or human-to-machine activities requiring judgment and a high level of intelligence and training. But the rest, whose innate intelligence or training is not of the highest, what will they do? We can foresee a nation with a large portion of its people doing, directly or indirectly, the endless public tasks that the welfare state needs and the government will not allow to be cybernated because of the serious unemployment that would result. These people will work short hours, with much time for the pursuit of leisure activities.

Even with a college education, what will they do all their long lives, day after day, four-day week-end after week-end, vacation after vacation, in a more and more crowded world? (There is a population explosion to face in another ten to thirty years.) What will they believe in and aspire to as they work their shorter hours and, on the outside, pursue their "self-fulfilling" activities, whatever they may be? No one has every seriously envisioned what characteristics these activities might have in order to be able to engross most men and women most of their adult lives. What will be the relationship of these people to government, to the "upper intellectuals," to the rest of the world, to themselves?

Obviously, attitudes toward work, play, and social responsibility will have changed greatly. Somehow we shall have to cope emotionally with the vast gap in living standards that will then typify the difference between us and the have-not nations. We shall presumably have found some way to give meaning to the consumption of mass leisure. It would seem that a life oriented to private recreation might carry with it an attitude of relative indifference to public responsibility. This indifference, plus the centralization of authority, would seem to imply a governing élite and a popular acceptance of such an élite.

If this world is to exist as a coherent society, it will have to have its own "logic," so that it will make sense to its inhabitants. Today, for most of our population, our society makes sense, even though some other eyes hardly see us as logical in the formal sense of the word and the eyes of some of our own people look on us as a more or less pointless society. We make and solve our problems chiefly by other than mathematical-logical standards, and so must the cybernated generations. What these standards might be, we do not know. But if they are inadequate, the frustration and pointlessness that they produce may well evoke, in turn, a war of desperation—ostensibly against some external enemy but, in fact, a war to make the world safe for human beings by destroying most of society's sophisticated technological base. One thing is clear: if the new "logic" is to resolve the problems raised here, it will have to generate beliefs, behavior, and goals far different from those which we have held until now and which are driving us more and more inexorably into a contradictory world run by (and for?) ever more intelligent, ever more versatile slaves.

from
*The Guaranteed Income**

There is widespread confusion about the reasoning which lies behind the proposal for a guaranteed income, and many of the studies now being published threaten to perpetuate, and even deepen, the causes of misunderstanding. The confusion results from the rapidly changing reactions toward the idea since it was first detailed by me in my 1963 book *Free Men and Free Markets*. I described this evolution in the preface of the 1965 paperback edition: "The bulk of the criticism in early 1963 evaluated *Free Men and Free Markets,* title notwithstanding, as an extreme left-wing text. By mid-1963, it was increasingly considered a modern restatement of New Dealer philosophy. By early 1964, following the publication of *The Triple Revolution* and the consequent association of my name with the 33 other signers of the document who together comprised the Ad Hoc Committee, the book was rather generally evaluated as 1964 liberalism. Finally, after mid-1964, the analysis and indeed the proposals are being characterized with increasing frequency as conservative and even reactionary."

This evolution has continued during the last two years. Thus an idea which was first rejected by almost all commentators as too extreme to be worthy of practical consideration is today being rejected by many of those who are most convinced of the need for a new socioeconomic order on the grounds that it promises no fundamental change in the present socioeconomy.

What brought about this dramatic shift in opinions? Certainly the most striking factor has been the acceptance of direct payments to the poor by Professor Milton Friedman, Senator Goldwater's economic adviser in the 1964 campaign. It has been increasingly argued that if Milton Friedman is in favor of the measure, all those concerned with the welfare of the individual should automatically reject the idea. Such *ad hominem* arguments should, of course, have no place in the debate.

It is therefore essential that the areas of agreement and disagreement among those supporting direct payments to the poor should

*Excerpt from the Introduction to *The Guaranteed Income* edited by Robert Theobald. Copyright © 1965, 1966 by Doubleday & Company, Inc. Reprinted by permission of the publisher.

be sharply differentiated. The first area of agreement is that the initial step on the way to eliminate poverty is to supply money rather than moral uplift, cultural refinements, extended education, retraining programs or makework jobs. In addition, it is agreed that the prime criterion for the distribution of funds should be the poverty of the individual rather than whether Congress is willing to pass special legislation supporting him: it is agreed, as a corollary, that many programs such as those in agriculture which were originally designed to help the poor have become methods of subsidizing the rich. There is another area of agreement which is crucial. It is seen as vital that funds should be provided as an absolute right—that the size of grants should be determined on the basis of objective criteria rather than on the whims and prejudices of the bureaucrat. An absolute guarantee of payment should be incorporated in the legislation setting up direct payments to the poor.

Certain people have tried to undermine this last key element of the guaranteed income proposal. They have stated that we should introduce the idea of direct payments to the poor but that the availability of payments should be based on a bureaucratic determination of the eligibility of the individual for such payments. Such an elimination of the guarantee destroys the crucial element in the proposal and would threaten ever greater intervention in the personal life of the individual.

The recognition of the need to provide *guaranteed direct* payments to the poor on the basis of their *existing income levels* must necessarily be shared by all the proponents of a guaranteed income. Their motivations for suggesting such a scheme may, however, be very different: this can be most clearly seen by contrasting the approach of Milton Friedman with my own. Professor Friedman sees the fundamental economic problem as resulting from increasing government intervention in the economic system. He finds this development deeply disturbing for he believes that the economic system can only be expected to work efficiently if each individual is free to seek his own economic advantage. Perceiving as he does that much of the increase in government intervention in the economy results from the fact that it is impossible for the rulers of a modern state to allow any group of citizens to starve, Professor Friedman believes that we should devise measures which would ensure a minimum income for all and thus eliminate the major present cause of government intervention in the economy. It is essential, in his view, that the level of income not be set so high that it would detract from the incentive to work. While he has not proposed a precise level for grants, his illustrations have been couched in terms of an income floor of $1,600 for a family of four.

DIFFERENCES WITH FRIEDMAN

Professor Friedman hopes that once such an allowance is available, society would not only cease to demand the introduction of further measures of government intervention but would acquiesce in the dismantling of the vast majority of the measures already in existence which were passed to help those less able to help themselves. He anticipates that as government measures are rescinded, and what he sees as the barriers to "self-help" are removed, the country would benefit from an access of the drives which made the nineteenth century so successful. The proposal of Professor Friedman can therefore be explained by his belief that we should re-create the conditions in which the individual can strive to maximize his economic satisfaction with the greatest degree of freedom and the minimum outside intervention.

While I agree with Professor Friedman that one of the main threats to the survival of freedom is the rapidly growing intervention of government bureaucracies in individual lives, my object in providing the individual with a guaranteed income is not to move back to unrestricted economic competition but rather to move forward into a new societal order. In my view, therefore, the guaranteed income must provide a standard of living adequate for decency—I believe that we should start with a minimum income of $3,200 for a family of four and provide for an annual increase of at least five percent. In addition, we must accept the certainty of a number of other changes in the distribution of resources. The first of these will be measures to protect those in the middle-income groups who lose their jobs as a consequence of cybernation.

For me, therefore, the guaranteed income represents the possibility of putting into effect the fundamental philosophic belief which has recurred consistently in human history—that each individual has a right to a minimal share in the production of his society. The perennial shortage of almost all the necessities of life prevented the application of this belief until recent years: the coming of relative abundance in the rich countries gives man the power to achieve the goal of providing a minimum standard of living for all.

It is not enough, however, to state that it is *possible* for the society to provide a minimal standard of living for all; it is *essential* to do so. The present late-industrial age is burdened with problems arising from the mismatch between the needs of the human society and the pressures exerted by an economic production, distribution and consumption system so complex and interrelated as to need the whole of the national culture to be organized around it. While we allow this process to continue, the economic system will increasingly become a parasite on the total environment, depriving the men who create it of their psychological and social sustenance and, in return, only providing them with economic gains.

The current late-industrial system, whether factory or farm, no longer needs many of the workers whose undereducation previously served it. The truth of this statement is now being dramatically demonstrated. We now know that the economic tools developed by John Maynard Keynes make it possible for any society to keep demand growing as rapidly as available supply. It should be added, however, that the historical record still suggests that America may only be willing to pass the necessary measures to ensure a balance between supply and demand in times of war. The degree of aggressiveness which will be required in coming years to preserve such a balance is much greater than in the past. Potential supply can rise and every year by 5-5½ percent: this must be balanced by increases in demand of 5-5½ percent if recessions and slumps are to be avoided.

Recent developments have confirmed the theoretical judgment of Professor Charles Killingsworth of Michigan State University that even when the government is successful in balancing potential demand with available supply, it will still be impossible to employ all those with low skills and inadequate education. This view has so far been rejected by the Administration and most economists on the ground that the pace of improvement in educational accomplishments will counterbalance the increase in the efficiency of machines, and that special education and retraining programs will be adequate to deal with the relatively few people who require further help.

But this forecast underestimates both the growing impact of advanced machinery and the results of continuing increases in the amount and coverage of the minimum wage. Despite the obvious social desirability of better minimum wage provisions, the evidence becomes ever clearer that increases in the minimum wage decrease the attractiveness of marginal employees. A special census report of the South Los Angeles area following the rioting in Watts in 1965 showed that during the boom period of 1960-65, conditions in South Los Angeles were no better than static and that some key indicators actually showed declines. For example, the male unemployment rate for South Los Angeles was 11.3 percent in 1960 and 10.1 percent in 1965: nationally the unemployment rate for nonwhite males dropped from 12 to 6 percent during the same period. Median family income in South Los Angeles actually declined during a period in which the typical American family's income rose substantially.

The August 1966 data on the labor force show clearly that even substantial movements toward full employment are no longer effective in drawing all of the labor force into employment and that it is the disadvantaged who suffer most severely. While overall unemployment dropped from 4.6 percent in the May-August 1965 period to 4 percent in the May-August 1966 period, the unemployment rates for unskilled nonfarm workers only dropped from 7.8 to 7.6 percent, while the unemployment rate for Negro teen-agers remained constant at 27 percent.

A severe problem of unemployability appears to be emerging. Certain types of workers have insufficient inherent capacities to be worth employing at any job for the socially determined wage rate. In these circumstances, employers can be expected to claim that there is a severe shortage of workers even at times when large numbers of people assert that they cannot find jobs.

THE OBEDIENT CONSUMER

The available statistics understate the social crisis which is now upon us, for many other workers theoretically "at work" in "jobs" perform little activity and none that gives meaning to their lives. Others still cling to the self-respect and societal esteem attached to their middle-income "skilled" or "management" job, but know that a machine system or computer will shortly be ready to replace them. New tasks and new, more complex processes which would never be accomplished by man are being assigned to the new, manless technology. In many areas man, the master, is less than technology, his servant. Conversely, we are witnessing a downgrading of human creativity as compared with the innovative potential of machine systems. Somehow, in any given area where man and machine compete, the output of the computer is more "authoritative," more "correct" than man's. So man's role is rapidly becoming that of obedient consumer, prompt obeyer of punch-card demands, apathetic observer of environmental abuse and human degradation, of water pollution, lethal air, the continuing waste of natural resources, the aimless misery of the unemployed and the underpaid, the neurotic defense mechanisms of the occupationally threatened middle class.

Man's structuring into the economic necessities of the present age cannot be reversed without the guaranteed income which aims to provide rights to resources adequate for the dignified life. Today's socioeconomic system uses a very simple mechanism for distributing resources: it assumes that the overwhelming proportion of those seeking jobs will find them and that the incomes received will allow the jobholder to live in dignity. Such a distribution mechanism requires that enough effective demand exists to take up all the goods and services that can be produced by all the capital and labor that can be effectively used.

INCENTIVES TO WORK

Keynes has shown why this chain must be preserved if the industrial socioeconomy is to function, and economists have therefore come to concentrate on the necessity of balancing supply and demand and thus ensuring the availability of sufficient jobs. This has been generally acceptable because it has been believed that more consumption led to higher standards of living: that "enough" is $1,000 more than present income. Recent experimentation, however, has confirmed the significance of the problem of sensory overload: that is, of an inability to absorb more than a certain amount of experience in a given time. This can be illustrated on one level by the new anesthesia technique, used particularly in dentistry, of providing earphones to the patients and then raising the level of sound to the point at which pain ceases to be felt. A similar phenomenon occurs during world tours: it becomes impossible to absorb more sights and sounds. The implications of this understanding of sensory overload are critical because there is increasingly general agreement that creativity depends upon a period of low sensory activity; in other words, upon an opportunity to reflect. As individuals come to realize the reality of sensory overload, they can be expected voluntarily to restrict their input of sensory perceptions; this will inevitably force limits on purchases and on travel.

In addition, society will be forced to limit waste by changing its patterns of rewards and sanctions. Arguments on this subject cannot be based, in my opinion, on an assumed shortage of raw materials, for man's ability to produce raw materials through physics and chemistry could grow at least as fast as his need for materials. Rather the need for limiting waste—whether caused by exaggerated rates of obsolescence, the development of a throwaway culture, the acceptance of polluting by-products or other reasons—will be based on our growing knowledge of ecology; on the necessity to limit the degree of change in the environment if man is to survive.

The guaranteed income is therefore essential for both short-run and long-run reasons. In the short run, it is required because an ever-growing number of people—blue-collar, white-collar, middle-management and professional—cannot compete with machines. In the absence of the guaranteed income the number of people in hopeless, extreme poverty will increase. In the long run, we will require a justification for the distribution of resources which is not based on job-holding, because this is the only way we can break the present necessity to ensure that supply and demand remain in balance—a necessity which is incompatible with continued development of the individual and continued survival of the world.

Both of these justifications are commonly attacked on the grounds that any adequate guaranteed-income scheme would limit incentives. However, the historical and anthropological record makes it clear that economic motivation is not the only way to get people to work—indeed there is considerable evidence that it is not necessarily the most effective way. The inevitable increase in wealth over the next decades will itself largely destroy the financial incentive. If the average family income (in 1966 prices) is of the order of $28,000 by the year 2000 as seems probable, most people will be motivated less by the possibility of increasing their income and more by other potentials. Indeed, this pattern is already emerging in the upper-income brackets.

Professor Friedman emphasizes the need to study the type of tax system which could be used to introduce direct payments to the poor but leads one essentially to ignore the long-run potentials of such a step for the socioeconomy. This consequence is inevitable for Professor Friedman has assumed that the guaranteed income is being introduced to preserve, and strengthen, the industrial age socioeconomy. It therefore appears irrelevant to examine what changes the guaranteed income would cause. While my approach certainly leads to a recognition of the need for studies about the appropriate tax system, it also results in a concentration on the long-run impact of the guaranteed income, for it involves a belief that the necessary evolution and the desirable goal for the American socioeconomy is *full unemployment rather than full employment*—a socioeconomy where choices are made on the basis of individual values rather than on constrained obedience. In this context the guaranteed income becomes the initial point of leverage in changing from the industrial age to the cybernetic era.

10

◀ ROBERT L. HEILBRONER* ▶

The Future of Capitalism (1966)

Operating within a modified Keynesian framework, Heilbroner starts his analysis in the following article with the assumption that capitalism will be maintained as the dominant socioeconomic organization for the next several generations. Whether or not this assumption of the semipermanence of capitalism is more reasonable than the opposite premise of its transiency is, of course, a moot point. Unless the existing system is beset by innumerable and obvious contradictions, it always appears more reasonable to assume continuity rather than a rupture of the status quo. This was as true of long periods under slavery and feudalism as it is now under the present modified capitalist system.

Heilbroner is concerned with exploring the limits of change within the bounds of capitalism. He recognizes that in America a system of privilege is grounded in capitalist institutions and is therefore a source of resistance to social and economic change. Although aware of many aspects of Marxian analysis, Heilbroner eschews its theory of history based on class conflict and replaces it with a technological deterministic theory of social change, in which the strategic group in society is the technological elite rather than powerful wealth holders or a proletariat. The latter group, in fact, nowhere appears as an active agent in Heilbroner's scheme. Rather he stresses the continuing ten-

---

*Professor of Economics, New School for Social Research.

sion between the former two groups as the dominant shaper of history. The organized knowledge and scientific technology of the new elite are thought of by Heilbroner as ultimately subverting the capitalist order, since their mentality and outlook are geared to social control and planning. The long-run decline of capitalism is thus intimately related to the development of a scientific and technological elite. In the short run, however, he admits that the skills of this elite are used to buttress the capitalist order. A missing link in Heilbroner's analysis is how the "technocracy" which supports capitalist institutions in the short run is antagonistic to these same institutions in the long run. His position is, at best, a questionable one. Although it is quite possible that individual members of the scientific elite may feel an ideological incompatibility with the materialistic and nationalistic aims of the social system, the overwhelming number show every evidence of being willingly co-opted into business and government where they occupy a privileged position. To claim that important historical changes are to be engineered by these groups is to adopt an elitist view of history in which the masses are passively moved by forces they neither understand nor control. Although Heilbroner's approving comment that "conscious social control in more and more areas of life will be a marked feature of society in the future" would appear to transcend liberalism, it is belied by his elitist frame of reference.

The merit of Heilbroner is that he, like Galbraith, has assiduously tried to make economics more socially relevant by directing its focus on how capitalism actually operates rather than spinning imaginary theories about an imaginery competitive market model. He notes with considerable acumen that the dominant corporate sector attempts through planning to insulate itself against disruptive market forces, and is more and more prone to accept a government with widespread supervisory and regulatory powers. His claim that considerable economic planning on a governmental level is compatible with a capitalist structure, and that technology creates a need for more societal organization, places Heilbroner on the left end of the liberal spectrum. Heilbroner believes that the capitalist system used with Keynesian type intelligence is capable of maintaining effective demand at high employment levels, gradually redistributing income sufficiently to end poverty, utilizing technology without serious disruptive effects in the short run, and achieving a peaceful accord with Russia—although Heilbroner acknowledges the presence of a "semi-militarized economy" in the United States and predicts the likelihood of Communist expansion in undeveloped countries during the next decade. One has to admire Heilbroner's courage in the hazardous game of crystal ball gazing. It remains to be seen whether or not the capitalist model is capable of delivering all that he optimistically claims for it. His view of the long run demise of capitalism because of the sapping of its ideological underpinnings is in marked contrast to his short run forecasts.

———M. L.

The Future of Capitalism*

For roughly the last century and a half the dominant system of economic organization in most of the West has been that of capitalism. In all likelihood, barring the advent of a catastrophic war, capitalism will continue as the dominant system of the Western world during the remainder of this century and well into the next. Although it will inevitably change, will likely suffer considerable duress over the next decades, and in the longer run will gradually give way to a very different kind of social order, for our lives and for those of our children, capitalism bids fair to confront us as the prevailing form of social organization in those nations where it is now solidly entrenched.

It seems to me that all serious social analysis and prediction must start from some such premise. At any rate, it is my premise, and I propose to explore—with all the uncertainties and risks inherent in such an enterprise—the social changes available to us within the limits of capitalism in the future.

But how can we establish these "limits"? Perhaps we can shed an initial light on the question if we imagine asking some perceptive observer in, say, 13th-century France what were the limits of feudalism. Our observer might be hard put to find an answer, particularly if he looked about him at the striking variety of forms that feudalism assumed in the various domains of Europe. Yet undoubtedly we could have suggested an answer to him that would have sounded reasonable. It is that certain kinds of economic and social change were unimaginable —indeed impossible—in 13th-century France because they would have implied the establishment of some totally different form of social organization. To take a central instance, it would have been impossible to have replaced the traditional ties, established customs, and fixed obligations by which the manorial economy hung together with some radically different system, such as the cash markets that were already disrupting the settled tenor of feudal economic life, because a change of this dimension would have critically undermined the power of the

*Robert Heilbroner, "The Future of Capitalism." Reprinted from *Commentary*, by permission; copyright © 1966 by the American Jewish Committee. This essay was included in somewhat different form in Heilbroner's book, *The Limits of American Capitalism*, New York: Harper & Row, 1966.

lord, elevated out of all proportion that of the parvenu class of merchants, and thereby destroyed the fixed hierarchy of status that was the very backbone of the feudal social structure. Thus, one meaning we can give to the idea of "limits" in a society is very simple: It is those boundaries of change that would so alter the functional base of a society, or the structure of privilege built on that base, as to displace a given social order by a new one.

In terms of the immediate subject of our essay, this draws the broad limits of American capitalism in the last third of the 20th century with reasonable fixity. To take a few examples: it is certainly beyond the present limits of capitalism to replace the guiding principle of production for profit by that of production for use; it is impossible to nationalize the great corporations or to end the private ownership of the means of mass communication; and it is impossible to end the concentration of wealth in private hands. One can debate whether all or any of these changes are desirable, but there is little point in debating whether they are realizable. Barring only some disaster that would throw open the gates to a radical reconstruction of society, they are not.

What we have established thus far, however, is only the first and most obvious answer to the question of what we mean by the "limits" of social change. For if we now return to the 13th century, we could imagine suggesting to our medieval observer another approach to the idea of feudal limits. Rather than pointing out to him the contemporary incompatibility of the market system, we might be able to show him the immense long-term historical momentum of the emergent forces of the monetized economy. Indeed, we might even be able to bring him to see that by the end of another four or five centuries, feudalism would have virtually disappeared, and that an economic organization of society once incompatible with feudalism would have triumphed over it.

From such a perspective, the task of delineating the limits of feudalism becomes a different one. It is no longer to discover what cannot be done in the short run, but to explore what *can* be done, and how, in doing it, the social structure may slowly and subtly alter, making possible still further change in the future.

It need hardly be said that one cannot project such a long evolutionary—or possibly revolutionary—advance in close detail. The precise route to be taken, the pace of progress, the roadblocks where the invading forces of a new society may be temporarily halted or even thrown back—all this surpasses any power of analysis we now have.

But the grand line of march is not beyond our ability to foresee. Looking back at 13th-century France, we can see how defenseless were its castle walls against the insinuating influence of the market system. In similar fashion, it should be possible to explore the limits of capitalism in America, not alone in terms of changes that cannot now be accommodated by the business system, but in terms of those forces that are altering capitalism, like feudalism in an earlier day, in ways that will eventually cause its social and economic structure to be displaced by another.

We cannot, however, explore change until we answer a prior question: Why do societies resist change? A full explanation of social inertia must reach deep into the psychological and technical underpinnings of the human community. But in the process of gradual social adjustment it is clear enough where to look for the main sources of the resistance to change. They are to be found in the structure of privilege inherent in all social systems.

Privilege is not an attribute we are accustomed to stress when we consider the construction of *our* social order. When pressed, we are, of course, aware of its core institutions in capitalism—the right to reap private benefits from the use of the means of production and the right to utilize the dynamic forces of the marketplace for private enrichment. The element of privilege in these institutions, however—that is, their operative result in favoring certain individuals and classes—is usually passed over in silence in favor of their purely functional aspects. Thus, private property is ordinarily explained as being no more than a convenient instrumentality for the efficient operation of an economic system, or the market elements of Land, Labor, and Capital as purely neutral "factors of production."

Now these institutions and relationships do indeed fulfill the purposes for which they are advertised. But this is not the only use they have. Land, Labor, and Capital are not just functional parts of a mechanism but are categories of social existence that bring vast differences in life chances with them. It is not just Labor on the one hand, and Land or Capital on the other; it is the Bronx on the one hand and Park Avenue on the other. Similarly, private property is not merely a pragmatic arrangement devised for the facilitation of production, but a social institution that brings to some members of the community a style of life qualitatively different from that afforded to the rest. In a word, the operation of capitalism as a *functional* system results in a structure of wealth and income characteristic of capitalism as a *system of privilege*—a structure in which the top two per cent of American families own between two-thirds and three-quarters of all corporate stock, and enjoy incomes roughly ten times larger than the average received within the nation as a whole.

The mere presence of these concentrations of wealth or large disparities of income does not in itself differentiate the system of privilege under capitalism from those of most other societies in history. Rather, what marks off our system is that wealth and income within capitalism are not mainly derived from non-economic activity, such as war, plunder, extortionate taxation, etc., but arise from the activity of marketers or the use of property by its owners.

This mixture of the functional and the privileged aspects of capitalism has a curious but important political consequence. It is that privilege under capitalism is much less "visible," especially to the favored groups, than privilege under other systems. The upper classes in feudalism were keenly alive to the gulf that separated them from the lower classes, and perfectly open about the need for preserving it. The upper groups under capitalism, on the other hand, are typically unaware that the advantages accruing to them from following the paths of the market economy constitute in any sense or fashion a privilege.

This lack of self-awareness is rendered even more acute by virtue of another differentiating characteristic of privilege under capitalism. It is that privilege is limited to the advantages inherent in the economic structure of society. That is, the same civil and criminal law, the same duties in war and peace, apply to both economically privileged and unprivileged. It would be a mistake to concentrate on obvious differences in the application of the law as being of the essence. Rather, one must contrast the single system of law and obligation under capitalism —however one-sidedly administered—with the *differing* systems that apply to privileged and unprivileged in other societies.

The divorce of economic from political or social privilege brings up the obvious fact that, at least in democratic societies like America, the privileged distribution of economic rewards is exposed to the corrective efforts of the democratic electorate. The question is, however, why the structure of privilege has remained relatively intact, despite so long an exposure to the potentially leveling influences of the majority.

In part, we can trace the answer to the very "invisibility" of privilege we have just described. Furthermore, in all stable societies the structure of privilege appears to the general public not as a special dispensation, but as the natural order of things, with which their own interests and sentiments are identified. This is especially true under capitalism, where the privileges of wealth are open, at least in theory, and to some extent in practice, to all comers. Finally, the overall results of capitalism, particularly in America during the entire 20th century and recently in Europe as well, have been sufficiently rewarding to hold anticapitalist sentiment to a relatively small segment of the population.

That the defense of privilege is the active source of resistance to social and economic change may appear so obvious as scarcely to be worth emphasizing. Obvious or not, it is a fact too often passed over in silence. It seems to me impossible to analyze the nature of the opposition to change without stressing the vulgar but central fact that every person who is rich under capitalism is a beneficiary of its inherent privileges. Taking the American system as it now exists, it seems fair to assert that the chance to own and acquire wealth constitutes a primary—perhaps even a dominating—social motivation for most men, and that those who enjoy or aspire to these privileges will not readily acquiesce in changes that will substantially lessen their chances of maintaining or gaining them.

The touchstone of privilege provides an indispensable key when we now return to our main theme. If it does not give us an exact calculus by which to compute what changes will and will not be acceptable, it does give us an angle of entry, a point of view, without which attempts to cope with the problem of social change are apt to have no relevance at all.

Take, for example, the problem of the poverty that now afflicts some 30 or 40 million Americans. Our alleged cause of this poverty has always directly stressed the privileges of capitalism. This is the view that poverty under capitalism is largely ascribable to wage exploitation. There is clearly an element of truth here, in that the affluence of the favored groups in capitalism does indeed stem from institutions that divert income from the community at large into the channels of dividends, interest, rent, monopoly returns, etc. It is by no means clear, however, that the amount of this diversion, if redistributed among the masses, would spell the difference between their poverty and their well-being. On the contrary, it is now generally acknowledged that the level of wages reflects workers' productivity more than any other single factor, and that this productivity in turn is primarily determined by the quantity and the quality of the capital equipment of the economic system.

Certainly, the productivity of the great mass of workers under capitalism has steadily increased, and so have their real wages. Today, for example, industrial workers in America cannot be classified as "poor" by prevailing absolute standards, if we take $4,000 a year as defining a level of minimum adequacy for a small family. Although wage poverty is clearly present in capitalism, it is primarily restricted to the argicultural areas and to the lowest categories of skills in the service trades. No small part of it is accounted for by discrimination against Negroes, and by the really shocking levels of income of Negro farm and service labor. On the other hand, the proportion of the labor force that is afflicted with this poverty is steadily diminishing. Farmers, farm managers, and farm laborers together will probably constitute only 5 per cent of the labor force within a decade. The low-paid non-farm common laborer, who constituted over 12 per cent of the working force in 1900, makes up only 5 per cent of it today and will be a smaller percentage tomorrow.

There remains, nevertheless, the question of how much the existing level of wages could be increased if the categories of capitalist privilege did not exist. Since it is difficult to estimate accurately the total amount of "privileged" income under capitalism, let us take as its convenient representation the sum total of all corporate profits before tax. In the mid 1960's, these profits exceeded $70 billion a year. If this sum were distributed equally among the 70 million members of the work force, the average share would be $1,000. For the lowest-paid workers, such as migrant farm laborers, this would represent an increase in annual incomes of 100 per cent or more—an immense gain. For the average industrial worker, however, the gain would be in the neighborhood of 20-25 per cent, certainly a large increase but not one that would fundamentally alter his living standards.

Thus, insofar as the institutions of capitalism constitute a drain upon non-privileged groups, it can be fairly said that they are only marginally responsible for any inadequacy in the prevailing general level of income. Individual companies may indeed be capable of vastly improving the lot of their workers—General Motors makes nearly as much gross profit on a car as it pays out in wages, and "could," therefore, virtually double its wages. But for the economy as a whole, no such large margin of redistribution is possible. So long, then, as the defense of these privileges does not result in substantially *increasing* the share of national income accruing to the privileged elements of the nation, it seems fair to conclude that the level of material well-being under capitalism is limited mainly by the levels of productivity it can reach. If the trend of growth of the past century is continued, the average level of real wages for industrial labor should double in another two to three decades. This would bring average earnings to a level of about $10,000 and would effectively spell the abolition of wage poverty, under any definition.

This conclusion does not close our investigation into the relationship between poverty and privilege, but rather directs it toward what is now revealed as the principal cause of poverty. This is the fact that large groups within the population—the aged, the handicapped, the sick, the unemployed, the castaways in rural backwaters—have no active tie into the market economy and must therefore subsist at the very meager levels to which non-participants in the work process are consigned. There is only one way that their condition can be quickly alleviated, but that one way would be very effective indeed. This is to redistribute to them enough income earned or received by more favored members of the community to bring them to levels of economic decency. A program with this objective would require some $10- to $12 billion above the public assistance that the poor now receive in this country. Such a sum would amount to approximately a seventh of corporate profits before tax. Alternatively, shared among the 11- or 12 million consumer units who constitute the top 20 per cent of the nation's income receivers, it would require an average additional tax of roughly $1,000 on incomes that average $16,000.

In both cases, in other words, a program to eliminate sheer need among the poor would constitute a sizable incursion into the incomes enjoyed by favored groups, although hardly such an invasion as to constitute the elimination of these privileges. Thus, the failure to carry out such a program cannot be laid to the "objective" or functional difference that such a redistribution would entail, but simply to the general unwillingness of those who enjoy higher incomes to share their good fortune with those who do not. As Adam Walinsky has very aptly put it, "The middle class knows that the economists are right when they say that poverty could be eliminated if we only will it; they simply do not will it."

To what extent does that conclusion, then, lead to the prospect of alleviating poverty within the next generation or so? In the short run the outlook is not very hopeful. Given the temptations of luxury consumption and the general lack of deep concern in a nation lulled by middle-class images of itself, it is doubtful that very effective programs of social rescue can be launched within the next decade or two. Yet, of all the problems confronting capitalism, poverty seems the least likely to be blocked permanently by the resistance of privilege. Tax receipts are now growing at the rate of some $6 billion a year simply as a consequence of the growth of the level of output, and this flow of funds to the government will increase over the future. It may be that these receipts will be used for larger arms expenditures for some years, but assuming that full-scale war will be averted, sooner or later the arms budget must level off. Thereafter the funds will become available for use either in the form of tax reductions—an operation which normally favors the well-to-do—or as the wherewithal for a major assault on the slums, etc. In this choice between the claims of privilege and those of social reform, the balance is apt to be tipped by the emerging new national elites, especially from government. In addition, a gradual liberalization of the prevailing business ideology is likely to ease opposition to measures that clearly promise to improve the quality of society without substantially affecting its basic institutions of privilege.

It is idle to predict when Harlem will be reconstructed and Appalachia reborn, since so much depends on the turn of events in the international arena. Yet it seems to me that the general dimensions of the problem make it possible to envisage the substantial alleviation—perhaps even the virtual elimination—of massive poverty within the limits of capitalism three or four decades hence, or possibly even sooner.

The elimination of poverty is, however, only part of a larger problem within capitalism—the problem of income distribution. Hence, we might now look to the chances that capitalism will alter the moral anomalies of wealth as well as those of poverty.

Here it is not so easy to foresee a change in the operational results of the system of privilege. Since the 1930's, the political intent of the public has clearly been to bring about some lessening of the concentration of income that goes to the very rich, and some diminution of the enclaves of family wealth that have passed intact from one generation to the next. Thus, we have seen the introduction of estate taxes that levy imposts of about one-third on net estates of only $1 million, and of fully half on net estates of $5 million; and these rates have been supplemented by measures to prevent the tax-free passage of wealth before death by gift.

Since the enactment of these taxes, a full generation has passed, and we would therefore expect to see some impact of the legislation in a significant lowering of the concentration of wealth among the top families. Instead, we find that the share held by the top families has decreased only slightly—from 33 per cent of all personal wealth in 1922, to 29 per cent in 1953 (the last year for which such calculations exist). Concentration of stock—the single most important medium for the investment of large wealth—has shown no tendency to decline since 1922. Equally recalcitrant before egalitarian measures is the flow of income to topmost groups. Legal tax rates on top incomes have risen from 54 per cent under President Hoover to over 90 per cent in the 1940's and early 1950's, and to 72 per cent in the mid 1960's. The presumed higher incidence of taxes at the peak of the income pyramid has, however, been subverted by innumerable stratagems of trusts, family sharing of income, capital gains, deferred compensation, or other means of tax avoidance or outright tax evasion.

There is no indication that this resistive capacity of the system of privilege is likely to weaken, at least within the time span of a generation. Nor is there any sign that the "natural workings" of the system will lessen the flow of income to the top. The statistics of income distribution clearly show a slow but regular drift of income *toward* the upper end of the spectrum. Three per cent of all income was received by income receivers in the $15,000-and-up brackets in 1947; in 1963, in terms of constant dollars, this fraction had grown to eight. This determined self-perpetuation of large concentrations of private wealth is likely to continue—afflicting the social order with that peculiar irresponsibility that is the unhappy hallmark of the system. The power of wealth is by no means the only source of power in America and may, in fact, be expected to decline. But the voice of money still speaks very loudly, and the capacity of wealth to surmount the half-acquiescent opposition of a democratic political system promises that it will continue to resound in America for a long while to come.

The maldistribution of income and the social problems that spring from it can no longer be said to threaten the viability—although it may seriously jeopardize the social peace—of capitalism. This cannot be said, however, of a second problem—the economic malfunction that has periodically racked capitalism over the last hundred years and that nearly caused its demise in the 1930's.

The persistent breakdowns of the capitalist economy can all be traced to a single underlying cause: the anarchic or planless character of capitalist production. So long as the output of individual firms is guided solely by the profitable opportunities open to each, without regard to the state of the market as a whole, economic short-circuits must result whenever the output of all firms fails to dovetail with the structure of demand, or when the production plans of the business community as a whole are not adequate to cope with the independently formulated savings plans of the community at large. In a milieu of huge enterprises and enormous fixed investments, such miscalculations or imbalances carry the potential of a major disruptive impact.

Hence, it is not surprising that reformers have long advocated planning as the remedy for capitalist depressions or stagnation. The trouble has been, however, that much of the planning which its partisans have urged upon it has been incompatible with the institutions of capitalism. For example, proposals to nationalize the core of heavy industry or to convert the biggest corporations into quasi-public utilities, may have much to recommend them along strictly economic lines, but they all infringe the preserves of private property or of the market to a degree intolerable to the American business community.

This does not mean, however, that planning is therefore ruled out. On the contrary, a great deal of planning is virtually inevitable over the coming decades, but it is likely to be used in support of the main institutions of capitalism rather than as a means of replacing them.

One such planning instrument is certain to be the reliance on the government's fiscal powers to maintain aggregate demand. Although we are still only in the early stages of experience with public demand-creation, there is little doubt that a bold use of fiscal mechanisms can virtually guarantee a steady or rising level of total expenditure. Moreover, since demand-creation involves little or no interference with individual markets or business, it impinges little, if at all, on the preserves of privilege. Tax cuts, for example, are certain to be welcomed by business and upper-income groups. Additional spending, so long as it is within the established areas of public concern—arms, roads, schools, rivers and harbors, conservation, and perhaps now social welfare—is also welcomed as a source of new business.

There remains, to be sure, a body of ideological resistance to the use of fiscal measures of a compensatory sort, compounded of an ignorance of public finance and a shrewd foreboding that the assumption of public economic responsibility, no matter how useful at the moment, is freighted with serious long-term implications. Yet it seems likely that this is a view of dwindling importance. A very considerable segment of business backed the controversial Kennedy tax cut, and the undoubted success of that policy should pave the way for further measures of the same kind. In addition, the non-business elites, especially from the academic and government establishments, are strongly in favor of fiscal controls to buoy up the system, and their influence in securing the bold use of these measures may be very important or even decisive. Thus, there seems a reasonable expectation that measures to safeguard the economy against the collapse of effective demand lie well within the ambit of capitalism today.

What is more difficult to judge is the extent to which capitalism will be able to go beyond general fiscal planning into planning on a more detailed basis for the achievement of broad welfare objectives. Here the experience of Europe since the war is relevant. In nearly every nation of Europe we have seen the formulation of planning techniques that go considerably beyond the mere application of fiscal leverage, to the conscious "design" of the economic future. The very fact that European capitalism has taken this turn puts it beyond argument that a considerable amount of indirect planning is compatible with the main institutions of capitalism.

On the other hand, the growth of European planning owes much to the particular traditions of European capitalism, including the more or less formalized structures of employers' federations and the pronounced "étatist" tradition in many states. The absence of comparable institutions and history makes doubtful the possibility of a wholesale transplantation of European forms of planning to America. Furthermore, unlike its sister capitalisms across the Atlantic, the United States has not become accustomed to the public ownership of transportation or utilities, or to a large public-housing sector, or to the development of a strong system of public welfare.

As a result, the United States has always entertained an exaggerated suspicion of all invasions by the public authority into private terrain. Hence the extent and speed with which American capitalism may evolve in the direction of detailed economic planning would seem to depend primarily on whether circumstances arise that require such techniques. If, for example, the continued incursion of technology, coupled with a very large inflow of young people into the labor market, should create an employment crisis during the next decade, some form of industrial planning would quite possibly emerge as an instrument of social policy. In that case, policies designed deliberately to create employment through a substantial enlargement of public activities at state or local levels, or—looking farther ahead—the designation of a civil sector, such as the rebuilding of the cities, as the peacetime equivalent of the military sector, might well show up as part of the practicable social agenda.

Capitalism, then, can achieve considerable change within the boundaries imposed by its market mechanisms and privileges of pri-

vate property. But there are also important limits beyond which it cannot go—at least within the foreseeable future. Primary among these is
the continuing requirement that the economic participants in a capitalist
world—even in a planned capitalist world—behave in the manner that
is required of them if the market mechanism is to work. That is, they
must act as "economic men," buying cheap and selling dear, allowing
relative remunerations to weigh heavily in their choices of occupations
or employment, setting acquisitive aims high in the hierarchy of life
goals. These marketing traits are not merely pervasive private idiosyn-
crasies that can be dispensed with if they are no longer esteemed. They
are integral to, and necessary for, the successful operation of a market
system. In a setting of bare subsistence and newly-risen entrepreneurs
there is little difficulty in adducing the acquisitive behavior required to
run a capitalist economy. But in a more advanced and affluent society,
where the primary drives of self-preservation begin to fail, the necessary
marketing behavior must be sustained by supplementary motives of
emulation and competitive striving. Thus, the endless and relentless
exacerbation of economic appetites in advanced capitalism is not merely
a surface aberration, but a deeply-rooted functional necessity to provide
the motivations on which the market system depends.

This thralldom to an overweening economic imperative of sales
and profits and its accompanying worship of a calculus of income are
features of capitalism that cannot be eliminated by planning. A planned
capitalism of the future, however rid of its gross malfunctions, will
nonetheless be one in which men are subservient to the economic demands of a market environment.

Nowhere is this apt to pose a more serious problem than along
the extended frontier where technology interacts with society. This
interaction takes two forms. One, which we may call the *direct effect,*
is revealed as the immediate change in the environment brought about
by the application of a new technique such as the computerized control
of production, or the use of a new product such as a jet transport. This
effect, as we know from experience, may bring radical changes into
economic or social life, but these changes have, at least, been consciously
introduced into society (although often with inadequate appreciation
of their immediate impact).

But there is as well an *indirect effect* of technology that diffuses
throughout society as the secondary consequences of new machinery or
new processes. Thus, the indirect effect of the new technology of auto-

mation is unemployment; the indirect effect of the new technology of medicine and health is an aging population; the indirect effect of the technology of war is the creation of a military-industrial economic sector. Not least we find, as a general indirect effect of all modern technology, an increasing complexity, size, and hierarchical organization of production, which gives rise in turn to a growing need for public intervention into the economic process itself.

Against this tremendous invasion of technology, a market economy offers but one instrument of control—the profit or loss stemming from the direct effect of a particular technology. As to its side-effects, the market mechanism proper has no controls whatsoever. As a result, the invasion of technology becomes an essentially disruptive force, continuously upsetting the patterns of life in a haphazard manner. Under a system that abdicates as much decision-making as possible to the rule of profit, the possibilities for a rational restraint over this force that rearranges our lives thus shrinks to a minimum. Capitalism is essentially defenseless before the revolutionizing impact of its technical drive. Of all the limits to which capitalism is subject, this is the most unyielding —although, as we shall see, it is this very helplessness of the system before the technological onslaught that holds out the most important promise for the long-term remaking of capitalism itself.

Our next concern lies with the reach and inhibitions of what we might call the *capitalist imagination.*

The quality of this imagination is most clearly revealed if we think for a moment of the "visionary" glimpse of the future often spelled out for us by business spokesmen—a future of enormous affluence, technical marvels, widespread leisure, etc. There is, in these vistas, much that is genuinely new and rich with possibilities for material betterment. But there is also something inherent in all these visions that remains unmentioned. It is that these imagined societies of the future still depend on "workers," however well off, who work for "businessmen," however enlightened, in a system motivated and directed by the commercial impulse, however tempered or refined. A society in which there were no workers or businessmen as we understand the terms; or in which the categories of privilege had been fundamentally altered; or where the pressures of the marketplace had been replaced by some other means of assuring economic continuity—all these possibilities are absent from the capitalist imagination. More than that, they are dismissed as "utopian."

Albeit unwittingly, this is set forth all too clearly in the peroration of a recent book by Frederick R. Kappel, President of A.T.&T.:

> We are involved in one of the great ideological struggles of all times. Essentially it is a contest between two quite basic concepts. One is that men are capable of faith in ideas that lift their minds and hearts, ideas that raise their sights and give them hope, energy, and enthusiasm. Opposing this is the belief that the pursuit of material ends is all that life on this earth is about.

The words are eloquent enough, but alas, what do they reveal? Which side, ours or theirs, is the side of "ideas that lift minds and hearts," which the side that believes "the pursuit of material ends is all that life on this earth is about"? In the breathtaking ambiguity of this intended affirmation of business faith, the unseeing confusion of identities meant to be so clearly polarized, lies an all too clear exposition of the weakness that inhabits the very center of the capitalist imagination.

We cannot be sure what effects such a constricted view of the future may have on the aspirations and attitudes of most American citizens. It is likely that for the majority who are understandably concerned with their material lot, it would make no difference whatsoever. But for a not unimportant minority—I think of college youth and of the intellectual community—the absence of any transcendent secular goal is apt to present an oppressive limitation to thought and spirit. Indeed, in my opinion the present anarchic mood of youth may well be due to just such a lack of a visionary future to which to bend its hopes and efforts.

Whatever the ultimate effect of this stifling at home, there is another area where the limitations of the capitalist imagination are likely to be of very great importance. This is in the contest with Communism for the guidance of future world society.

It is hardly necessary to speak of the power of Communism as a force bearing on American capitalism. Yet in appraising that force, we often fail to articulate that which is most threatening about it to ourselves as members or protagonists of the capitalist way of life. This is the presence of Communism as a viable social system that has dispensed with our institutions of privilege, and that therefore faces capitalism with the living refutation of their necessity. In this fundamental sense, Communism puts capitalism on trial before the bar of history.

In this trial it matters not that Communism has its own system of privilege, in some ways more primitive than our own. Nor does it count for much that capitalist performance on many fronts is manifestly superior to that of Communism. What matters is that Communism has demonstrated the mutability and historic transiency of our particular social order, and that that social order can never again feel entirely secure in its claims to permanence and legitimacy.

I believe it is this sense of historic unease that lies behind the deep, uncritical, and often unreasoning hostility of America toward Communism. The reasons we cite for our fear and hatred—the undeniable acts of cruelty and repression, of aggression and intolerance, of intrigue and untrustworthiness—can be duplicated in many non-Communist countries: in Portugal, in Spain, in the Union of South Africa, in various Latin American dictatorships, past and present. There, however, they have never roused in us the fervor or revulsion they do when discovered in the Communist world. In part, this is no doubt because these other nations are small and weak and do not constitute centers of national power comparable to Russia or China (although hardly Cuba); in part, because they do not seek to export their particular world-views. But more deeply, especially among the conservative interests of this country, I think it is because the existence of Communism frightens American capitalism, as the existence of Protestantism once frightened the Catholic Church; or the French Revolution the English aristocracy.

The fundamental threat of Communism is not likely to decline over the next generation. Rather, it is apt to grow. In Russia, the prospect is clearly for substantial economic expansion; for the gradual improvement of the still dreary life of its people; for a continuation of its massive scientific advances; for further intellectual, and perhaps political, liberalization. For China, no such sanguine assurances can be given, but its continuing emergence as the unquestioned leader of Asia seems hardly likely to be reversed. In Latin America and Africa, the outlook can only be for political turmoil as the aspirations of excited masses outdistance any conceivable pace of progress. In the ensuing unrest, radical leaders are bound to emerge, and it would be a miracle if they were not inclined, to some degree, toward Communism or some kind of national collectivism.

This tendency is apt to be reinforced by the very ideological limitations of capitalism we have been concerned with. If we look to the developing nations, we find in nearly all of them a yearning, not alone for material progress, but for a great social and political, even spiritual, transformation. However millennial these hopes, however certain to be dashed, they are not to be lightly disregarded. The leaders and elites of the young nations, like those of our own youth, are looking for a model of a society that will fire them to great efforts, and it is unlikely that they will find this model in the market-based and wealth-protecting philosophy of capitalism.

All these considerations point to the very great likelihood that Communism or radical national collectivism will make substantial inroads during the coming generation or two, perhaps by conquest or subversion, but more probably by the decay of existing orders unable to handle the terrible demands of political awakening and economic reformation.

Given this grave outlook, what would be its impact on America?

We have already witnessed the initial impact in the substantial militarization of American capitalism. The so-called military-industrial complex (to which should be added "political" as an equal partner) today contributes between eight and ten per cent to the Gross National Product. In the 1960's, military expenditure has regularly exceeded the sum total of all personal income taxes, has accounted for one-fourth of all federal public works, has directly employed some 3.2 million workers in defense industries and another 1.1 million as civilian employees of the Defense Department and the services, has subsidized about one-third of all research in the United States; and not least, has come to be accepted as a normal and permanent fixture of American life by all groups, including the academic. The fact is that American capitalism is now a semi-militarized economy and will very probably become even more so during the next decade.

In this dangerous situation, it is important for us to clarify the specific influence over the direction of events that can be ascribed to the business interest in society. According to Marxism—or more properly Leninism—the business structure itself inherently presses the state toward armed conflict. The fierce economic conflicts of capitalist nations prior to World War II, the long history of capitalist suppression of colonials continuing down to the present in some parts of Africa, the huge and jealously guarded interests of the United States and other capitalist nations in the oil regions of the Near East or Latin America —all make it impossible to dismiss such a picture of a belligerent capitalist imperialism. At the same time, even a cursory review of the nations initiating aggressive actions since 1945 should raise doubts as to the exclusive capitalist predisposition to war. More important, an analysis of the roots of belligerency in the more warlike capitalisms, specifically pre-war Germany or Japan, must emphasize the leading role played by purely military or lingering feudal elements, and the largely passive, although not always reluctant, part taken by capitalist groups.

On somewhat more Marxian lines, Victor Perlo has made a determination of the direct economic interest of the top American corporations in war or peace. He concludes that the economic self-interest of the biggest corporations is more or less evenly divided, with half profiting from a defense economy, and half—including such giants as General Motors and U.S. Steel—being penalized by it. Assuming that big businessmen would be motivated to oppose or support disarmament on such grounds, it is important to note that nothing like a monolithic "pro-war" economic interest can be said to exist within American capitalism.

Further, the imperialist thrust that increased both the chances and the causes of war in the late 19th century seems to be giving way to less dangerous forms of international relationship. Property interests that once had to be defended by force of arms are now protected by government insurance. International relationships that formerly allowed large capitalist enterprises to intervene directly into the economic and political life of colonial nations have been succeeded by relationships in which the independence of action of foreign companies is severely restricted. In a word, the politics of nationalism has asserted its preeminence over the economics of imperialism, with the salutary consequence of a diminution in the role of business as the active initiator of foreign economic policy.

Thus, the role of business proper in the struggle for world power does not seem intrinsically warlike. Unfortunately, that does not mean the chances for conflict are therefore small. Business is not the only power center within capitalist societies, and in America the military and the civil branches of government contain more than their share of belligerent-minded leaders who are in a position to influence foreign policy. Then, too, we must reckon with the generalized hatred of Communism among the lower and middle classes, a hatred that may originally have been implanted but that now flourishes as a self-maintaining source of aggression.

In this situation, given the reciprocal posture of the other side, it is difficult to see how a major conflict could be avoided, were not the consequences of all-out warfare so terrifying. On both sides, only the instinct of self-preservation—fortunately the single most powerful instinct —holds back the military-minded, the fundamentalist, the ambitious, or simply the self-righteous. As a result, the most probable outlook becomes a continuation of the military-political struggle on the scale of Korea or Vietnam. The danger is that a succession of such involvements may encourage the rise of a strict garrison state, one that is marked by an atmosphere of internal repression and external belligerence.

This grave possibility may well be the single most dangerous eventuality during the next decade or two, when the chances of Communist "take-overs" will be greatest. But the longer-term future is far from foreclosed along such lines. On both sides of the great divide, forces are at work that can lessen the intensity of hostilities. One of these is the enhanced prospect for international stabilization, once the worst is over and those nations that are going to go Communist or national-collectivist have done so. A second hopeful possibility is the growth of a greater degree of isolationism in American politics—or perhaps one should say a lesser degree of interventionism—compounded in part of disillusion, in part of fear, and in part of a more realistic appreciation of our inability to affect the unruly tides of world history. Yet another force for peaceful accommodation is the possibility that the specter of Communist "world domination" will be dispelled by the sight of Communist nations in intense rivalry, just as the Communist world may be relieved by the continuing evidence of inter-capitalist frictions.

And finally, we can hope that within a generation or so, new concerns posed by enormous world populations, interlocked global technical devices for communications, transport, power, and other uses, vanishing fossil fuel supplies, a worldwide polluted atmosphere, etc., will cause the present ideological fervor to subside under more pressing problems, just as did the great religious animosities of the past.

Not all the preconditions for such a turn of events lie in our own hands. Much depends on the continuation of the present trend toward the fragmentation and gradual liberalization of the Communist world. But given this opportunity, there seems at least a reasonable chance that American and European capitalism can find a *modus vivendi* with the other side. There again, I believe, the critical determination of direction is apt to reside with the new elites rising within capitalism. Indeed, if there are limits to the adaptability of capitalism before the untoward development of world events, these limits appear to reside, more than is the case with the other challenges before the system, in the quality of the "new men" who are rising to positions of power within it.

It is time to revert to the question we set ourselves at the outset. What limits, we asked, were inherent in the capitalist system as such? The answer at which we have arrived is necessarily of a speculative nature. Yet, it does not appear entirely fanciful. What seems possible is to bring about social change that stops short of a direct assault on the economic machinery of privilege that all elites—indeed, that even the general public—in a capitalist society are normally eager to protect. This enables us to draw the general boundaries of short-term evolution for capitalism. The distribution of wealth can be corrected at the bottom, albeit slowly, but not at the top. The control over output can be improved very greatly but the essential commercial character of a market system, with its surrender to the acquisitive impulse, is incorrigible. A considerable accommodation can be made with the non-capitalist world, but the imagination of that world cannot be captured by a basically conservative outlook. There are, in a word, deep-seated attributes to the quality of life that constitute an impregnable inner keep of the system of American capitalism as we know it.

And yet, if we now recall our earlier concern with feudalism, we will recall that despite the seeming impregnability of its institutions in the 13th century, by the 18th century, somehow, the system had nonetheless changed out of all recognition. How did feudalism expire? It gave way to capitalism as part of a subversive process of historic change in which a newly-emerging attribute of daily life proved to be as irresistibly attractive to the privileged orders of feudalism as it was to be ultimately destructive of them. This subversive influence was the gradual infiltration of commercial relationships and cash exchanges into the everyday round of feudal life, each act of marketing binding men more fully into the cash nexus and weakening by that degree the traditional duties and relationships on which feudalism was based. Against this progressive monetization the old order struggled in vain, for the temptations and pleasures of the cash economy were greater than the erosion of privileges that went with it.

Could there be in our day an equivalent of that powerfully disintegrative and yet constitutive force—a force sufficiently overwhelming to render impotent the citadel of capitalism, and yet as irresistibly attractive to it as the earlier current of change was to feudalism? I think there is such a force, and that it already bulks very large within our world. This revolutionary power is the veritable explosion of organized knowledge, and its applied counterpart, scientific technology.

The extraordinary rate of expansion of this explosion is sufficiently familiar to require only a word of exposition. There is, for instance, the often-quoted but still astonishing statement that of all the scientists who have ever lived in all of history, half are alive today. There is the equally startling calculation that the volume of scientific publication during the last ten to fifteen years is as large as, or larger than, that of all previous ages. Such examples serve accurately enough to convey the notion of the exponential growth of scientific inquiry in our day. As to the equally phenomenal growth of the powers of the technology, if that needs any demonstration, there is the contrast cited by Kenneth Boulding between the centuries needed to recuperate from the physical destruction that accompanied the collapse of the Roman Empire, and the scant twenty years in which the shattered and burned cities of modern Europe and Japan were rebuilt after the Second World War.

This explosion of science and technology is often thought of as a product of capitalism, insofar as it arose in an age dominated by capitalism. Yet the association was far more one of coexistence than of causal interrelation. At best we can say that the secular air of bourgeois culture was compatible with, perhaps even conducive to, scientific investigation, but we can hardly credit the acceleration of scientific activities around the middle of the 19th century to the direct stimulus or patronage of capitalism itself.

Even scientific technology exhibits but little debt to the existence of capitalism. The technology on which capitalism began its long course of growth was strictly of a pragmatic, intuitive, pre-scientific kind. Watt, for example, invented the steam engine over fifty years before the basic formulation of the law of thermodynamics. The English textile, iron and steel, or chemical industries were founded and prospered with no "scientific" underpinnings at all. The same is true for the young railroad industry, for canal building, or road-laying. The deliberate employment of scientific investigation to create or refine the technology of production was considerably delayed in arriving. In this country the first private industrial laboratory was not built until 1900 by the General Electric company, and organized research and development on a large scale did not really get under way until 1913.

Thus, we find the flowering of science and the application of science to technology—the very hallmarks of the modern era—to be currents that arose *within* capitalism, but that do not owe their existence directly to capitalism. Rather, science and its technology emerge as a great underground river whose tortuous course has finally reached the surface during the age of capitalism, but which springs from far distant sources. Having now surfaced, that river must cut its own channels through the existing social landscape. Indeed, if we ask what force in our day might in time be strong enough to undercut the bastions of privilege of capitalism and to create its own institutions and social structures in their place, the answer must surely be the one force that dominates our age–the power of science and of scientific technology.

There is, I suspect, little to argue about as to the commanding pressure of science in modern times. What is likely to be a good deal less readily accepted, however, is the contention that this force will cause drastic modifications in, or even the eventual supersession of, capitalism. For at first glance this new current of history seems to have imparted an immense momentum to capitalism by providing it with a virtually inexhaustible source of invention and innovation to insure its economic growth. Merely to review in our minds the broad areas of investment and economic output that owe their existence *entirely* to the laboratory work of the last three decades—the nuclear and space establishments, electronics, the computerization of industry, the creation of new materials such as plastics—is to reveal the breadth of this new gulf stream of economic nourishment.

Yet, like the attractions of the cash market for the feudal lord, the near-term advantages of science and technology conceal long-term conflicts and incompatibilities between this new force of history and its host society. Indeed, the insinuation of science and technology into the interstices of business enterprise promises to alter the fundamental working arrangements of capitalism.

At least one of these alterations is already familiar to us. This is the tendency of technology to create social problems that require public controls to correct or forestall. In part, these agencies of control are contained and concealed *within* the centers of production themselves, where they show up as rising echelons of corporate administration and supervision. In part, the controls show up in the familiar bureaus of government that cope, with greater or lesser success, with the social repercussions of transportation, nuclear energy, drugs, air pollution, etc.

In still a different aspect, the controls invade areas of social life rather than production, as in the astonishing network of government required solely to manage the automobile (an effort that requires the labor of one out of every ten persons employed by all state and local governments). Meanwhile, in the background of the social system the controls are manifest as the growing apparatus of regulation over wages and prices, and over the total flow of economic activity—all ultimately traceable to the need to intervene more closely into an economy of increasing technological disruption.

Not that the disruptive effect of technology is itself a new phenomenon. The dislocations of the technology of the pre-scientific age—say the spinning jenny—were quite as great as those of the modern age. The difference is that in an earlier age the repair of technological disturbances was largely consigned to the adaptive powers of the individual and his family, to the ameliorative efforts of small-scale local government, and to the annealing powers of the market itself. Today, however, these traditional agencies of social repair can no longer cope effectively with the entrance of technology. The individual, now typically a member of a small urban family rather than of a large extended rural family, is much less capable of withstanding economic displacement without external assistance. The local community, faced with large-scale problems of unemployment or ecological maladjustment brought about by technical change, has no recourse but to turn to the financial help and expertise available only from larger government units. The market, which no longer "clears" when the marketers are enormous firms rather than atomistic business units, also discovers that the only antidote to grave economic disjunction is the countervailing influence or *force majeur* of the central governing authority. In a word, technology seems to be exerting a steady push from many levels and areas of the economy in the direction of a society of *organization.*

To this well-known effect of technical progress we must now add another—the capacity of technology to render redundant the physical energies of man. That is, machines do man's work for him, thereby freeing him from the bonds of toil and, not less important in the context of our inquiry, from the hegemony of the market process.

We see this disemployment effect most dramatically in the case of agriculture. But equally startling is the labor-displacing effect of modern technology in that congeries of activities associated with the extraction of basic materials from nature and their fabrication, assembly, conversion, or transport to point of sale. Since 1900, science and technology have given us a stupendous array of new products, each requiring large quantities of human effort—the automobile, the whole range of consumer durables, the communications industry, office machinery, new metals, fabrics, and materials of all kinds, to name but a few. Yet at the end of that period, the total requirements on the labor force for all these goods-centered industries had risen by only *two percentage points*. During the era of the greatest increase in factory production ever known, virtually no increase in the distribution of labor in favor of the goods sector was needed—indeed, since the hours of work fell, there was actually a *relatively decreased* need for human effort in the output of these goods.

Today we stand at the threshold of a new stage in the application of scientific technology to human activities: automation. What is most threatening about this technology is that it has begun to invade a sanctuary of hitherto relatively unmechanized work—the vast numbers of jobs in the office, administrative, and service occupations. By 1960, more than half the labor force was in these jobs. And now, into this varied group of occupations, technology is starting to penetrate in the form of machines as complex as those that can read and sort checks, or as relatively simple as those that dispense coffee and sandwiches.

This is not to maintain that no new areas of employment exist. Certainly there remain very large and still untapped possibilities for work in the reconstruction of the cities; the provision of education; the improvement of health and recreation facilities; the counseling of the young and the care of the aged; the beautification of the environment. Provided only that demand can be marshaled for these activities, there is surely no dearth of job prospects for the coming generation.

But that is precisely the point. The incursion of technology has pushed the frontiers of work into a spectrum of jobs whose common denominator is that they require *public action and public funds* for their initiation and support. The employment-upsetting characteristics of technology thus act to speed capitalism along the general path of planning and control down which it is simultaneously impelled by the direct environment-upsetting impact of technological change.

If we look further ahead, the necessity for planning is apt to become still more pressing. The day of a "fully automated" society is by no means a fantasy, although its realization may well require another century, or more. That is to say, we can, without too much difficulty, imagine a time when as small a proportion of the labor force as now suffices to overprovide us with food, will serve to turn out the manufactured staples, the houses, the transportation, the retail services, even the governmental supervision that will be required.

What the leisured fraction of the population will then do with itself is an interesting and important question. It may possibly find avenues of remuneration that are resistive to mechanical duplication, so that instead of taking in one another's wash, we buy one another's paintings. But even in this best outcome, the underlying process of production, now enormously mechanized and intricately interconnected, would require some form of coordination other than the play of market forces. If we think of the network of controls over output and disposal that now characterize the agricultural sector, we catch some idea of the controls required to operate an economy where manpower requirements generally would have been reduced to a level comparable to that of farming today. And, if the leisured population does not find adequate remuneration in unmechanizable private employments, it will have to be given the direct right to share in society's output—another vital infringement on the market's function.

But the erosion of the market goes deeper yet. For the introduction of technology has one last effect whose ultimate implications for the metamorphosis of capitalism are perhaps greatest of all. This is the effect of technology in steadily raising the average level of well-being, thereby gradually bringing to an end the condition of material need as an effective stimulus for human behavior.

Everyone recognizes that the end to want would represent the passage over an historic watershed for mankind. But it must be equally clear that such a passage will also represent a basic revision of the existential situation that has hitherto provided the main impetus for work. As needs diminish, the traditional stimuli of capitalism begin to lose their force, occupations become valued for their intrinsic pleasures rather than for their extrinsic rewards. The very decision to work or not becomes a matter of personal preference rather than of economic necessity. More telling, the drive for profit—the nuclear core of capitalist energy—becomes blunted, as the purchasable distinctions of wealth decline. In a society of the imaginable wealth implicit in another hundred years of technical progress, who will wish to be the rich man's servant at any price?

All this is no doubt a gain in human dignity. But that is not an end to it. As a result of this inestimable gain in personal freedom, a fundamental assurance for social viability also vanishes, for the market stimuli that bring about social provisioning are no longer met with obedient responses. One has but to imagine employees in an industry of central importance going on strike, not with the slim backing of unemployment insurance and a small union supplement, as today, but with liquid assets sufficient to maintain them, if need be, for a year or more, to envisage the potential for social disorder inherent in the attainment of a genuinely widespread and substantial affluence.

Yet it is precisely such an affluence that is within clear sight, provided that the impetus of science and technology continue to propel the economy for another century. In this impasse there is but one possible solution. *Some authority other than the market must be entrusted with the allocation of men to the essential posts of society, should they lack for applicants.*

We have concerned ourselves so far only with the curious two-edged effect of science and technology on the functional aspects of capitalism. Now we must pay heed to a second and perhaps even more critical effect, the conquest of the capitalist imagination by science and scientific technology.

I think it is fair to say that capitalism as an *idea* has never garnered much enthusiasm. All efforts to raise money-making to the level of a positive virtue have failed. The self-interest of the butcher and the baker to which Adam Smith appealed in lieu of their benevolence may serve as powerful sources of social energy, but not as powerful avatars of the social imagination.

By way of contrast, I think it is also fair to say that science *is* the burning idea of the 20th century, comparable in its impact on men's minds to the flush of democratic enthusiasm of the late 18th century or to the political commitment won by Communism in the early 20th. The altruism of science, its "purity," the awesome vistas it opens and the venerable path it has followed, have won from all groups exactly that passionate interest and conviction that is egregiously lacking to capitalism as a way of life.

It is not alone that science carries a near-religious ethos of conviction and even sacrifice. Within Communism as within capitalism, the new elites arising within the framework of the old society owe their ascendancy and their allegiance in large part to science. The scientific cadres proper, the social scientists, the government administrative personnel—even the military—look to science not merely as the vehicle of their expertise, but as the magnetic North of their compass of values.

These new elites have not as yet divorced their social goals from those of the society to which they are still glad to pay allegiance, and no more than the 13th-century merchants huddled under the walls of a castle, do they seem themselves as the potential architects and lords of a society built around their own functions. But as with the merchants, we can expect that such notions will in time emerge and assert their primacy over the aims of the existing order.

What sorts of notions are these apt to be?

One general direction of thought will surely be the primacy of scientific discovery as a central purpose of society, a *raison d'être* for its existence, perhaps even a vehicle for its religious impulses. No doubt the distribution of social resources and of privileges will reflect this basic orientation toward scientific exploration and application. Not less characteristic will be an emphasis on rational solutions to social problems. The key word of the new society is apt to be *control*. Not alone economic affairs (which should become of secondary importance), but the numbers and location of the population and its genetic quality, the manner of social domestication of children, the choice of life-work—even the very duration of life itself—are all apt to become subjects for scientific investigation and direction.

It is tempting, but idle, to venture beyond these few suggestions. What manner of life, what institutions, what ideologies may serve the purposes of a society dedicated to the accumulation of scientific knowledge and power, we cannot foretell; variations may well be as great as those observable in societies dedicated to the accumulation of material wealth. Nor does there seem to be much point in attempting to foresee by what precise stratagems the elites and ideas of the future may finally assert their claims. Historic projection is rarely, if ever, a matter of simple extrapolation from the present and recent past. Should there arise radical parties in America, broadly-based and aimed at a rational reorganization of economic affairs, the pace of transition would be quicker. Should there not, changes will still occur, but more slowly. Veblen was too impatient for his engineers to take over; Schumpeter, more realistic when he advised the intelligentsia to be prepared to wait in the wings for possibly a century, a "short run" in affairs of this kind, he said.

So, too, the examples of the past discourage us from attempting to prophesy the manner of demise of the system to be superseded. The new protagonists of social and economic control will lack for some time an articulate conception of a purposively constituted and consciously directed social system. The old ideas of the proper primacy of economic aims will linger side-by-side with newer ideas of the priority of scientific interests. And no doubt the privileges of the older order will endure side-by-side with those of the new, just as titles of nobility exist to this very day. It is conceivable that violence may attend the transfer of power and responsibility from one elite to another, but more probably the transfer will be imperceptible; managed by the sons of the old elite entering the profession of the new.

All these are the merest speculations, difficult to avoid entirely, not to be taken too literally. Only one thing is certain. It is the profound incompatibility between the new idea of the active use of science within society and the idea of capitalism.

The conflict lies in the ideas that ultimately inform both worlds. The world of science as it is applied to society is committed to the idea of man as a being who shapes his collective destiny; the world of capitalism to an idea of man as one who permits his common social destination to take care of itself. The essential idea of a society built on scientific engineering is to impose human will on the social universe; that of capitalism to allow the social universe to unfold as if it were beyond human interference.

Before the activist philosophy of science as a social instrument, this inherent social passivity of capitalism becomes archaic, and eventually intolerable. The "self-regulating" economy that is its highest social achievement stands condemned by its absence of meaning and intelligence, and each small step taken to correct its deficiencies only advertises the inhibitions placed on the potential exercise of purposeful thought and action by its remaining barriers of ideology and privilege. In the end, capitalism is weighed in the scale of science and found wanting, not alone as a system but as a philosophy.

That an ascendant science, impatient to substitute reason for blind obedience, inquiry for ideology, represents a great step forward for mankind, I do not doubt. Yet it seems necessary to end on a cautionary note. Just as the prescient medievalist might have foreseen in capitalism the possibilities for the deformation of human life as well as for its immense improvement, so the approaching world of scientific predominance has its darker sides. There lurks a dangerous collectivist tinge in the prospect of controls designed for the enlargement of man but inherently capable of his confinement as well. But beyond that, there is, in the vista of scientific quest grimly pursued for its own sake, a chilling reminder of a world where economic gains are relentlessly pursued for their own sake. Science is a majestic driving force from which to draw social energy and inspiration, but its very impersonality, its "value-free" criteria, may make its tutelary elites as remote and unconcerned as the principles in whose name they govern.

Against these cold and depersonalizing tendencies of a scientifically organized world, humanity will have to struggle in the future, as it has had to contend against not dissimilar excesses of economic involvement in this painful—but also liberating—stage of human development. Thus, if the dawn of an age of science opens larger possibilities for mankind than it has enjoyed heretofore, it does not yet promise a society in which the overriding aim of mankind will be the cultivation and enrichment of all human beings, in all their diversity, complexity and profundity. That is the struggle for the very distant future, which must be begun, nonetheless, today.

11

◀ DANIEL P. MOYNIHAN* ▶

The Professionalization of Reform (1965)

Daniel P. Moynihan, along with John K. Galbraith and Arthur Schlesinger, Jr., is a charter member of America's eastern liberal establishment. On leave from academic positions, these three men rallied to the support of President Kennedy and became part of the inner circle that influenced the direction of American foreign and domestic policies. Only Moynihan managed to stay on through the Johnson Great Society programs and now, at the time of this writing, has become part of the Nixon administration as the President's special assistant for Urban Affairs. Moynihan is in a unique position to describe the inner philosophy of the vast bureaucracy which operates the social and economic programs of the federal government. In the article presented here, he describes the movement toward the professionalization of reform within this bureaucracy. Although the modern reform movement, according to Moynihan, lacks the outside ideological push of past eras, meaningful progress can still be made because the internal structure of the government has developed a direction of its own. Bolstered by the vast amount of statistical data collected by governmental agencies, and the theoretical work of the academic community, the professionals within the government initiate programs to attack America's social and economic problems. Thus external pressure

---

*Special Assistant for Urban Affairs to President Richard M. Nixon. Formerly Urbanologist at Harvard University and M.I.T.

groups, such as the labor unions, need no longer be relied upon
to provide leadership for reform, because within the structure of
the government there has arisen a bureaucracy with a social conscience which means to use the power of the federal government
to correct the misallocations of the market system. Although Moynihan
states that there is always the danger of an all-too-powerful government, he is quick to assure us that the new style of reform
provides a "promise of social sanity and stability" for the future.
According to Moynihan, Keynesian economics, through its ability
to control the level of economic activity, has enabled the government to generate a fiscal dividend to finance social reform. This
dividend arises from the tendency for government tax revenues to
rise at a faster rate than government expenditures for current programs, during periods of economic expansion. As the frequency of
business cycles is lessened, the professional decision makers can calculate the amount of the dividend that the tax system will produce
and plan their social programs accordingly. The problem that Moynihan does not face up to is that this fiscal dividend may be continually
drained off for military expenditures or be given back to the private
sector through tax reductions or subsidies. In spite of the availability
of adequate programs, politicians may find it more expedient to
counter recessions or dispose of future fiscal dividends by reducing
taxes rather than by increasing government expenditures. Galbraith
has labeled this use of Keynesian economics as "reactionary," because
it threatens the already inadequate level of public expenditures and
worsens the social imbalance.*

As Moynihan shows, and conservatives warn, the use of institutionalized planning has become an important trend in America.
Whether it is ultimately responsible to the people remains an open
question, but to Moynihan, and in direct contrast to Hayek,† the short-
run perils are outweighed by the long-run prospects.

——R. R.

The Professionalization of Reform‡

Our best hope for the future lies in the extension to social
organization of the methods that we already employ in
our most progressive fields of effort. In science and in in-

*See introduction to chapter 8.

†See chapter 2.

‡Reprinted from Daniel P. Moynihan, "The Professionalization of Reform,"
The Public Interest, No. 1 (Fall, 1965), 6–16. © 1965 by National Affairs, Inc.

dustry ... we do not wait for catastrophe to force new ways upon us. ... We rely, and with success, upon quantitative analysis to point the way; and we advance because we are constantly improving and applying such analysis.

The passage above, as succinct a case for social planning as could be made, is not a product of either the thought or the institutions of the liberal left. It is, rather, a statement by the late mathematical economist Wesley C. Mitchell. And it has recently been approvingly reprinted at the beginning of a report on "The Concept of Poverty" published by—the Chamber of Commerce of the United States.

The report itself, the work of businessmen and scholars, is perhaps the most competent commentary on the government's anti-poverty program yet to appear. It is replete with citations of articles in *Social Research* and *Land Economics,* and of data from *The Statistical Abstract of the United States;* the perspective ranges from friendly references to the works of Friedrich Engels, to more detached assessments of contemporary tracts. ("Michael Harrington, author of a widely read book on poverty, *The Other America,* has written, 'Any gain for America's minorities will immediately be translated into an advance for all the unskilled workers. One cannot raise the bottom of society without benefiting everyone above.' This is almost precisely wrong.") But the report is less significant for what it says than for what it is: an example of the evolving technique and style of reform in the profoundly new society developing in the United States. Lacking a better term, it might be described as the professionalization of reform.

Writing for the British journal, *The New Society,* just prior to the assassination of President Kennedy, Nathan Glazer described the process:

Without benefit of anything like the Beveridge report to spark and focus public discussion and concern, the United States is passing through a stage of enormous expansion in the size and scope of what we may loosely call the social services—the public programs designed to help people adapt to an increasingly complex and unmanageable society. While Congress has been painfully and hesitantly trying to deal with two great measures—tax reform and a civil rights bill —and its deliberations on both have been closely covered by the mass media, it has also been working with much less

publicity on a number of bills which will contribute at
least as much to changing the shape of American society.

The vast Mental Retardation Facilities and Community Mental Health
Centers Construction Act had just become law. The no less enormous
vocational education bill was moving steadily through the Congress.
The Kennedy Administration had earlier obtained such measures as
the Area Redevelopment Act, the Manpower Development and Training Act, and the Public Welfare Amendments of 1962. "Waiting in
the wings" were a domestic peace corps and an ambitious youth conservation corps, while the community action programs developed by
the President's Committee on Juvenile Delinquency and Youth Crime,
established in 1961, were scheduled for new and expanded funding.

It is a special mind that can as much as keep the titles of these
programs straight. But the most interesting thing about all this sudden
expansion of social services was that it had behind it, as Glazer noted,
"nothing like the powerful political pressure and long-sustained intellectual support that produced the great welfare measures of the New
Deal—Social Security, Unemployment Insurance, Public Welfare, Public Housing." The "massive political support and intellectual leadership
that produced the reforms of the thirties" simply did not exist; yet the
reforms were moving forward.

Glazer accounted for this in terms of the emergence of a large
body of professional persons and professional organizations that had
taken on themselves the concern for the 20 to 30 per cent of the
population that was outside the mainstream of American prosperity.
Intellectuals knew little about the subject, and were not much interested. Organized labor, while both concerned and knowledgeable, had
had but limited success in involving its membership in such efforts.
As a result

> the fate of the poor is in the hands of the administrators
> and the professional organizations of doctors, teachers,
> social workers, therapists, counselors and so forth. It is
> these, who, in a situation where the legislation and programs
> become ever more complex, spend the time to find out—
> or rather have brought home to them—through their work
> the effects of certain kinds of measures and programs, and
> who propose ever more complex programs which Congress
> deliberates upon in the absence of any major public interest.
> When Congress argues these programs, the chief pressures

upon it are not the people, but the organized professional
interests that work with that segment of the problem, and
those who will benefit from or be hurt by the legisation.

The antipoverty program that was being developed even as
Glazer wrote is far the best instance of the professionalization of reform
yet to appear. In its genesis, its development, and now its operation, it
is a prototype of the social technique of action that will almost certainly
become more common in the future. It is a technique that will not appeal to everyone, and in which many will perceive the not altogether
imaginary danger of a too-powerful government. But it is also a technique that offers a profound promise of social sanity and stability in time
to come.

There are two aspects of the poverty program which distinguish it from earlier movements of its kind: The initiative came largely
from within. The case for action was based on essentially esoteric
information about the past and probable future course of events.

The most distinctive break with the past is with regard to
initiative. War on poverty was not declared at the behest of the poor.
Just the opposite. The poor were not only invisible, as Michael Harrington described them, they were also for the most part silent. John
F. Kennedy ventured into Appalachia searching for Protestant votes,
not for poverty. There he encountered the incredible pauperization of
the mountain people, most particularly the soft coal miners, an industrial work force whose numbers had been reduced by nearly two-thirds
in the course of a decade—but with hardly a sound of protest. The
miners were desperately poor, shockingly unemployed, but neither
radical nor in any significant way restive. It may be noted that in 1964,
in the face of the historic Democratic sweep, Harlan County, Kentucky,
returned a freshman Republican Congressman.

True, the civil rights movement was well established and highly
effective during this period, but it was primarily concerned with just
that: the demand for the recognition of the civil rights of the Negro
American. While the movement would clearly in time turn to the
problem of poverty and of the economic position of the Negro, it had
only begun to do so, as in the March on Washington in August 1963,
and its economic demands were still general and essentially traditional,
as for example, an increased minimum wage.

Apart from the always faithful labor movement, the only major
lobbies working for any of the programs that came together to form

the War on Poverty were the conservationists supporting the youth conservation camps, and the National Committee on the Employment of Youth, an organization representing a variety of groups in the social welfare field. The essential fact is that the main pressure for a massive government assault on poverty developed within the Kennedy-Johnson Administration, among officials whose responsibilities were to think about just such matters. These men now exist, they are well paid, have competent staffs, and have access to the President. (Many of these officials, of course, were originally brought to Washington by the New Deal: they are by no means all *nuovi uomini*.) Most importantly, they have at their command an increasing fund of information about social conditions in the United States.

Almost all this information is public, but the art of interpreting it is, in a sense, private. Anyone is free to analyze income statistics, or employment data, or demographic trends to his heart's content. But very few persons in the beginning years of the present decade were able to perceive in those statistics the gradual settling of a poverty class in America. A number of officials in the Federal government (mostly academicians on leave) were. Leaving aside the question of whether or not they were right—a question which must always be open —it is clear that the judgment they reached was quite at variance, almost poles apart, from the general public understanding of the time.

Whereas the public, both high and low in the intellectual hierarchy, saw income distribution steadily compressing, saw the Negro American more and more winning his rightful place in society, saw prosperity spreading through the land, the men in the government saw something quite different: an income distribution gap that had not budged since the end of the war, and had in fact worsened sharply for Negroes, a rising measure of social disorganization among poor families and poor communities, a widening gap between the prospects of the poor and those of the middle class.

In President Johnson these officials found a chief executive who knew a good deal about poverty, and seemingly everything about politics. In a matter of weeks from the time he assumed office, the array of programs and bills Glazer had described as "waiting in the wings" were mustered into a coherent legislative program, reinforced by some entirely new ideas, and moved out under the banner of War on Poverty. It was an issue that united rather than divided, and the ranks of its supporters if anything swelled as it moved through the legislative process.

There is nothing, as such, startling about these developments. They have been foreseen, with either hope or fear, by many persons for many years. However, in recent times a number of events have occurred which very much hasten the process, and make it of greater moment. These have to do with the almost sudden emergence of the fact that the industrial nations of the world seem finally about to learn how to manage their economies, with the professionalization of the middle class, and with the exponential growth of knowledge.

THE ECONOMIC REVOLUTION

Recent years, with the steady advance of technology, have given birth to a good number of neo-apocalyptic views of the future of the American economy, most of them associated with the concept of automation. No one should doubt there is something called automation going on, and that it does change things. However, there is no evidence whatever that it is in fact transforming American society, or any other society. It is simply the newest phase in a process that has been under way for at least two centuries, and will presumably go on and on, past any immediate concern of this age or the next.

At the same time, there is a good deal of evidence, if that is the term for what are little more than everyday impressions, that in the area of economic policy there has occurred a genuine discontinuity, a true break with the past: Men are learning how to make an industrial economy work.

What is involved is something more permanent than simply a run of good luck, or specially refined intuitions on the part of persons responsible for the economic affairs of one nation, or a group of nations. Rather it is the fact that for two decades now, since the end of World War II, the industrial democracies of the world have been able to operate their economies on a high and steadily expanding level of production and employment. Nothing like it has ever happened before in history. It is perhaps the central fact of world politics today. The briefest recollection of what happened to those economies in the two decades that followed World War I will suggest why.

Moreover, it is a development that has all the markings of a scientific event, of a profound advance in knowledge, as well as of an improvement in statecraft.

In the beginning was the theory. With but little data either to support or confound them, economic theories multiplied and conflicted.

But gradually more and better data accumulated: progress begins on social problems when it becomes possible to measure them. As the data accumulated and technology made it possible to calculate more rapidly, the theories gradually became able to explain more, and these in turn led to the improvement in the data. John Maynard Keynes at King's College, Cambridge, and Wesley C. Mitchell at the National Bureau of Economic Research in New York, are supremely good symbols of the two processes that ended up in a deeply symbiotic relationship. And then one day it all more or less hangs together and the world is different, although of course not quite aware of the change. Governments promise full employment—and then produce it. (In 1964 unemployment, adjusted to conform more or less to United States' definitions, was 2.9 per cent in Italy, 2.5 per cent in France and Britain, and 0.4 per cent in Germany. Consider the contrast with post-World War I.) Governments undertake to expand their economy at a steady rate—and do so. (In 1961 the members of the Organization for Economic Cooperation and Development, which grew out of the Marshall Plan, undertook to increase their output by 50 per cent during the decade of the 1960s. The United States at all events is right on schedule.)

The ability to predict events, as against controlling them, has developed even more impressively—the Council of Economic Advisers' forecast of GNP for 1964 was off by only $400 million in a total of $623 billion; the unemployment forecast was on the nose.

There is a temptation, of course, to go too far in presuming what can be done with the economy. The international exchange system is primitive, and at the moment menacing. The stock market can be wildly irrational. There are, as Hyman Lewis points out, competing theories of investment which could bring us unsettling dilemmas. We in the United States have not achieved full employment. We have accepted the use of federal taxing and spending powers as a means of social adjustment, but so far only in pleasant formulations. Our willingness to raise taxes, for example, is yet to be tested. In general, the political component of political economy remains very much uncertain. Thus the British, again to cite Lewis, have the best economists, but one of the less successful economies. But the fact remains that economics is approaching the status of an applied science.

In the long run this econometric revolution, assuming it works itself out, is bound to have profound effects on the domestic politics of all the nations involved. The central political issue of most industrial nations over the past century and a half has been how to make an economy work. Almost every conceivable nostrum, from the nationalization of the means of production, distribution, and exchange, to the free coinage of silver, has been proposed, and most have been tried. Usually without success. In the United States, for one administration after another, economic failure has led to political failure. But if henceforth the business cycle has a longer sweep, and fewer abrupt downturns, the rise and fall of political fortunes may follow the same pattern. Once in power, a party may be much more likely to remain so. Or in any event, the issues that elect or defeat governments could be signficantly different from those of the past.

The more immediate impact of this econometric revolution in the United States is that the federal government will be endowed, more often than not, with a substantial, and within limits predictable, rise in revenues available for social purposes. Significantly, the War on Poverty began in the same year of the great tax cut. The President was not forced to choose between the measures; he was able to proceed with both. In that sense, the War on Poverty began not because it was necessary (which it was), but because it was possible.

The singular nature of the new situation in which the federal government finds itself is that the immediate *supply* of resources available for social purposes might actually outrun the immediate *demand* of established programs. Federal expenditures under existing programs rise at a fairly predictable rate. But, under conditions of economic growth, revenues rise faster. This has given birth to the phenomenon of the "fiscal drag"—the idea that unless the federal government disposes of this annual increment, either by cutting taxes or adding programs, the money taken out of circulation by taxes will slow down economic growth, and could, of course, at a certain point stop it altogether.

Thus, assuming the continued progress of the economy in something like the pattern of recent years, there is likely to be $4-5 billion in additional, unobligated revenue coming in each year. *But* this increment will only continue to come on conditions that it is disposed of. Therefore one of the important tasks to which an Administration must address itself is that of devising new and responsible programs for expending public funds in the public interest.

This is precisely the type of decision making that is suited to the techniques of modern organizations, and which ends up in the hands of persons who make a profession of it. They are less and less political decisions, more and more administrative ones. They are decisions that can be reached by consensus rather than conflict.

THE PROFESSIONALIZATION OF THE MIDDLE CLASS

"Everywhere in American life," Kenneth S. Lynn reports, "the professions are triumphant." The period since the G.I. Bill has witnessed an extraordinary expansion of higher education. In the United States, a quarter of the teenage population now goes on to some kind of college, and among specific class and ethnic groups the proportion is as high as three quarters. The trend is unmistakable and probably irresistible: in the course of the coming decades some form of higher education will become near to universal. But most importantly, for more and more persons the form of education will involve professional training. This is not the same thing as traditional higher education; it does not produce the same types of persons.

The difference has been most succinctly stated by Everett C. Hughes: "Professionals *profess*. They profess to know better than others the nature of certain matters, and to know better than their clients what ails them or their affairs." And he continues:

> Lawyers not only give advice to clients and plead their cases for them; they also develop a philosophy of law— of its nature and its functions, and of the proper way in which to administer justice. Physicians consider it their prerogative to define the nature of disease and of health, and to determine how medical services ought to be distributed and paid for. Social workers are not content to develop a technique of casework; they concern themselves with social legislation. Every profession considers itself the proper body to set the terms in which some aspect of society, life or nature is to be thought of, and to define the general lines, or even the details, of public policy concerning it.

As the number of professionals increase, so also do the number of professions, or neo-professions. More and more, middle-class persons are attracted by the independence of judgment, esoteric knowledge, and immunity to outside criticism that characterize professionals. As Everett Hughes puts it: "The YMCA secretary wants his occupation recognized not merely as that of offering young men from the country a pleasant road to Protestant righteousness in the city, but as a more universal one of dealing with groups of young people. All that is learned of adolescence, of behavior in small groups, of the nature and organization of community life is considered the intellectual basis of his work."

There are now an extraordinary number of such persons in America. Those Americans classified as professional and technical workers have just passed the nine million mark—more than the number of "managers, officials, and proprietors," more than the craftsmen and foremen. And of this group, an enormous number is involved in various aspects of social welfare and reform. Through sheer numbers they would tend to have their way; but as professionals in a professionalizing society, they are increasingly *entitled* to have their way. That is how the system works.

One of the more powerful demonstrations of the influence of professional thinking on programs of social reform is the provision of the Economic Opportunity Act that community action programs be carried out with the "maximum feasible participation" of the poor themselves. This is one of the most important and pioneering aspects of the entire antipoverty program. But typically this demand was inserted in the legislation not because of any demand of the poor, but because the intellectual leaders of the social reform profession had come to the conclusion that this was indispensable to effective social action. Typically also, the literature describes the process in terms of the use of the "indigenous nonprofessional"—persons identified by the fact that they are *not* professional. A somewhat ironical turn of events in this area is the role the community action programs are playing in re-creating the ethnic political-social organizations of the big city slums— the dismantling of which was for so long the object of political and social reformers in the United States!

The prospect of large-scale opposition to the new professions is, for the moment at least, limited because the professionalization of the middle class has led to a no less extraordinary opening up of careers to talent. The time when any considerable number of persons of great ability and ambition have found their way out of poverty blocked by their inability to obtain an education has all but passed. (There are still many, many persons whose natural abilities are stunted by poverty, but that is another matter.) A nationwide survey of 1960 high school graduates, Project Talent, found that about 97 per cent of those in the top 1 per cent of aptitude and 93 per cent of those in the top 5 per cent, entered college within a year. Among the next 5 per cent (the 90th to 94th percentile) 86 per cent did so. As a general proposition, ability is recognized and rewarded in America today as at no time in history. (Michael Young's forecast of the revolt of the lower quartile against the ultimate injustice of a society based on merit may not be discounted, but it is not on the other hand scheduled until 2031.)

It is possible that this process, just because it is successful in drawing up talent from lower economic and social groups, will deprive those groups of much of their natural leadership, and make them all the more dependent on professionals. Kenneth Clark has noted that the degree of recruitment of civil rights leaders into "establishment" organizations verges on raiding—and has raised suspicions of hidden motives! On the other hand, there is rather a pronounced tendency for persons from such groups, when they do rise to the middle class, to settle into professions which involve work with the very groups they left behind. Thus, in a certain sense the poor are not so much losing their natural leaders as obtaining them through different routes.

THE EXPONENTIAL GROWTH OF KNOWLEDGE

Among the complexities of life is the fact that the American business community, in a period when it was fiercely opposed to the idea of economic or social planning, nonetheless supported, even pressed for, the development of a national statistical system which has become the best in the world and which now makes certain types of planning and regulation—although quite different from the collective proposals of earlier eras—both feasible and in a measure inevitable. Much as mountains are climbed, so statistics are used if they are there. As an example, trade union wage settlements in recent years have been profoundly influenced by the wage-price guidelines set by the federal government. This could not possibly have occurred on an essentially voluntary basis were it not that the Bureau of Labor Statistics has developed the technique of measuring productivity—and has done so, accompanied, step by step, by the business and labor advisory committees that work with the bureau. A measure of the near quantum change that has only recently occurred in the information available for social planning in the United States (the development work began long ago, but the pay-off has been rather recent) may be suggested by the fact that the nation went through the great depression of the 1930s without ever really knowing what the rate of unemployment was! This was then a measurement taken but once every ten years, by the census. Today, of course, employment and unemployment data are collected monthly, and debated in terms of the decimal points. Similarly, the census has been quietly transformed from a ten-times-a-century proceeding to a system of current accounts on a vast range of social data.

Most of the information that went into the development of the antipoverty program was essentially economic, but the social data available to the President's task force was of singular importance in shaping the program, and in turn the program will greatly stimulate the collection of more such. The nation is clearly on the verge of developing a system of social statistics comparable to the now highly developed system of economic statistics.

The use of all such statistics is developing also. A vast "industry of discovery," to use William Haber's description of events in the physical sciences, is developing in the social sciences as well. Computer technology has greatly enhanced the possible use of such data. Just as the effort to stimulate the American economy is now well advanced, the simulation of social processes, particularly in decision making, is also begun, and may be expected to produce important, if not indeed revolutionary insights. Such prospects tend to stir some alarm in thoughtful persons, but it may be noted the public has accepted with calm, even relish, the fact that the outcome of elections is now predicted with surpassing accuracy. If that most solemn of democratic rituals may be simulated without protest, there is not likely to be much outcry against the simulation of various strategies of housing integration, or techniques of conflict resolution, or patterns of child rearing.

Expenditure for social science research was somewhere between $500 and $600 million in 1964. This was only 10 per cent of the $6 billion spent in the same year on the life and physical sciences (including psychology), and much less a proportion of the $19 billion spent on research and development altogether. Nonetheless it represents a sixfold growth in a decade. There is, moreover, some indication that social scientists are not yet thinking in the money terms that are in fact available to them. Angus Campbell suggested recently that social scientists still think in budgets of thousands of dollars when they should be thinking of millions. "The prevailing format for social research is still the exploitation of opportunities which are close at hand, easily manageable, and inexpensive." But, he adds, "there are a good many social scientists who know very well how to study social change on a broad scale and are intensely interested in going about it." The Survey Research Center at the University of Michigan, which Campbell directs, has, for example, under way a year-long panel survey of the impact of the 1964 tax cut on the nation's taxpayers, a specific example of the use of social science techniques in the development of economic policy.

All in all, the prospect is for a still wider expansion of knowledge available to governments as to how people behave. This will be accompanied by further improvement of the now well-developed techniques of determining what they think. Public opinion polls are already a daily instrument of government decision-making (a fact which has clearly affected the role of the legislature). In combination, these two systems of information make it possible for a government to respond intelligently and in time to the changing needs and desires of the electorate. The day when mile-long petitions and mass rallies were required to persuade a government that a popular demand existed that things be done differently is clearly drawing to a close. Indeed, the very existence of such petitions and rallies may in time become a sign that what is being demanded is *not yet* a popular demand.

THE PERILS OF PROGRESS

The professionalization of reform will proceed, regardless of the perils it presents. Even in the face of economic catastrophe, which is certainly conceivable if not probable, the response will be vastly more systematic and informed than any of the past.

A certain price will be paid, and a considerable risk will be incurred. The price will be a decline in the moral exhilaration of public affairs at the domestic level. It has been well said that the civil rights movement of the present time has at last provided the youth of America with a moral equivalent of war. The more general effect of the civil rights movement has been a much heightened public concern for human dignity and welfare. This kind of passion could seep out of the life of the nation, and we would be the less for it.

The risk is a combination of enlightenment, resources, and skill which in the long run, to use Harold D. Laswell's phrase, becomes a "monocracy of power."

But the potential rewards are not less great. The creation of a society that can put an end to the "animal miseries" and stupid controversies that afflict most peoples would be an extraordinary achievement of the human spirit. The argument may be made, for example, that had the processes described in this article not progressed as far as they had by 1961, the response of the federal government to the civil rights revolution would have been thoroughly inadequate: that instead of joining with and helping to direct the movement, the national government would have trailed behind with grudging, uncomprehending, and increasingly inadequate concessions that could have resulted in the problem of the Negro American becoming insoluble in terms of existing American society.

The prospect that the more primitive social issues of American politics are at last to be resolved need only mean that we may now turn to issues more demanding of human ingenuity than that of how to put an end to poverty in the richest nation in the world. Many such issues might be in the area of foreign affairs, where the enormity of difficulty and the proximity of disaster is sufficient to keep the citizens and political parties of the nation fully occupied. And there is also the problem of perfecting, to the highest degree possible, the *quality* of our lives and of our civilization. We may not be accustomed to giving political priority to such questions. But no one can say they will be boring or trivial!

BIBLIOGRAPHY

(In addition to the works included in the body of this section, the editors also recommend the following.)

Berle, Adolf A. *The Twentieth Century Capitalist Revolution.* New York: Harcourt, Brace, and World, 1954.

Clark, John M. *Social Control of Business.* New York: McGraw-Hill, 1939.

Galbraith, John Kenneth. *American Capitalism: The Concept of Countervailing Power.* Boston: Houghton, Mifflin, 1956.

————. *The Affluent Society.* Boston: Houghton, Mifflin, 1958.

Hansen, Alvin. *The American Economy.* New York: McGraw-Hill, 1957.

Harris, Seymour E. *Economics of the Kennedy Years and a Look Ahead.* New York: Harper & Row, 1964.

Heller, Walter W. *New Dimensions of Political Economy.* New York: W. W. Norton & Co., 1967.

Lekachman, Robert. *The Age of Keynes.* New York: Random House, 1966.

Myrdal, Gunnar. *Beyond the Welfare State.* New Haven: Yale University Press.

Rostow, Walter W. *The Stages of Economic Growth.* London: Cambridge University Press, 1960.

Samuelson, Paul. Weekly column in *Newsweek*.

Shonfield, Andrew. *Modern Capitalism: The Changing Balance of Public and Private Power*. New York: Oxford University Press, 1965.

Young, James P. *The Politics of Affluence*. San Francisco: Chandler Publishing, 1968.

PART 3

THE RADICAL VIEW

INTRODUCTION

What is a radical? If someone is against the status quo, he might be considered a radical. Such a position would validate the claims of someone like Ayn Rand to being a "radical for capitalism." No one more than a modern conservative such as Friedman wishes to see changes within present-day America capitalism. But the changes he hopes for are on the opposite end of the spectrum from the changes which the radicals presented in this section would like to see. Whereas modern conservatives want a movement back to a purer form of capitalism (laissez-faire), radicals, as the term is used here, call for the elimination of the basic capitalist institutions altogether. Both groups are concerned with maximizing individual freedom, and the conflict between the two often resolves itself in the issue of capitalism versus socialism. To modern conservatives, maximum economic efficiency and a high degree of individual freedom are best achieved under a system of competitive capitalism. To radicals, capitalism is incapable of delivering a future that is just and equitable. They view the profit-driven market system with its base of private property and privilege as preventing the emergence of a just and equitable society. Even liberal attempts to "patch up" capitalism are viewed with disdain, because as the radicals see it the abuses of capitalism are an inherent part of the system, and only the replacement of the system itself will eliminate these abuses. In contrast then to the conservative's desire for a purer form of capitalism, the radical wants a structural transformation of the existing capitalist system into some form of socialism.

As with the other two views presented above, there is a wide range of opinions within the radical camp. The spectrum of opinion runs from the reform socialists such as Michael Harrington, who are concerned with encouraging a gradual movement toward the welfare state, to the more revolutionary socialists such as Marx, Baran, and Sweezy. Harrington is about as close to the liberal position as an avowed socialist can be. Although he is not the revolutionist that Marx is, neither does Harrington seem to believe that the form of democratic socialism that he affirms as the proper goal of society will evolve out of the present system. In fact the very fear that the modern corporation will consistently sacrifice the public good for its own has compelled Harrington to become a political activist. What he is searching for is a new political action group which will work within the existing party structure to consciously direct the economy toward socialism. In his role as a skilled journalist and speaker he has shown himself to be more of an influence on modern American liberals and "New Leftists" than on the hard core of radical thinkers.

Between Harrington and the Marxists lies a wide range of opinion which would include the views of Thorstein Veblen. He has been described by some as America's most important twentieth-century social scientist. While seeing the downfall of capitalism as inevitable, Veblen did not make clear his preferences for any alternative system. He emphasized that the basic conflict within capitalism was between the efficiency of modern technology in producing goods and the attempts of businessmen to restrict output in order to increase profits. Like the other radicals presented here, Veblen is very critical of the goals of the modern corporation, claiming that they are inconsistent with the goals of society. To him contradictions and conflicts grow out of the fact that conservative business institutions tend to get out of phase with the dynamic machine technology. Unlike Marx, Veblen was not a revolutionary socialist and believed that the replacement of the capitalist system would be an evolutionary process. Marx of course is also concerned with the evolution of economic systems and views capitalism as merely a stage in this evolution. For Marx the course of history is shaped by the economic pressure of the changing forces of production on the class structure. In contrast to Veblen, Marx sees an end to the evolutionary process in the estabment of a communist society (characterized by the ultimate disappearance of the state) and is willing to help speed the process along through revolution. The *Communist Manifesto* is a call to action for such a movement.

Baran and Sweezy update Marx's treatment of the structure and irrationalities of modern capitalism by attempting to demonstrate, among other things, the crucial function of imperialism and militarism in maintaining a viable economy. While no less revolutionary than Marx himself, these two modern American Marxists no longer look for revolution in the advanced capitalist countries but have turned their attention to the less developed areas of the world.

George Stigler, a well-known modern economist, has claimed that the study of economics makes people politically conservative. In general the writers in this section would surely reject this position in favor of the view that as one matures he realizes the futility of expecting meaningful change within the existing system. The future of capitalism is dependent on what position the majority of its citizens take on this issue. Given the present state of affairs radicals must be led to conclude that thus far the American people have been lulled into a short-sighted position.

——R. R.

12

◀ KARL MARX* and FRIEDRICH ENGELS† ▶

from
A Contribution to the Critique of Political Economy (1859)

from
Anti-Dühring (1878)

from
The Communist Manifesto (1848)

from
Capital (1867)

Marxian theory represents an intellectual reaction to the social, political, and economic conditions of nineteenth-century Europe, the period historians refer to as the Industrial Revolution. The transformation of society during this process of industrialization was truly a revolutionary one. With the movement from the self-sufficient rural areas to the mushrooming urban factory areas, the workers were made dependent on the sale of their labor services for survival, since they no longer owned the means of production. The social disorganization caused by the early capitalistic process of industrialization was unparalleled. Under the new rigid discipline of the machine, labor power

---

*(1818–1883)
†(1820–1895)

became a commodity to be bought and sold like any other commodity. Long hours of labor under barbarian working conditions, at little more than subsistence-level wages, resulted in what many saw as exploitation of the working masses. Against this background, Marx set his savage pen.

The kernel of Marxist thought is the idea that capitalism is merely a stage in the historical progress of mankind, having been successively preceded by primitive communism, slavery, and feudalism. Marx was interested in examining the dynamic development of capitalism ("the laws of motion") and the relations into which people enter in the process of production. From this historically-oriented study, using a method he referred to as dialectical materialism, Marx predicted the fall of capitalism. This analytic technique represented an improvement of considerable proportions compared to previous schools of economic thought, who had, with the partial exception of John Stuart Mill, assumed the eternal nature of capitalism, and viewed this system, moreover, as continually tending towards a norm of full employment.

The core of the capitalist system, according to Marx, is found in how the propertyless proletariat must sell its labor power to those who have accumulated capital. This is why Marx refers to capital as a "social power" in addition to its usual technical definition. Exploitation of the worker occurred because the capitalists derived a surplus through the worker's creation of commodities whose value was greater than the value the workers received for their labor services (under normal conditions and in the long run). Whenever it was profitable to do so, the capitalist introduced technological improvements into the production process, which took the form of labor-saving devices. Technologically-displaced labor became, according to Marx, part of the "reserve army" of unemployed. The existence of this surplus pool of labor, competing for the available jobs, kept wages close to a social subsistence level. The consequence of this exploitation and unemployment, as Marx saw it, was that the consuming power of the working class was held down. At the same time, the capitalists restricted their own present consumption so as to accumulate more capital (i.e. they saved part of their income and invested it in labor-saving machinery, steel mills, mines, buildings, etc., which would facilitate the production of still more goods in the future). Accumulating more and more capital therefore means adding to society's productive capacity and subsequently to its "reserve army" of unemployed. One Marxist economist said that we can observe the paradox under capitalism of stepping on the brake as far as consumption is concerned and on the accelerator as far as production is concerned. In addition the intricate relationship between the capital goods sector and the consumer goods sector gets disrupted. These are the basic internal economic contradictions in the capitalist system. Marx said that this leads to depressions, imperialism, wars, and a class struggle of ever-increasing severity. The result was the eventual overthrow of the bourgeoisie by a politically-organized, class-conscious proletariat constantly growing in size and importance, and the setting up of a system based on common ownership of the means of production and distribution. In brief this is the Marxian system including the theory of social change that emerges from its operation.

A proper assessment of the Marxian system involves an analysis of its predictive ability. On the one hand Marx insightfully predicted the rise of monopoly capital and a mass labor movement at a time when there were only dim foreshadowings of such developments. On the other hand he proved to be an incorrect prophet in several important areas: (1) He expected capitalism to break down in the most advanced industrial countries rather than in the lesser developed nations. In point of fact, the system under the stress of war broke at its weakest link—Czarist Russia—and not at its strongest points—England, Germany, and the United States. (2) Growth of labor unions led to somewhat more equal bargaining power with management, and the State, under pressure, was able and willing to introduce a wide variety of reformist programs. Both these factors created much less class-consciousness among the working class than Marx anticipated. (3) In a similar fashion nationalism and racial discrimination served to divide the workers, thus weakening still further their revolutionary potential on both a national and an international level.

These developments were reinforced by limited improvements in the economic status of the workers in the industrially advanced countries by the latter decades of the Victorian era. The savings and capital formation of the early industrialization period made possible a greater output of consumer goods, which helped to raise the standard of living of the broad masses despite recurring business cycles and a lopsided distribution of wealth and income. Marxists still believe that the "stability" of capitalism is more temporary than permanent, more apparent than real. They assert that the contradictions besetting capitalism, both abroad and at home, are growing in intensity, and thus it is only a question of time before the gathering revolutionary forces yield the expected Marxian results. They also note that the gap between the rich nations and poor nations continues to widen.

There has been a degree of revival of interest in Marxism in recent years (perhaps triggered by the growing ideological competition between capitalism and socialism in the third world) and a growing amount of dialogue between Marxists and non-Marxists (such as Joan Robinson, C. Wright Mills, William A. Williams, and Robert Heilbroner). This is a fruitful development that hopefully will strengthen the trend towards more realism and analytical rigor in the social sciences. Marxism has several unique contributions to make, particularly concerning the dynamic relationship between class conflict and economic development, and recognition of this fact is slowly asserting itself in intellectual circles.

———M. L.

from

A Contribution to the Critique of Political Economy*

I [Marx] was led by my studies to the conclusion that legal relations as well as forms of state could neither be understood by themselves, nor explained by the so-called general progress of the human mind, but that they are rooted in the material conditions of life, which are summed up by Hegel after the fashion of the English and French of the eighteenth century under the name "civic society;" the anatomy of that civic society is to be sought in political economy. . . . The general conclusion at which I arrived and which, once reached, continued to serve as the leading thread in my studies, may be briefly summed up as follows.

In the social production which men carry on they enter into definite relations that are indispensable and independent of their will; these relations of production correspond to a definite stage of development of their material powers of production. The sum total of these relations of production constitutes the economic structure of society— the real foundation, on which rise legal and political superstructures and to which correspond definite forms of social consciousness. The mode of production in material life determines the general character of the social, political and spiritual processes of life. It is not the consciousness of men that determines their existence, but, on the contrary, their social existence determines their consciousness. At a certain stage of their development, the material forces of production in society come in conflict with the existing relations of production, or—what is but a legal expression for the same thing—with the property relations within which they had been at work before. From forms of development of the forces ·of production these relations turn into their fetters. Then comes the period of social revolution. With the change of the economic foundation the entire immense superstructure is more or less rapidly transformed. In considering such transformations the distinction should always be made between the material transformation of the economic conditions of production which can be determined with the precision of natural science, and the legal, political, religious, esthetic or philosophic—in short ideological forms in which men become con-

---

*From Karl Marx, *A Contribution to the Critique of Political Economy* (Chicago, 1904), pp. 11–13. First published 1859.

scious of this conflict and fight it out. Just as our opinion of an individual is not based on what he thinks of himself, so can we not judge of such a period of transformation by its own consciousness; on the contrary, this consciousness must rather be explained from the contradictions of material life, from the existing conflict between the social forces of production and the relations of production. No social order ever disappears before all the productive forces, for which there is room in it, have been developed; and new higher relations of production never appear before the material conditions of their existence have matured in the womb of the old society. Therefore, mankind always takes up only such problems as it can solve; since, looking at the matter more closely, we will always find that the problem itself arises only when the material conditions necessary for its solution already exist or are at least in the process of formation. In broad outlines we can designate the Asiatic, the ancient, the feudal, and the modern bourgeois methods of production as so many epochs in the progress of the economic formation of society. The bourgeois relations of production are the last antagonistic form of the social process of production—antagonistic not in the sense of individual antagonism, but of one arising from conditions surrounding the life of individuals in society; at the same time the productive forces developing in the womb of bourgeois society create the material conditions for the solution of that antagonism. This social formation constitutes, therefore, the closing chapter of the prehistoric stage of human society. . . .

from

Anti-Duhring*

The materialistic conception of history starts from the principle that production, and with production the exchange of its products, is the basis of every social order; that in every society which has appeared in history the distribution of the products, and with it the division of society into classes or estates, is determined by what is produced and how it is produced, and how the product is exchanged. According to this conception, the ultimate causes of all social changes and political revolutions

---

*Friedrich Engels, Anti-Duhring. First published 1878.

are to be sought, not in the minds of men, in their increasing insight into eternal truth and justice, but in changes in the mode of production and exchange; they are to be sought not in the *philosophy* but in the *economics* of the epoch concerned. The growing realization that existing social institutions are irrational and unjust, that reason has become nonsense and good deeds a scourge, is only a sign that changes have been taking place quietly in the methods of production and forms of exchange, with which the social order, adapted to previous economic conditions is no longer in accord. This also involves that the means through which the abuses that have been revealed can be got rid of must likewise be present, in more or less developed form, in the altered conditions of production. These means are not to be *invented* by the mind, but *discovered* by means of the mind in the existing material facts of production.

Where then, on this basis, does modern socialism stand?

The existing social order, as is now fairly generally admitted, is the creation of the present ruling class, the bourgeoisie. The mode of production peculiar to the bourgeoisie—called, since Marx, the capitalist mode of production—was incompatible with the local privileges and the privileges of birth as well as with the reciprocal personal ties of the feudal system; the bourgeoisie shattered the feudal system, and on its ruins established the bourgeois social order, the realm of free competition, freedom of movement, equal rights for commodity owners, and all the other bourgeois glories. The capitalist mode of production could now develop freely. From the time when steam and the new toolmaking machinery had begun to transform the former manufacture into large-scale industry, the productive forces evolved under bourgeois direction developed at a pace that was previously unknown and to an unprecedented degree. But just as manufacture, and the handicraft industry which had been further developed under its influence, had previously come into conflict with the feudal fetters of the guilds, so large-scale industry, as it develops more fully, comes into conflict with the barriers within which the capitalist mode of production holds it confined. The new forces of production have already outgrown the bourgeois form of using them; and this conflict between productive forces and mode of production is not a conflict which has arisen in men's heads, as for example the conflict between original sin and divine justice; but it exists in the facts, objectively, outside of us, independently of the will or purpose even of the men who brought it about. Modern socialism is nothing but the reflex in thought of this actual conflict, its ideal reflec-

tion in the minds first of the class which is directly suffering under it—
the working class. . . .

The seizure of the means of production by society puts an end
to commodity production, and therewith to the domination of the
product over the producer. Anarchy in social production is replaced by
conscious organization on a planned basis. The struggle for individual
existence comes to an end. And at this point, in a certain sense, man
finally cuts himself off from the animal world, leaves the conditions of
animal existence behind him and enters conditions which are really
human. The conditions of existence forming man's environment, which
up to now have dominated man, at this point pass under the dominion
and control of man, who now for the first time becomes the real conscious master of nature, because and in so far as he has become master
of his own social organization. The laws of his own social activity, which
have hitherto confronted him as external, dominating laws of nature,
will then be applied by man with complete understanding, and hence
will be dominated by man. Men's own social organization, which has
hitherto stood in opposition to them as if arbitrarily decreed by nature
and history, will then become the voluntary act of men themselves. The
objective, external forces which have hitherto dominated history, will
then pass under the control of men themselves. It is only from this
point that men, with full consciousness, will fashion their own history;
it is only from this point that the social causes set in motion by men
will have, predominantly and in constantly increasing measure, the effects willed by men. It is humanity's leap from the realm of necessity
into the realm of freedom.

In conclusion, let us briefly sum up our sketch of the course of
development:

1. Medieval Society—Individual production on a small scale.
Means of production adapted for individual use, hence primitively
clumsy, petty, dwarfed in action. Production for immediate consumption,
either of the producer himself or of his feudal lord. Only where an
excess of production over his consumption occurs is such excess offered
for sale and enters into exchange. Production of commodities, therefore, only in its infancy; but it already contains within itself, in embryo,
anarchy in social production.

2. Capitalist Revolution—Transformation of industry, at first
by means of simple co-operation and manufacture. Concentration of
the means of production, hitherto scattered, into large workshops. As
a consequence, their transformation from individual into social means
of production—a transformation which on the whole does not affect

the forms of exchange. The old forms of appropriation remain in force. The *capitalist* appears: in his quality of owner of the means of production he also appropriates the products and turns them into commodities. Production has become a social act, exchange and with it appropriation remain individual acts, the acts of separate individuals. *The social product is appropriated by the individual capitalist.* Fundamental contradiction, from which arise all the contradictions in which present-day society moves and which modern industry brings to light.

(a) Severance of the producer from the means of production. Condemnation of the worker to wage labor for life. *Antagonism of proletariat and bourgeoisie.*

(b) Growing emphasis and increasing effectiveness of the laws governing commodity production. Unbridled competitive struggle. *Contradiction between social organization in the individual factory and social anarchy in production as a whole.*

(c) On the one hand, perfecting of machinery, owing to competition, made a compulsory commandment for each individual manufacturer, and equivalent to a continually increasing displacement of workers: *industrial reserve army*—on the other hand, unlimited extension of production, likewise a compulsory law of competition for every manufacturer—on both sides, unheard of development of productive forces, excess of supply over demand, overproduction, glutting of the markets, crises every ten years, vicious circle: excess here of means of production and products, excess there of workers without employment and means of existence. But these two levers of production and of social well-being are unable to work together, because the capitalist form of production prevents the productive forces from working and the products from circulating, unless they are first turned into capital: which their very superabundance prevents. The contradiction has become heightened into an absurdity. *The mode of production rebels against the form of exchange.* The bourgeoisie is convicted of incapacity further to manage their own social productive forces.

(d) Partial recognition of the social character of the productive forces forced upon the capitalists themselves. Taking over of the great institutions for production and communication, first by *joint stock companies,* later by *trusts,* then by the *state.* The bourgeoisie shows itself to be a superfluous class; all its social functions are now performed by hired employees.

3. Proletarian Revolution—Solution of the contradictions. The proletariat seizes the public power and by means of this power transforms the socialized means of production, slipping from the hands of

the bourgeoisie, into public property. By this act, the proletariat frees the means of production from the character of capital hitherto borne by them, and gives their social character complete freedom to assert itself. A social production upon a predetermined plan now becomes possible. The development of production makes the further existence of different classes of society an anachronism. In proportion as anarchy in social production vanishes, the political authority of the state also dies away. Man, at last the master of his own form of social organization, becomes at the same time the lord over nature, master of himself—free.

To carry through this world-emancipating act is the historical mission of the modern proletariat. And it is the task of scientific social-ism, the theoretical expression of the proletarian movement, to establish the historical conditions and, with these, the nature of this act, and thus to bring to the consciousness of the now oppressed class the conditions and nature of the act which it is its destiny to accomplish.

from

The Communist Manifesto*

A spectre is haunting Europe—the spectre of Communism. All the powers of old Europe have entered into a holy alliance to exorcise this spectre: Pope and Czar, Metternich and Guizot, French Radicals and German police-spies.

Where is the party in opposition that has not been decried as communistic by its opponents in power? Where the Opposition that has not hurled back the branding reproach of Communism, against the more advanced opposition parties, as well as against its reactionary adversaries?

Two things result from this fact:

I. Communism is already acknowledged by all European pow-ers to be itself a power.

II. It is high time that Communists should openly, in the face of the whole world, publish their views, their aims, their tendencies, and meet this nursery tale of the spectre of Communism with a manifesto of the party itself.

*From Karl Marx and Friedrich Engels, *Manifesto of the Communist Party*. First published 1848. Reprinted by permission of International Publishers Co., Inc., Copyright © 1932. Pp. 3–31.

To this end, Communists of various nationalities have assembled in London, and sketched the following manifesto, to be published in the English, French, German, Italian, Flemish, and Danish languages.

Bourgeois and Proletarians

The history of all hitherto existing society is the history of class struggles.

Freeman and slave, patrician and plebian, lord and serf, guild-master and journeyman, in a word, oppressor and oppressed, stood in constant opposition to one another, carried on an uninterrupted, now hidden, now open fight, a fight that each time ended, either in a revolutionary reconstitution of society at large, or in the common ruin of the contending classes.

In the earlier epochs of history, we find almost everywhere a complicated arrangement of society into various orders, a manifold gradation of social rank. In ancient Rome we have patricians, knights, plebeians, slaves; in the Middle Ages, feudal lords, vassals, guild-masters, journeymen, apprentices, serfs; in almost all of these classes, again, subordinate gradations.

The modern bourgeois society that has sprouted from the ruins of feudal society, has not done away with class antagonisms. It has but established new classes, new conditions of oppression, new forms of struggle in place of the old ones.

Our epoch, the epoch of the bourgeoisie, possesses, however, this distinctive feature: It has simplified the class antagonisms. Society as a whole is more and more splitting up into two great hostile camps, into two great classes directly facing each other—bourgeoisie and proletariat.

From the serfs of the Middle Ages sprang the chartered burghers of the earliest towns. From these burgesses the first elements of the bourgeoisie were developed.

The discovery of America, the rounding of the Cape, opened up fresh ground for the rising bourgeoisie. The East-Indian and Chinese markets, the colonisation of America, trade with the colonies, the increase in the means of exchange and in commodities generally, gave to commerce, to navigation, to industry, an impulse never before known, and thereby, to the revolutionary element in the tottering feudal society, a rapid development.

The feudal system of industry, in which industrial production was monopolised by closed guilds, now no longer sufficed for the growing wants of the new markets. The manufacturing system took its place. The guild-masters were pushed aside by the manufacturing middle class; division of labor between the different corporate guilds vanished in the face of division of labor in each single workshop.

Meantime the markets kept ever growing, the demand ever rising. Even manufacture no longer sufficed. Thereupon, steam and machinery revolutionised industrial production. The place of manufacture was taken by the giant, modern industry, the place of the industrial middle class, by industrial millionaires—the leaders of whole industrial armies, the modern bourgeois.

Modern industry has established the world market, for which the discovery of America paved the way. This market has given an immense development to commerce, to navigation, to communication by land. This development has, in its turn, reacted on the extension of industry; and in proportion as industry, commerce, navigation, railways extended, in the same proportion the bourgeoisie developed, increased its capital, and pushed into the background every class handed down from the Middle Ages.

We see, therefore, how the modern bourgeoisie is itself the product of a long course of development, of a series of revolutions in the modes of production and of exchange.

Each step in the development of the bourgeoisie was accompanied by a corresponding political advance of that class. An oppressed class under the sway of the feudal nobility, it became an armed and self-governing association in the mediaeval commune; here independent urban republic (as in Italy and Germany), there taxable "third estate" of the monarchy (as in France); afterwards, in the period of manufacture proper, serving either the semi-feudal or the absolute monarchy as a counterpoise against the nobility, and, in fact, corner-stone of the great monarchies in general—the bourgeoisie has at last, since the establishment of modern industry and of the world market, conquered for itself, in the modern representative state, exclusive political sway. The executive of the modern state is but a committee for managing the common affairs of the whole bourgeoisie.

The bourgeoisie has played a most revolutionary rôle in history.

The bourgeoisie, wherever it has got the upper hand, has put an end to all feudal, patriarchal, idyllic relations. It has pitilessly torn asunder the motley feudal ties that bound man to his "natural superiors," and has left no other bond between man and man than naked self-interest, than callous "cash payment." It has drowned the most heavenly ecstasies of religious fervor, of chivalrous enthusiasm, of philistine sentimentalism, in the icy water of egotistical calculation. It has resolved personal worth into exchange value, and in place of the numberless indefeasible chartered freedoms, has set up that single, unconscionable freedom—Free Trade. In one word, for exploitation, veiled by religious and political illusions, it has substituted naked, shameless, direct, brutal exploitation.

The bourgeoisie has stripped of its halo every occupation hitherto honored and looked up to with reverent awe. It has converted the physician, the lawyer, the priest, the poet, the man of science, into its paid wage-laborers.

The bourgeoisie has torn away from the family its sentimental veil, and has reduced the family relation to a mere money relation.

The bourgeoisie has disclosed how it came to pass that the brutal display of vigor in the Middle Ages, which reactionaries so much admire, found its fitting complement in the most slothful indolence. It has been the first to show what man's activity can bring about. It has accomplished wonders far surpassing Egyptian pyramids, Roman aqueducts, and Gothic cathedrals; it has conducted expeditions that put in shade all former migrations of nations and crusades.

The bourgeoisie cannot exist without constantly revolutionising the instruments of production, and thereby the relations of production, and with them the whole relations of society. Conservation of the old modes of production in unaltered form, was, on the contrary, the first condition of existence for all earlier industrial classes. Constant revolutionising of production, uninterrupted disturbance of all social conditions, everlasting uncertainty and agitation distinguish the bourgeois epoch from all earlier ones. All fixed, fast-frozen relations, with their train of ancient and venerable prejudices and opinions, are swept away, all new-formed ones become antiquated before they can ossify. All that is solid melts into air, all that is holy is profaned, and man is at last compelled to face with sober senses his real conditions of life and his relations with his kind.

The need of a constantly expanding market for its products chases the bourgeoisie over the whole surface of the globe. It must nestle everywhere, settle everywhere, establish connections everywhere.

The bourgeoisie has through its exploitation of the world market given a cosmopolitan character to production and consumption in every country. To the great chagrin of reactionaries, it has drawn from under the feet of industry the national ground on which it stood. All old-established national industries have been destroyed or are daily being destroyed. They are dislodged by new industries, whose introduction becomes a life and death question for all civilised nations, by industries that no longer work up indigenous raw material, but raw material drawn from the remotest zones; industries whose products are consumed, not only at home, but in every quarter of the globe. In place of the old wants, satisfied by the production of the country, we find new wants, requiring for their satisfaction the products of distant lands and climes. In place of the old local and national seclusion and self-sufficiency, we have intercourse in every direction, universal interdependence of nations. And as in material, so also in intellectual production. The intellectual creations of individual nations become common property. National one-sidedness and narrow-mindedness become more and more impossible, and from the numerous national and local literatures there arises a world literature.

The bourgeoisie, by the rapid improvement of all instruments of production, by the immensely facilitated means of communication, draws all nations, even the most barbarian, into civilisation. The cheap prices of its commodities are the heavy artillery with which it batters down all Chinese walls, with which it forces the barbarians' intensely obstinate hatred of foreigners to capitulate. It compels all nations, on pain of extinction, to adopt the bourgeois mode of production; it compels them to introduce what it calls civilisation into their midst, i.e., to become bourgeois themselves. In a word, it creates a world after its own image.

The bourgeoisie has subjected the country to the rule of the towns. It has created enormous cities, has greatly increased the urban population as compared with the rural, and has thus rescued a considerable part of the population from the idiocy of rural life. Just as it has made the country dependent on the towns, so it has made barbarian and semi-barbarian countries dependent on the civilised ones, nations of peasants on nations of bourgeois, the East on the West.

More and more the bourgeois keeps doing away with the scattered state of the population, of the means of production, and of property. It has agglomerated population, centralised means of production, and has concentrated property in a few hands. The necessary consequence of this was political centralisation. Independent, or but loosely connected provinces, with separate interests, laws, governments and systems of taxation, became lumped together into one nation, with one government, one code of laws, one national class interest, one frontier and one customs tariff.

The bourgeoisie, during its rule of scarce one hundred years, has created more massive and more colossal productive forces than have all preceding generations together. Subjection of nature's forces to man, machinery, application of chemistry to industry and agriculture, steam-navigation, railways, electric telegraphs, clearing of whole continents for cultivation, canalisation of rivers, whole populations conjured out of the ground—what earlier century had even a presentiment that such productive forces slumbered in the lap of social labor?

We see then that the means of production and of exchange, which served as the foundation for the growth of the bourgeoisie, were generated in feudal society. At a certain stage in the development of these means of production and of exchange, the conditions under which feudal society produced and exchanged, the feudal organisation of agriculture and manufacturing industry, in a word, the feudal relations of property became no longer compatible with the already developed productive forces; they became so many fetters. They had to be burst asunder; they were burst asunder.

Into their place stepped free competition, accompanied by a social and political constitution adapted to it, and by the economic and political sway of the bourgeois class.

A similar movement is going on before our own eyes. Modern bourgeois society with its relations of production, of exchange and of property, a society that has conjured up such gigantic means of production and of exchange, is like the sorcerer who is no longer able to control the powers of the nether world whom he has called up by his spells. For many a decade past, the history of industry and commerce is but the history of the revolt of modern productive forces against modern conditions of production, against the property relations that are the conditions for the existence of the bourgeoisie and of its rule. It is enough to mention the commercial crises that by their periodical return put the existence of the entire bourgeois society on trial, each time more threateningly. In these crises a great part not only of the existing products, but also of the previously created productive forces, are periodically destroyed. In these crises there breaks out an epidemic that, in all earlier epochs, would have seemed an absurdity—the epidemic of over-production. Society suddenly finds itself put back into a state of momentary barbarism; it appears as if a famine, a universal war of devastation had cut off the supply of every means of subsistence; industry and commerce seem to be destroyed. And why? Because there is too much civilisation, too much means of subsistence, too much industry, too much commerce. The productive forces at the disposal of society no longer tend to further the development of the conditions of bourgeois property; on the contrary, they have become too powerful for these conditions, by which they are fettered, and no sooner do they overcome these fetters than they bring disorder into the whole of bourgeois society, endanger the existence of bourgeois property. The conditions of bourgeois society are too narrow to comprise the wealth created by them. And how does the bourgeoisie get over these crises? On the one hand by enforced destruction of a mass of productive forces; on the other, by the conquest of new markets, and by the more thorough exploitation of the old ones. That is to say, by paving the way for more extensive and more destructive crises, and by diminishing the means whereby crises are prevented.

The weapons with which the bourgeoisie felled feudalism to the ground are now turned against the bourgeoisie itself.

But not only has the bourgeoisie forged the weapons that bring death to itself; it has also called into existence the men who are to wield those weapons—the modern working class—the proletarians.

In proportion as the bourgeoisie, i.e., capital, is developed, in the same proportion is the proletariat, the modern working class, developed—a class of laborers, who live only so long as they find work, and who find work only so long as their labor increases capital. These laborers, who must sell themselves piecemeal, are a commodity, like every other article of commerce, and are consequently exposed to all the vicissitudes of competition, to all the fluctuations of the market.

Owing to the extensive use of machinery and to division of labor, the work of the proletarians has lost all individual character, and, consequently, all charm for the workman. He becomes an appendage of the machine and it is only the most simple, most monotonous, and most easily acquired knack, that is required of him. Hence, the cost of production of a workman is restricted, almost entirely, to the means of subsistence that he requires for his maintenance, and for the propagation of his race. But the price of a commodity, and therefore also of labor, is equal to its cost of production. In proportion, therefore, as the repulsiveness of the work increases, the wage decreases. Nay more, in proportion as the use of machinery and division of labor increases, in the same proportion the burden of toil also increases, whether by prolongation of the working hours, by increase of the work exacted in a given time, or by increased speed of the machinery, etc.

Modern industry has converted the little workshop of the patriarchal master into the great factory of the industrial capitalist. Masses of laborers, crowded into the factory, are organised like soldiers. As privates of the industrial army they are placed under the command of a perfect hierarchy of officers and sergeants. Not only are they slaves of the bourgeois class, and of the bourgeois state; they are daily and hourly enslaved by the machine, by the overlooker, and, above all, by the individual bourgeois manufacturer himself. The more openly this despotism proclaims gain to be its end and aim, the more petty, the more hateful and the more embittering it is.

The less the skill and exertion of strength implied in manual labor, in other words, the more modern industry develops, the more is the labor of men superseded by that of women. Differences of age and sex have no longer any distinctive social validity for the working class. All are instruments of labor, more or less expensive to use, according to their age and sex.

No sooner has the laborer received his wages in cash, for the moment escaping exploitation by the manufacturer, than he is set upon by the other portions of the bourgeoisie, the landlord, the shopkeeper, the pawnbroker, etc.

The lower strata of the middle class—the small tradespeople, shopkeepers, and retired tradesmen generally, the handicraftsmen and peasants—all these sink gradually into the proletariat, partly because their diminutive capital does not suffice for the scale on which modern industry is carried on, and is swamped in the competition with the large capitalists, partly because their specialised skill is rendered worthless by new methods of production. Thus the proletariat is recruited from all classes of the population.

The proletariat goes through various stages of development. With its birth begins its struggle with the bourgeoisie. At first the contest is carried on by individual laborers, then by the work people of a factory, then by the operatives of one trade, in one locality, against the individual bourgeois who directly exploits them. They direct their attacks not against the bourgeois conditions of production, but against the instruments of production themselves; they destroy imported wares that compete with their labor, they smash machinery to pieces, they set factories ablaze, they seek to restore by force the vanished status of the workman of the Middle Ages.

At this stage the laborers still form an incoherent mass scattered over the whole country, and broken up by their mutual competition. If anywhere they unite to form more compact bodies, this is not yet the consequence of their own active union, but of the union of the bourgeoisie, which class, in order to attain its own political ends, is compelled to set the whole proletariat in motion, and is moreover still able to do so for a time. At this stage, therefore, the proletarians do not fight their enemies, but the enemies of their enemies, the remnants of absolute monarchy, the landowners, the nonindustrial bourgeois, the petty bourgeoisie. Thus the whole historical movement is concentrated in the hands of the bourgeoisie; every victory so obtained is a victory for the bourgeoisie.

But with the development of industry the proletariat not only increases in numbers; it becomes concentrated in greater masses, its strength grows, and it feels that strength more. The various interests and conditions of life within the ranks of the proletariat are more and more equalised, in proportion as machinery obliterates all distinctions of labor and nearly everywhere reduces wages to the same low level. The growing competition among the bourgeois, and the resulting commercial crises, make the wages of the workers ever more fluctuating. The unceasing improvement of machinery, ever more rapidly developing, makes their livelihood more and more precarious; the collisions between individual workmen and individual bourgeois take more and more the character of collisions between two classes. Thereupon the workers begin to form combinations (trade unions) against the bourgeoisie; they club together in order to keep up the rate of wages; they found permanent associations in order to make provision beforehand for these occasional revolts. Here and there the contest breaks out into riots.

Now and then the workers are victorious, but only for a time. The real fruit of their battles lies, not in the immediate result, but in the ever expanding union of the workers. This union is furthered by the improved means of communication which are created by modern industry, and which place the workers of different localities in contact with one another. It was just this contact that was needed to centralise the numerous local struggles, all of the same character, into one national struggle between classes. But every class struggle is a political struggle. And that union, to attain which the burghers of the Middle Ages, with their miserable highways, required centuries, the modern proletarians, thanks to railways, achieve in a few years.

This organisation of the proletarians into a class, and consequently into a political party, is continually being upset again by the competition between the workers themselves. But it ever rises up again, stronger, firmer, mightier. It compels legislative recognition of particular interests of the workers, by taking advantage of the divisions among the bourgeoisie itself. Thus the ten-hour bill in England was carried.

Altogether, collisions between the classes of the old society further the course of development of the proletariat in many ways. The bourgeoisie finds itself involved in a constant battle. At first with the aristocracy; later on, with those portions of the bourgeoisie itself whose interests have become antagonistic to the progress of industry; at all times with the bourgeoisie of foreign countries. In all these battles it sees itself compelled to appeal to the proletariat, to ask for its help, and thus, to drag it into the political arena. The bourgeoisie itself, therefore, supplies the proletariat with its own elements of political and general education, in other words, it furnishes the proletariat with weapons for fighting the bourgeoisie.

Further, as we have already seen, entire sections of the ruling classes are, by the advance of industry, precipitated into the proletariat, or are at least threatened in their conditions of existence. These also supply the proletariat with fresh elements of enlightenment and progress.

Finally, in times when the class struggle nears the decisive hour, the process of dissolution going on within the ruling class, in fact within the whole range of old society, assumes such a violent, glaring character, that a small section of the ruling class cuts itself adrift, and joins the revolutionary class, the class that holds the future in its hands. Just as, therefore, at an earlier period, a section of the nobility went over to the bourgeoisie, so now a portion of the bourgeoisie goes over to the proletariat, and in particular, a portion of the bourgeois ideologists, who have raised themselves to the level of comprehending theoretically the historical movement as a whole.

Of all the classes that stand face to face with the bourgeoisie today, the proletariat alone is a really revolutionary class. The other classes decay and finally disappear in the face of modern industry; the proletariat is its special and essential product.

The lower middle class, the small manufacturer, the shopkeeper, the artisan, the peasant, all these fight against the bourgeoisie, to save from extinction their existence as fractions of the middle class. They are therefore not revolutionary, but conservative. Nay more, they are reactionary, for they try to roll back the wheel of history. If by chance they are revolutionary, they are so only in view of their impending transfer into the proletariat; they thus defend not their present, but their future interests; they desert their own standpoint to adopt that of the proletariat.

The "dangerous class," the social scum (*Lumpenproletariat*), that passively rotting mass thrown off by the lowest layers of old society, may, here and there, be swept into the movement by a proletarian revolution; its conditions of life, however, prepare it far more for the part of a bribed tool of reactionary intrigue.

The social conditions of the old society no longer exist for the proletariat. The proletarian is without property; his relation to his wife and children has no longer anything in common with bourgeois family relations; modern industrial labor, modern subjection to capital, the same in England as in France, in America as in Germany, has stripped him of every trace of national character. Law, morality, religion, are to him so many bourgeois prejudices, behind which lurk in ambush just as many bourgeois interests.

All the preceding classes that got the upper hand, sought to fortify their already acquired status by subjecting society at large to their conditions of appropriation. The proletarians cannot become masters of the productive forces of society, except by abolishing their own previous mode of appropriation, and thereby also every other previous mode of appropriation. They have nothing of their own to secure and to fortify; their mission is to destroy all previous securities for, and insurances of, individual property.

All previous historical movements were movements of minorities, or in the interest of minorities. The proletarian movement is the self-conscious, independent movement of the immense majority, in the interest of the immense majority. The proletariat, the lowest stratum of our present society, cannot stir, cannot raise itself up, without the whole superincumbent strata of official society being sprung into the air.

Though not in substance, yet in form, the struggle of the proletariat with the bourgeoisie is at first a national struggle. The proletariat of each country must, of course, first of all settle matters with its own bourgeoisie.

In depicting the most general phases of the development of the proletariat, we traced the more or less veiled civil war, raging within existing society, up to the point where that war breaks out into open revolution, and where the violent overthrow of the bourgeoisie lays the foundation for the sway of the proletariat.

Hitherto, every form of society has been based, as we have already seen, on the antagonism of oppressing and oppressed classes. But in order to oppress a class, certain conditions must be assured to it under which it can, at least, continue its slavish existence. The serf, in the period of serfdom, raised himself to membership in the commune, just as the petty bourgeois, under the yoke of feudal absolutism, managed to develop into a bourgeois. The modern laborer, on the contrary, instead of rising with the progress of industry, sinks deeper and deeper below the conditions of existence of his own class. He becomes a pauper, and pauperism develops more rapidly than population and wealth. And here it becomes evident, that the bourgeoisie is unfit any longer to be the ruling class in society, and to impose its conditions of existence upon society as an over-riding law. It is unfit to rule because it is incompetent to assure an existence to its slave within his slavery, because it cannot help letting him sink into such a state, that it has to feed him, instead of being fed by him. Society can no longer live under this bourgeoisie, in other words, its existence is no longer compatible with society.

The essential condition for the existence and sway of the bourgeois class, is the formation and augmentation of capital; the condition for capital is wage-labor. Wage-labor rests exclusively on competition between the laborers. The advance of industry, whose involuntary promoter is the bourgeoisie, replaces the isolation of the laborers, due to competition, by their revolutionary combination, due to association. The development of modern industry, therefore, cuts from under its feet the very foundation on which the bourgeoisie produces and appropriates products. What the bourgeoisie therefore produces, above all, are its own grave-diggers. Its fall and the victory of the proletariat are equally inevitable.

PROLETARIANS AND COMMUNISTS

In what relation do the Communists stand to the proletarians as a whole?

The Communists do not form a separate party opposed to other working class parties.

They have no interests separate and apart from those of the proletariat as a whole.

They do not set up any sectarian principles of their own, by which to shape and mould the proletarian movement.

The Communists are distinguished from the other working class parties by this only: 1. In the national struggles of the proletarians of the different countries, they point out and bring to the front the common interests of the entire proletariat, independently of all nationality. 2. In the various stages of development which the struggle of the working class against the bourgeoisie has to pass through, they always and everywhere represent the interests of the movement as a whole.

The Communists, therefore, are on the one hand, practically, the most advanced and resolute section of the working class parties of every country, that section which pushes forward all others; on the other hand, theoretically, they have over the great mass of the proletariat the advantage of clearly understanding the line of march, the conditions, and the ultimate general results of the proletarian movement.

The immediate aim of the Communists is the same as that of all the other proletarian parties: formation of the proletariat into a class, overthrow of bourgeois supremacy, conquest of political power by the proletariat.

The theoretical conclusions of the Communists are in no way based on ideas or principles that have been invented, or discovered, by this or that would-be universal reformer.

They merely express, in general terms, actual relations springing from an existing class struggle, from a historical movement going on under our very eyes. The abolition of existing property relations is not at all a distinctive feature of Communism.

All property relations in the past have continually been subject to historical change consequent upon the change in historical conditions.

The French Revolution, for example, abolished feudal property in favor of bourgeois property.

The distinguishing feature of Communism is not the abolition of property generally, but the abolition of bourgeois property. But modern bourgeois private property is the final and most complete expression of the system of producing and appropriating products that is based on class antagonisms, on the exploitation of the many by the few.

In this sense, the theory of the Communists may be summed up in the single sentence: Abolition of private property.

We Communists have been reproached with the desire of abolishing the right of personally acquiring property as the fruit of a man's own labor, which property is alleged to be the groundwork of all personal freedom, activity, and independence.

Hard-won, self-acquired, self-earned property! Do you mean the property of the petty artisan and of the small peasant, a form of property that preceded the bourgeois form? There is no need to abolish that;

the development of industry has to a great extent already destroyed it, and is still destroying it daily.

Or do you mean modern bourgeois private property?

But does wage-labor create any property for the laborer? Not a bit. It creates capital, i.e., that kind of property which exploits wage-labor, and which cannot increase except upon condition of begetting a new supply of wage-labor for fresh exploitation. Property, in its present form, is based on the antagonism of capital and wage-labor. Let us examine both sides of this antagonism.

To be a capitalist, is to have not only a purely personal, but a social *status* in production. Capital is a collective product, and only by the united action of many members, nay, in the last resort, only by the united action of all members of society, can it be set in motion.

Capital is therefore not a personal, it is a social, power.

When, therefore, capital is converted into common property, into the property of all members of society, personal property is not thereby transformed into social property. It is only the social character of the property that is changed. It loses its class character.

Let us now take wage-labor.

The average price of wage-labor is the minimum wage, i.e., that quantum of the means of subsistence which is absolutely requisite to keep the laborer in bare existence as a laborer. What, therefore, the wage-laborer appropriates by means of his labor, merely suffices to prolong and reproduce a bare existence. We by no means intend to abolish this personal appropriation of the products of labor, an appropriation that is made for the maintenance and reproduction of human life, and that leaves no surplus wherewith to command the labor of others. All that we want to do away with is the miserable character of this appropriation, under which the laborer lives merely to increase capital, and is allowed to live only insofar as the interest of the ruling class requires it.

In bourgeois society, living labor is but a means to increase accumulated labor. In Communist society, accumulated labor is but a means to widen, to enrich, to promote the existence of the laborer.

In bourgeois society, therefore, the past dominates the present; in Communist society, the present dominates the past. In bourgeois society capital is independent and has individuality, while the living person is dependent and has no individuality.

And the abolition of this state of things is called by the bourgeois, abolition of individuality and freedom! And rightly so. The abolition of bourgeois individuality, bourgeois independence, and bourgeois freedom is undoubtedly aimed at.

By freedom is meant, under the present bourgeois conditions of production, free trade, free selling and buying.

But if selling and buying disappears, free selling and buying disappears also. This talk about free selling and buying, and all the other "brave words" of our bourgeoisie about freedom in general, have a meaning, if any, only in contrast with restricted selling and buying, with the fettered traders of the Middle Ages, but have no meaning when opposed to the Communist abolition of buying and selling, of the bourgeois conditions of production, and of the bourgeoisie itself.

You are horrified at our intending to do away with private property. But in your existing society, private property is already done away with for nine-tenths of the population; its existence for the few is solely due to its non-existence in the hands of those nine-tenths. You reproach us, therefore, with intending to do away with a form of property, the necessary condition for whose existence is the non-existence of any property for the immense majority of society.

In a word, you reproach us with intending to do away with your property. Precisely so; that is just what we intend.

From the moment when labor can no longer be converted into capital, money, or rent, into a social power capable of being monopolised, i.e., from the moment when individual property can no longer be transformed into bourgeois property, into capital, from that moment, you say, individuality vanishes.

You must, therefore, confess that by "individual' you mean no other person than the bourgeois, than the middle-class owner of property. This person must, indeed, be swept out of the way, and made impossible.

Communism deprives no man of the power to appropriate the products of society; all that it does is to deprive him of the power to subjugate the labor of others by means of such appropriation.

It has been objected, that upon the abolition of private property all work will cease, and universal laziness will overtake us.

According to this, bourgeois society ought long ago to have gone to the dogs through sheer idleness; for those of its members who work, acquire nothing, and those who acquire anything, do not work. The whole of this objection is but another expression of the tautology: There can no longer be any wage-labor when there is no longer any capital.

All objections urged against the Communist mode of producing and appropriating material products, have, in the same way, been urged against the Communist modes of producing and appropriating intellectual products. Just as, to the bourgeois, the disappearance of class property is the disappearance of production itself, so the disappearance of class culture is to him identical with the disappearance of all culture.

That culture, the loss of which he laments, is, for the enormous majority, a mere training to act as a machine.

But don't wrangle with us so long as you apply, to our intended abolition of bourgeois property, the standard of your bourgeois notions of freedom, culture, law, etc. Your very ideas are but the outgrowth of the conditions of your bourgeois production and bourgeois property, just as your jurisprudence is but the will of your class made into a law for all, a will whose essential character and direction are determined by the economic conditions of existence of your class.

The selfish misconception that induces you to transform into eternal laws of nature and of reason, the social forms springing from your present mode of production and form of property—historical relations that rise and disappear in the progress of production—this misconception you share with every ruling class that has preceded you. What you see clearly in the case of ancient property, what you admit in the case of feudal property, you are of course forbidden to admit in the case of your own bourgeois form of property.

Abolition of the family! Even the most radical flare up at this infamous proposal of the Communists.

On what foundation is the present family, the bourgeois family, based? On capital, on private gain. In its completely developed form this family exists only among the bourgeoisie. But this state of things finds its complement in the practical absence of the family among the proletarians, and in public prostitution.

The bourgeois family will vanish as a matter of course when its complement vanishes, and both will vanish with the vanishing of capital.

Do you charge us with wanting to stop the exploitation of children by their parents? To this crime we plead guilty.

But, you will say, we destroy the most hallowed of relations, when we replace home education by social.

And your education! Is not that also social, and determined by the social conditions under which you educate, by the intervention of society, direct or indirect, by means of schools, etc.? The Communists have not invented the intervention of society in education; they do but seek to alter the character of that intervention, and to rescue education from the influence of the ruling class.

The bourgeois claptrap about the family and education, about the hallowed co-relation of parent and child, becomes all the more disgusting, the more, by the action of modern industry, all family ties among the proletarians are torn asunder, and their children transformed into simple articles of commerce and instruments of labor.

But you Communists would introduce community of women, screams the whole bourgeoisie in chorus.

The bourgeois sees in his wife a mere instrument of production. He hears that the instruments of production are to be exploited in common, and, naturally, can come to no other conclusion than that the lot of being common to all will likewise fall to the women.

He has not even a suspicion that the real point aimed at is to do away with the status of women as mere instruments of production.

For the rest, nothing is more ridiculous than the virtuous indignation of our bourgeois at the community of women which, they pretend, is to be openly and officially established by the Communists. The Communists have no need to introduce community of women; it has existed almost from time immemorial.

Our bourgeois, not content with having the wives and daughters of their proletarians at their disposal, not to speak of common prostitutes, take the greatest pleasure in seducing each other's wives.

Bourgeois marriage is in reality a system of wives in common and thus, at the most, what the Communists might possibly be reproached with is that they desire to introduce, in substitution for a hypocritically concealed, an openly legalised community of women. For the rest, it is self-evident, that the abolition of the present system of production must bring with it the abolition of the community of women springing from that system, i.e., of prostitution both public and private.

The Communists are further reproached with desiring to abolish countries and nationality.

The workingmen have no country. We cannot take from them what they have not got. Since the proletariat must first of all acquire political supremacy, must rise to be the leading class of the nation, must constitute itself *the* nation, it is, so far, itself national, though not in the bourgeois sense of the word.

National differences and antagonisms between peoples are vanishing gradually from day to day, owing to the development of the bourgeoisie, to freedom of commerce, to the world market, to uniformity in the mode of production and in the conditions of life corresponding thereto.

The supremacy of the proletariat will cause them to vanish still faster. United action, of the leading civilised countries at least, is one of the first conditions for the emancipation of the proletariat.

In proportion as the exploitation of one individual by another is put an end to, the exploitation of one nation by another will also be put an end to. In proportion as the antagonism between classes within the nation vanishes, the hostility of one nation to another will come to an end.

The charges against Communism made from a religious, a philosophical, and, generally, from an ideological standpoint, are not deserving of serious examination.

Does it require deep intuition to comprehend that man's ideas, views, and conceptions, in one word, man's consciousness, changes with every change in the conditions of his material existence, in his social relations, and in his social life?

What else does the history of ideas prove, than that intellectual production changes its character in proportion as material production is changed? The ruling ideas of each age have ever been the ideas of its ruling class.

When people speak of ideas that revolutionise society, they do but express the fact that within the old society the elements of a new one have been created, and that the dissolution of the old ideas keeps even pace with the dissolution of the old conditions of existence.

When the ancient world was in its last throes, the ancient religions were overcome by Christianity. When Christian ideas succumbed in the 18th century to rationalist ideas, feudal society fought its death-battle with the then revolutionary bourgeoisie. The ideas of religious liberty and freedom of conscience, merely gave expression to the sway of free competition within the domain of knowledge.

"Undoubtedly," it will be said, "religious, moral, philosophical and juridical ideas have been modified in the course of historical development. But religion, morality, philosophy, political science, and law, constantly survived this change.

"There are, besides, eternal truths, such as Freedom, Justice, etc., that are common to all states of society. But Communism abolishes eternal truths, it abolishes all religion, and all morality, instead of constituting them on a new basis; it therefore acts in contradiction to all past historical experience."

What does this accusation reduce itself to? The history of all past society has consisted in the development of class antagonisms, antagonisms that assumed different forms at different epochs.

But whatever form they may have taken, one fact is common to all past ages, viz., the exploitation of one part of society by the other. No wonder, then, that the social consciousness of past ages, despite all the multiplicity and variety it displays, moves within certain common forms, or general ideas, which cannot completely vanish except with the total disappearance of class antagonisms.

The Communist revolution is the most radical rupture with traditional property relations; no wonder that its development involves the most radical rupture with traditional ideas.

But let us have done with the bourgeois objections to Communism.

We have seen above, that the first step in the revolution by the working class, is to raise the proletariat to the position of ruling class, to establish democracy.

The proletariat will use its political supremacy to wrest, by degrees, all capital from the bourgeoisie, to centralise all instruments of production in the hands of the state, i.e., of the proletariat organised as the ruling class; and to increase the total of productive forces as rapidly as possible.

Of course, in the beginning, this cannot be effected except by means of despotic inroads on the rights of property, and on the conditions of bourgeois production; by means of measures, therefore, which appear economically insufficient and untenable, but which, in the course of the movement, outstrip themselves, necessitate further inroads upon the old social order, and are unavoidable as a means of entirely revolutionising the mode of production.

These measures will of course be different in different countries.

Nevertheless in the most advanced countries, the following will be pretty generally applicable.

1. Abolition of property in land and application of all rents of land to public purposes.

2. A heavy progressive or graduated income tax.

3. Abolition of all right of inheritance.

4. Confiscation of the property of all emigrants and rebels.

5. Centralisation of credit in the hands of the state, by means of a national bank with state capital and an exclusive monopoly.

6. Centralisation of the means of communication and transport in the hands of the state.

7. Extension of factories and instruments of production owned by the state; the bringing into cultivation of waste lands, and the improvement of the soil generally in accordance with a common plan.

8. Equal obligation of all to work. Establishment of industrial armies, especially for agriculture.

9. Combination of agriculture with manufacturing industries; gradual abolition of the distinction between town and country, by a more equable distribution of the population over the country.

10. Free education for all children in public schools. Abolition of child factory labor in its present form. Combination of education with industrial production, etc.

When, in the course of development, class distinctions have disappeared, and all production has been concentrated in the hands of a vast association of the whole nation, the public power will lose its political character. Political power, properly so called, is merely the organised power of one class for oppressing another. If the proletariat during its contest with the bourgeoisie is compelled, by the force of circumstances, to organise itself as a class; if, by means of a revolution, it makes itself the ruling class, and, as such, sweeps away by force the old conditions of production, then it will, along with these conditions, have swept away the conditions for the existence of class antagonisms, and of classes generally, and will thereby have abolished its own supremacy as a class.

In place of the old bourgeois society, with its classes and class antagonisms, we shall have an association, in which the free development of each is the condition for the free development of all. . . .

from

Capital*

PRIMITIVE ACCUMULATION

. . . Through capital surplus-value is made, and from surplus-value more capital. But the accumulation of capital presupposes surplus-value; surplus-value presupposes capitalistic production; capitalistic pro-

---

*From Karl Marx, *Capital*, Vol. I. First published 1867.

duction presupposes the pre-existence of considerable masses of capital and of labor power in the hands of producers of commodities. The whole movement, therefore, seems to turn in a vicious circle, out of which we can only get by supposing a primitive accumulation preceding capitalistic accumulation; an accumulation not the result of the capitalist mode of production, but its starting point.

Political Economy explains the origin of this primitive accumulation as an anecdote of the past. In times long gone by there were two sorts of people; one, the diligent, intelligent, and above all, frugal élite; the other, lazy rascals, spending their substance, and more, in riotous living. Thus it came to pass that the former sort accumulated wealth, and the latter sort had at last nothing to sell except their own skins. And from this original sin dates the poverty of the great majority that, despite all its labor, has up to now nothing to sell but itself, and the wealth of the few that increases constantly although they have long ceased to work. In actual history it is notorious that conquest, enslavement, robbery, murder, briefly force, play the great part. In the tender annals of Political Economy, the idyllic reigns from time immemorial. Right and "labor" were from all time the sole means of enrichment, the present year of course always excepted. As a matter of fact, the methods of primitive accumulation are anything but idyllic.

The capitalist system presupposes the complete separation of the laborers from all property in the means by which they can realise their labor. As soon as capitalist production is once on its own legs, it not only maintains this separation, but reproduces it on a continually extending scale. The process, therefore, that clears the way for the capitalist system, can be none other than the process which takes away from the laborer the possession of his means of production. The so-called primitive accumulation, therefore, is nothing else than the historical process of divorcing the producer from the means of production.

The economic structure of capitalistic society has grown out of the economic structure of feudal society. The dissolution of the latter set free the elements of the former.

The laborer could only dispose of his own person after he had ceased to be attached to the soil and ceased to be the slave, serf, or bondman of another. To become a free seller of labor power, who carries his commodity wherever he finds a market, he must further have escaped from the regime of the guilds, their rules for apprentices and journeymen, and the impediments of their labor regulations. Hence, the historical movement which changes the producers into wageworkers, appears, on the one hand, as their emancipation from serfdom and from the fetters of the guilds, and this side alone exists for our bourgeois historians. But, on the other hand, these new freemen became sellers of themselves only after they had been robbed of all their own means of production, and of all the guarantees of existence afforded by the old feudal arrangements. And the history of this, their expropriation, is written in the annals of mankind in letters of blood and fire.

The industrial capitalists, these new potentates, had on their part not only to displace the guild masters of handicrafts, but also the feudal lords, the possessors of the sources of wealth. In this respect their conquest of social power appears as the fruit of a victorious struggle both against feudal lordship and its revolting prerogatives, and against the guilds and the fetters they laid on the free development of production and the free exploitation of man by man. The *chevaliers d'industrie,* however, only succeeded in supplanting the knights of the sword by making use of events of which they themselves were wholly innocent. They have risen by means as vile as those by which the Roman freed-man once on a time made himself the master of his *patronus.*

The starting-point of the development that gave rise to the wage-laborer as well as to the capitalist, was the servitude of the laborer. The advance consisted in a change of form of this servitude, in the transformation of feudal exploitation into capitalist exploitation. To understand its march, we need not go back very far. Although we come across the first beginnings of capitalist production as early as the 14th or 15th century, sporadically, in certain towns of the Mediterranean, the capitalist era dates from the 16th century. Wherever it appears, the abolition of serfdom has been long effected, and the highest development of the middle ages, the existence of sovereign towns, has been long on the wane.

In the history of primitive accumulation, those moments are particularly important, when great masses of men are suddenly and forcibly torn from their means of subsistence, and hurled as free and "unattached" proletarians on the labor market. The expropriation of the peasant from the soil, is the basis of the whole process. . . .

WHAT CAPITALIST ACCUMULATION LEADS TO

What does the primitive accumulation of capital, *i.e.,* its historical genesis, resolve itself into? In so far as it is not immediate transformation of slaves and serfs into wage-laborers, and therefore a mere

change of form, it only means the expropriation of the immediate producers, *i.e.,* the dissolution of private property based on the labor of its
owner.

The private property of the laborer in his means of production
is the foundation of petty industry; petty industry, again, is an essential
condition for the development of social production and of the free individuality of the laborer himself. Of course, this petty mode of production exists also under slavery, serfdom, and other states of dependence.
But it flourishes, it lets loose its whole energy, only where the laborer
is the private owner of his own means of labor set in action by himself:
the peasant of the land which he cultivates, the artisan of the tool which
he handles as a virtuoso. This mode of production presupposes parcelling
of the soil, and scattering of the other means of production. As it excludes the concentration of these means of production, so also it excludes cooperation, division of labor within each separate process of
production, the control over and the productive application of the forces
of nature by society, and the free development of the social productive
powers. It is compatible only with a system of production, and a society,
moving within narrow and more or less primitive bounds. To perpetuate
it, would be to decree universal mediocrity. At a certain stage of development it brings forth the material agencies for its own dissolution. From
that moment new forces and new passions spring up in the bosom of
society; but the old social organisation fetters them and keeps them
down. It must be annihilated; it is annihilated.

Its annihilation, the transformation of the individualised and
scattered means of production into socially concentrated ones, of the
pigmy property of the many into the huge property of the few, the expropriation of the great mass of the people from the soil, from the
means of subsistence and from the means of labor, this fearful and
painful expropriation of the mass of people forms the prelude to the
history of capital. Self-earned private property, that is based, so to say,
on the fusing together of the isolated, independent laborer with the
conditions of his labor, is supplanted by capitalistic private property,
which rests on exploitation of the nominally free labor of others, *i.e.,*
on wages-labor.

As soon as the process of transformation has sufficiently decom-
posed the old society from top to bottom, as soon as the laborers are
turned into proletarians, their means of labor into capital, as soon as
the capitalist mode of production stands on its own feet, then the further
socialisation of labor and the further transformation of the land and
other means of production, as well as the further expropriation of pri-

vate proprietors, takes a new form. That which is now to be expropriated is no longer the laborer working for himself, but the capitalist exploiting many laborers. This expropriation is accomplished by the action of the immanent laws of capitalistic production itself, by the centralisation of capital. One capitalist always kills many.

Hand in hand with this centralisation, or this expropriation of many capitalists by few, develops, on an ever extending scale, the co-operative form of the labor-process, the conscious technical application of science, the economising of all means of production by combined, socialised labor, the entanglement of all peoples in the net of the world-market, and with this, the international character of the capitalistic regime.

Along with the constantly diminishing number of the magnates of capital, who usurp and monopolise all advantages of this process of transformation, grows the mass of misery, oppressions, slavery, degradation, exploitation; but with this too grows the revolt of the working-class, always increasing in numbers, and disciplined, united, organised by the very mechanism of the process of capitalist production itself. The monopoly of capital becomes a fetter upon the mode of production, which has sprung up and flourished along with, and under it. Centralisations of the means of production and socialisation of labor at last reach a point where they become incompatible with their capitalist integument. This integument is burst asunder. The knell of capitalist private property sounds. The expropriators are expropriated.

The capitalist mode of appropriation, the result of the capitalist mode of production, capitalist private property, is the first negation of individual private property, as founded on the labor of the proprietor. But capitalist production begets, with the inexorability of a law of nature, its own negation. This does not re-establish private property, but individual property based on the acquisitions of the capitalist era: i. .e., on cooperation and the possession in common of the land and of the means of production produced by labor itself.

The transformation of scattered private property, arising from individual labor, into capitalist private property was, naturally, a process incomparably more protracted, violent, and difficult, than the transformation of capitalistic private property, already practically resting on socialised production, into socialised property. In the former case, we had the expropriation of the mass of the people by a few usurpers; in the latter, we have the expropriation of a few usurpers by the mass of the people.

13

◀ THORSTEIN VEBLEN* ▶

from

The Theory of Business Enterprise (1904)

from

The Engineers and the Price System (1921)

Veblen was the ideological father of the institutionalist school in American economic thought. Whereas his followers (like Wesley Mitchell and John R. Commons) were inclined to champion the accumulation of empirical data and the shifting forms of social control necessary to deal with the limited problems of a developing market society, Veblen's critique of American capitalism was uncompromising and revolutionary. Writing at the turn of the twentieth century, during the first wave of business mergers which was engineered by a rising class of investment bankers, Veblen reacted strongly against the marginalist school of economics, firmly entrenched in academia at that time. The thrust of his critique was that orthodox economics was overly concerned with value and price phenomena instead of the more important evolutionary considerations of the cumulative growth of changing institutions. Furthermore, the former theory was based on a questionable psychological base—hedonism—in which man's actions are attributed to an alleged pleasure-pain calculus. In addition

---

* (1857–1929)

to this pecuniarily based drive Veblen held that man's activities were influenced by an instinct of workmanship (drive for purposeful or useful work), parental bent (concern for continuity of the group), and idle curiosity (desire for systematic knowledge). Man, to Veblen, thus appears as a multi-dimensioned animal operating in a dynamic social universe, as opposed to the orthodox concept of the "economic man" in a static personal universe.

Fundamental to Veblen's attempt to discover the laws of change within capitalism is his claim that the two basic institutions of American society are the business enterprise system and technology. He characterized their relationship as a clashing one. While the businessmen were concerned with the maximization of private profit, the engineers and technicians operating the machine technology (industry) were concerned with the most efficient utilization of resources. Veblen's writings in this area foreshadow later work on imperfect competition and welfare economics. He contrasted the welfare needs of the community for maximum productivity—greater output at lower cost—with the consistent practice of the business interests of restricting output to increase their profits. Under capitalism, according to Veblen, the interests of industry and the welfare needs of the community were sacrificed in favor of the interests of business. This was Veblen's way of saying that our vast accumulation of knowledge and technology, which ought to be the common heritage of all men, was being misused to further the economic interests of a small propertied class. As a result of this conflict Veblen foresaw the probable shift of the control of industry from the businessman to the engineers and technicians. The selection presented here reflects this feeling. The major part of it is taken from one of Veblen's last works, *The Engineers and the Price System,* and reflects a more moderate position than that of his earlier writings. In the end Veblen did not seem to hold out much hope that changing technology would affect man's thinking enough to place the control of industry into the hands of the engineers. Although he was not fully in favor of any alternative type of socioeconomic system, Veblen was without doubt hostile to capitalism; it was wasteful, predatory, prone towards economic crises, and based on irrational drives like religion, salesmanship, and patriotism.

Although few Marxists have embraced Veblen, there is much in common in their critiques of capitalist society. Both Marx and Veblen had a "materialist" conception of history with the stress on technology (Marx uses the term forces of production) as the prime agent in the evolution of institutions. They both held that capitalism could not permanently coexist with advanced technology. Noneconomic factors affected the pace and direction of social change, but the economic organization was viewed as decisive by both. Veblen, however, was more aware of the importance of noneconomic factors in guiding man's thinking and action; instead of turning to socialism the masses could be co-opted into the pursuit of "conspicuous consump-

tion," "devout observances," "sportsmanship," and "chauvinism."
There is less inevitability in Veblen's evolutionary approach than in
Marx's. This reflects Veblen's Darwinian influence. Unlike Marx he
views history as a "scheme of blindly cumulative causation, in which
there is no trend, no final term, no consummation." They do, however,
agree that the current capitalist regime is a temporary phase. For
Veblen the economic pressure which shapes the course of history is
the disciplinary effect of changing technology on prevailing social
habits, whereas for Marx, the key economic pressure is the effect of
changing conditions of production on social classes. Veblen was a
reporter of the social scene, standing apart from the events he described, while Marx was both a reporter and an active participant,
determined to speed up the evolutionary process towards socialism.

——M. L.

from

The Theory of Business Enterprise*

THE NATURAL DECAY OF BUSINESS ENTERPRISE

Broadly, the machine discipline acts to disintegrate the institutional heritage, of all degrees of antiquity and authenticity—whether
it be the institutions that embody the principles of natural liberty or
those that comprise the residue or more archaic principles of conduct
still current in civilized life. It thereby cuts away that ground of law
and order on which business enterprise is founded. The further cultural
bearing of this disintegration of the received order is no doubt sufficiently serious and far-reaching, but it does not directly concern the
present inquiry. It comes in question here only in so far as such a
deterioration of the general cultural tissues involves a set-back to the
continued vigor of business enterprise. But the future of business enterprise is bound up with the future of civilization, since the cultural
scheme is, after all, a single one, comprising many interlocking elements, no one of which can be greatly disturbed without disturbing
the working of all the rest.

In its bearing on the question in hand, the "social problem"
at large presents this singular situation. The growth of business enterprise rests on the machine technology as its material foundation. The

---

*From Thorstein Veblen, *The Theory of Business Enterprise* (1904).

machine industry is indispensable to it; it cannot get along without the machine process. But the discipline of the machine process cuts away the spiritual, institutional foundations of business enterprise; the machine industry is incompatible with its continued growth; it cannot, in the long run, get along with the machine process. In their struggle against the cultural effects of the machine process, therefore, business principles cannot win in the long run; since an effectual mutilation or inhibition of the machine system would gradually push business enterprise to the wall; whereas with a free growth of the machine system business principles would presently fall into abeyance.

The institutional basis of business enterprise—the system of natural rights—appears to be a peculiarly unstable affair. There is no way of retaining it under changing circumstances, and there is no way of returning to it after circumstances have changed. It is a hybrid growth, a blend of personal freedom and equality on the one hand and of prescriptive rights on the other hand. The institutions and points of law under the natural-rights scheme appear to be of an essentially provisional character. There is relatively great flexibility and possibility of growth and change; natural rights are singularly insecure under any change of circumstances. The maxim is well approved that eternal vigilance is the price of (natural) liberty. When, as now, this system is endangered by socialistic or anarchistic disaffection there is no recourse that will carry the institutional apparatus back to a secure natural-rights basis. The system of natural liberty was the product of a peaceful régime of handicraft and petty trade; but continued peace and industry presently carried the cultural growth beyond the phase of natural rights by giving rise to the machine process and the large business; and these are breaking down the structure of natural rights by making these rights nugatory on the one hand and by cutting away the spiritual foundations of them on the other hand. Natural rights being a by-product of peaceful industry, they cannot be reinstated by a recourse to warlike habits and a coercive government, since warlike habits and coercion are alien to the natural-rights spirit. Nor can they be reinstated by a recourse to settled peace and freedom, since an era of settled peace and freedom would push on the dominance of the machine process and the large business, which break down the system of natural liberty.

When the question is cast up as to what will come of this conflict of institutional forces—called the Social Problem—it is commonly made a question of remedies: What can be done to save civilized mankind from the vulgarization and disintegration wrought by the machine industry?

Now, business enterprise and the machine process are the two prime movers in modern culture; and the only recourse that holds a promise of being effective, therefore, is a recourse to the workings of business traffic. And this is a question, not of what is conceivably, ideally, idyllically possible for the business community to do if they will take thought and act advisedly and concertedly toward a chosen cultural outcome, but of what is the probable cultural outcome to be achieved through business traffic carried on for business ends, not for cultural ends. It is a question not of what ought to be done, but of what is to take place.

Persons who are solicitous for the cultural future commonly turn to speculative advice as to what ought to be done toward holding fast that which is good in the cultural heritage, and what ought further to be done to increase the talent that has been intrusted to this generation. The practical remedy offered is commonly some proposal for palliative measures, some appeal to philanthropic, esthetic, or religious sentiment, some endeavor to conjure with the name of one or another of the epiphenomena of modern culture. Something must be done, it is conceived, and this something takes the shape of charity organizations, clubs and societies for social "purity," for amusement, education, and manual training of the indigent classes, for colonization of the poor, for popularization of churches, for clean politics, for cultural missionary work by social settlements, and the like. These remedial measures whereby it is proposed to save or to rehabilitate certain praiseworthy but obsolescent habits of life and of thought are, all and several, beside the point so far as touches the question in hand. Not that it is hereby intended to cast a slur on these meritorious endeavors to save mankind by treating symptoms. The symptoms treated are no doubt evil, as they are said to be; or if they are not evil, the merits of that particular question do not concern the present inquiry. The endeavors in question are beside the point in that they do not fall into the shape of a business proposition. They are, on the whole, not so profitable a line of investment as certain other ventures that are open to modern enterprise. Hence, if they traverse the course of business enterprise and of industrial exigencies, they are nugatory, being in the same class with the labor of Sisyphus; whereas if they coincide in effect with the line along which business and industrial exigencies move, they are a work of supererogation, except so far as they may be conceived to accelerate a change that is already under way. Nothing can deflect the sweep of business enterprise, unless it be an outgrowth of this enterprise itself or of the industrial means by which business enterprise works.

Nothing can serve as a corrective of the cultural trend given by the machine discipline except what can be put in the form of a business proposition. The question of neutralizing the untoward effects of the machine discipline resolves itself into a question as to the cultural work and consequences of business enterprise, and of the cultural value of business principles in so far as they guide such human endeavor as lies outside the range of business enterprise proper. It is not a question of what ought to be done, but of what is the course laid out by business principles; the discretion rests with the business men, not with the moralists, and the business men's discretion is bounded by the exigencies of business enterprise. Even the business men cannot allow themselves to play fast and loose with business principles in response to a call from humanitarian motives. The question, therefore, remains, on the whole, a question of what the business men may be expected to do for cultural growth on the motive of profits.

Something they are doing, as others are, from motives of benevolence, with a well-advised endeavor to maintain the cultural gains of the past and to make the way of life smoother for mankind in the future. But the more secure and substantial results to be looked for in this direction are those that follow incidentally, as by-products of business enterprise, because these are not dependent on the vagaries of personal preference, tastes, and prejudices, but rest on a broad institutional basis.

The effects of business enterprise upon the habits and temper of the people, and so upon institutional growth, are chiefly of the nature of sequelæ. . . . The discipline of business employments is of a conservative nature, tending to sustain the conventions that rest on natural-rights dogma, because these employments train the men engaged in them to think in terms of natural rights. . . In its severer, more unmitigated form, this discipline in pecuniary habits of thought falls on a gradually lessening proportion of the population. The absolute number of business men, counting principals and subordinates, is, of course, not decreasing. The number of men in business pursuits, in proportion to the population, is also apparently not decreasing; but within the business employments a larger proportion are occupied with office routine, and so are withdrawn from the more effectual training given by business management proper. If such a decrease occurs in any country, it is almost certainly not to be found in any other country than America.

This business discipline is somewhat closely limited both in scope and range. (1) It acts to conserve, or to rehabilitate, a certain restricted line of institutional habits of thought, viz. those preconceptions of natural rights which have to do with property. What it conserves, therefore, is the bourgeois virtues of solvency, thrift, and dissimulation. The nobler and more spectacular aristocratic virtues, with their correlative institutional furniture, are not in any sensible degree fortified by the habits of business life. Business life does not further the growth of manners and breeding, pride of caste, punctilios of "honor," or even religious fervor. (2) The salutary discipline of business life touches the bulk of the population, the working classes, in a progressively less intimate and less exacting manner. It can, therefore, not serve to correct or even greatly to mitigate the matter-of-fact bias given these classes by the discipline of the machine process.

As a direct disciplinary factor the machine process holds over the business employments, in that it touches larger classes of the community and inculcates its characteristic habits of thought more unremittingly. And any return to more archaic methods of industry, such as is sometimes advocated on artistic grounds, seems hopeless, since business interests do not countenance a discontinuance of machine methods. The machine methods that are corrupting the hearts and manners of the workmen are profitable to the business men, and that fact seems to be decisive on the point. A direct, advised return to handicraft, or any similar discontinuance of the machine industry, is out of the question; although something in the way of a partial return to more primitive methods of industry need not be impracticable as a remote and indirect consequence of the working of business enterprise. . . .

from

The Engineers and the Price System*

THE CAPTAINS OF FINANCE AND THE ENGINEERS

In more than one respect the industrial system of today is notably different from anything that has gone before. It is eminently a system, self-balanced and comprehensive; and it is a system of interlocking mechanical processes, rather than of skilful manipulation. It is mechanical rather than manual. It is an organization of mechanical powers

*From The Engineers and the Price System. Copyright 1921 by B. W. Huebsch, Inc., renewed 1949 by Ann B. Sims and Becky Meyers. Reprinted by permission of The Viking Press, Inc.

and material resources, rather than of skilled craftsmen and tools; although the skilled workmen and tools are also an indispensable part of its comprehensive mechanism. It is of an impersonal nature, after the fashion of the material sciences, on which it constantly draws. It runs to "quantity production" of specialized and standardized goods and services. For all these reasons it lends itself to systematic control under the direction of industrial experts, skilled technologists, who may be called "production engineers," for want of a better term.

This industrial system runs on as an inclusive organization of many and diverse interlocking mechanical processes, interdependent and balanced among themselves in such a way that the due working of any part of it is conditioned on the due working of all the rest. Therefore it will work at its best only on condition that these industrial experts, production engineers, will work together on a common understanding; and more particularly on condition that they must not work at cross purposes. These technological specialists whose constant supervision is indispensable to the due working of the industrial system constitute the general staff of industry, whose work it is to control the strategy of production at large and to keep an oversight of the tactics of production in detail.

Such is the nature of this industrial system on whose due working depends the material welfare of all the civilized peoples. It is an inclusive system drawn on a plan of strict and comprehensive interdependence, such that, in point of material welfare, no nation and no community has anything to gain at the cost of any other nation or community. In point of material welfare, all the civilized peoples have been drawn together by the state of the industrial arts into a single going concern. And for the due working of this inclusive going concern it is essential that that corps of technological specialists who by training, insight, and interest make up the general staff of industry must have a free hand in the disposal of its available resources, in materials, equipment, and man power, regardless of any national pretensions or any vested interests. Any degree of obstruction, diversion, or withholding of any of the available industrial forces, with a view to the special gain of any nation or any investor, unavoidably brings on a dislocation of the system; which involves a disproportionate lowering of its working efficiency and therefore a disproportionate loss to the whole, and therefore a net loss to all its parts.

And all the while the statesmen are at work to divert and obstruct the working forces of this industrial system, here and there, for the special advantage of one nation and another at the cost of the rest; and the captains of finance are working, at cross purposes and in collusion, to divert whatever they can to the special gain of one vested interest and another, at any cost to the rest. So it happens that the industrial system is deliberately handicapped with dissension, misdirection, and unemployment of material resources, equipment, and man power, at every turn where the statesmen or the captains of finance can touch its mechanism; and all the civilized peoples are suffering privation together because their general staff of industrial experts are in this way required to take orders and submit to sabotage at the hands of the statesmen and the vested interests. Politics and investment are still allowed to decide matters of industrial policy which should plainly be left to the discretion of the general staff of production engineers driven by no commercial bias.

No doubt this characterization of the industrial system and its besetting tribulations will seem overdrawn. However, it is not intended to apply to any date earlier than the twentieth century, or to any backward community that still lies outside the sweep of the mechanical industry. Only gradually during the past century, while the mechanical industry has progressively been taking over the production of goods and services, and going over to quantity production, has the industrial system taken on this character of an inclusive organization of interlocking processes and interchange of materials; and it is only in the twentieth century that this cumulative progression has come to a head with such effect that this characterization is now visibly becoming true. And even now it will hold true, visibly and securely, only as applies to the leading mechanical industries, those main lines of industry that shape the main conditions of life, and in which quantity production has become the common and indispensable rule. Such are, e.g., transport and communication; the production and industrial use of coal, oil, electricity and water power; the production of steel and other metals; of wood pulp, lumber, cement and other building materials; of textiles and rubber; as also grain-milling and much of the grain-growing, together with meat-packing and a good share of the stock-raising industry.

There is, of course, a large volume of industry in many lines which has not, or only in part and doubtfully, been drawn into this network of mechanical processes and quantity production, in any direct and conclusive fashion. But these other lines of industry that still stand over on another and older plan of operation are, after all, outliers and subsidiaries of the mechanically organized industrial system, dependent on or subservient to those greater underlying industries which make up the working body of the system, and which therefore set the pace for the rest. And in the main, therefore, and as regards these greater mechanical industries on whose due working the material welfare of the community depends from day to day, this characterization will apply without material abatement.

But it should be added that even as regards these greater, primary and underlying, lines of production the system has not yet reached a fatal degree of close-knit interdependence, balance, and complication; it will still run along at a very tolerable efficiency in the face of a very appreciable amount of persistent derangement. That is to say, the industrial system at large has not yet become so delicately balanced a mechanical structure and process that the ordinary amount of derangement and sabotage necessary to the ordinary control of production by business methods will paralyze the whole outright. The industrial system is not yet sufficiently close-knit for that. And yet, that extent and degree of paralysis from which the civilized world's industry is suffering just now, due to legitimate businesslike sabotage, goes to argue that the date may not be far distant when the interlocking processes of the industrial system shall have become so closely interdependent and so delicately balanced that even the ordinary modicum of sabotage involved in the conduct of business as usual will bring the whole to a fatal collapse. The derangement and privation brought on by any well organized strike of the larger sort argues to the same effect.

In effect, the progressive advance of this industrial system towards an all-inclusive mechanical balance of interlocking processes appears to be approaching a critical pass, beyond which it will no longer be practicable to leave its control in the hands of business men working at cross purposes for private gain, or to entrust its continued administration to others than suitably trained technological experts, production engineers without a commercial interest. What these men may then do with it all is not so plain; the best they can do may be good enough; but the negative proposition is becoming sufficiently plain, that this mechanical state of the industrial arts will not long tolerate the continued control of production by the vested interests under the current business-like rule of incapacity by advisement.

In the beginning, that is to say during the early growth of the machine industry, and particularly in that new growth of mechanical industries which arose directly out of the Industrial Revolution, there was no marked division between the industrial experts and the business managers. That was before the new industrial system had gone far on the road of progressive specialization and complexity, and before business had reached an exactingly large scale; so that even the business men of that time, who were without special training in technological matters, would still be able to exercise something of an intelligent oversight of the whole, and to understand something of what was required in the mechanical conduct of the work which they financed and from which they drew their income. Not unusually the designers of industrial processes and equipment would then still take care of the financial end, at the same time that they managed the shop. But from an early point in the development there set in a progressive differentiation, such as to divide those who designed and administered the industrial processes from those others who designed and managed the commercial transactions and took care of the financial end. So there also set in a corresponding division of powers between the business management and the technological experts. It became the work of the technologist to determine, on technological grounds, what could be done in the way of productive industry, and to contrive ways and means of doing it; but the business management always continued to decide, on commercial grounds, how much work should be done and what kind and quality of goods and services should be produced; and the decision of the business management has always continued to be final, and has always set the limit beyond which production must not go.

With the continued growth of specialization the experts have necessarily had more and more to say in the affairs of industry; but always their findings as to what work is to be done and what ways and means are to be employed in production have had to wait on the findings of the business managers as to what will be expedient for the purpose of commercial gain. This division between business management and industrial management has continued to go forward, at a continually accelerated rate, because the special training and experience required for any passably efficient organization and direction of these industrial processes has continually grown more exacting, calling for special knowledge and abilities on the part of those who have this work to do and requiring their undivided interest and their undivided attention to the work in hand. But these specialists in technological knowledge, abilities, interests, and experience, who have increasingly come into the case in this way—inventors, designers, chemists, mineralogists, soil experts, crop specialists, production managers and engineers of many kinds and denominations—have continued to be employees of the captains of industry, that is to say, of the captains of finance, whose work it has been to commercialize the knowledge and abilities of the industrial experts and turn them to account for their own gain.

It is perhaps unnecessary to add the axiomatic corollary that the captains have always turned the technologists and their knowledge to account in this way only so far as would serve their own commercial profit, not to the extent of their ability; or to the limit set by the material circumstances; or by the needs of the community. The result has been, uniformly and as a matter of course, that the production of goods and services has advisedly been stopped short of productive capacity, by curtailment of output and by derangement of the productive system. There are two main reasons for this, and both have operated together throughout the machine era to stop industrial production increasingly short of productive capacity. (a) The commercial need of maintaining a profitable price has led to an increasingly imperative curtailment of the output, as fast as the advance of the industrial arts has enhanced the productive capacity. And (b) the continued advance of the mechanical technology has called for an ever-increasing volume and diversity of special knowledge, and so has left the businesslike captains of finance continually farther in arrears, so that they have been less and less capable of comprehending what is required in the ordinary way of industrial equipment and personnel. They have therefore, in effect, maintained prices at a profitable level by curtailment of output rather than by lowering production-cost per unit of output, because they have not had such a working acquaintance with the technological facts in the case as would enable them to form a passably sound judgment of suitable ways and means for lowering production-cost; and at the same time, being shrewd business men, they have been unable to rely on the hired-man's-loyalty of technologists whom they do not understand. The result has been a somewhat distrustful blindfold choice of processes and personnel and a consequent enforced incompetence in the management of industry, a curtailment of output below the needs of the community, below the productive capacity of the industrial system, and below what an intelligent control of production would have made commercially profitable.

Through the earlier decades of the machine era these limitations imposed on the work of the experts by the demands of profitable business and by the technical ignorance of the business men, appears not to have been a heavy handicap, whether as a hindrance to the continued development of technological knowledge or as an obstacle to its ordinary use in industry. That was before the mechanical industry had gone far in scope, complexity, and specialization; and it was also before the continued work of the technologists had pushed the industrial system to so high a productive capacity that it is forever in danger of turning out a larger product than is required for a profitable business. But gradually, with the passage of time and the advance of the industrial arts to a wider scope and a larger scale, and to an increasing specialization and standardization of processes, the technological knowledge that makes up the state of the industrial arts has called for a higher degree of that training that makes industrial specialists; and at the same time any passably efficient management of industry has of necessity drawn on them and their special abilities to an ever-increasing extent. At the same time and by the same shift of circumstances, the captains of finance, driven by an increasingly close application to the affairs of business, have been going farther out of touch with the ordinary realities of productive industry; and, it is to be admitted, they have also continued increasingly to distrust the technological specialists, whom they do not understand, but whom they can also not get along without. The captains have per force continued to employ the technologists, to make money for them, but they have done so only reluctantly, tardily, sparingly, and with a shrewd circumspection; only because and so far as they have been persuaded that the use of these technologists was indispensable to the making of money.

One outcome of this persistent and pervasive tardiness and circumspection on the part of the captains has been an incredibly and increasingly uneconomical use of material resources, and an incredibly wasteful organization of equipment and man power in those great industries where the technological advance has been most marked. In good part it was this discreditable pass, to which the leading industries had been brought by these one-eyed captains of industry, that brought the régime of the captains to an inglorious close, by shifting the initiative and discretion in this domain out of their hands into those of the investment bankers. By custom the investment bankers had occupied a position between or overlapping the duties of a broker in corporate securities and those of an underwriter of corporate flotations—such a position, in effect, as is still assigned them in the standard writings on corporation finance. The increasingly large scale of corporate enterprise, as well as the growth of a mutual understanding among these business concerns, also had its share in this new move. But about this time, too, the "consulting engineers" were coming notably into evidence in many of those lines of industry in which corporation finance has habitually been concerned.

So far as concerns the present argument the ordinary duties of these consulting engineers have been to advise the investment bankers as to the industrial and commercial soundness, past and prospective, of any enterprise that is to be underwritten. These duties have comprised a painstaking and impartial examination of the physical properties involved in any given case, as well as an equally impartial auditing of the accounts and appraisal of the commercial promise of such enterprises, for the guidance of the bankers or syndicate of bankers interested in the case as underwriters. On this ground working arrangements and a mutual understanding presently arose between the consulting engineers and those banking houses that habitually were concerned in the underwriting of corporate enterprises.

The effect of this move has been twofold: experience has brought out the fact that corporation finance, at its best and soundest, has now become a matter of comprehensive and standardized bureaucratic routine, necessarily comprising the mutual relations between various corporate concerns, and best to be taken care of by a clerical staff of trained accountants; and the same experience has put the financial houses in direct touch with the technological general staff of the industrial system, whose surveillance has become increasingly imperative to the conduct of any profitable enterprise in industry. But also, by the same token, it has appeared that the corporation financier of nineteenth-century tradition is no longer of the essence of the case in corporation finance of the larger and more responsible sort. He has, in effect, come to be no better than an idle wheel in the economic mechanism, serving only to take up some of the lubricant.

Since and so far as this shift out of the nineteenth century into the twentieth has been completed, the corporation financier has ceased to be a captain of industry and has become a lieutenant of finance; the captaincy having been taken over by the syndicated investment bankers and administered as a standardized routine of accountancy, having to do with the flotation of corporation securities and with their fluctuating values, and having also something to do with regulating the rate and volume of output in those industrial enterprises which so have passed under the hand of the investment bankers.

By and large, such is the situation of the industrial system today, and of that financial business that controls the industrial system. But this state of things is not so much an accomplished fact handed on out of the recent past; it is only that such is the culmination in which it all heads up in the immediate present, and that such is the visible drift of things into the calculable future. Only during the last few years has the state of affairs in industry been obviously falling into the shape so outlined, and it is even yet only in those larger and pace-making lines of industry which are altogether of the new technological order that the state of things has reached this finished shape. But in these larger and underlying divisions of the industrial system the present posture and drift of things is unmistakable. Meantime very much still stands over out of that régime of rule-of-thumb, competitive sabotage, and commercial log-rolling, in which the businesslike captains of the old order are so altogether well at home, and which has been the best that the captains have known how to contrive for the management of that industrial system whose captains they have been. So that wherever the production experts are now taking over the management, out of the dead hand of the self-made captains, and wherever they have occasions to inquire into the established conditions of production, they find the ground cumbered with all sorts of incredible makeshifts of waste and inefficiency—such makeshifts as would perhaps pass muster with any moderately stupid elderly layman, but which look like blindfold guesswork to these men who know something of the advanced technology and its working-out.

Hitherto, then, the growth and conduct of this industrial system presents this singular outcome. The technology—the state of the industrial arts—which takes effect in this mechanical industry is in an eminent sense a joint stock of knowledge and experience held in common by the civilized peoples. It requires the use of trained and instructed workmen—born, bred, trained, and instructed at the cost of the people at large. So also it requires, with a continually more exacting insistence, a corps of highly trained and specially gifted experts, of divers and various kinds. These, too, are born, bred, and trained at the cost of the community at large, and they draw their requisite special knowledge from the community's joint stock of accumulated experience. These expert men, technologists, engineers, or whatever name may best suit them, make up the indispensable General Staff of the industrial system; and without their immediate and unremitting guidance and correction the industrial system will not work. It is a mechanically organized structure of technical processes designed, installed, and conducted by these production engineers. Without them and their constant attention the industrial equipment, the mechanical appliances of industry, will foot up to just so much junk. The material welfare of the community is unreservedly bound up with the due working of this industrial system, and therefore with its unreserved control by the engineers, who alone are competent to manage it. To do their work as it should be done these men of the industrial general staff must have a free hand, unhampered by commercial considerations and reservations; for the production of the goods and services needed by the community they neither need nor are they in any degree benefited by the supervision or interference from the side of the owners. Yet the absentee owners, now represented, in effect, by the syndicated investment bankers, continue to control the industrial experts and limit their discretion, arbitrarily, for their own commercial gain, regardless of the needs of the community.

Hitherto these men who make up the general staff of the industrial system have not drawn together into anything like a self-directing working force; nor have they been vested with anything more than an occasional, haphazard, and tentative control of some disjointed sector of the industrial equipment, with no direct or decisive relation to that personnel of productive industry that may be called the officers of the line and the rank and file. It is still the unbroken privilege of the financial management and its financial agents to "hire and fire." The final disposition of all the industrial forces still remains in the hands of the business men, who still continue to dispose of these forces for other than industrial ends. And all the while it is an open secret that with a reasonably free hand the production experts would today readily increase the ordinary output of industry by several fold,—variously estimated at some 300 per cent. to 1200 per cent. of the current output. And what stands in the way of so increasing the ordinary output of goods and services is business as usual.

Right lately these technologists have begun to become uneasily "class-conscious" and to reflect that they together constitute the indispensable General Staff of the industrial system. Their class consciousness has taken the immediate form of a growing sense of waste and confusion in the management of industry by the financial agents of the absentee owners. They are beginning to take stock of that all-pervading mismanagement of industry that is inseparable from its control for commercial ends. All of which brings home a realization of their own shame and of damage to the common good. So the engineers are beginning to draw together and ask themselves, "What about it?"

This uneasy movement among the technologists set in, in an undefined and fortuitous way, in the closing years of the nineteenth century; when the consulting engineers, and then presently the "efficiency engineers," began to make scattered corrections in detail, which showed up the industrial incompetence of those elderly laymen who were doing a conservative business at the cost of industry. The consulting engineers of the stardard type, both then and since then, are commercialized technologists, whose work it is to appraise the industrial value of any given enterprise with a view to its commercial exploitation. They are a cross between a technological specialist and a commercial agent, beset with the limitations of both and commonly not fully competent in either line. Their normal position is that of an employee of the investment bankers, on a stipend or retainer, and it has ordinarily been their fortune to shift over in time from a technological footing to a frankly commercial one. The case of the efficiency engineers, or scientific-management experts, is somewhat similar. They too have set out to appraise, exhibit, and correct the commercial shortcomings of the ordinary management of these industrial establishments which they investigate, to persuade the business men in charge how they may reasonably come in for larger net earnings by a more closely shorn exploitation of the industrial forces at their disposal. During the opening years of the new century a lively interest centered on the views and expositions of these two groups of industrial experts; and not least was the interest aroused by their exhibits of current facts indicating an all-pervading lag, leak, and friction in the industrial system, due to its disjointed and one-eyed management by commercial adventurers bent on private gain.

During these few years of the opening century the members of this informal guild of engineers at large have been taking an interest in this question of habitual mismanagement by ignorance and commercial sabotage, even apart from the commercial imbecility of it all. But it is the young rather than the old among them who see industry in any other light that its commercial value. Circumstances have decided that the older generation of the craft have become pretty well commercialized. Their habitual outlook has been shaped by a long and unbroken apprenticeship to the corporation financiers and the investment bankers; so that they still habitually see the industrial system as a contrivance for the roundabout process of making money. Accordingly, the established official Associations and Institutes of Engineers, which are officered and engineered by the elder engineers, old and young, also continue to show the commercial bias of their creators, in what they criticize and in what they propose. But the new generation which has been coming on during the present century are not similarly true to that tradition of commercial engineering that makes the technological man an awestruck lieutenant of the captain of finance.

By training, and perhaps also by native bent, the technologists find it easy and convincing to size up men and things in terms of tangible performance, without commercial afterthought, except so far as their apprenticeship to the captains of finance may have made commercial afterthought a second nature to them. Many of the younger generation are beginning to understand that engineering begins and ends in the domain of tangible performance, and that commercial expediency is another matter. Indeed, they are beginning to understand that commercial expediency has nothing better to contribute to the engineer's work than so much lag, leak, and friction. The four years' experience of the war has also been highly instructive on that head. So they are beginning to draw together on a common ground of understanding, as men who are concerned with the ways and means of tangible performance in the way of productive industry, according to the state of the industrial arts as they know them at their best; and there is a growing conviction among them that they together constitute the sufficient and indispensable general staff of the mechanical industries, on whose unhindered team-work depends the due working of the industrial system and therefore also the material welfare of the civilized peoples. So also, to these men who are trained in the stubborn logic of technology, nothing is quite real that cannot be stated in terms of tangible performance; and they are accordingly coming to understand that the whole fabric of credit and corporation finance is a tissue of make-believe.

Credit obligations and financial transactions rest on certain principles of legal formality which have been handed down from the eighteenth century, and which therefore antedate the mechanical industry and carry no secure conviction to men trained in the logic of that industry. Within this technological system of tangible performance corporation finance and all its works and gestures are completely idle; it all comes into the working scheme of the engineers only as a gratuitous intrusion which could be barred out without derangement of the work at any point, provided only that men made up their mind to that effect—that is to say, provided the make-believe of absentee ownership were discontinued. Its only obvious effect on the work which the engineers have to take care of is waste of materials and retardation of the work. So the next question which the engineers are due to ask regarding this timeworn fabric of ownership, finance, sabotage, credit and un-earned income is likely to be: Why cumbers it the ground? And they are likely to find the scriptural answer ready to their hand.

It would be hazardous to surmise how, how soon, on what prov-ocation, and with what effect the guild of engineers are due to realize that they constitute a guild, and that the material fortunes of the civi-lized people already lie loose in their hands. But it is already sufficiently plain that the industrial conditions and the drift of conviction among the engineers are drawing together to some such end.

Hitherto it has been usual to count on the interested negotia-tions continually carried on and never concluded between capital and labor, between the agents of the investors and the body of the work-men, to bring about whatever readjustments are to be looked for in the control of productive industry and in the distribution and use of its product. These negotiations have necessarily been, and continue to be, in the nature of business transactions, bargaining for a price, since both parties to the negotiation continue to stand on the consecrated ground of ownership, free bargain, and self-help; such as the com-mercial wisdom of the eighteenth century saw, approved and certified it all, in the time before the coming of this perplexing industrial system. In the course of these endless negotiations between the owners and their workmen there has been some loose and provisional syndication of claims and forces on both sides; so that each of these two recognized parties to the industrial controversy has come to make up a loose-knit vested interest, and each speaks for its own special claims as a party in interest. Each is contending for some special gain for itself and trying to drive a profitable bargain for itself, and hitherto no disinterested spokesman for the community at large or for the industrial system as a going concern has seriously cut into this controversy between these contending vested interests. The outcome has been businesslike con-cession and compromise, in the nature of bargain and sale. It is true, during the war, and for the conduct of the war, there were some half-concerted measures taken by the Administration in the interest of the nation at large, as a belligerent; but it has always been tacitly agreed that these were extraordinary war measures, not to be countenanced in time of peace. In time of peace the accepted rule is still business as usual; that is to say, investors and workmen wrangling together on a footing of business as usual.

These negotiations have necessarily been inconclusive. So long as ownership of resources and industrial plant is allowed, or so long as it is allowed any degree of control or consideration in the conduct of industry, nothing more substantial can come of any readjustment than a concessive mitigation of the owners' interference with production. There is accordingly nothing subversive in these bouts of bargaining between the federated workmen and the syndicated owners. It is a game of chance and skill played between two contending vested interests for private gain, in which the industrial system as a going concern enters only as a victim of interested interference. Yet the material welfare of the community, and not least of the workmen, turns on the due working of this industrial system, without interference. Concessive mitigation of the right to interfere with production, on the part of either one of these vested interests, can evidently come to nothing more substantial than a concessive mitigation.

But owing to the peculiar technological character of this industrial system, with its specialized, standardized, mechanical, and highly technical interlocking processes of production, there has gradually come into being this corps of technological production specialists, into whose keeping the due functioning of the industrial system has now drifted by force of circumstance. They are, by force of circumstance, the keepers of the community's material welfare; although they have hitherto been acting, in effect, as keepers and providers of free income for the kept classes. They are thrown into the position of responsible directors of the industrial system, and by the same move they are in a position to become arbiters of the community's material welfare. They are becoming class-conscious, and they are no longer driven by commercial interest, in any such degree as will make them a vested interest in that commercial sense in which the syndicated owners and federated workmen are vested interests. They are, at the same time, numerically and by habitual outlook, no such heterogeneous and unwieldy body as the federated workmen, whose numbers and scattering interest has left all their endeavors substantially nugatory. In short, the engineers are in a position to make the next move.

By comparison with the population at large, including the financial powers and the kept classes, the technological specialists which come in question here are a very inconsiderable number; yet this small number is indispensable to the continued working of the productive industries. So slight are their numbers, and so sharply defined and homogeneous is their class, that a sufficiently compact and inclusive organization of their forces should arrange itself almost as a matter of course, so soon as an appreciable proportion of them shall be moved by any common purpose. And the common purpose is not far to seek, in the all-pervading industrial confusion, obstruction, waste, and retardation which business as usual continually throws in their face. At the same time they are the leaders of the industrial personnel, the workmen, of the officers of the line and the rank and file; and these are coming into a frame of mind to follow their leaders in any adventure that holds a promise of advancing the common good.

To these men, soberly trained in a spirit of tangible performance and endowed with something more than an even share of the sense of workmanship, and endowed also with the common heritage of partiality for the rule of Live and Let Live, the disallowance of an outworn and obstructive right of absentee ownership is not likely to seem a shocking infraction of the sacred realities. That customary right of ownership by virtue of which the vested interests continue to control the industrial system for the benefit of the kept classes, belongs to an older order of things than the mechanical industry. It has come out of a past that was made up of small things and traditional make-believe. For all the purposes of that scheme of tangible performance that goes to make up the technologist's world, it is without form and void. So that, given time for due irritation, it should by no means come as a surprise if the guild of engineers are provoked to put their heads together and, quite out of hand, disallow that large absentee ownership that goes to make the vested interests and to unmake the industrial system. And there stand behind them the massed and rough-handed legions of the industrial rank and file, ill at ease and looking for new things. The older commercialized generation among them would, of course, ask themselves: Why should we worry? What do we stand to gain? But the younger generation, not so hard-bitten by commercial experience, will be quite as likely to ask themselves: What do we stand to lose? And there is the patent fact that such a thing as a general strike of the technological specialists in industry need involve no more than a minute fraction of one per cent. of the population; yet it would swiftly bring a collapse of the old order and sweep the timeworn fabric of finance and absentee sabotage into the discard for good and all.

Such a catastrophe would doubtless be deplorable. It would look something like the end of the world to all those persons who take their stand with the kept classes, but it may come to seem no more than an incident of the day's work to the engineers and to the rough-handed legions of the rank and file. It is a situation which may well be deplored. But there is no gain in losing patience with a conjunction of circumstances. And it can do no harm to take stock of the situation and recognize that, by force of circumstance, it is now open to the Council of Technological Workers' and Soldiers' Deputies to make the next move, in their own way and in their own good time. When and what this move will be, if any, or even what it will be like, is not something on which a layman can hold a confident opinion. But so much seems clear, that the industrial dictatorship of the captain of finance is now held on sufferance of the engineers and is liable at any time to be discontinued at their discretion, as a matter of convenience. . . .

WHAT MAKES FOR A CHANGE

. . . Any question of a revolutionary overturn, in America or in any other of the advanced industrial countries, resolves itself in practical fact into a question of what the guild of technicians will do. In effect it is a question whether the discretion and responsibility in the management of the country's industry shall pass from the financiers, who speak for the Vested Interests, to the technicians, who speak for the industrial system as a going concern. There is no third party qualified to make a colorable bid, or able to make good its pretensions if it should make a bid. So long as the vested rights of absentee ownership remain intact, the financial powers—that is to say the Vested Interests —will continue to dispose of the country's industrial forces for their own profit; and so soon, or so far, as these vested rights give way, the control of the people's material welfare will pass into the hands of the technicians. There is no third party.

The chances of anything like a Soviet in America, therefore, are the chances of a Soviet of technicians. And, to the due comfort of the Guardians of the Vested Interests and the good citizens who make up their background, it can be shown that anything like a Soviet of Technicians is at the most a remote contingency in America.

It is true, so long as no such change of base is made, what is confidently to be looked for is a régime of continued and increasing shame and confusion, hardship and dissension, unemployment and privation, waste and insecurity of person and property—such as the rule of the Vested Interests in business has already made increasingly familiar to all the civilized peoples. But the vested rights of absentee

ownership are still embedded in the sentiments of the underlying population, and still continue to be the Palladium of the Republic; and the
assertion is still quite safe that anything like a Soviet of Technicians
is not a present menace to the Vested Interests in America.

By settled habit the technicians, the engineers and industrial
experts, are a harmless and docile sort, well fed on the whole, and
somewhat placidly content with the "full dinner-pail" which the lieutenants of the Vested Interests habitually allow them. It is true, they
constitute the indispensable General Staff of that industrial system which
feeds the Vested Interests; but hitherto at least, they have had nothing
to say in the planning and direction of this industrial system, except as
employees in the pay of the financiers. They have, hitherto, been quite
unreflectingly content to work piecemeal, without much of an understanding among themselves, unreservedly doing job-work for the Vested
Interests; and they have without much reflection lent themselves and
their technical powers freely to the obstructive tactics of the captains
of industry; all the while that the training which makes them technicians is but a specialized extension of that joint stock of technological
knowledge that has been carried forward out of the past by the
community at large.

But it remains true that they and their dear-bought knowledge
of ways and means—dear-bought on the part of the underlying community—are the pillars of that house of industry in which the Vested
Interests continue to live. Without their continued and unremitting
supervision and direction the industrial system would cease to be a
working system at all; whereas it is not easy to see how the elimination of the existing businesslike control could bring anything but relief
and heightened efficiency to this working system. The technicians are
indispensable to productive industry of this mechanical sort; the Vested
Interests and their absentee owners are not. The technicians are indispensable to the Vested Interests and their absentee owners, as a working
force without which there would be no industrial ouput to control or
divide; whereas the Vested Interests and their absentee owners are
of no material consequence to the technicians and their work, except
as an extraneous interference and obstruction.

It follows that the material welfare of all the advanced industrial peoples rests in the hands of these technicians, if they will only
see it that way, take counsel together, constitute themselves the self-
directing General Staff of the country's industry, and dispense with the

interference of the lieutenants of the absentee owners. Already they are strategically in a position to take the lead and impose their own terms of leadership, so soon as they, or a decisive number of them, shall reach a common understanding to that effect and agree on a plan of action.

But there is assuredly no present promise of the technicians' turning their insight and common sense to such a use. There need be no present apprehension. The technicians are a "safe and sane" lot, on the whole; and they are pretty well commercialized, particularly the older generation, who speak with authority and conviction, and to whom the younger generation of engineers defer, on the whole, with such a degree of filial piety as should go far to reassure all good citizens. And herein lies the present security of the Vested Interests, as well as the fatuity of any present alarm about Bolshevism and the like; for the whole-hearted co-operation of the technicians would be as indispensable to any effectual movement of overturn as their unwavering service in the employ of the Vested Interests is indispensable to the maintenance of the established order.

14

◀ PAUL BARAN* AND PAUL SWEEZY ▶

from

Monopoly Capital (1966)

     Paul Sweezy, editor of the independent socialist magazine, *Monthly Review,* is the most prominent modern American Marxist economist. His collaborator in the following selection, the late Paul Baran, was one of the few avowed Marxists in academic circles. Their book *Monopoly Capital* is without a doubt the most important addition to Marxist economic thought in the last generation. It attempts to remedy an important deficiency in Marx's economic writings; although Marx foreshadowed important aspects of the transition from competitive capitalism to monopoly capitalism, he did not develop a full-fledged theory of monopoly capitalism. Although their analysis has a general Marxist character (the class struggle is the underlying theme) Baran and Sweezy make several important modifications of Marxist doctrine.

     To begin with, they conclude that the center of revolution has shifted from the developed countries to the undeveloped countries and that the key revolutionary agents are the peasantry and a thin stratum of workers in the latter, rather than the industrial working class in the former. The material basis for the loss of revolutionary elan among the advanced industrial labor force, according to Baran and Sweezy, is the trickling down of the economic benefits of colonialism and imperialism to the white working class in the Western

---

*Former professor at Stanford University. (Died in 1964.)

capitalist countries. This is why the authors hold that "the class struggle in our time has been thoroughly internationalized." Orthodox Marxists still adhere to the view that the working class, defined in a broad sense of the term, is the ultimate decisive force driving society towards a revolutionary restructuring, and that although the nationalist struggle against colonialism should be supported, it is of second-order importance. The near seizure of power by a worker-student alliance in industrial, relatively affluent France in May-June 1968 lends some credence to this orthodox view, although the continued lack of class consciousness among the American working class (particularly its white section) supports the Baran-Sweezy "revisionist" thesis.

Baran and Sweezy also modify Marx's doctrine that an important factor causing a secular decline of capitalism was a tendency towards a falling rate of profit. They present an alternative formulation which they call the secular tendency for economic surplus (they discard Marx's term "surplus value") to rise under a regime of monopoly capitalism. Economic surplus refers to "the difference between total social output and the socially necessary costs of producing it." This surplus has to be absorbed in order to maintain economic stability. The methods employed in our "irrational system," according to Baran and Sweezy, are the capitalists' consumption and investment, the sales effort, civilian government spending, and, increasingly, militarism and imperialism.

The authors predict increasing military intervention by our corporate-dominated society to stem the worldwide tide of revolutionary protest. It is worth noting that many people view the method, and perhaps the purpose, of the intervention of the Russian non-capitalist society in Czechoslovakia as strikingly similar to that of the intervention of the American capitalist society in Vietnam. It is not unreasonable to suppose that there are powerful economic and/or political groups in both societies that stand to gain through a militaristic stance and attempt to develop governmental policies to carry out their own interests.

Baran and Sweezy assign the same commanding post to the supersize corporation that Galbraith, Heilbroner, and Schumpeter do, although Baran and Sweezy are considerably less sympathetic to this institution than this liberal trio. A comparison is revealing: Baran and Sweezy reject the liberal argument that the modern corporation is less profit-oriented since corporate management has become increasingly socialized. They state that, "The big corporation, if not more profit-oriented than the individual entrepreneur, is at any rate better equipped to follow a policy of profit maximization. . . . The economy of large corporations is more, not less, dominated by the logic of profit-making than the economy of small entrepreneurs ever was." Many liberals, particularly Galbraith*, stress the separation of ownership and control in the modern corporation as well as the difference

*See chapter 8.

in interests between the owners and the managers. Baran and Sweezy claim that this dichotomy is only valid on a technical level. "Because of the strategic positions they (the managers) occupy, they function as the protectors and spokesmen for all large scale property. Far from being a separate class, they constitute in reality the leading echelon of the property-owning class." Another important point of divergence can be observed in the relationship of corporate planning and economic stability. Galbraith suggests that technology necessitates the superceding of the market place and the institutionalization of economic planning by the large-scale corporations aided by governmental policies that closely reflect the needs of these corporations. While Baran and Sweezy would very willingly agree about the tightly knit bonds between government and the leading corporations, their adherence to the Marxist position is seen in their statement, "The function of the State is to serve the interests of monopoly capital." They would not agree that capitalism has been made more stable by corporate economic planning. They conclude that although the individual large-scale enterprise (particularly the conglomerate) may have become more stable than smaller business units, the system as a whole remains vulnerable, unstable, and dependent on a war type economy. They said, "Except in war and periods of war related prosperity, stagnation is now the normal state of the United States economy." This dismal picture of an "intolerable social order" which progressively dehumanizes man is presented in sharp contrast to a growing world revolutionary movement aimed at overthrowing it and establishing a humane, planned society. Whether this vision of the limited potential of a capitalist order and the limitless potential of a post-capitalist order is a correct projection remains to be seen.   ——M. L.

from

*Monopoly Capital**

THE GIANT CORPORATION

1

Scientific understanding proceeds by way of constructing and analyzing "models" of the segments or aspects of reality under study. The purpose of these models is not to give a mirror image of reality,

*Copyright © 1966 by Paul M. Sweezy. Reprinted by permission of the copyright owner from Paul A. Baran and Paul M. Sweezy, *Monopoly Capital*, Monthly Review Press, 1966.

not to include all its elements in their exact sizes and proportions, but rather to single out and make available for intensive investigation those elements which are decisive. We abstract from nonessentials, we blot out the unimportant to get an unobstructed view of the important, we magnify in order to improve the range and accuracy of our observation. A model is, and must be, unrealistic in the sense in which the word is most commonly used. Nevertheless, and in a sense paradoxically, if it is a good model it provides the key to understanding reality.

There are no rules for model-building, and, as the literature of economics attests, it is much easier to build a bad one than a good one—a bad model being one which abstracts from essentials and therefore leads to neither insight nor understanding.[1] Nor are there any simple *a priori* tests by which a model can be judged. The proof of the pudding is in the eating. We can only start with certain hypotheses and ideas; we can use them to separate the unimportant from the important; out of the residue of the important we can shape what look like the parts and elements of a system; we can assemble the parts and elements, refining and polishing as we proceed. When we finally get our model, there is one test to which we must subject it: does it help to make sense of the real world? Or, to put the matter in another way, does it help us to see connections to which we were previously blind, to relate effects to causes, to replace the arbitrary and the accidental by the regular and the necessary? In a word, does it help us to understand the world and act in it intelligently and effectively?

These are the general ideas and aims by which we have been guided in constructing a model of the monopoly capitalist economy. It is intended to put at the center of the stage and play the spotlight on those features which, despite all diversity and underneath whatever overlay of detail, make the system what it is. And in order to accomplish this, we start, . . . with an analysis of the typical unit of Big Business, the modern giant corporation.

Once again: we are not interested in realism of a photographic kind. There undoubtedly are corporations which correspond closely to the "ideal type"—to use Max Weber's expression—with which we shall be concerned, but the analysis would lose none of its relevance even if there were not. The point is that the decisive units of the economy are unmistakably moving toward a definite, recognizable pattern,

---

[1] As Duesenberry rightly says: "Knowing how to simplify one's description of reality without neglecting anything essential is the most important part of the economist's art." James S. Duesenberry, *Business Cycles and Economic Growth,* New York, 1958, pp. 14–15.

and this pattern itself is much more important than any of the concrete approximations to it. A model of which the major component
parts are corporations of the ideal type will display with sharpness and
clarity what may appear in everyday economic life in a disguised form,
difficult to recognize and easy to misinterpret.

2

The corporate paradigm on which we wish to focus attention
has a number of characteristic features, of which we may single out
the following:

(1) Control rests in the hands of management, that is to say,
the board of directors plus the chief executive officers. Outside interests are often (but not always) represented on the board to facilitate
the harmonization of the interests and policies of the corporation with
those of customers, suppliers, bankers, etc.; but real power is held by
the insiders, those who devote full time to the corporation and whose
interests and careers are tied to its fortunes.

(2) Management is a self-perpetuating group. Responsibility
to the body of stockholders is for all practical purposes a dead letter.
Each generation of managers recruits its own successors and trains,
grooms, and promotes them according to its own standards and values.
The corporate career recognizes two characteristic forms of advance:
rising from lower to higher positions within a given company, and
moving from a smaller company to a larger one. The acme of success is the presidency or board chairmanship of one of the biggest
corporations.

(3) Each corporation aims at and normally achieves financial independence through the internal generation of funds which
remain at the disposal of management. The corporation may still, as a
matter of policy, borrow from or through financial institutions, but it
is not normally forced to do so and hence is able to avoid the kind
of subjection to financial control which was so common in the world
of Big Business fifty years ago.

Before we investigate the behavior of giant corporations of this
type, a few words of explanation and clarification may be useful.

In the first place, there is no implication in our description of
the corporate paradigm that great wealth, or family connections, or
large personal or family stockholdings are unimportant in the recruiting and promotion of management personnel—that, for example, the

chances of a David Rockefeller's getting a job at the Chase Manhattan Bank and rising to the top position are the same as those of anyone else with similar personal and intellectual attributes. On the contrary, wealth and connections are of the utmost importance, and it may indeed be taken for granted that they are normally decisive. What we are implying is something quite different: that stock ownership, wealth, connections, etc., do not as a rule enable a man to control or exercise great influence on a giant corporation from the outside. They are rather tickets of admission to the inside, where real corporate power is wielded. Mills put the essential point in a nutshell:

> Not great fortunes, but great corporations are the important units of wealth, to which individuals of property are variously attached. The corporation is the source of, and the basis of the continued power and privilege of wealth. All the men and the families of great wealth are now identified with large corporations in which their property is seated.[2]

What needs to be emphasized is that the location of power inside rather than outside the typical giant corporation renders obsolete the conception of the "interest group" as a fundamental unit in the structure of capitalist society. In traditional usage, an interest group is a number of corporations under common control, the locus of power being normally an investment or commercial bank or a great family fortune.[3] Thus a Morgan company was one under the control of the investment banking firm of J. P. Morgan & Company, a Rockefeller company one under the control of the Rockefeller family, and so on. The members of an interest group would naturally coordinate their policies; and in the case of conflicts, the interests of the controlling power (or of the whole group as interpreted by the controlling power) would prevail.

A whole series of developments have loosened or broken the ties that formerly bound the great interest groups together. The power of the investment banker was based on the urgent need of the early

---

[2]C. Wright Mills, *The Power Elite,* New York, 1956, p. 116.

[3]An analysis of interest groups in the American economy as of the mid-1930's will be found in Appendix 13 to Part 1 of the National Resources Committee's well-known report *The Structure of the American Economy,* Washington, 1939 (reprinted in Paul M. Sweezy, *The Present as History,* New York, 1953, Chapter 12).

corporate giants, at the time of foundation and in the first stages of growth, for outside financing. Later this need declined in importance or disappeared altogether as the giants, reaping a rich harvest of monopoly profits, found themselves increasingly able to take care of their financial needs from internally generated funds. At the same time, the domineering founders of family fortunes were dying off, leaving their stockholdings to numerous heirs, foundations, charities, trust funds, and the like, so that the ownership unit which once exercised absolute control over many enterprises became increasingly amorphous and leaderless. Thus the larger corporations gradually won more and more independence from both bankers and dominant stockholders, and their policies accordingly were geared to an ever greater extent each to its own interests rather than being subordinated to the interests of a group.

We are not of course maintaining that interest groups have disappeared or are no longer of any importance in the United States economy. We do hold that they are of rapidly diminishing importance and that an appropriate model of the economy no longer needs to take account of them. . . .

3

What pattern of behavior can we expect from huge, management-controlled, financially independent corporations?

Formal economic theory has largely ignored this question, continuing to operate with the assumption of the profit-maximizing individual entrepreneur who has occupied the central role in theories of the capitalist system since well before the time of Adam Smith. Retaining this assumption amounts in effect to making another: that in all respects that matter to the functioning of the system the corporation acts like an individual entrepreneur.

If one stops to think about it, this seems unlikely on the face of it. Furthermore, while economic theorists have largely ignored the corporation, other social scientists have devoted much time and energy to its study. So far as we know, none of them has ever supported the proposition that the modern corporation is merely an enlarged version of the classical entrepreneur. On the other hand, there is a voluminous literature dating back to the turn of the century and reaching its culmination in the famous work of Berle and Means which argues most emphatically that the modern corporation represents a qualitative break with the older form of individual enterprise and that radically different types of behavior are to be expected from it. According to Berle and Means:

> It is conceivable—indeed it seems almost inevitable if the corporate system is to survive—that the "control" of the great corporations should develop into a purely neutral technocracy, balancing a variety of claims by various groups in the community and assigning to each a portion of the income stream on the basis of public policy rather than private cupidity.[4]

What Berle and Means described as "conceivable" a quarter of a century ago is taken for granted as an accomplished fact by many present-day observers of the business scene. Thus Carl Kaysen, in a paper delivered at the 1956 annual meeting of the American Economic Association, speaks of "the wide-ranging scope of responsibility assumed by management" as one of the "characteristic features of behavior" of the modern corporation, and proceeds as follows:

> No longer the agent of proprietorship seeking to maximize return on investment, management sees itself as responsible to stockholders, employees, customers, the general public, and, perhaps most important, the firm itself as an institution. . . . From one point of view, this behavior can be termed responsible: there is no display of greed or graspingness; there is no attempt to push off onto workers or the community at large part of the social costs of the enterprise. The modern corporation is a soulful corporation.[5]

According to this view, which is certainly very widespread nowadays, the maximization of profits has ceased to be the guiding principle of business enterprise. Corporate managements, being self-

---

[4] *The Modern Corporation and Private Property,* New York, 1932, p. 356.

[5] Carl Kaysen, "The Social Significance of the Modern Corporation," *American Economic Review,* May 1957, pp. 313–314. See also M. J. Rathbone, President of Standard Oil of New Jersey, in the *Saturday Review,* April 16, 1960: "Managements of large companies must harmonize a wide span of obligations: to investors, customers, suppliers, employees, communities and the national interest. Thus the large organization may actually have a narrower range for its decision-making than the small, closely held corporation which is not so much in the public eye and hence not so exposed to criticism."

appointed and responsible to no outside group, are free to choose their aims and in the typical case are assumed to subordinate the old-fashioned hunt for profits to a variety of other, quantitatively less precise but qualitatively more worthy, objectives.

The implications of this doctrine of the "soulful corporation" are far-reaching. The truth is that if it is accepted, the whole corpus of traditional economic theory must be abandoned and the time-honored justification of the existing social order in terms of economic efficiency, justice, etc., simply falls to the ground. This has been most effectively pointed out by Edward S. Mason:

> But if profit maximization is not the directing agent, how are resources allocated to their most productive uses, what relation have prices to relative scarcities, and how do factors get remunerated in accordance with their contribution to output? Assume an economy composed of a few hundred large corporations, each enjoying substantial market power and all directed by managements with a "conscience." Each management wants to do the best it can for society consistent, of course, with doing the best it can for labor, customers, suppliers, and owners. How do prices get determined in such an economy? How are factors remunerated, and what relation is there between remuneration and performance? What is the mechanism, if any, that assures effective resource use, and how can corporate managements "do right by" labor, suppliers, customers, and owners while simultaneously serving the public interests?[6]

Economists have made no attempt to answer these questions, and indeed it is doubtful whether it even makes sense to ask them in relation to an economy such as Mason postulates, that is to say, one made up of or dominated by a few hundred soulful corporations. Prices and incomes would be indeterminate, and there would be no theoretically definable tendencies toward equilibrium. To be sure, economic life in such a society might settle down into routines and patterns which could be analyzed by historians, sociologists, and statisticians, but it seems reasonably clear that today's economic theorists would be out of a job.

---

[6]Edward S. Mason, "The Apologetics of 'Managerialism,'" *The Journal of Business,* January 1958, p. 7.

One school of thought, associated especially with the name of Herbert A. Simon of Carnegie Institute of Technology, seems already to have drawn these conclusions and is attempting to study the big corporation and its implications by means of what Simon calls "organization theory." According to this theory, corporations do not try to maximize anything but merely to achieve "satisfactory" results. Thus, to the maximizing behavior which was assumed to characterize the old-fashioned entrepreneur, Simon contrasts what he calls the "satisficing" behavior of modern corporate managements. At the annual meetings of the American Economic Association in 1956, a paper by Simon expounding this view was answered by James Earley of the University of Wisconsin who had been engaged for a number of years on a study of the management policies of a sample of large and successful American corporations. Summing up a wealth of carefully collected and analyzed empirical material, Earley had little difficulty in disposing of Simon's theory; what is more significant from our point of view is that he went on to give a most useful and illuminating description of how modern corporate managements really behave. This statement is so good that it seems worthwhile to rescue large parts of it from the untitled obscurity of the Economic Association's *Papers and Proceedings.* After noting some points of agreement and others of minor disagreement with Simon, Earley proceeds as follows:

> I have more serious reservations concerning what appears to be the major economic theorem Simon arrives at; namely, that the business enterprise looks for merely satisfactory solutions of its problems and specifically seeks merely satisfactory profits. That his approach has led so directly to this conclusion is one of the facts that makes me especially doubt that it is a satisfactory one. Whatever may be true of individuals or of other types of organization, I cannot square Simon's "satisficing" behavior with the behavior of the large-scale American business firm. I agree that the conventional notion of profit maximization and of general "optimization" must be modified. I contend this is carrying the change much too far. Let me briefly catalogue the main types of evidence that lead me to reject the "satisficing" postulate.
>
> (1) As a part of my research, I have made a study of recent management literature, both general and specialized, one of my hypotheses in doing so being that this literature

will reveal the frames of reference and mores of advanced business management. A striking characteristic of this literature (except where public relations is an evident objective) is its systematic focus on cost reduction, the expansion of revenue, and the increase of profits. There is, of course, much reference to standards and to the need of remedying unsatisfactory situations. The drive is always toward the better and frequently the best, not just the good. Like Samuel Gompers' ideal union leader, the exemplary man of management seems to have "More!" for at least one of his mottoes.

(2) Secondly, my questionnaire studies of the practices and policies of leading so-called "excellently managed" companies lead me toward generally similar conclusions. I have published the major results of the first of these studies and will not review them here.[7]

(3) The third fact that makes me doubt Simon's postulate as applied to the firm is the rapidly growing use of economists, market analysts, other types of specialists, and management consultants by our larger businesses. The main function of most of these people is to help the firm reduce costs, find superior methods, choose the most profitable alternatives, and uncover new profit opportunities. As these sophisticated gentlemen gain in influence in business councils—and I confidently believe they will—profit oriented rationality is likely to be more and more representative of business behavior.

(4) Most of all I am impressed by the rapid development of analytical and managerial techniques that both stimulate and assist the business firms to find the least costly ways of doing things and the most profitable things to do. Operations research and mathematical programming are only the more fancy of this growing genus. There are also greatly improved forms of accounting and budgeting, improved methods of market analysis, refinements in business forecasting, and interesting types of nonmathematical programming. The unifying character of these new techniques is that they seek to apply the principles of rational problem-solving to business planning and decision making.

---

[7]The author's reference here is to James S. Earley, "Marginal Policies of 'Excellently Managed' Companies," *The American Economic Review,* March 1956.

Let me conclude by briefly sketching the notion of business behavior that seems to be emerging from my own studies. It falls somewhere between the old postulate of profit maximization and Simon's "satisfactory profit." It fully recognizes the limited informational and computational resources of the firm. It also incorporates his suggested concept of the "aspiration level" and a modified principle of "viability." My behavioral postulate could best be briefly described as "a systematic temporal search for highest practicable profits.'

The theory underlying it runs, very briefly, as follows:

The major goals of modern large-scale business are high managerial incomes, good profits, a strong competitive position, and growth. Modern management does not view these goals as seriously inconsistent but rather, indeed, as necessary, one to the other. Competitive strength and even survival, management believes, require large innovative and substantial growth expenditures in the rapidly changing technical and market conditions of the present day. Since growth by merger is hazardous and frequently impossible, large and more or less continuous capital expenditures are necessary. For well-recognized reasons, management wishes to minimize outside financing, so the funds for most of these expenditures must be internally generated. This requires high and growing profits above dividend levels. So, too, do high managerial rewards. High and rising profits are hence an instrument as well as a direct goal of great importance.

With these goals and needs in view, advanced management plans for profit through time, using coordinated programs stretching as far ahead as practicable. The profit targets incorporated in these programs are sufficient to finance not only good dividends but also desired innovative and growth expenditures. The programs are revised frequently, as experience accrues and new opportunities are discovered.

The tendency toward profit maximization (i.e., highest practicable profit) appears in this system along several dimensions. In the process of revising and reformulating programs, more expensive and less profitable activities are pruned or dropped and cheaper or more profitable ones are added. Less costly processes and the more profitable product and market sectors serve as the standards toward which others are expected to converge or be replaced. By steadily selecting those methods and sectors that promise better returns, these standards are kept high and, if possible, rising. Finally, the overall profit and growth targets of the enterprise as a whole are raised through time, unless adversity prevents.

These goals and programs and standards, it is true, represent at any time certain "aspiration levels," and the efforts to satisfy them receive prime attention. But the two major points about them are that (1) they are likely to be hard to reach and (2) they will ordinarily recede (i.e., grow larger) through time. Even in good times the firm's aspiration levels, therefore, are fairly taut, and they are highly elastic upward. On the other hand, there is great resistance to adjusting profit and other standards downward, so that in bad times the business firm tries even harder to make the highest practicable profits.

I readily agree that I have sketched the behavior of what might be called the "exemplary firm" rather than the firm that is quantitatively representative of the present business population. But my main point is that the management techniques and the *expertise* than can validate my notion are developing rapidly, are increasingly being made available to business, and are being rapidly adopted by leading firms. Consequently, I suspect, the exemplary firm will be the representative firm of the future. If so, its behavior will be more rather than less appropriately analyzed by some of our time-honored theoretical notions, such as profit maximization. . . .[8]

Two aspects of this admirable statement call for comment. First, it introduces a healthy corrective to what Earley calls "the conventional notion of profit maximization and general 'optimization.'" This conventional notion has been tied to a more or less explicitly stated assumption that the maximizing entrepreneur has complete knowledge of all alternatives open to him and of the consequences of choosing any combination of them. Given this assumption, he can always select the combination of alternatives which yields an absolute

[8]*American Economic Review,* May 1957, pp. 333–335.

maximum. Further, if it is assumed that his knowledge remains equally complete in the face of changing conditions, it follows logically that he can always make instantaneous and appropriate adjustments to new circumstances. What is involved here is an assumption of omniscience on the part of the entrepreneur, which, far from being a useful abstraction, is of course an absurdity. In practice, to be sure, economists have usually given a more sensible meaning to the maximization principle, but by failing expressly to repudiate the omniscience postulate, by failing to spell out what is and what is not involved in the assumption of profit maximization, they have left themselves vulnerable to attacks of the kind mounted by Simon. It is therefore valuable to have Earley's carefully considered statement. By stressing the "limited informational and computational resources of the firm," he makes clear that no assumption of complete knowledge is involved, and his entire argument is based on the rejection of any idea of an absolute maximum or optimum. The firm (whether individual entrepreneur or corporation makes no difference) always finds itself in a given historical situation, with limited knowledge of changing conditions. In this context it can never do more than improve its profit position. In practice, the search for "maximum" profits can only be the search for the greatest *increase* in profits which is possible in the given situation, subject of course to the elementary proviso that the exploitation of today's profit opportunities must not ruin tomorrow's. This is all there is to the profit maximization principle, but it also happens to be all that is necessary to validate the "economizing" behavior patterns which have been the very backbone of all serious economic theory for the last two centuries.

The second aspect of Earley's statement which we want to emphasize, and the one most relevant to our present purpose, is the convincing demonstration that the big corporation, if not more profit-oriented than the individual entrepreneur (he quite properly leaves this question open), is at any rate better equipped to pursue a policy of profit maximization. The result is much the same: the economy of large corporations is more, not less, dominated by the logic of profit-making than the economy of small entrepreneurs ever was.

It might be thought that this is enough to dispose of the soulful corporation and at the same time to justify the procedure of those economists who have altogether ignored the rise of the corporate form of enterprise and continued to reason in terms of the individual entrepreneur. This is not so, however, and for two reasons: First, the alleged soulfulness of the corporation relates not only to its attitude toward the acquisition of profits but also to its attitude toward the utilization of profits, and there is still much to be said on the latter subject. Second, there are undoubtedly differences between individual enterprise and corporate enterprise which have little to do with the goal of profit maximization but which still are of great importance for economic theory.... [Let] us probe somewhat more deeply into the motivational and behavioral patterns of corporate management....

4

Big corporations are run by company men. What kind of people are they? What do they want and why? What position do they hold in the class structure of American society?

There is a widespread impression, and much literature to support and propagate it, that the managements of big corporations form some sort of separate, independent, or "neutral" social class. This view we have already encountered in an elementary form in the "neutral technocracy" of Berle and Means and the "soulful corporation" of Carl Kaysen; it is developed more elaborately in such works as James Burnham's *The Managerial Revolution* and Berle's *The 20th-Century Capitalist Revolution*. Most of the variants of this theory have interesting and enlightening insights to contribute, but in our view they all share a common defect: the basic idea is wrong.

The fact is that the managerial stratum is the most active and influential part of the propertied class. All studies show that its members are largely recruited from the middle and upper reaches of the class structure; they overlap with what C. Wright Mills calls the "very rich"; with few and negligible exceptions, they are wealthy men in their own right, quite apart from the large incomes and extensive privileges which they derive from their corporate connections.[9] It is of course true, as we have emphasized, that in the typical big corporation the management is not subject to stockholder control, and in this sense the "separation of ownership from control" is a fact. But there is no justification for concluding from this that managements in general are divorced from ownership in general. Quite the contrary, managers are

---

[9]By far the best treatment of these subjects will be found in C. Wright Mills, *The Power Elite*, especially Chapters 6, 7, and 8.

among the biggest owners; and because of the strategic positions they occupy, they function as the protectors and spokesmen for all large-scale property. Far from being a separate class, they constitute in reality the leading echelon of the property-owning class.

This is not to argue that managers have no distinctive interests *qua* managers. Like other segments of the propertied class, they do. But the conflicts of interest that arise in this way are between managers and small property owners rather than between managers and large property owners. The clearest case in point has to do with dividend policy.

It is generally assumed that the desire of managers to generate the largest feasible volume of internal corporate funds leads to an interest in a low dividend payout rate, while stockholders' concern to maximize their disposable cash income leads to an interest in a high payout rate. Actually, this is much too simple. Most managers are themselves big owners of stock (in their own and other companies) and as such have the same interest in dividends as other big stockholders. This interest is neither in a minimum nor a maximum payout rate but somewhere in between: stockholdings should yield a reasonable cash income (for managers this is particularly important as a guarantee of family security after they retire or die); on the other hand, they should also steadily appreciate in value. The first requirement calls for dividends, the second for plowing back of earnings. Nevertheless, the special managerial interest in a low payout rate does exist and is undoubtedly important. But the point to be emphasized is that this makes managers the allies of the very largest stockholders for whom a minimum payout rate is also a desideratum. The reason of course is that the very rich save a large part of their incomes in any case, and it is to their advantage for the corporations in which they own stock to do the saving for them rather than pay out dividends from which to do their own saving. Corporate saving results in an increase in the value of their stocks. If at any time they need the cash, either to spend or for some other investment, they can sell part or all of their shares, realizing the increment of value in the form of a capital gain taxable at the maximum rate of 25 percent. On the other hand, if they receive more in the form of dividends they have to pay taxes at the much higher rates applicable to their brackets, which of course cuts down their effective rate of saving.

Pressure for higher payout rates generally comes from small

stockholders. Only rarely is it effectively exerted on managements via the formal corporate voting machinery, but this does not mean that the small stockholder is without influence. Socially the seven million or so small stockholders in the United States are an important group: they are quite likely to be solid citizens, leaders of public opinion with local political influence. Since the tiny upper echelon of the propertied class (including its leading element, the managers of the big corporations) is always politically vulnerable, it naturally wants to have the support and loyalty of the small stockholder. A moderate, and perhaps even more important a steady, dividend policy is the most effective way of insuring this support.

In practice, dividend policies are the outcome of a compromise between the desire of managements and large stockholders for a low payout rate and the desire of small stockholders for a high rate. Moreover, as would be expected, there is considerable variation from one company to another. Those which are largely owned by a few rich individuals or families tend to have the lowest payout rates; while the highest rates of all are likely to be paid by companies which both have a large number of small stockholders and are also situated in what may be called "public-relations-sensitive" areas of the economy. As would also be expected, managements as a rule hold the upper hand in determining the terms of the compromise, maintaining payout rates of 50 percent or less in most management-controlled industrial corporations. When profits rise, moreover, managements deliberately delay the adjustment of dividends to the new profit level, so that in time of prosperity the actual as distinct from the target payout rate tends to decline.[10] All of which testifies to the combined power of management and the very rich: the two are in fact integrated into a harmonious interest group at the top of the economic pyramid.

5

The company man is dedicated to the advancement of his company. This does not mean, however, that he is any more or less *homo economicus,* any more or less selfish, any more or less altruistic than either the tycoon or the individual owner-entrepreneur before him. . . .

---

[10]For more complete quantitative data, see the excellent study of John Lintner, "Distribution of Incomes of Corporations Among Dividends, Retained Earnings, and Taxes," *American Economic Review,* May 1956.

To be a going concern, a social order must instill in its members the ambition to be a success in its own terms. Under capitalism the highest form of success is business success, and under monopoly capitalism the highest form of business is the big corporation. In this system the normal procedure for an ambitious young man must be to work himself up to as near the top as possible of as big a corporation as possible. Once he enters a given corporation, he devotes himself to two ends: ascending the managerial ladder and advancing the relative status of his company in the corporate world. In practice these two ends are indistinguishable: the young man's rise in the company depends on his contribution to improving the position of the company. This is the crux of the matter, and this is why we can say without qualification that the company man is dedicated to the advancement of his company: he is dedicated to the advancement of his company precisely to the extent that he is dedicated to advancing himself.

This remains true even after he has reached the top of a given company. If he makes a good record, he may be "called" to a larger company. And even if he is not, or has no hope of being, he is still just as much interested in improving the position of the company he heads; for standing, prestige, and power in the business world are not personal attributes but rather are conferred on the individual businessman by the standing, prestige, and power of his company and by his position in that company. . . .

. . . Size is not the only index of corporate status: this is an oversimplification. Other important indexes are rate of growth and "strength" as measured by such standards as credit rating and the price of a company's securities. Thus, assuming equal size, one company will rank ahead of others if it is stronger and growing more rapidly; and strength and rapid growth may even offset a big size differential if the larger company is stagnant or declining. The primary objectives of corporate policy—which are at the same time and inevitably the personal objectives of the corporate managers—are thus strength, rate of growth, and size. There is no general formula for quantifying or combining these objectives—nor is there any need for one. For they are reducible to the single common denominator of profitability. Profits provide the internal funds for expansion. Profits are the sinew and muscle of strength, which in turn gives access to outside funds if and when they are needed. Internal expansion, acquisition, and merger are the ways in which corporations grow, and growth is the road to size. Thus profits, even though not the ultimate goal, are the necessary means to all ultimate goals. As such, they become the immediate, unique, unifying, quantitative aim of corporate policies, the touchstone of corporate rationality, the measure of corporate success. Here is the real—the socio-structural as distinct from individual-psychological—explanation of the kind of profit-maximizing behavior so ably described by Earley. . . .

To sum up: Business is an ordered system which selects and rewards according to well understood criteria. The guiding principle is to get as near as possible to the top inside a corporation which is as near as possible to the top among corporations. Hence the need for maximum profits. Hence the need to devote profits once acquired to enhancing financial strength and speeding up growth. These things become the subjective aims and values of the business world because they are the objective requirements of the system. The character of the system determines the psychology of its members, not vice versa. . . .

. . . The real capitalist today is not the individual businessman but the corporation. What the businessman does in his private life, his attitude toward the getting and spending of his personal income—these are essentially irrelevant to the functioning of the system. What counts is what he does in his company life and his attitude toward the getting and spending of the company's income. And here there can be no doubt that the making and accumulating of profits hold as dominant a position today as they ever did. . . .

The replacement of the individual capitalist by the corporate capitalist constitutes an institutionalization of the capitalist function. The heart and core of the capitalist function is accumulation: accumulation has always been the prime mover of the system, the locus of its conflicts, the source of both its triumphs and its disasters. . . .

6

We have tried to show that the giant corporation of today is an engine for maximizing profits and accumulating capital to at least as great an extent as the individual enterprise of an earlier period. But it is not merely an enlarged and institutionalized version of the personal capitalist. There are major differences between these types of business enterprise, and at least two of them are of key importance to a general theory of monopoly capitalism: the corporation has a longer time horizon than the individual capitalist, and it is a more rational calculator. Both differences are fundamentally related to the incomparably larger scale of the corporation's operations. . . .

The long corporate time horizon and the rationalization of

management generate certain characteristic attitudes and modes of behavior. Of these perhaps the most important are (1) a systematic avoidance of risk-taking, and (2) an attitude of live-and-let-live toward other members of the corporate world. In both respects the change from the old-fashioned individual enterprise is so great in quantity as to amount to a change in quality. . . .

. . . In the early days when Big Business was emerging from the jungle of small-scale competition, corespective behavior was rare indeed. Even the railroads had to go through a series of exhausting rate wars before they finally got it into their corporate heads that roadbeds and tracks and locomotives and cars would go on being used to carry passengers and freight whatever might happen to security owners or rival managements. The original tycoons, faced with the consequences of cutthroat competition, sought a way out through a policy of ruthless monopolization. The victims of this drive, however, were numerous and not without influence. By entering into a temporary alliance with dissatisfied farmers and workers, they succeeded in getting the antitrust laws passed, which, though far from achieving their avowed aim of preserving (or restoring) free competition, nevertheless put very real roadblocks in the way of full monopolization. For this reason, as well as others of a technological and economic nature, there were few cases in which one corporation or even one financial interest group succeeded in establishing effective control over an entire market.

It was under these circumstances that Big Businessmen began to learn the virtues of corespective behavior. The process of learning was hastened as the highly individualistic tycoon passed from the scene and the company man gradually took his place as the typical representative of corporate business. Today there are probably fewer genuine monopolies than there were at the turn of the century, but there is also infinitely less cutthroat competition. . . .

THE TENDENCY OF SURPLUS* TO RISE

1

Monopoly capitalism is a system made up of giant corporations. This is not to say that there are no other elements in the system or

---

* (The difference between total output and the socially necessary costs of producing total output.)

that it is useful to study monopoly capitalism by abstracting from everything except giant corporations. It is both more realistic and more enlightening to proceed from the outset by including, alongside the corporate-monopoly sector, a more or less extensive smaller-business sector, the reason being that smaller business enters in many ways into the calculations and strategies of Big Business. To abstract from smaller business would be to exclude from the field of investigation some of the determinants of Big Business behavior.

One must, however, be careful not to fall into the trap of assuming that Big Business and smaller business are qualitatively equal or of coordinate importance for the *modus operandi* of the system. The dominant element, the prime mover, is Big Business organized in giant corporations. These corporations are profit maximizers and capital accumulators. They are managed by company men whose fortunes are identified with the corporations' success or failure. They—and here the pronoun stands for both the corporations and the men—look ahead and calculate with care. It is their initiative that sets the economy in motion, their power that keeps it moving, their policies that get it into difficulties and crises. Smaller business is on the receiving end, reacting to the pressures of Big Business, to a certain extent shaping and channeling them, but without effective power to counter them and still less to exercise an independent initiative of its own. From the point of view of a theory of monopoly capitalism, smaller business should properly be treated as a part of the environment within which Big Business operates rather than as an actor on the stage.

Within the corporation, relations are direct, hierarchical, bureaucratic. Here genuine planning holds sway, with directives flowing from the top down and responsibility from the bottom up. For the system as a whole, however, such relations are absent. Not even the largest corporations produce more than a very small fraction of society's total output. Take General Motors, for example, which, measured in terms of sales, is the biggest industrial corporation in the country. In 1957, GM's total of wages, overhead costs, and profits, which corresponds closely to the company's contribution to the Gross National Product, amounted to just over $4 billion, about 1 percent of GNP for that year. It is of course true that several giant corporations often act in concert, but they do so for the purpose of serving their own ends rather than for the purpose of influencing, not to say controlling, the functioning of the system as a whole.

Overall, monopoly capitalism is as unplanned as its competitive predecessor. The big corporations relate to each other, to consumers, to labor, to smaller business primarily through the market. The way the system works is still the unintended outcome of the self-regarding actions of the numerous units that compose it. And since market relations are essentially price relations, the study of monopoly capitalism, like that of competitive capitalism, must begin with the workings of the price mechanism.

The crucial difference between the two is well known and can be summed up in the proposition that under competitive capitalism the individual enterprise is a "price taker," while under monoply capitalism the big corporation is a "price maker." When we say that giant corporations are price makers, we mean that they can and do choose what prices to charge for their products. The typical giant corporation, however, is one of several corporations producing commodities which are more or less adequate substitutes for each other. When one of them varies its price, the effect will immediately be felt by others. . . . A wrong guess about rivals' reactions would throw the whole calculation off and necessitate readjustments which in turn would provoke further moves by rivals, and so on, the whole process quite possibly degenerating into mutually destructive price warfare.

Unstable market situations of this sort were very common in the earlier phases of monopoly capitalism, and still occur from time to time, but they are not typical of present-day monopoly capitalism. And clearly they are anathema to the big corporations with their penchant for looking ahead, planning carefully, and betting only on the sure thing. To avoid such situations therefore becomes the first concern of corporate policy, the *sine qua non* of orderly and profitable business operations.

This objective is achieved by the simple expedient of banning price cutting as a legitimate weapon of economic warfare. . . . With price competition banned, sellers of a given commodity or of close substitutes have an interest in seeing that the price or prices established are such as to maximize the profits of the group as a whole. . . . And it means that the appropriate general price theory for an economy dominated by such corporations is the traditional monopoly price theory of classical and neo-classical economies. What economists have hitherto treated as a special case turns out to be, under conditions of monopoly capitalism, the general case. . . . [Since] prices tend to be stickier on the downward side than on the upward side, this fact introduces a significant upward bias into the general price level in a monopoly capitalist economy. . . .

2

Now under monopoly capitalism it is true as it was in Marx's day that "the executive power of the . . . state is simply a committee for managing the common affairs of the entire bourgeois class."[11] And the common affairs of the entire bourgeois class include a concern that no industries which play an important role in the economy and in which large property interests are involved should be either too profitable or too unprofitable. Extra large profits are gained not only at the expense of consumers but also of other capitalists (electric power and telephone service, for example, are basic costs of all industries), and in addition they may, and at times of political instability do, provoke demands for genuinely effective antimonopoly action. Abnormally low profits in a major branch of the economy such as agriculture, on the other hand, damage the interests of a large and politically powerful group of property owners who are able through pressure and bargaining with the other capitalists to enlist the necessary support for remedial action. It therefore becomes a state responsibility under monopoly capitalism to insure, as far as possible, that prices and profit margins in the deviant industries are brought within the range prevailing among the general run of giant corporations.

This is the background and explanation of the innumerable regulatory schemes and mechanisms which characterize the American economy today—commission regulation of public utilities, prorationing of oil production, price supports and acreage controls in agriculture, and so on. In each case of course some worthy purpose is supposed to be served—to protect consumers, to conserve natural resources, to save the family-size farm—but only the naive believe that these fine sounding aims have any more to do with the case than the flowers that bloom in the spring. There is in fact a vast literature, based for the most part on official documents and statistics, to prove that regulatory commissions protect investors rather than consumers, that oil prorationing wastes rather than conserves natural resources, that the family-size farm is declining faster than in any previous period of American history.[12]

[11]*Communist Manifesto,* Part 1, paragraph 12.

[12]A considerable body of the relevant material is conveniently assembled and summarized in Walter Adams and Horace M. Gray, *Monopoly in America: The Government as Promoter,* New York, 1955.

All of this is fully understandable once the basic principle is grasped that under monopoly capitalism the function of the state is to serve the interests of monopoly capital. As two champions of free competition have so truthfully said: "With every advance of monopoly toward greater economic power and more general social acceptance the federal government becomes more subservient to it, more dependent on it, more disposed to favor it with grants of privilege, protection, and subsidy."[13]

Consequently the effect of government intervention into the market mechanisms of the economy, whatever its ostensible purpose, is to make the system work more, not less, like one made up exclusively of giant corporations acting and interacting in the manner analyzed [previously].

3

Strengthening monopoly and regularizing its operations is of course not the only function of the state under monopoly capitalism. . . . The state, through its taxing and spending activities and through its policies toward the rest of the world, plays a decisive role in the way the system operates. The question therefore arises: Would it not be better to adopt from the outset terminology which calls attention to and emphasizes the role of the state in this social system? There is ample precedent for doing so. In *State and Revolution* (1917) Lenin spoke of "the epoch of the development of monopoly capitalism into state monopoly capitalism," and it is now the accepted view in the Communist world that the advanced capitalist countries have long since passed through this transitional stage and entered that of state monopoly capitalism.

We have chosen not to follow this precedent but rather to use the terms "monopoly capital" and "monopoly capitalism" without qualification for two reasons. In the first place, the state has always played a crucial role in the development of capitalism, and while this role has certainly increased quantitatively we find the evidence of a qualitative change in recent decades unconvincing. Under the circumstances, to lay special emphasis on the role of the state in the present stage of monopoly capitalism may only mislead people into assuming that it was of negligible importance in the earlier history of capitalism. Even more important is the fact that terms like "state capitalism" and "state monopoly capitalism" almost inevitably carry the connotation that the

---

[13]*Ibid.,* p. 1.

state is somehow an *independent* social force, coordinate with private business, and that the functioning of the system is determined not only by the cooperation of these two forces but also by their antagonisms and conflicts. This seems to us a seriously misleading view—in reality, what appear to be conflicts between business and government are reflections of conflict within the ruling class—and we think it desirable to avoid terminology which tends to give it currency.

4

The abandonment of price competition does not mean the end of all competition: it takes new forms and rages on with ever increasing intensity. Most of these new forms of competition come under the heading of what we call the sales effort. . . . [and] to those forms of competition which have a direct bearing on costs of production and hence on the magnitude of the surplus.

If it is true, as we have argued, that oligopolies succeed in attaining a close approximation to the theoretical monopoly price and if their never-ceasing efforts to cut costs, so much stressed by James Earley, are generally successful, then it follows with inescapable logic that surplus must have a strong and persistent tendency to rise. But before this conclusion can be accepted, we must ask whether the *system* of oligopolies generates pressures which force corporate managers to cut costs and improve efficiency. We know that this is the case in the competitive system: as Marx expressed it, "competition makes the immanent laws of capitalist production to be felt by each individual capitalist as external coercive laws."[14] Is this true of the kind of competition that exists among giant corporations? Or must we say about them what Adam Smith said about joint stock companies, which he identified with monopoly: "Monopoly is a great enemy to good management, which can never be universally established but in consequence of that free and universal competition which forces everybody to have recourse to it for the sake of self-defense."[15]

These are extremely important questions for an understanding of monopoly capitalism, and we must be careful in answering them not to take at face value the literature which emanates from the corporate establishment itself. We know that the managers of giant corporations

---

[14]*Capital,* Volume 1, Chapter 22, Section 3.
[15]*The Wealth of Nations,* Book 1, Chapter 11, Part 1.

and their spokesmen have every interest in projecting an image of technological progressiveness and organizational efficiency. We also know that such images are often mere rationalizing ideologies. What needs to be determined is not what corporate managements want us to believe but what modes of behavior are imposed upon them by the workings of the system itself.

There are, it seems to us, two aspects of non-price competition which are of decisive importance here. The first has to do with what may be called the dynamics of market sharing. The second has to do with the particular form which the sales effort assumes in the producer goods industries.

To begin with, the firm with lower costs and higher profits enjoys a variety of advantages over higher-cost rivals in the struggle for market shares. (This fact seems to have been largely overlooked by economists,[16] but it is perfectly clear to businessmen.) The firm with the lowest costs holds the whip hand; it can afford to be aggressive even to the point of threatening, and in the limiting case precipitating, a price war. It can get away with tactics (special discounts, favorable credit terms, etc.) which if adopted by a weak firm would provoke retaliation. It can afford the advertising, research, development of new product varieties, extra services, and so on, which are the usual means of fighting for market shares and which tend to yield results in proportion to the amounts spent on them. Other less tangible factors are involved which tend to elude the economist's net but which play an important part in the business world. The lower-cost, higher-profit company acquires a special reputation which enables it to attract and hold customers, bid promising executive personnel away from rival firms, and recruit the ablest graduates of engineering and business schools. For all these reasons, there is a strong positive incentive for the large corporation in an oligopolistic industry not only to seek continuously to cut its costs but to do so faster than its rivals.

Here is where the self-defense factor considered so crucial by Adam Smith comes into play. Any company which falls behind in the race to cut costs is soon in trouble. Its power to fight back against attack is undermined, its freedom of maneuver curtailed, its ability to use the normal weapons of the competitive struggle weakened. Playing a more and more passive role, it finds its position progressively deteri-

---

[16]Duesenberry is an exception; see his *Business Cycles and Economic Growth,* especially pp. 124–125.

orating, and eventually it is faced with some unpleasant but unavoidable alternatives: it can merge, on unfavorable terms of course, with a stronger firm; it can attempt a reorganization and comeback, usually under new management and with new capital; or it can give up the ghost and leave the field to its more successful rivals. This sort of thing happens very often in the business world, and every manager knows of numerous cases and lives in constant fear that a similar fate will overtake him if his company falls behind in the cost race. The stick of failure thus complements the carrot of success in an oligopolistic system no less than in a competitive one.

There is an additional reason, in our judgment as important as it is neglected, why a tendency for costs of production to fall is endemic to the entire monopoly capitalist economy, even including those areas which if left to themselves would stagnate technologically. It stems from the exigencies of non-price competition in the producer goods industries. Here, as in industries producing consumer goods, sellers must be forever seeking to put something new on the market. But they are not dealing with buyers whose primary interest is the latest fashion or keeping up with the Joneses. They are dealing with sophisticated buyers whose concern is to increase profits. Hence the new products offered to the prospective buyers must be designed to help them increase their profits, which in general means to help them reduce their costs. If the manufacturer can convince his customers that his new instrument or material or machine will save them money, the sale will follow almost automatically.

Probably the clearest example of the cost-reducing effects of the innovating activity of manufacturers of producer goods is to be found in agriculture. As Galbraith has pointed out, "there would be little technical development and not much progress in agriculture were it not for government-supported research supplemented by the research of the corporations which devise and sell products to the farmer."[17] No doubt, as this statement implies, government research has been the main factor behind the spectacular reduction in agricultural costs during the last two decades, but the sales-hungry manufacturers of farm machinery, fertilizers, pesticides, etc., have also played an important part in the process. Similarly, producers of machine tools, computers and computer systems, business machines, automatic control equipment,

---

[17]J. K. Galbraith, *American Capitalism*, Boston, 1952, pp. 95–96.

loading and transfer machinery, new plastics and metal alloys, and a thousand and one other kinds of producer goods are busy developing new products which will enable their customers—comprising literally the entire business world—to produce more cheaply and hence to make more profits. In a word: producers of producer goods make more profits by helping others to make more profits. The process is self-reinforcing and cumulative, and goes far toward explaining the extraordinarily rapid advance of technology and labor productivity which characterizes the developed monopoly capitalist economy.

We conclude, then, that with regard to the cost discipline which it imposes on its members the monopoly capitalist economy is no less severe than its competitive predecessor, and that in addition it generates new and powerful impulses to innovation. There can therefore be no doubt about the downward trend of production costs under monopoly capitalism.

On the face of it this would seem to be an argument for monopoly capitalism's being considered a rational and progressive system. And if its cost-reducing proclivities could somehow be disentangled from monopoly pricing and a way could be found to utilize the fruits of increasing productivity for the benefit of society as a whole, the argument would indeed be a powerful one. But of course this is just what cannot be done. The whole motivation of cost reduction is to increase profits, and the monopolistic structure of markets enables the corporations to appropriate the lion's share of the fruits of increasing productivity directly in the form of higher profits. This means that under monopoly capitalism, declining costs imply continuously widening profit margins. And continuously widening profit margins in turn imply aggregate profits which rise not only absolutely but as a share of national product. If we provisionally equate aggregate profits with society's economic surplus, we can formulate as a law of monopoly capitalism that the surplus tends to rise both absolutely and relatively as the system develops.[18]

---

[18]As a matter of fact, statistically recorded profits are far from comprising the entire economic surplus. Interest and rent are also forms of surplus; and under monopoly capitalism still other forms assume decisive importance. Up to this point, however, we have used the term "profits" to mean simply the difference between sales revenue and costs of production, and the aggregate of profits in this sense is a legitimate first approximation to a fully developed concept of the economic surplus.

This law immediately invites comparison, as it should, with the classical-Marxian law of the falling tendency of the rate of profit. Without entering into an analysis of the different versions of the latter, we can say that they all presuppose a competitive system. By substituting the law of rising surplus for the law of falling profit, we are therefore not rejecting or revising a time-honored theorem of political economy: we are simply taking account of the undoubted fact that the structure of the capitalist economy has undergone a fundamental change since that theorem was formulated. What is most essential about the structural change from competitive to monopoly capitalism finds its theoretical expression in this substitution. . . .

. . . The persistent rise in the unemployment rate in recent years lends strong support to the view that the problem of realizing surplus value is indeed more chronic today that it was in Marx's time. The truth would seem to be that except in war and periods of war-related prosperity stagnation is now the normal state of the United States economy.

THE ABSORPTION OF SURPLUS

1

. . . Under monopoly capitalism, owing to the nature of the price and cost policies of the giant corporations, there is a strong and systematic tendency for surplus to rise, both absolutely and as a share of total output. We now come to the problem of the absorption or utilization of the surplus.

In general, surplus can be absorbed in the following ways: (1) it can be consumed, (2) it can be invested, and (3) it can be wasted. . . .

2

To the extent that surplus is consumed by capitalists, the amount available for investment is correspondingly reduced. . . . The question therefore [is]: does capitalists' consumption tend to rise as a share of surplus? If not, the investment-seeking part of surplus must rise relatively to total income [in order to absorb the surplus].

Let us assume that capitalists consume the entire amount of distributed profits. This is not true, of course, but if it can be shown that even in this case capitalists' consumption does not tend to rise as a share of surplus, then the conclusion which follows will hold *a fortiori* for cases in which capitalists save out of their distributed profits.

The problem is now quite simply whether there is in fact a tendency for the distributed share of surplus (dividends) to rise, remain constant, or fall as surplus itself expands. And here the evidence leaves no doubt about the answer.

. . . Most large companies have a target dividend payout rate which remains remarkably constant over long periods of time (50 percent seems to be the most common figure). When profits rise, however, they do not immediately adjust dividends to maintain the target rate. For example, if a company has been earning $2 a share for some time and is paying a dividend of $1, and if earnings then rise to $4, the dividend will be raised to $2 not in one year but over a period of several years. In the meantime, the actual payout rate will lag behind the target rate. If this pattern is adhered to—and there is every indication that it is a deeply rooted aspect of corporate behavior—it follows that a continuous rise in earnings would be accompanied by an equally continuous decline in the payout rate.

Under these circumstances, capitalists' consumption would increase absolutely, which of course is to be expected, but it would decline as a proportion of surplus and even more as a proportion to total income. Since these conclusions hold *a fortiori* to the extent that capitalists save out of their dividend incomes, it is clear that no solution of the problem of surplus absorption can be expected from this quarter.

3

Not only surplus, then, but also the investment-seeking part of surplus tends to rise as a proportion of total income. Whether this tendency will be realized, however, is another question. In attempting to answer it, we must first determine whether the system normally provides investment outlets large enough to absorb a rising share of a rising surplus.

The logic of the situation is as follows: if total income grows at an accelerating rate, then a larger and larger share has to be devoted to investment; and, conversely, if a larger and larger share is devoted to investment, total income must grow at an accelerating rate.[19] What

---

[19]See Evsey Domar, *Essays in the Theory of Economic Growth,* New York, 1957, pp. 127–128.

this implies, however, is nonsensical from an economic standpoint. It means that a larger and larger volume of producer goods would have to be turned out for the sole purpose of producing a still larger and larger volume of producer goods in the future. Consumption would be a diminishing proportion of output, and the growth of the capital stock would have no relation to the actual or potential expansion of consumption.[20]

Quite apart from the fact that such an explosive growth process would sooner or later exceed the physical potentialities of any conceivable economy, there is simply no reason to assume that anything like it has ever occurred or is likely to occur in the real world. Manufacturers of producer goods do not provide each other with an infinitely expanding market for each others' output, and they know it. In particular, it is sheer fantasy to imagine the cautious, calculating giant corporations of monopoly capitalism planning and carrying out the kind of snowballing expansion programs which this case presupposes.

If accelerating growth is ruled out as totally unrealistic, one is left with the inescapable conclusion that the actual investment of an amount of surplus which rises relatively to income must mean that the economy's capacity to produce grows more rapidly than its output. Such an investment pattern is certainly not impossible; indeed, it has frequently been observed in the history of capitalism. But what is impossible is that it should persist indefinitely. Sooner or later, excess capacity grows so large that it discourages further investment. When investment declines, so do income and employment and hence also surplus itself. In other words, this investment pattern is self-limiting and ends in an economic downturn—the beginning of a recession or depression. . . .

. . . On the other hand, if the economy moves up from a position of less-than-capacity production, both surplus and the investment-seeking segment of surplus swell absolutely and relatively. . . . Surplus swells when capacity is fully utilized and surplus rapidly shrinks when investment outlets fail and aggregate demand declines. As surplus shrinks, the investment-seeking part of it shrinks more than in proportion. On the downswing, in other words, the ratio of consumption to both surplus and total output rises, and this sooner or later puts a stop

[20]This is essentially the case analyzed by Tugan-Baranowsky in his well-known attempt to refute all underconsumption theories of economic crisis. For the relevant references, as well as a discussion of Tugan's theory, see Paul M. Sweezy, *The Theory of Capitalist Development,* New York, 1942, Chapter 10, Section 2.

to the contraction. The lower turning point is reached when the amount of surplus seeking investment is exactly absorbed by available investment outlets. At this point, a temporary equilibrium is reached which is characterized by the existence of excess productive capacity and unemployed workers. The reverse side of the coin is that an upswing, however initiated, generates a similar rapid absolute and relative increase of surplus. As soon as the investment-seeking part of surplus exceeds available investment outlets, the expansion comes to an end. And it should be remembered that this upper turning point may be reached long before full utilization of capacity or full employment of labor is achieved. . . .

We have seen that...mechanisms tend to generate a steady rising supply of investment-seeking surplus, but that in the nature of the case they cannot generate a corresponding rise in the magnitude of investment outlets. . . .

4

. . . A large part of investment over the years has been embodied in improved or altogether new types of producer goods. Does this mean that technological progress automatically provides outlets for investment-seeking surplus and that any shortage of outlets could in principle be overcome by an appropriate increase in the rate of technological progress? . . .

. . . Under monopoly capitalism there is no necessary correlation, as there is in a competitive system, between the rate of technological progress and the volume of investment outlets. Technological progress tends to determine the *form* which investment takes at any given time rather than its amount.[21]

This is not a rigid rule to which there are no exceptions. Particularly in the case of new products, as distinct from new versions of existing products, there may be a rush to get into the market first in order to enjoy for a time an unchallenged monopoly position. A "key feature of new products," says [a] McGraw-Hill survey, "is that they

---

[21] It is one of Steindl's great merits to have seen this relationship clearly (*Maturity and Stagnation in American Capitalism* (1952), p. 133), but he made the mistake of formulating it as a general proposition applicable to all stages of capitalism. That it is true under oligopoly is recognized and emphasized by Paolo Sylos Labini in his stimulating work, *Oligopoly and Technical Progress,* Cambridge, Massachusetts, 1962, especially pp. 148–149.

usually carry very high profit margins. When a company is first in the field, it can set a relatively high price . . . and hope to earn a high return—far higher, in most cases, than on standard products for which markets are intensively competitive. There is, therefore, every incentive to take quick advantage of new product developments by the construction of new plant capacity.[22] The importance of this point should not be exaggerated, however, for the same study, in discussing the lag between scientific discovery and economic application, indicates that there are also factors which work in the opposite direction, inhibiting bursts of investment associated with the introduction of new products:

> Capital investment particularly tends to lag because the expenditures required to begin output of a *new product* are usually quite small. Often existing facilities, or a part of them, can be converted to turn out trial quantities of the new product. And the really heavy expenditures required to build a complete new plant are not made until a year or two later. Similarly, expenditures to introduce a *new process* are not usually made until there is a relatively large production volume to justify these outlays. Especially in our heavy industries, new processes tend to be introduced (and, in fact, designed) as the low-cost way of adding new capacity. [In other words, they merely determine the form of investment which would have been made anyway.] Therefore, capital outlays for both new products and new processes tend to be delayed beyond the time of strictly scientific development, until sales prospects justify the building of large-scale facilities.[23]

---

[22]Dexter M. Keezer and others, *New Forces in American Business,* New York, 1958, p. 34. Just how profitable a new product can be is well illustrated by the success story of the Xerox Corporation. In an article devoted to Xerox and its products, *Newsweek* (September 9, 1964) speaks of "the breathtaking profit potential of what has amounted to a monopoly in electrostatic copiers. A 914, for instance, costs something less than $2,500 to manufacture. Yet Xerox leases most of them, recovers even the manufacturing cost through depreciation—and each leased machine is returning an average of at least $4,000 a year. If a customer wants to buy, the price is $29,500. Even Wilson [President of Xerox] has remarked: 'I keep asking myself when I am going to wake up.' The indicated profit margin of over 1000 percent on sales must be something like a record.

[23]*New Forces in American Business,* p. 62n.

To the extent that this argument applies, there is little reason to distinguish between new products and new processes: both tend to be introduced in a controlled fashion and to determine the form which investment takes rather than its magnitude. The new product takes the place of the old, just as the new process takes the place of the old; there is little of that "creative destruction" which Schumpeter saw as the chief dynamic force of the capitalist economy. . . .

. . . Where the amount of depreciation is very large, as in present-day monopoly capitalism, it is quite possible that business can finance from this source alone all the investment it considers profitable to make in innovations (both new products and new processes), leaving no "innovational" outlets to help absorb investment-seeking surplus. Technological progress may, in other words, do little more than shape the most profitable uses for funds made available to corporate managements through their own "generous" depreciation policies. To the extent that this is so, technological progress makes no contribution at all to solving the problem of outlets for the "visible" part of invesment-seeking surplus: whatever investment may be required to embody available innovations may well be less than enough to absorb the rising tide of depreciation allowances. . . .

Our conclusion is that technological progress is no more likely than population growth to make a significant contribution to solving the problem of surplus absorption. . . .

Twist and turn as one will, there is no way to avoid the conclusion that monopoly capitalism is a self-contradictory system. It tends to generate ever more surplus, yet it fails to provide the consumption and investment outlets required for the absorption of a rising surplus and hence for the smooth working of the system. Since surplus which cannot be absorbed will not be produced, it follows that the *normal* state of the monopoly capitalist economy is stagnation. With a given stock of capital and a given cost and price structure, the system's operating rate cannot rise above the point at which the amount of surplus produced can find the necessary outlets. And this means chronic under-utilization of available human and material resources. . . .

5

Counteracting forces do exist. If they did not, the system would indeed long since have fallen of its own weight. It therefore becomes a matter of the greatest importance to understand the nature and implications of these counteracting forces . . . .

The self-contradictory character of monopoly capitalism—its chronic inability to absorb as much surplus as it is capable of producing —impresses itself on the ordinary citizen in a characteristic way. To him, the economic problem appears to be the very opposite of what the textbooks say it is: not how best to utilize scarce resources but how to dispose of the products of superabundant resources. And this holds regardless of his wealth or position in society. If he is a worker, the ubiquitous fact of unemployment teaches him that the supply of labor is always greater than the demand. If he is a farmer, he struggles to stay afloat in a sea of surpluses. If he is a businessman, his sales persistently fall short of what he could profitably produce. Always too much, never too little.

This condition of affairs is peculiar to monopoly capitalism. The very notion of "too much" would have been inconceivable to all pre-capitalist forms of society; and even in the competitive stage of capitalism, it described a temporary derangement, not a normal condition. In a rationally ordered socialist society, no matter how richly endowed it might be with natural resources and technology and human skills, "too much" could only be a welcome signal to shift attention to an area of "too little." Only under monopoly capitalism does "too much" appear as a pervasive problem affecting everyone at all times.

From this source stem a whole series of attitudes and interests of crucial importance for the character and functioning of monopoly capitalist society. On the one hand, there is a stubborn spirit of restrictionism which pervades the institutional structure.[24] Union featherbedding and Henry Wallace's plowing under of little pigs are only the best publicized example of practices which are all but universal in business and government: the most primitive reaction to an excess of supply is simply to cut back. During the 1930's, when "too much" took on the dimensions of a universal disaster, primitive restrictionism acquired, in the National Industrial Recovery Act and the National Recovery Administration, the dignity and sanction of official national policy.

But cutting back as a remedy for "too much," even if beneficial to particular groups or individuals, only aggravates the situation as a

---

[24]This is what the French, by a somewhat attenuated logic, call Malthusianism.

whole. A secondary and more sophisticated set of attitudes and policies therefore emerges, gropingly and slowly at first but with increasing purposefulness and momentum as monopoly capitalism develops. Their rationale derives from the simple fact that the obverse of "too much" on the supply side is "too little" on the demand side; instead of cutting back supply they aim at stimulating demand.

The stimulation of demand—the creation and expansion of markets—thus becomes to an ever greater degree the leitmotif of business and government policies under monopoly capitalism. But this statement, true as it is, can easily be misleading. There are many conceivable ways of stimulating demand. If a socialist society, for example, should find that through some planning error more consumer goods were being produced than could be sold, given the existing structure of prices and incomes, the simplest and most direct remedy would clearly be to cut prices.[25] This would reduce the amount of surplus at the disposal of the planning authorities and correspondingly raise the purchasing power of consumers. The threatened glut could be quickly and painlessly averted: everyone would be better off, no one worse off. Such a course of action is obviously not open to a monopoly capitalist society, in which the determination of prices is the jealously guarded prerogative of the giant corporations. Each makes its own decisions with a view to maximizing its own private profit. Except for short periods of all-out war, when inflationary pressures threaten the entire economic and social fabric, there is no agency charged with controlling prices. Moreover, every attempt to maintain or establish such an agency in peacetime has resulted either in ignominious failure (witness the fiasco of price control after the Second World War) or in the thinly disguised legalization of monopoly pricing practices in "regulated" industries. The plain fact is that the pricing process is controlled by the most powerful vested interests in monopoly capitalist society. To imagine that it could possibly be regulated in the public interest would be to imagine away the very characteristics of that society which make it what it is.

If stimulation of demand through price reduction is impossible within the framework of monopoly capitalism, this cannot be said of other possible methods. Take, for example, advertising and related forms of salesmanship ... Every giant corporation is driven by the logic of its situation to devote more and more attention and resources to the

---

[25]See Kalecki, *Theory of Economic Dynamics,* London, 1954, pp. 62–63.

sales effort. And monopoly capitalist society as a whole has every interest in promoting rather than restricting and controlling this method of creating new markets and expanding old ones.

Just as with price cutting and salesmanship, other forms of stimulating demand either are or are not compatible with the pattern of interests, the structure of power, the web of ideology that constitute the essence of monopoly capitalist society. Those which are compatible will be fostered and promoted; those which are incompatible will be ignored or inhibited. The question for monopoly capitalism is not whether to stimulate demand. It must, on pain of death.

The question is how to stimulate demand. And here, . . . the system has its own built-in selective mechanisms which have the most far-reaching consequences for every aspect of life in monopoly capitalist society. . . .

6

. . . With the law of rising surplus replacing the law of the falling tendency of the rate of profit, and with normal modes of surplus utilization patently unable to absorb a rising surplus, the question of other modes of surplus utilization assumes crucial importance. That they should be there in large and growing volume becomes a life-and-death issue for the system. And as they grow relative to capitalists' consumption and accumulation, they increasingly dominate the composition of social output, the rate of economic growth, and the quality of society itself.

One of these alternative modes of utilization we call the sales effort. . . . In its impact on the economy, it is outranked only by militarism. In all other aspects of social existence, its all-pervasive influence is second to none.

The tremendous growth of the sales effort and the spectacular intensification of its sway stem from its having undergone a far-reaching qualitative change. Price competition has largely receded as a means of attracting the public's custom, and has yielded to new ways of sales promotion: advertising, variation of the products' appearance and packaging, "planned obsolescence," model changes, credit schemes, and the like.

In an economic system in which competition is fierce and relentless and in which the fewness of the rivals rules out price cutting, advertising becomes to an ever increasing extent the principal weapon of the competitive struggle. . . .

7

... What indeed would happen to a market continually plagued by insufficient demand? And what would happen to an economic system suffering from chronic underconsumption, underinvestment, and underemployment? For the economic importance of advertising lies not primarily in its causing a reallocation of consumers' expenditures among different commodities but in its effect on the magnitude of aggregate effective demand and thus on the level of income and employment. This has been readily grasped by professors of marketing and advertising as well as by business journalists, but with few exceptions it has been ignored by economic theorists. . . .

The direct impact of the sales effort on the income and output structure of the economy is therefore similar to that of government spending financed by tax revenue. This impact, measured by what has come to be called in economic literature the "balanced budget multiplier," is to expand aggregate income and output by an amount as large as the original revenue (and outlay). And of course the expansion of aggregate income is associated with higher employment of unproductive workers in advertising agencies, advertising media, and the like. . . . The function of advertising, perhaps its dominant function today, thus becomes that of waging, on behalf of the producers and sellers of consumer goods, a relentless war against saving and in favor of consumption. And the principal means of carrying out this task are to induce changes in fashion, create new wants, set new standards of status, enforce new norms of propriety. The unquestioned success of advertising in achieving these aims has greatly strengthened its role as a force counteracting monopoly capitalism's tendency to stagnation and at the same time marked it as the chief architect of the famous "American Way of Life."

. . . Just as advertising, product differentiation, artificial obsolescence, model changing, and all the other devices of the sales effort do in fact promote and increase sales, and thus act as indispensable props to the level of income and employment, so the entire apparatus of "finance, insurance, and real estate" is essential to the normal functioning of the corporate system and another no less indispensable prop to the level of income and employment. The prodigious volume of resources absorbed in all these activities does in fact constitute necessary costs of capitalist production. What should be crystal clear is that an economic system in which *such* costs are socially necessary has long ceased to be a socially necessary economic system. . . .

8

In the preceding [paragraphs] it was shown that the sales effort absorbs, directly and indirectly, a large amount of surplus which otherwise would not have been produced. . . .

Under monopoly capitalism, . . . the normal condition is less than capacity production. The system simply does not generate enough "effective demand" (to use the Keynesian term) to insure full utilization of either labor or productive facilities. If these idle resources can be put to work, they can produce not only necessary means of subsistence for the producers but also additional amounts of surplus. Hence if government creates more effective demand, it can increase its command over goods and services without encroaching on the incomes of its citizens. This creation of effective demand can take the form of direct government purchases of goods and services, or of "transfer payments" to groups which can somehow make good their claims for special treatment (subsidies to businessmen and farmers, doles to the unemployed, pensions to the aged, and so on) . . . .

. . . The vast and growing amounts of surplus absorbed by government in recent decades are not, we repeat, deductions from what would otherwise be available to corporations and individuals for their private purposes. The structure of the monopoly capitalist economy is such that a continually mounting volume of surplus simply could not be absorbed through private channels; if no other outlets were available, it would not be produced at all. What government absorbs is in addition to, not subtracted from, private surplus. Even more: since a larger volume of government spending pushes the economy nearer to capacity operation, and since up to this point surplus grows more rapidly than effective demand as a whole, it follows that both the government and the private segments of surplus can and indeed typically do grow simultaneously. It is only when government absorption continues to expand even after full utilization has been reached, as during the later years of the Second World War, that private surplus is encroached upon. . . .

The American ruling class, at any rate its leading echelon of managers of giant corporations, has learned these lessons through the rich experience of three decades of depression, war, and Cold War. And its attitude toward taxation and government spending has undergone a fundamental change. The older hostility to any expansion of government activities has not of course disappeared. In the realm of ideology, deeply rooted attitudes never disappear quickly. Moreover, in some sections of the ruling class—especially rentiers and smaller businessmen —hatred of the tax collector dominates feelings about the role of government. But the modern Big Businessman, though he sometimes speaks the traditional language, no longer takes it so seriously as his ancestors. To him, government spending means more effective demand, and he senses that he can shift most of the associated taxes forward onto consumers or backward onto workers. In addition—and this point is of great importance in understanding the subjective attitudes of Big Businessmen—the intricacies of the tax system, specially tailored to fit the needs of all sorts of special interests, open up endless opportunities for speculative and windfall gains. . . .

9

During the interval 1929–1957, total government spending increased from roughly one tenth to one quarter of GNP, most of the difference representing absorption of surplus which would otherwise not have been produced. . . .

It is of course in the area of defense purchases that most of the expansion has taken place—from less than 1 percent of GNP to more than 10 percent, accounting for about two thirds of the total expansion of government spending relative to GNP since the 1920's. This massive absorption of surplus in military preparations has been the key fact of postwar American economic history. Some six or seven million workers, more than 9 percent of the labor force, are now dependent for jobs on the arms budget. If military spending were reduced once again to pre-Second World War proportions, the nation's economy would return to a state of profound depression, characterized by unemployment rates of 15 percent and up, such as prevailed during the 1930's. . . .

The New Deal managed to push government spending up by more than 70 percent, but this was nowhere near enough to bring the economy to a level at which human and material resources were fully employed. Resistance of the oligarchy to further expansion in civilian spending hardened and held with unemployment still well above 15 percent of the labor force. By 1939 it was becoming increasingly clear that liberal reform had sadly failed to rescue United States monopoly capitalism from its own self-destructive tendencies. As Roosevelt's second term approached its end, a profound sense of frustration and uneasiness crept over the country.

Then came the war, and with it salvation. Government spending soared and unemployment plummeted. . . .

... The need of the American oligarchy for a large and growing military machine is a logical corollary of its purpose to contain, compress, and eventually destroy the rival world socialist system. ...

... What really interests the giant multinational corporations which dominate American policy. What they want is *monopolistic control* over foreign sources of supply and foreign markets, enabling them to buy and sell on specially privileged terms, to shift orders from one subsidiary to another, to favor this country or that depending on which has the most advantageous tax, labor, and other policies—in a word, they want to do business on their own terms and wherever they choose. And for this what they need is not trading partners but "allies" and clients willing to adjust their laws and policies to the requirements of American Big Business. ...

It would be misleading to leave the impression that only the oligarchy has favored the steady increase in military spending during these years. If one assumes the permanence of monopoly capitalism, with its proved incapacity to make rational use for peaceful and humane ends of its enormous productive potential, one must decide whether one prefers the mass unemployment and hopelessness characteristic of the Great Depression or the relative job security and material well-being provided by the huge military budgets of the 1940's and 1950's. Since most Americans, workers included, still do assume without question the permanence of the system, it is only natural that they should prefer the situation which is personally and privately more advantageous. And in order to rationalize this preference, they have accepted the official ideology of anti-Communism which appears to justify an unlimited expansion of the military establishment as essential to national survival.

10

... The real battlefields between capitalism and socialism have for years now been in Asia, Africa, and Latin America—in Korea, Vietnam, Algeria, Cuba, the Congo. The United States has been directly and militarily involved in most of these battles, and there is every reason to think that the leaders of the American oligarchy expect to go on being involved on an increasing scale in the future. This is the plain meaning of the increasing emphasis within the American military establishment on conventional arms, on building up so-called "counter-insurgency" and "special" forces, on the type of military planning and deployment of troops and supplies. ...

These activities will continue and grow. They will undoubtedly lead to a long series of catastrophes, crises, and confrontations—of a kind with which we are already all too familiar. What does not seem likely is that they can provide any substitute for the nuclear arms race as an object for military spending. The fateful question "on what?" to which monopoly capitalism can find no answer in the realm of civilian spending has crept subversively into the military establishment itself. From all present indications there is no answer there either.

THE IRRATIONAL SYSTEM

. . . Behind the emptiness, the degradation, and the suffering which poison human existence in this society lies the profound irrationality and moral bankruptcy of monopoly capitalism itself. No outraged protests, no reforms within the monopoly capitalist framework can arrest the decay of the whole. And as becomes clearer every day, this decay makes increasingly problematical the rationality of even the most spectacular advances in scientific knowledge and technical and organizational skills. Improvements in the means of mass communication merely hasten the degeneration of popular culture. The utmost perfection in the manufacture of weapons of destruction does not make their production rational. The irrationality of the end negates all improvements of the means. Rationality itself becomes irrational. We have reached a point where the only true rationality lies in action to overthrow what has become a hopelessly irrational system.

Will such action be forthcoming in sufficient volume and intensity to accomplish its purpose? The future of the United States and of monopoly capitalism obviously depends on the answer. So also, though more indirectly, does the future of mankind itself for a long time to come.

The answer of traditional Marxian orthodoxy—that the industrial proletariat must eventually rise in revolution against its capitalist oppressors—no longer carries conviction. Industrial workers are a diminishing minority of the American working class, and their organized cores in the basic industries have to a large extent been integrated into the system as consumers and ideologically conditioned members of the society. They are not, as the industrial workers were in Marx's day, the system's special victims, although they suffer from its elementality and irrationality along with all other classes and strata—more than some, less than others.

The system of course has its special victims. They are the unemployed and the unemployable, the migrant farm workers, the inhabitants of the big city ghettos, the school dropouts, the aged subsisting on meager pensions—in a word, the outsiders, those who because of their limited command over purchasing power are unable to avail themselves of the gratifications, such as they are, of consumption. But these groups, despite their impressive numbers, are too heterogeneous, too scattered and fragmented, to constitute a coherent force in society. And the oligarchy knows how, through doles and handouts, to keep them divided and to prevent their becoming a lumpen-proletariat of desperate starvelings.[26]

If we confine attention to the inner dynamics of advanced monopoly capitalism, it is hard to avoid the conclusion that the prospect of effective revolutionary action to overthrow the system is slim. Viewed from this angle, the more likely course of development would seem to be a continuation of the present process of decay, with the contradiction between the compulsions of the system and the elementary needs of human nature becoming ever more insupportable. The logical outcome would be the spread of increasingly severe psychic disorders leading to the impairment and eventual breakdown of the system's ability to function even on its own terms.[27]

. . . Advanced monopoly capitalism does not exist in isolation, and any speculation about its future which takes account only of its inner laws and tendencies is certain to be misleading. The United States dominates and exploits to one extent or another all the countries and territories of the so-called "free world" and correspondingly meets with

---

[26]These are of course the objectives of the Johnson administration's so-called war on poverty.

[27]That we may already be entering such a stage is suggested by the findings of the so-called Midtown Manhattan Study, by far the most thorough investigation yet undertaken of the mental health of a large population sample. Based on eight years of research in a relatively well-to-do, all-white area in New York City, and referring only to adults between ages 20 and 59, this Study found that only 18.5 percent of the sample could be classified as Well, i.e., free from significant symptoms. The Mild and Moderate levels of symptom formation accounted for 36.3 and 21.8 percent of the sample respectively. The Marked, Severe, and Incapacitated were 13.2, 7.5, and 2.7 percent respectively. Thus over four fifths of the sample were found to be suffering from some identifiable form of mental disturbance, and nearly a quarter were "in the impaired range of the mental health continuum." Leo Srole and others, *Mental Health in the Metropolis: The Midtown Manhattan Study,* New York, Toronto, London, 1962, p. 342.

varying degrees of resistance. The highest form of resistance is revolutionary war aimed at withdrawal from the world capitalist system and the initiation of social and economic reconstruction on a socialist basis. Such warfare has never been absent since the Second World War, and the revolutionary peoples have achieved a series of historic victories in Vietnam, China, Korea, Cuba, and Algeria. These victories, taken together with the increasingly obvious inability of the underdeveloped countries to solve their problems within the framework of the world capitalist system, have sown the seeds of revolution throughout the continents of Asia, Africa, and Latin America. Some of these seeds will sprout and ripen rapidly, others slowly, still others perhaps not until after a long period of germination. What seems in any case clear is that they are now implanted beyond any prospect of extirpation. It is no longer mere rhetoric to speak of the world revolution: the term describes what is already a reality and is certain to become increasingly the dominant characteristic of the historical epoch in which we live.

The implications of this fact for the future of monopoly capitalism are only beginning to become apparent. The ruling class of the United States understands, instinctively and through experience, that every advance of the world revolution is a defeat—economic, political and moral—for itself. It is determined to resist such advances wherever they may threaten, by whatever means may be available; and it counts on its enormous superiority in the technology of warfare to bring it victory. But the truth is that in this struggle there can be no real victories for the counter-revolutionary side. Underlying the revolutionary upsurge are real economic, social, and demographic problems; and it is the very nature of counter-revolution to prevent these problems from being rationally attacked, let alone solved. Counter-revolution may win, indeed already has won, many battles, but the war goes on and inexorably spreads to new peoples and new regions. And as it spreads so does the involvement of the United States.

No one can now foresee all the consequences for the United States of this increasing commitment to the cause of world counter-revolution, but equally no one can doubt that it will profoundly affect the inner as well as the outer course of events. In the long run its main impact may well be on the youth of the nation. The need for military manpower seems certain to rise sharply; it may soon be normal for young Americans to spend several years of their lives, if they are lucky enough to survive, fighting in the jungles and mountains of Asia, Africa, and Latin America. The psychic stress and physical suffering experienced by them and their families will add a new dimension to the agony inflicted by an anti-human social order. Will the effect be merely to hasten the process of decay already so far advanced? Will the shock perhaps awaken more and more people to the urgent need for basic change? Or will, as some believe, the increasingly evident hopelessness of its cause lead the American ruling class to the ultimate irrationality of unleashing nuclear holocaust?

That no one can now answer these questions means that all the options are not foreclosed, that action aimed at altering the course of events has a chance to succeed. There are even indications, especially in the Negro freedom movement in the South, in the uprisings of the urban ghettos, and in the academic community's mounting protest against the war in Vietnam, that significant segments of the American people are ready to join an active struggle against what is being cumulatively revealed as an intolerable social order. If this is so, who can set limits to the numbers who may join them in the future?

But even if the present protest movements should suffer defeat or prove abortive, that would be no reason to write off permanently the possibility of a real revolutionary movement in the United States. As the world revolution spreads and as the socialist countries show by their example that it is possible to use man's mastery over the forces of nature to build a rational society satisfying the human needs of human beings, more and more Americans are bound to question the necessity of what they now take for granted. And once that happens on a mass scale, the most powerful supports of the present irrational system will crumble and the problem of creating anew will impose itself as a sheer necessity. This will not happen in five years or ten, perhaps not in the present century: few great historical dramas run their course in so short a time. But perhaps even fewer, once they are fairly started, change their nature or reverse their direction until all their potentialities have been revealed. The drama of our time is the world revolution; it can never come to an end until it has encompassed the whole world.

In the meantime, what we in the United States need is historical perspective, courage to face the facts, and faith in mankind and its future. Having these, we can recognize our moral obligation to devote ourselves to fighting against an evil and destructive system which maims, oppresses, and dishonors those who live under it, and which threatens devastation and death to millions of others around the globe.

15

◀ MICHAEL HARRINGTON* ▶

from

The Accidental Century (1965)

The fact that Michael Harrington is a member of the American Socialist Party would be enough to qualify him as a radical to many Americans. Socialism is still an ill-defined and often unacceptable word in this country, although most Americans are convinced that we are somehow headed toward it. In one important respect, however, they are wrong, for socialism necessarily implies the ownership and control of the means of production by the community as a whole. This is clearly not the case in America where the ownership and control of the means of production remains in the hands of private interests. Although nationalization is still a part of the socialists' general program, to Harrington ownership is not as vital as bringing the production and distribution of wealth under democratic control. He notes that "one of the most basic tendencies of the contemporary technological revolution [is] to collectivize economic and social life." The control of this increasingly collective society by a corporate elite is described by Harrington as undemocratic and antisocialist. Thus, according to Harrington, the use to which technology will be put cannot be left to the private interests of the corporate managers, but must be directed toward social needs by conscious and democratic

---

*Chairman of the board of the League for Industrial Democracy.

means. It is the unplanned use of technology which has given the twentieth century its present accidental character.*

Harrington maintains that the solutions to social problems such as housing, clean air, education, and ghetto employment, are not well suited to the goals of the profit-motivated private sector. This is chiefly because the solutions to these problems will most often require uneconomical decisions which the business community is not trained to make. Even if the benevolent corporation did appear, its actions, according to Harrington, would still not be subject to the control of society. Harrington clearly resists what he sees as an "evolutionary trend toward subordinating the social good to private purpose." Reacting against the growing cooperation between government and business in an attempt to cure social ills, Harrington has stated that "government power under the present system tends to promote the common good by granting unjust rewards to the special interests of business." Harrington fears this social–industrial complex as much as he does the military–industrial one, because it places the control over, and planning for, social programs in the hands of "self-interested executives and ambitious bureaucrats" who increasingly make decisions without taking society into account. To Harrington the government should have the responsibility of setting up national priorities within which the productive sector would play a subordinate role. It is through the planning of these priorities that the community would be able to exercise control over the allocation of productive resources in the economy. If the future is to be a truly democratic one, Harrington calls for Americans to realize that the obligations of the public and private sectors are separate and that they must be willing to set up the democratic institutions "which can make the humane although often commercially wasteful decisions that America needs."

Harrington perceives that the solution to social problems is a political question. His willingness to work within the existing system of political parties clearly places him on the right wing of the radical movement. Harrington has correctly characterized himself as a "radical who belongs to the liberal community." Liberals on the whole view him as "rather respectable," and he has had a noticeable influence on the professional reformers described in Moynihan's article.† *The Other America,* his most well-known book to date, is often credited with

---

*"This accidental revolution is the sweeping and unprecedented technological transformation of the Western environment which has been, and is being, carried out in a casual way. In it, this technology is essentially under private control and used for private purposes. . . . In following their individual aims, industrialists blundered into a social revolution. There is indeed an invisible hand in all of this. Only it is shaping an unstable new world rather than Adam Smith's middle-class harmony."

†See chapter 12.

motivating the War on Poverty. Unlike many radicals Harrington has outlined a political program of action to direct American capitalism along the lines which he feels it must go. His insistence that the movement toward a democratically-controlled collectivist society must be a gradual, evolutionary, one separates him from other radicals and makes him politically palatable to liberals. Although Harrington cannot claim credit for originating such an approach, his pragmatic nature separates him from many other radicals who expect immediate and uncompromising change. Harrington's willingness to debate the critical issues of our time and to promote change within the existing system may very well propel his ideas into the mainstream of liberalism. If this happens, as it already has in a limited way, then Harrington may well prove to be one of the most influential socialists in American history.

—R. R.

from

*The Accidental Century**

The average nineteenth-century prophet thought that capitalism would end volcanically. Its contradictions, it was said, would one day burst the system asunder.

Now, another metaphor may become more apt: Capitalism is moving toward its end massively, imperceptibly, like a glacier. Its decadence is cold, not hot.

Thomas Mann's images of disorder were, from World War I on, evoked by the violent apocalypse. But in *Buddenbrooks,* he wrote of a less dramatic change, the defeat of the merchant oligarchs by the new businessmen. That development, which Mann only glimpsed, was but the beginning of a process: the pacific war of capitalism against capitalism, the gentle apocalypse. This quiet decadence persisted as a possibility when the economic breakdowns, revolutions, and counter-revolutions did not destroy the established order. And since its progress is recorded by statistical increments rather than by masses in the street, since it is gradual enough to allow the old rhetoric to mask the new reality, it is more difficult to observe than the collapse of a nation or the disintegration of a social class.

---

*Reprinted with permission of The Macmillan Company from *The Accidental Century* by Michael Harrington. Copyright © Michael Harrington, 1965.

Three aspects of the cold decadence of capitalism suggest its character. The capitalist economy is destroying the capitalist civilization and personality; in the process, businessmen are building a collective society for private profit; and, as a result, it is the corporation rather than the Communist Party which is the major Western institution moving toward a convergence with the Soviet example.

I

The civilization of capitalism—not its economic mechanism, but its culture, its morality, its idealism—is being destroyed by the capitalist economy. The expropriation of traditional values is thus being carried out by unwitting businessmen rather than by revolutionary proletarians.

Historically, capitalism appeared as an ethic as well as a system of production. The competitive individual with his absolute right to private property served his fellowmen by seeking his own profit. It was the free market, an invisible hand fixing prices, allocating resources to their best use and so on, which vectored all the antagonistic personal greeds into a common good. In such a theory, the making of money was a virtue since it promoted individualism, innovation and the wealth of the entire society.

In the Protestant version of the capitalist morality, riches were the reward of the righteously ascetic. In the French Physiocrat's view, private property was the very basis of freedom itself. As A. A. Berle summarized this doctrine, "if a man was to be free, able to speak his own mind, depict his own thought and develop his own personality, he would have to have a base apart from one that was politically or ecclesiastically organized and controlled." That base was private property.

The idyll described in these visions did not, of course, exist. The millions who were degraded in the teeming new cities were the victims of the accident of their birth rather than the products of an economic selection of the fit and unfit. They demonstrated this fact when they formed the labor and socialist movement and educated the wealthy in some of the fundamentals of humanity. And yet, there was some relationship between the workings of the economy and the right-eousness felt by the entrepreneur. If business early learned the value of state subsidy and tariff protection, there was still competition. The

invisible hand of the market regularly misallocated resources and precipitated depressions, but over the long run (with the modifications imposed upon it by the supposedly incompetent majority), more and
more goods were manufactured and distributed.

Under such circumstances, it did not take utter hypocrisy or
ignorance to profess the capitalist faith sincerely.

At the same time, the predictions of violent capitalist breakdown were tenable enough to corroborate the traditional socialist
expectation. For most of the twentieth century it did indeed seem that
the system would end apocalyptically. In the thirty-one years between
1914 and 1945, there were two world wars, the Russian Revolution,
aborted revolutions throughout Central Europe, the Great Depression,
Italian fascism, and the barbaric retrogression of Nazism. The data
gave comfort to the "catastrophic optimism" of Karl Marx (the phrase
is Raymond Aron's).

After World War II, however, events altered the classic perspective. The United States did not undergo its scheduled depression
and instead reconverted to prosperity. This allowed it to subsidize the
reorganization of capitalism in Western Europe. The renaissance of
the Continental economy profoundly affected the labor and socialist
movements. They largely abandoned the doctrine of the class struggle
and accepted the welfare state and mixed economy as their ideal.

Capitalism enjoyed an unprecedented internal security from
everything but itself.

It was in this period that the capitalist economy took the most
vigorous measures against the capitalist ideology. And perhaps the
twenty years of postwar capitalist success destroyed more of the capitalist ethic than the thirty-one years of intrawar capitalist failure.
This was the process of the cold decadence.

The capitalist destruction of the capitalist ethic took place primarily through the private collectivization of the Western economy for
minority profit.

A few anticipated this process and many have described it
after the fact. The industrialist and mystic, Walter Rathenau, talked
as early as 1917 (in a book entitled *Von Kommenden Dingen—Of
Coming Things*) of an economy in which corporations would generate
their own resources, free themselves from any real relation to the
individual investor or the market, and become anonymous, self-sufficient
automatons. Vatican sociology has often expressed a similar fear. In
Mater et Magistra, John XXIII wrote, "In fact, by its own deep-seated

and, as it were, intrinsic tendencies, free competition has almost destroyed itself. It has brought about a great accumulation of wealth
and a corresponding concentration of economic power in the hands
of a few 'who are frequently not the owners but only the trustees and
managers of invested funds, which they administer at their own
pleasure.' " (The quotation is from Pius XI in 1931.)

There are many statistical descriptions of this process and there
is no point in rehearsing them at any length here. A few figures should
suffice to outline a reality which is daily becoming more and more
unmistakable. Their relevance to this chapter is that each one of these
changes in economic structure marks an ethical event, the passing of
a virtue.

In the place of the old competition, there is now a "corporate
socialism" (the phrase is Estes Kefauver's) or a "collective capitalism"
(Gardiner C. Means). Instead of a multiplicity of producers confronting one another in the market, there were in 1962 in America 500
corporations with $229.1 billion in sales—or more than half the sales
and 70 percent of the total profit of the economy. The United States,
as the most advanced industrial nation, became the most anticapitalist
without knowing it.

This enormous concentration of corporate power had been particularly dynamic in the post-World War II period. Between 1947 and
1954, the 100 largest companies had increased their share of manufacturing from 23 percent to 30 percent; and the 200 top units
controlled fully 37 percent of manufacturing. In American slang, one
spoke of the Big Three in automobiles (actually, the Big Two and
nearly the Big One), of the Big Four in steel, the Big Three in
chemicals, and so on.

In 1964 the U.S. News & World Report, a conservative business magazine, announced that 25 percent of all American profit had
gone to seven companies: General Motors, the American Telephone
and Telegraph Company, Standard Oil of New Jersey, Texaco, Ford,
Gulf Oil, and International Business Machines. In 1956, the same seven
corporations had cornered "only" 16.6 percent of the profits. In short,
the concentration of the rewards of production was even more acute
than the concentration of the volume of production.

There were attempts to explain this development away by
arguing that it had been accompanied by the diffusion of stock ownership. In part, this was simply less true than the proponents of the
thesis thought. In a 1963 National Bureau of Economic Research

study, Robert J. Lampmann pointed out that 1.6 percent of the adult population of the United States held 82.4 percent of the publicly held shares. Insofar as a larger number of people did hold some stock, this represented a growth in the total of helpless, impotent small stockholders whose fragmented "ownings" had little to do with how corporations acted.

As a result of this concentration of corporate power, more and more companies were freed from the law of supply and demand. The most dramatic form of this development was the "administered price," in which the cost of an item on the market was determined, not by how much how many buyers were willing to pay, but in order to return a set profit. So it was that a Senate Committee in the 1950's revealed that General Motors "targeted" its profits for a "20% rate of return on the net worth after taxes at a predetermined level of production, or standard volume." Actually, the intention in this case was modest, since the company in question regularly reached profit levels of 25 percent and above.

Gardiner C. Means, one of the first American economists to theorize about this transformation, estimates that General Electric and Du Pont also have target rates of 20 percent after taxes, that Union Carbide seeks a 15 percent, and that U.S. Steel in the fifties increased its target from a traditional 8 percent to a goal of perhaps as high as 15 percent.

There is a most instructive irony in all of this, one which reveals how a businessman can be a revolutionist without noticing it.

During the New Deal, when most of management was talking of the destruction of cherished values, the Administration set up a National Planning Board. It explored the possibilities of "facilitative planning" (a rough equivalent of the "indicative planning" practiced in France, to be described shortly). In the course of its work, the Board developed production-consumption patterns which indicated how people would spend their money at different levels of economic activity and what the production and employment requirements would be at these levels.

Gardiner Means, who was the Board's Director of Research, notes that the main practical use of this technique by the Government was made during World War II. The military sector was analyzed in terms of production-consumption relationships, and input-output analysis was employed in one of the vastest industrial efforts of all time. After the war, some of these ideas survived, but modestly, in the

Employment Act of 1946 and the activities of the Council of Economic Advisers.

But, and here the irony surfaces, the large corporations had become so huge that they could take up these methods which had been worked out for the national economy. Thus, General Electric estimated the demand for electrical appliances at full employment, and then decided what proportion of the market it would plan to supply. This same company is one of the most politically conservative in the United States, and would be appalled if the Government were to emulate the planning techniques of the profit-making corporations, techniques which the Government itself has developed. General Electric, and many giants like it, has emancipated itself from most of the capitalist verities but not the capitalist rhetoric.

This contradiction in which businessmen consciously violate the economic laws that they proclaim is not limited to a few of the largest corporations. Texas oilmen, the most aggressive of America's millionaire conservatives, invest mightily in the propagation of *laissez-faire,* pure and simple, and especially simple. They are able to do so because they operate in an industry in which production is strictly controlled under law and with their support. The Farm Bureau, the organization which represents the wealthy American farmers who receive over $4 billion in annual subsidy, predictably opposes degrading "handouts" to poor farmers. This near-comic opposition of greed and principle is only one aspect of the historic corruption of capitalism by capitalism. Occasionally, though, someone does talk of the *Emperor's Clothes.*

In the thirties, Russell Leffingwell of Morgan's told an investigating committee, "The growth of corporate enterprise has been drying up individual independence and initiative. . . . We are becoming a nation of hired men. Hired by great aggregates of capital."

With the corporate giants able to remove price and profit from the vagaries of the free market, they were also able to collectivize inventiveness. In the United States, where military research and development played such a major role in the postwar economy, some two-thirds of this technological pioneering was financed directly or indirectly by the Government. In every Western nation, inventive genius had become rationalized through research bureaucracies.

A similar process took place in another area where business was theoretically supposed to submit to the judgment of the free economy: the money market. In fulfillment of Rathenau's 1917 prophecy that the corporation would be able to divorce itself from the individual investor, the American companies more and more raised their capital from themselves. A. A. Berle has estimated that, from 1947 to 1956, the United States economy raised $292 billion in investment funds. Of this enormous sum, 60 percent was financed from retained profits, and 40 percent from "outside" the corporations. But even this latter figure was deceptive, since the "outside" was not primarily composed of thinking, judging risktakers, but of insurance companies, mutual funds, pension trusts, and other institutions whose adventurousness is limited by law or tradition.

Some of the elements of capitalist collectivization, then, are the concentration of economic power, the consequent ability to "administer" prices to an economy rather than responding to the law of supply and demand, the utilization of profit targets and planning techniques, the statification of inventiveness, and the abolition of risk in the money market. Making money had been declared virtuous because it promoted individualism, inventiveness, and the productive taking of chances. Now, each one of these qualities had been largely negated by the system. Adam Smith had thought that the corporation was hopelessly medieval, since it represented the anonymous control of someone else's money, and this contradicted the spiritual essence and genius of capitalism. By the mid-twentieth century, the corporation was capitalism.

The developing new system created new kinds of people.

In *The Lonely Crowd,* David Riesman perceptively described the personality evoked by the old reality and ethic. The "inner-directed" entrepreneur lived on a social frontier between feudalism and capitalism. He therefore consciously chose his individualism and his values, operating on a sort of internal gyroscope. In the twentieth century, however, wealth had become a function of manipulation and organization. There appeared the "other-directed" man, the team player who needed radar rather than a gyroscope, who took his values from others —when he could find them.

C. A. R. Crosland described a similar change in England. "The old style capitalist was by instinct a tyrant and an aristocrat who cared for no one's approval. The new style executive prides himself on being a good committee man, and subconsciously longs for the approval of the sociologist." In France, Pierre Bauchet has documented the way in which the new directors, bureaucrats of capital rather than entrepreneurs, find it natural and useful to integrate their "private" activities into a state plan.

But perhaps the most poignant case in point came to light in William H. Whyte's study of *The Organization Man.* Whyte wrote his book while working for *Fortune,* a business magazine. Though honest about the reality of capitalism, he is hardly its ideological opponent, and this led him to a hopeless contradiction. Whyte candidly described the way in which the corporation was invading, and consciously rationalizing, the very lives of its employees. Even the romantic concept of marriage, one of the great moral accomplishments of capitalist civilization, is bureaucratized as the company calculates a man's wife along with the rest of the assets and liabilities.

Having described this relentless progress of the organization, Whyte can recommend no resistance more profound than an interior aloofness. He counsels the young executive to be a sort of good businessman Schweik, defeating the system by disloyally playing its game. This individual act of disaffiliation is as far as Whyte can go, and thus the true believer in the individualistic truths of the old capitalist ethic becomes a fifth columnist within the actual capitalist economy.

In America, then, one can watch the cold decadence of capitalism as it transforms and collectivizes the executive personality. In Europe, however, these changes have become explicitly political.

France is the most illuminating example of this juridical denial of capitalist laws by capitalist economies. In the Paris of the early sixties, a conservative and nationalist general presided over the Fourth Plan and prepared the Fifth. His prime minister was a banker. They were both committed to a directed economy in which state planning is a means of mobilizing the entire society behind politically determined goals. They were also in favor of capitalism, or at least of extracting private profit from public effort. In this dual purpose of state plan and corporate gain, De Gaulle and Pompidou presented one of the most advanced instances of private collectivization.

The French Plan began immediately after the Second World War. In part, it was a culmination of the social consciousness of the Resistance; in part, it was a necessity imposed upon a war-torn nation which had to restore the very structure of its economy. By the mid-fifties, French planning had transcended both of the motives that presided over its birth. It had become conservative, or at least technocratic, rather than militant and plebian as in the Resistance ideal. And it was starting to plan in a context of relative affluence rather than of poverty.

Even during the extreme parliamentary instability of the last days of the Fourth Republic, the French economy continued to register high rates of growth (annual increments of over 5 percent were common in the mid-fifties). When General de Gaulle took power, he inherited the accomplishments of the Plan and turned them into a vision of a paternalistic, directed, and planned economy which would restore grandeur to the nation. (He also developed a curious thesis of a classless France in which workers, peasants, and the bourgeoisie would no longer contend among themselves but be tutored, on television, by the Leader.)

The Plan which was at the center of this philosophy does not in any way change the system of ownership or profit in France. It is "indicative" rather than compulsory, and the businessman is free to ignore its suggestions. Indeed, as critics of the Plan like Pierre Mendès-France have documented, even the nationalized enterprises, like Renault or the public banks, often violate the very guidelines of the Government which "owns" them. (In a society dominated by private corporations, public corporations absorb the former's methods, morality and immorality.) Yet, the Government's control of 50 percent of new investment is a powerful lever with which to secure conformity to the Plan.

On paper, there is a wide participation of all classes in the society in the planning process (this is the basis for De Gaulle's claim to a classless, cooperative France). In fact, the Fourth Plan was elaborated by commissions which were weighted over 90 percent toward businessmen and state functionaries—the distinction between the two categories is not always clear—and about 8 percent for worker and peasant unionists. Still, even if there were numerical equality between corporate and popular representatives, the businessmen would be at an enormous advantage. They command professional, paid research staffs and are thus in a position to understand and shape the Plan. The unions, by virtue of the very income and power structure of the society, count for less in these deliberations, whatever the representational mathematics.

The chief concept of the French Plan was, and is, a denial of one of the basic propositions of capitalist economics. Rather than allowing the "invisible hand" of the marketplace to determine the allocation of resources and rewards, the planners make a conscious and political choice of a growth rate to be achieved over a period of several years. Supply and demand are then adjusted to this decision, rather than the other way around. The result was a more harmonious development of the entire economy and an increase in the profit of the corporations that now have the state as a center for market research. But, as Gilbert Mathieu, the economic correspondent of Le Monde, noted in 1963, the relative inequities of income distribution increased between 1956 and 1961.

Indeed, there is a sense in which this maldistribution of income under the Plan is inevitable. When the state intervenes in an economy in which rewards are still assigned on the basis of private profit, then an increase in the general integration and efficiency of the society will benefit the rich. This might be offset by a vigorous and progressive tax policy, but this is certainly not the case in France (which, if anything, provides more scope for tax avoidance by the wealthy than the United States). As it is, one comes up with a system that combines the collective mode of planning with the private appropriation of money, a hybrid that moves away from both capitalism and socialism. And in terms of the distribution of wealth, the effect is for the entire community to subsidize those who are best off.

In American discussions, the embarrassing French example is usually countered with the German "miracle." In that country, it is said, the "social market economy" has observed the classic rules and prospered accordingly. However, as *Business Week* noted in the early sixties, the reality is a little less Adam Smithian than the claim: 55 percent of all investment in plant, equipment, and construction was financed by the state, and more than 40 percent of aluminum and more than 40 percent of auto, lead, and zinc production were also statified. (According to a high official of the French Commissariat du Plan, conversations between French and German planners in 1963 indicated that the two nations had an equal government intervention, albeit in different forms.)

Given such facts, it becomes somewhat more understandable that the British Conservative Party, in the name of antisocialism, should introduce national planning in their country. As George Lichtheim concluded from this case and others, the directed economies of Europe "may still be capitalist" but they "cannot any longer be described as bourgeois." Capitalism is destroying capitalist motivation, ideology, and even personality.

In the United States, however, this process has been somewhat more disguised than in Europe. In the absence of open government planning, America has preferred to carry out its collectivizations in the name of something called "free enterprise." Ironically, the French Commissariat du Plan sends a technician to America in order to learn planning methods from the corporations. For in this country, the exigencies of production demand planning as much as in Europe, only the piety of tradition will not allow the word to be spoken openly.

Even so, in the mid-sixties there were signs that American theory would at least begin to catch up with American practice. A majority report of the Senate Subcommittee on Employment and Manpower in 1964 urged conscious planning. And in the Housing Message of 1964, President Lyndon B. Johnson declared, "By 1970, we shall have to build at least two million new homes a year to keep up with the growth of our population. We will need many new classrooms, uncounted miles of new streets and utility lines, and an unprecedented volume of water and sewage facilities. We will need stores and churches and libraries, distribution systems for goods, transporation systems for people and communications systems for ideas. . . .

"Now is the time to direct the productive capacity of our home building industry to the great needs of the neglected segments of our population. . . . In the tradition of the long-established partnership between private industry and community development, the Federal Government should encourage and facilitate these new and desirable approaches."

Such a statement recognized that the housing needs of the nation were so complex and interrelated that they required both anticipation and planning. But, significantly, after the Federal Government had accomplished what the free market was once supposed to do— direct a broad allocation of resources—and after it had laid down the plans for the new communities and provided their infrastructure, they would be turned over to private builders for their profit. Here again, innovation is collectivized and profit privatized.

While the Europeans were carrying out frank social planning for private profit, America was doing the same thing shamefacedly. As a result, a conservative movement could arise in the United States and, in the logical name of all the hallowed truths, make the preposterous proposal to go back to *laissez faire*. And many of the wealthiest businessmen who supported this fantasy were themselves the most successful practitioners of the capitalist anticapitalism. The spectacle would be humorous were it not dangerous, yet clearly a society cannot long pay such an astronomical price for its rhetoric. Along with the old-fashioned virtues, the old-fashioned vocabulary will have to vanish.

In short, in the spiritual name of courageous, inventive, and risk-taking individuals, bureaucratized corporations, supported and subsidized by governments, were planning in increasing independence of the laws of supply and demand or the judgments of investors. Economic life was more and more dominated by anonymous collectivities, and a relatively few directors were making decisions that effected the existence of almost every citizen. The civilization of capitalism, its ethics, its morality, its philosophy, was being destroyed by the practice of capitalism.

And businessmen, without giving too much thought to the matter, were shaping new environments and new types of men.

II

If Karl Marx was the great prophet of the apocalyptic decadence of capitalism, of its violent breakdown, it was Joseph Schumpeter who most profoundly expressed its cold decadence. His feat was all the more remarkable in that he was a partisan, not a foe, of the system whose strange doom he described. He was, as Daniel Bell has said, that rare being, an economist with a sense of the tragic.

Indeed, one of the most remarkable things about Schumpeter is that he wrote his *Capitalism, Socialism and Democracy* in a time of the worldwide breakdown of the capitalist economy, yet he predicted that the system would be destroyed, not by its failures, but by its very accomplishments. Capitalism, he said, "through its very success undermines the social institutions which protect it, and 'inevitably' creates conditions in which it will not be able to live and which strongly point to socialism as the heir 'apparent.'" Setting aside for the moment Schumpeter's prediction of the coming of socialism, let's examine the thesis of the evolutionary subversion of capitalism.

Perhaps Schumpeter's most poetic statement of the theme is contained in an analogy between the medieval warrior and the modern businessman. Among other things, the knight was rendered obsolete by a weapons technology, by guns which democratized the battlefield and made a peasant or an artisan as lethal as a prince. Similarly, the capitalist is the victim of a technological change which, and the notion has a poignance, he himself brings about. "Since capitalist enterprise, by its very achievements, tends to automate progress, we conclude that it tends to make itself superfluous—to break into pieces under the pressure of its own success. The perfectly bureaucratized giant industrial unit only ousts the small or medium-sized firm, but in the end it also ousts the entrepreneur and expropriates the bourgeoisie as a class which in the process stands to lose not only its income but also what is infinitely more important, its function."

Like the social psychologists who came after him, Schumpeter understood that these changes in structure implied transformations of personal and ethical values as well: "The capitalist process, by substituting a mere parcel of shares for the walls of, and machines in, a factory, takes the life out of the idea of property. It loses the grip that was once so strong—the grip in the sense of the legal right and the actual ability to do as one pleases with one's own. . . . And this evaporation of what we may term the material substance of property—its visible and touchable reality—affects not only the attitudes of the holder but also that of the workmen and public in general. Denaturized, defunctionalized and absentee ownership does not impress and call forth moral allegiance as the vital form of property did."

The capitalist economy, Schumpeter realized, expropriated the capitalist civilization. "The scheme of values in capitalist society," he wrote, "though causally related to economic success, is losing its hold not only upon the public mind but also upon the 'capitalist' stratum itself."

At this moment in his analysis, Schumpeter developed a profound insight in the form of a confused prophecy and a bad definition. Socialism, he said, was the successor to that capitalist system which destroyed itself by accomplishing too much.

For Schumpeter, any society which centralized economic decision and in which the public sphere dominated the private was socialist. By reducing the term to a simple description of a way of organizing an economy, he narrowed, and radically so, the meaning that the socialist movement itself had given to its ideal. In Western European history and, above all, in the American socialist vision of Eugene Victor Debs, socialism stood for equality, solidarity, the elimination of class distinction, cooperation, and the fulfillment of democracy at least as much as for the nationalization of the means of production.

What Schumpeter did was to confuse socialism, which was and is a democratic program for a collectivist age, with collectivism itself (after the triumph of Joseph Stalin, the world Communist movement propagandized in favor of this same error). And yet, his very imprecision contains an important understanding on his part. "A society," Schumpeter wrote, "may be fully and truly socialist and yet be led by an absolute ruler or be organized in the most democratic of all possible ways." If one takes Schumpeter's "socialism" as a reference, not to the historical socialist dream of a democratic life, but to the collectivism which emerges out of capitalism, a significant truth appears.

Schumpeter understood that the political issue was not *whether* the future was to be collective, but *how* it was to be so. Collectivism could be the basis of the "most democratic" organization. It was not, as conservatives had held, inevitably cruel and totalitarian. But then, it could also support absolutism and authoritarianism. It was not, as some socialists had thought, inevitably benign and libertarian.

And so Schumpeter concluded on a note of profound ambiguity. Collectivism was inexorably being created by the "Vanderbilts, Carnegies and Rockefellers" more than by the revolutionary proletariat. But the social content of this irresistible trend, whether it would be egalitarian or dictatorial, humane or antihumanist, was not predetermined. The quality of the life of the future was still to be fashioned, and by men and not by economic patterns. In short, the question of freedom had been posed, not settled, by contemporary history.

III

Schumpeter's insight can be deepened by way of a further irony. The *laissez faire* ideologists had always charged that any form of collectivism would inevitably be bureaucratic and unfree. Today in the West there is indeed the possibility for the emergence of such an anthill society. It is promoted by unwitting businessmen, the spiritual children of *laissez faire.*

The basis for this paradox is fairly simple to describe. Capitalists are now in control of the transition to a non- and anticapitalist order. Their training and background prepare them to carry out such a transition in the most confused and self-contradictory way. Left to themselves, the managers will create a bureaucratic form of collectivism and thus emphasize the convergence of the Western and Soviet systems much more effectively than any of the Communist parties of Europe and America.

The potential of this development comes more and more to the surface in the discussions of corporate "responsibility." A section of the business community, disturbed by the disappearance of any clear management responsibility to stockholders or to the law of supply and demand or to owners—or any other classic source of legitimacy for economic power—has been trying to decide to whom, or to what, the corporations owe fealty. For if the classic morality of private property no longer describes who rules, and should rule, what does?

Some of these theorists have come up with a most revealing answer, usually put affirmatively, happily. The corporation, they argue, is becoming responsible to the public. But if this is so, then the managers no longer fulfill the virtue of making money. Now, they are making public policy. And then, as an insightful observer put it, one is watching "the frightening spectacle of a powerful economic group whose future and perceptions are shaped in a tight materialistic context of money and things but which imposes its narrow ideas about a broad spectrum of unrelated non-economic subjects on the mass of men and society."

The ambiguities of this corporate collectivism are perhaps most accessible in the writings of A. A. Berle.

Berle's analysis is particularly important in that he writes as a friend of the capitalist order and proponent of the notion that the corporation must develop a conscience. In 1932, he had joined Gardiner C. Means in writing *The Modern Corporation and Private Property*, one of the very first empirical studies to hold that in the capitalist society the capitalist himself—the property owner—no longer managed his enterprise. In his place stood an administrator, an executive, who made decisions but did not own. Since this seminal analysis, many writers have developed aspects of the Berle and Means thesis of the separation of ownership and control in advanced capitalist society. And Berle has attempted to come to legal and ethical grips with the consequences of the system of "power without property" which he had helped define.

To whom are the managers responsible if ownership is no longer the source of their authority? Under the developed ideology of capitalism, it was possible for the manager not to own his enterprise, but then he was the agent of the stockholders and thus ultimately responsive to the claims of property. But if Berle is right in his factual description, the stockholders have become passive, have been excluded from the decision process, and the manager disposes of millions, and even billions, of dollars without being practically accountable to anyone.

Berle's answer to the theoretical problem inherent in this situation is straightforward. The corporation should, he affirms, develop a conscience. And in one way or another, major segments of American business have taken up this rhetoric, proclaiming through institutional advertisements that they are somehow trustees of the commonweal. One company, General Electric, raised this theme to the level of a corporate philosophy (called "Boulwareism") which combined community education with a concerted attempt to destroy trade unionism.

But then there is a basic anomaly in Berle's position, one which F. A. Hayek, among the best known of the contemporary defenders of the traditional capitalist wisdom, put bluntly: "So long as management is supposed to serve the interests of the stockholder, it is reasonable to leave control of its action to the stockholders. But if management is supposed to serve wider public interests, it becomes merely a logical consequence of this conception that the appointed representatives of the public interest should control management."

Hayek is right as against Berle in that the latter attempts to give a democratic legitimacy to the corporation—it is supposed to become an instrument of the people—but leaves it in the hands of a bureaucratic elite which is neither elected nor controlled by the people. Berle is right as against Hayek in that the traditional theory of the corporate rule of the stockholder applies less and less every day. In short, Berle's description of new forms of property is much more compelling than his vision of a new corporate ethic.

This confusion over the theoretical justification of the current system of production points to the kind of world which the corporation is, in fact, creating. It is not socialist, for, as Hayek notes, it is run by a managerial elite. It is increasingly not capitalist in the historically understood definition of the term, since it does not rest upon private property. It is a society whose trends are collectivist, and therefore anticapitalist, and bureaucratic and elitist and therefore antisocialist.

One might say that the corporation is moving toward a bureaucratic collectivist order, neither capitalist nor socialist.

When one leaves the ethical questions about this system of "power without property" and moves on to more empirical description, the issues become clearer. Here it is possible to determine the responsibility of the corporation as it actually manifests itself in day-to-day operation. A public corporation, for instance, would show a political struggle in its decision process. A corporation with a conscience would demonstrate situations in which ethical considerations overrode a calculus of gain. What, in fact, has been the conduct of the corporation?

Predictably, all of these changes in the structure of the economy have affected the way in which corporate decisions are made. In his authoritative *La Planification Francaise,* Pierre Bauchet describes the separation of ownership and control in France. Then, in an analysis which applies to the United States, he states some of the consequences of this fact. The managers, he says, "seek less a profit of the capitalist than a profit of the enterprise. The capitalist's profit is traditionally identified with immediate financial gain, while that of the enterprise develops over a long period of activity: the first is based upon the conservation and increase of the wealth of the owners, the second upon augmenting the power of the firm . . ." It is, Bauchet believes, because of this development that the corporations engage in long-term planning and are even willing to integrate their policies with those of the state. Their power is no longer personal; it has become collective.

Gardiner C. Means has a similar description of the mode of operation of the American corporation where "the directors . . . try to run it well for the same reasons that the trustees of a great university seek to run the university well . . ."

And yet, even though the old robber-baron psychology no longer operates, even though the aim is no longer a personal profit, the goal is still a private profit. Only now, the private recipient is not an individual or a family but the collective of managers itself. And the way in which this power has actually been exercised provides no warrant for the discovery of a corporate conscience.

Between 1958 and 1962, for instance, American manufacturers spent $13.3 billion on new investment—and let 18 percent of their productive capacity stand idle. Socially, one result of this pattern was to promote a high, chronic rate of unemployment. On a public or conscientious basis it would be impossible to justify such a squandering of resources, both human and material. But with their targeted profit rates, the corporations go on strike whenever they cannot gain their predetermined return. More than that, their targets are established on a long-run volume of production so they can make their money even while allowing their plants to work far under capacity.

The steel industry is an excellent example of this process. Dominated by a small group of corporations, it spent a fair portion of the 1950's running well under its capacity—and sometimes 50 percent under capacity. It was not that society had satisfied its social appetite for steel. Far from it. In the very same periods, unmet needs desperately required steel: low-cost housing, schools, hospitals, transportation systems, etc. According to the hallowed laws of the free market, the steel giants should have taken advantage of this demand by lowering prices, increasing volume, and thus creating a new market.

In reality, the steel corporations, particularly the industry leader, U.S. Steel, used this period to increase their targeted profits, as Gardiner C. Means suggests. They also increased prices, recommended wage restraint to workers whom they accused of being recklessly inflationary in their demands, and, when this curious concept of the public interest was mildly challenged by a Democratic President, reacted as if America had suddenly become a totalitarian society. All this took place in a sector of the economy whose decisions affect more of the life of the United States than most state governments and many acts of Federal legislation.

In short, the structures, techniques, and direction of the corporation have been more and more collectivized, and its policies are generally no longer made to further the interest of an individual or family. But the old principle of profit survives the passing of its ethical justifications and itself becomes collective, anonymous, and even more powerful. In the heart of the process, it is difficult to discern a conscience.

So far, the focus has been upon the collectivization of corporate production, personality, and decision-making. But there is another important collectivization: that of mass opinion and taste. This, of course, is accomplished by the most successful educational institution of contemporary capitalism, the advertising industry.

Much of the rage directed against advertising by intellectuals is unfair. These critics note that this industry has a systematic habit of degrading language, truth, and culture in general. They generally assume that this is primarily due to the personal corruption of those who direct the communications media in America. Yet this misses the more profound functions of advertising and implies the too simple theory that one is confronted by a conspiracy of traitorous college graduates. The reality goes much more deeply into the American economic system and the new, private collectivism.

The advertising industry now accounts for an expenditure of approximately $15 billion a year which puts it on a par with formal education as a social activity. As a standard text by S. Watson Dunn describes the situation, "Since the end of World War II, advertising expenditures have been rising faster than Gross National Product, national income, carloadings, or almost any barometer of business activity one might choose." Such a massive investment is clearly not made out of a Philistine hatred of culture.

Rather, this development takes place because the rationalization and collectivization of production require the rationalization and collectivization of taste. The child, in David Riesman's apt phrase, is turned into a "consumer trainee." And, as David M. Potter, one of the most perceptive commentators on the subject, has written, "advertising now competes with such long-standing institutions as the school and the church in the magnitude of its social influence." Just as the "free market" no longer allocates resources, determines prices, or raises the bulk of new investment funds, it no longer provides an open confrontation of buyer and seller. The consumer is taxed so that his own desires may be standardized enough to be run through a computing machine.

Even more basically, it is the role of advertising to make the misallocation of resources characteristic of corporate collectivism appear as the free choice of the society.

For example, the public sector of American life—health, governmentally financed housing, education, transportation, and the like —is considered a great burden by most Americans. Yet, this sector contains some of the most important necessities of modern life and is a fundamental constituent of a standard of living. The private sector, on the other hand, is thought of as an area of freedom. Here one may bid for competing detergents made by the same firm, purchase planned obsolescence in automobiles and household appliances, and pay interest rates which are carefully designed for maximum deception. The private sector advertises; the public sector, by far and large, does not.

It takes money and ingenuity to convince people to invest in luxuries which they do not need and to ignore their necessities. It also makes money to do so. And it is the advertising industry that makes this misallocation of resources seem rational and freely chosen.

This instance, and the other cases of planned waste for profit, should serve to throw light on Berle's hopes for the coming of a corporate conscience. Whatever the institutional advertisements about the public responsibilities of business, the corporation acts to promote its private, but collective, profit. It imposes itself upon the people rather than responding to their needs, producing on a basis of targeted greed. It no longer follows the classic capitalist virtues, but it has managed to retain the classic capitalist vice of irresponsibility.

It is a somewhat confused recognition of this reality that leads Berle to one of his most surprising statements. Again, it must be emphasized that he writes as a defender of capitalism (and, in foreign-policy terms, as one of the more rigid American opponents of the Soviet Union). Yet he asserts, "The private property system in production, which began with our great grandfather's farm and forge, has almost vanished in the vast area of the American economy dominated by this system [retained-profits financing and institutional investment—author's note]. Instead, we have something which differs from the Russian or socialist system *mainly in its philosophic content"* (emphasis added).

Even if one takes Berle's statement of the present convergence of the communist and capitalist systems as extreme, as I do, how is it that one can even talk of such a comparison? For if this were even a major tendency in the West, then the role of the Communist parties is being usurped by businessmen. To deal with this bizarre possibility, it is necessary to go back to some of the implications of Schumpeter's definition of "socialism."

In the Marxian version of the hot decadence of capitalism, the working class of the most advanced, technologically developed nations would seize power from owners who could no longer resolve the contradiction between the social character of the productive process and the private character of the system that directed it. History would make the capitalist weak and the workers desperately strong. Yet, it is quite possible that the movement toward collectivism (not socialism) in this century took place under the opposite conditions from the ones envisioned by Marx: in Russia, where the workers were weak; in the West, where the capitalists were strong.

If Russia in 1917 was ripe for a socialist revolution, it was almost totally unripe for socialism. Industrially backward, its tiny working class could, for specific historic reasons, lead the overthrow of the old ruler, but it did not have the numbers or the economic resources to build a new order. Lenin and Trotsky felt that their Revolution was only the beginning, that it was going to be rescued by socialist victories in the heart of Europe. That did not happen.

Instead, the first attempt actually to institute socialism was based upon the socialization of poverty rather than abundance. As Marx had predicted long before, such a project could not succeed democratically. The material basis for socialism was an already existent wealth, which was precisely what the Russians did not have. Stalin forced the restriction of consumption, feeding heavy industry rather than people. To exact such a sacrifice from the masses, he expropriated their political power and concentrated it in the hands of a bureaucratic elite with social and economic privileges.

The Russian rhetoric was socialist, the Russian reality was not. The state owned the means of production—but the people did not "own" the state. They could exercise such an "ownership" over the nationalized means of production only if they could determine who would direct them and with what policies. For them, democracy was the only title to social wealth, their equivalent of the capitalist stock certificate. Thus, the destruction of democratic freedoms by Stalin was not simply a denial of political rights but the end of the social and economic power of the people as well.

The new bureaucracy established its privileges through its totalitarian monopoly of political power. The bureaucrat played politics as the businessman plays the market—as a means to gain economic and social position. When the industrial backwardness of Russia was overcome, the wealth created by the labor of the many was concentrated in the hands of the few. This was a collectivization in the absence of a strong working class.

In the West, the bureaucratic and collectivist tendencies emerged from riches rather than from scarcity. The capitalist system automated and collectivized the old-fashioned capitalist out of existence, replacing him with a manager. The corporation bureaucrat became more powerful, but not as in Russia through a process of forced industrialization. His power grew as society was backing leisurely and unthinkingly into the future. The executive was a revolutionist but did [not] know it. The resulting structure—and it is still far from finished—was not identical to the Soviet system or anything like it. In Russia there was totalitarianism; in the West, limited democracy; under communism, resources were allocated by direct and centralized political decision; under capitalism, by indirect, though increasingly centralized, economic decision.

And yet, there is a possible convergence of these utterly different histories. As the West becomes more collectivized under a managerial elite and Russia becomes wealthier under a political elite, the conscious, self-seeking decisions of a minority could become the basis of both economies. In terms of their evolution, there would be tremendous contrasts between General Motors and a Commissariat of Transportation. In terms of economic function and practice, the two entities could come to resemble one another more and more.

And what the two cases would share, above all, would be that their collectivization would have been accomplished without the active, directing participation of the great mass of the people.

Marx, and the early socialist movement, has based the hope for a libertarian collectivism on the way in which socialization would take place: through the revolutionary struggle of the democratic majority. It would be humane, he argued, because the people, and the workers in particular, would be driven to brotherhood out of a daily necessity which they would turn into a social virtue. They would join together in unions, in a political movement; they would counterpose their superior numbers and ethic to the superior funds and egotism of business. The secret of their triumph, and consequently of the society they would fashion, would be free cooperation.

But assuming the very real possibility that Western collectivism will be introduced by businessmen, then Marx's method would point toward dark consequences. The conditions of life, the practical necessities, of the executive are material gain, authority, direction. The capitalist who accidentally stumbled into the revolutionizing of society would imbue it with the only values he knows, and the worst traditions of the past and the grimmest potential of the future would be united.

IV

But one need not look so far into the distance in order to discern the cold decadence of capitalism.

Practically every ethical, moral, and cultural justification for the capitalist system has now been destroyed by capitalism. The idyll of the free market, risktaking, inventiveness, the social virtue of making money, all these have been abolished by the very success of capitalism itself. In some cases, most particularly in the United States, this contradiction between rhetoric and reality has led to the appearance of an atavistic "conservatism" which seeks to repeal the modern world. As a social and economic program, this is preposterous; as a political movement, it might threaten the very peace of the earth.

But, most basically, the problem of the cold decadence of capitalism is not that it represents the decline of the values and ideologies of the past. It is that this system will transform itself without really noticing the fact, and that the businessman as revolutionist will corrupt, not simply himself, but the society of the future as well.

A HOPE

Either Western man is going to choose a new society—or a new society will choose, and abolish, him.

It is clear that the contemporary revolution will continue to reshape the human environment in the most radical way. If anything, time will speed up even more, for the cybernated technology of today proceeds by geometric leaps and bounds rather than by arithmetic progression. Short of an atomic holocaust, which would simply write an end to the whole process, there is no reason to think that it will slow down. . . . The consequences of this development are not merely material and scientific. They invade the spirit, the psychology, politics, and every other aspect of life.

In this context, America has for some time been engaged in the wrong argument. It has been debating as to whether or not the future should be collective and social, and ignoring the fact that the present is already becoming so. The real issue is not whether, but how, this future will arrive—unwittingly or consciously chosen.

If the new society imposes itself upon a people who do not notice a revolution, the moment will constitute the decadence of the Western ideal.

And yet, there is the possibility that the West will freely choose a new society.

No option which can be taken will solve all human problems. The most happy outcome could even be, as Norman Mailer has suggested, only that suffering will be raised from the level of fate to that of tragedy. For when there are no longer plagues, famines, and natural catastrophes to blame death and evil on, the essential finitude of men could become all the more stark and stripped of its accidental qualities. And, contrary to Marx, in a society where men die from death because they have been born, there could be a religious renaissance as well as a heroic atheism.

The claim put here is minimal. The free choice of the future will not abrogate the human condition. But it will provide the context in which autonomous human beings can grow in depth and understanding, which is all the West has really ever asked.

In order to choose the new society rather than being chosen by it, the West must make this accidental century conscious and truly democratic. And this goal I would call socialism.

There are many arguments against using the word "socialism." Most Americans do not understand it. Communism uses the term as a rhetorical mask for a bureaucratic minority that imposes its private desires upon a social technology. Worse yet, the Communists have attempted to identify socialism with totalitarianism. In the emergent nations, the word "socialism" is used to describe the socialization of poverty for the purposes of accumulating capital. These societies, as the great socialist theorists would have predicted, are far distant from the ideal of the free development of the individual which is of the socialist essence. And even in Western Europe where the Social Democratic parties have maintained the democratic content of socialism, they have often equated their vision with a welfare state more than with a new civilization.

Despite all these semantic and historic drawbacks, the term must be used. With the exception of the United States, socialism is what the most democratic forces in the West call their dream. And even more basically, the nineteenth-century socialists, for all their failures of prediction, were the first to anticipate the present plight and to attempt to resolve it. They were right when they said that the way in which men produce their worldly goods is becoming more and more social. They were right in asserting that this complex, interdependent technology could not be contained within a system of private decision-making. And if there is to be a humane outcome to the contemporary Western adventure, they will have to be made right in their faith that the people can freely and democratically take control of their own lives and society.

And this last idea is the heart of the socialist hope as I define it. From the very beginning, the socialists knew that modern technology could not be made just by dividing it up into tiny parcels of individual ownership. It is of the very nature of that technology to be concentrated and collective. Therefore, the socialists assigned a new and radical meaning to democracy. The people's title to the social means of production would be guaranteed, they said, not through stock certificates, but through votes. The basic economic decisions would be made democratically.

In this context, the nationalization of industry is a technique of socialism, not its definition. It is one extremely important way of abolishing the political and social power that results from concentrated private ownership. It also facilitates directing economic resources to the satisfaction of human needs. When the people "own" the state through political democracy, then public corporations are truly theirs, and nationalization is an instrument of freedom. But there are other ways to forward the democratization of economic and social power. Fiscal and monetary policy, a cooperative sector, and taxes are among them.

In these terms, the one set and undeviating aspect of socialism is its commitment to making the democratic and free choice of the citizens the principle of social and economic life. All other issues—the extent of nationalization, the mode of planning, and the like—have to be empirically tested and measured in the light of how they serve that end. For certainly the old popular definition of socialism as the simple and wholesale nationalization of the economy has not survived the experience of this century, and particularly the Communist experience. At the same time, it has become abundantly clear that the commanding heights of the economy—where decisions affect more of life than most laws of Congresses and Parliaments—cannot be left to private motives. . . .

. . . People . . . ignore the fact that the accidental revolution is already a powerful planning agency, and, that in the absence of a conscious and democratic plan, modern technology follows an unconscious and elitist plan of its own. Society is not growing organically, like the oaks and English lawns of the traditional conservative image. It is a human construct, it is accelerating, and if men do not plan the uses of the machines they make, then machines and their elite guardians will plan the lives of men . . . .

. . . I am suggesting that the only way the accidental revolution can become socially conscious of itself is through a profound economic and social deepening of democracy. This I call socialism. . . .

. . . These changes are impossible unless there is a conscious and democratic allocation of resources within the context of national planning. The market will not accomplish such a transformation and neither will the corporation. To achieve it, society has to opt for a conscious social criterion in [areas] of life already social in fact . . . [Among the areas where national planning is needed are education and housing.] . . .

. . . The fulfillment of this possibility is, of course, a political issue. With so many variables up in the air, it is impossible to set down a program and perspective for the Western nations in this regard. Yet, certain relevant generalizations can be made. In the United States, it is inconceivable that the country can face up to these issues on the basis of politics as usual. The American party system has been structured for some time so as to produce accommodations in the middle of the road and to avoid sharp conflicts. In some ways this trend became particularly marked in the elections of 1964 when Mr. Johnson projected his role as the "President of all the people" against Goldwater extremism. But there is a fateful, and increasingly untrue, assumption underlying such consensus politics in America: that all problems can be solved by conciliation.

If radical options are to intrude in the near future upon all the advanced nations, if the nature of work, the potential of democracy, and the very meaning of economics are in the midst of transformation, then the old wisdom will be inadequate. And what will be required is the appearance of a new party alignment—a new party—in the United States. As of now, there is an American Right and an American Center; but there is not really an American democratic Left. And only the emergence of a democratic Left holds out the possibility of the United States measuring up to its challenge.

For reasons of American history, it is probable that a radical political change will not happen radically. That is to say, if the necessary new party does come, it will not result from the sudden emergence of a full-blown third force, but through the conflict within the present party structure. The potential elements for such a change [are]: the racial minorities and the poor generally; the labor movement revived; the liberal middle class; both secular and religious humanism. Thus, in looking not to the far distance but the immediate American future, the struggle of the liberal wing of the Democratic Party seems to be the point of departure for any serious hope.

And yet, as all that has been said should make clear, the outcome of this development cannot stop at traditional liberalism. In the process of change, it must become clear that America is having the wrong debate, that the shibboleths about collectivism, balanced budgets, and bureaucracy are without real meaning. For the present premise of most of American politics is that the choice is between a resolute march to the rear in the name of anticollectivism and a cautious confrontation with the future in the name of a mixed economy. In reality, the past which is the dream of the American Right is beyond recall; and the present which is recognized by American liberalism is much more radical than is imagined. At some point, then, a new political movement must begin to talk of a new political program—the democratic and conscious control of a technology that is already collective and bureaucratic. . . .

The End

BIBLIOGRAPHY

(In addition to the works included in the body of this section, the editors also recommend the following.)

Baran, Paul. *The Political Economy of Growth.* New York: Monthly Review Press, 1957.

Dobb, Maurice. *Political Economy and Capitalism.* London: Routledge, Kegan Paul, 1937.

———. *Papers on Capitalism, Development and Planning.* New York: International Publishers, 1967.

Harrington, Michael. *Toward a Democratic Left.* New York: The Macmillan Co., 1968.

Horowitz, David (ed.). *Marx and Modern Economics.* New York: Monthly Review Press, 1968.

Kolko, Gabriel. *Wealth and Power in America.* New York: Praeger, 1962.

Magdoff, Harry. *The Age of Imperialism.* New York: Monthly Review Press, 1969.

Mandel, Ernest. *Marxist Economic Theory.* New York: Monthly Review Press, 1967.

Nkrumah, Kwame. *Neo-Colonialism: Last Stage of Imperialism.* New York: International Publishers, 1965.

Perlo, Victor. *Empire of High Finance.* New York: International Publishers, 1957.

Robinson, Joan. *An Essay on Marxian Economics.* London: Macmillan, 1942.

Strachey, John. *The Theory and Practice of Socialism.* New York: Random House, 1936.

———. *The Nature of Capitalist Crisis.* New York: Covici, Friede, 1935.

———. *The Coming Struggle for Power.* New York: Covici, Friede, 1933.

Sweezy, Paul. *The Theory of Capitalist Development.* New York: Monthly Review Press, 1942.

Veblen, Thorstein. *The Theory of the Leisure Class.* New York: Modern Library, 1934.

Views On Capitalism

The text of this book was designed by Bob Simon and typeset by The Typographic Service Company, Los Angeles, California, in 12-point Garamond No. 3 lite, with 2-point leading. The part and chapter headings are in 18-point Garamond Bold with 48-point Melior numerals. The printing was done by offset lithography by Publishers Press, Salt Lake City, Utah, and the paper is 50# Boise Cascade Wove. The book was bound by Mountain States Bindery, Salt Lake City, Utah, in 13-point Permalin Linenweave printed in 3-colors by offset lithography. The cover was designed by Glencoe Press.

11-401

38065